The Compl

Community
Chaplain's
Handbook

Mark Cress

Chris Hobgood   Dwayne Reece

ISBN 0-9786039-0-7
For Worldwide Distribution
Printed in the U.S.A.

Lanphier Press
U.S.A.
www.lanphierpress.com

Images and photo releases provided by Shutterstock.com and Corporate Chaplains of America.

Cover design and layout by Robin Crabtree.

The authors wish to acknowledge Jesus as the true Author and Finisher of their lives. He has given them collectively more than fifty years on this Earth with helpmates to whom they dedicate this book. They are:

Linda Cress   *Kimberly Hobgood*   *Debbie Reece*

Without their ministry as Jesus-filled wives, this book would never have been written.

Complete Handbook of Community Chaplaincy
Chapter Outline

Unit I: Mission Fields for the Community Chaplain: The first unit in this text highlights some of the specific areas in which a community chaplain may serve. As these target mission fields are explored, emphasis is placed on identifying an area of ministry, gaining access to the mission field, and assessing vital ministry needs related to the area of the community served.

Unit 2: Foundations of Community Chaplaincy: Like everything in life, chaplaincy must be built on a firm foundation. Unit 2 seeks to lay this firm footing by exploring the biblical and historical basis for community chaplaincy.

Unit 3: Core Principles of Community Chaplaincy: Unit 3 details the core principles that serve as the guiding force for the care provided by community chaplains.

Unit 4: Caring in Crisis: Unit 4 concludes with pragmatic principles for equipping the community chaplain to help in the many times of crisis encountered by those in their care.

Preface

Although this work may ultimately be found most often in an academic setting, it may surprise people that the authors did not set out to produce a scholarly treatise or defense of any kind. Rather, the objective was that readers be compelled to engage God, other people, and even themselves as they explore the ministry of chaplaincy in the United States through the eyes, ears, and hearts of those who have walked it out.

These pages are intended to provide a guidebook of not only the "why's", but also the "how-to's", for real-life, on-the-ground situations encountered every day in the work of community chaplaincy. They are also designed to facilitate the deeply probing questions that will focus and solidify one's efforts, as well as clarify and confront relationships and personal issues. In other words, this book is not for the faint of heart!

The authors have committed their lives to serving Christ through chaplaincy. In addition to their own twenty-plus years of service as chaplains, God has blessed them with a team of certified chaplains from which to draw rich and abiding training experiences.

Corporate Chaplains of America agreed in 2005 to work with a leading US seminary to assist in offering a course in the fundamentals of corporate chaplaincy for a future Master of Arts in Workplace Ministry degree program. One early challenge proved to be the fact that no text existed for such a class. Lanphier Press graciously stepped up to ensure a publication would be produced to allow the process to move forward.

The authors were tasked to create a volume that is both practical and thorough. Although no single work short of the Scriptures can ever hope to fully cover even a single subject of study, a textbook emerged that has since been used by schools of higher learning. Many of the principles found in workplace ministry are applicable to other areas of ministry. What follows is a set of ministry principles that can be applied in a variety of circumstances to utilize process management training in the greatest mission field: the sphere of influence in which God has placed you!

Acknowledgements

Pulling together a work like this is never accomplished in a vacuum. For every writer in a book project, there are always scores of players in the background who are rarely recognized for all the extra efforts necessary to make it a reality. The authors of this text wish to thank the precious people who have worked tirelessly to keep this project on target and to get it ultimately into your hands today.

Cindy Rice coordinated every word of this text between three authors and many revisions. She proofed every syllable and corrected many errors before the text was ever seen by other professionals on the team. Projects such as this do not happen without talented, caring people like Cindy.

Robin Crabtree artistically designed the cover and skillfully typeset the text. In addition, she offered edit references and technical assistance without which we would still be at ground zero.

Clay Summers and Mike Wolff contributed insightful writing and research support for chapters four and five.

As in every Lanphier project, Jeff Hilles provided leadership, insight, and warm friendship to every member of the textbook development team.

The following chaplains went the extra mile in providing case studies and anecdotal stories that add a richness and depth to this work: Albert Beltran, Greg Bennett, Gaylon Benton, Susan Hogan, Sherry Kiser, Brian Page, Gene Rund, Henry Sanchez, Jeff Seeger, Troy Talmadge, and Gary Williams.

It also takes many encouragers to pull off a task like this - folks who pray, call, cheer, support, egg on, push, and promote. They are very much appreciated and include: Danny Akin, Bruce Battle, Rick Butler, Paul Carlisle, Randy Clark, Danny Cox, Jess Duboy, Ron Duke, Jim Goldston, George King, Ellen McNally, Chuck Milian, Bob Pettus, Frank Reed, Steve Steff, and Tom Vande Gutche.

Also, special thanks to Howard Piekarz and the fine team at Edwards Brothers.

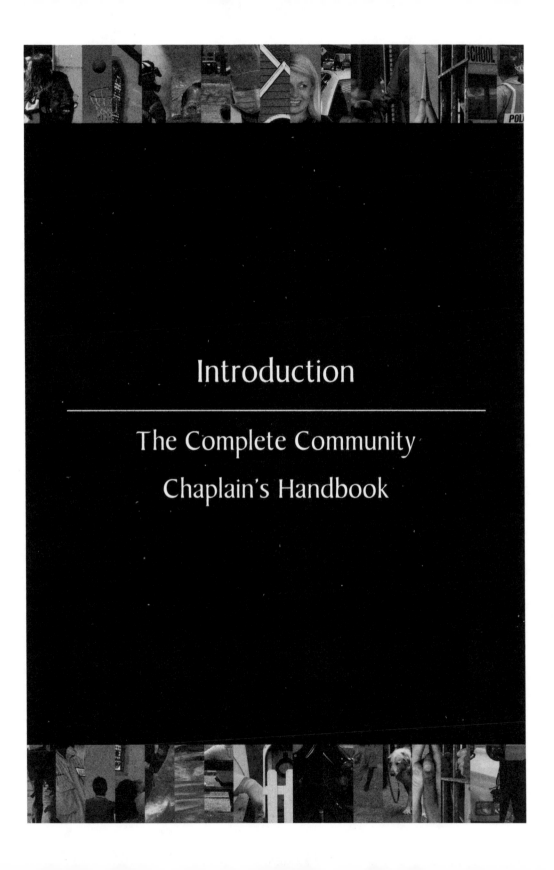

Introduction

The Complete Community

Chaplain's Handbook

INTRODUCTION

———————— The Complete Community Chaplain's Handbook ————————

C haplaincy is a concept that is often new to many people. Ask most people about chaplains and they will be familiar only with hospital chaplains or military chaplains. Put the words community and chaplain together to form the title "community chaplain," and most often you will be met with a look of puzzlement and the obvious question: "What is a community chaplain?" The goal of this book is not only to answer this question, but also to equip the prospective chaplain for the greatest of callings to serve in the greatest of mission fields - the sphere of influence in which God has placed him.

While the industry awareness may be quite low, the reality is that there are more than 4,000 chaplains serving in the American workplace today, and the trend toward the provision of chaplains caring for employees is on the upswing. Companies as small as Price's Auto Body & Paint Shop of Raleigh, NC with 25 employees, and companies as large as Southeastern Freight Lines employing over 7,000, are seeing the benefits of caring for their most valuable of assets - their associates. However, it is not just private Christian-owned-and-operated companies fueling this trend. Even publicly held companies utilize workplace chaplains. Tyson Foods relies on 130 part-time chaplains serving in 242 plants to care for its workforce of 114,000. John Tyson, the grandson of the founder of the company and current CEO, is the driving force behind the program. This trend of receptivity to faith in the workplace is extending to other areas where people spend time: on little league sports fields, in community swimming pools and clubhouses, in book clubs, public school systems, and even in city government.

The Complete Community Chaplain's Handbook was born out of a decade of providing genuine caring in the workplace through the work of Corporate Chaplains of America. The past ten years of experience has been invested in doing two things: first, serving the needs of employees and second, developing a process-managed approach to further the care of employees. The first goal is being accomplished every day as chaplains traverse cubicle aisles, loading docks, and office buildings across America seeking to impact the lives of associates in crisis. This experience and knowledge base has been applied to a larger audience than just the workplace. It can be used to

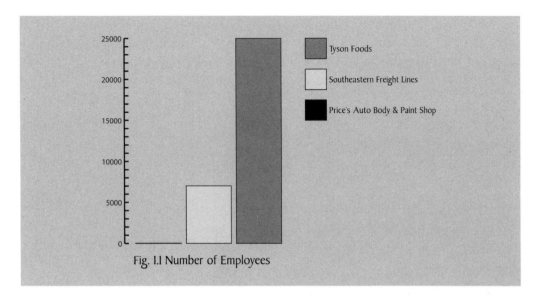

Fig. 1.1 Number of Employees

claim your community, your sphere of influence, for Christ. Within the pages of this book, this process-managed approach to chaplaincy has been distilled into workable teaching material. Our purpose in producing it is to contribute to the expansion of the chaplaincy movement, not only in the U.S. but throughout the world.

This volume explores, in exhaustive fashion, the chaplaincy movement from the Christian perspective. It will briefly trace the history of chaplaincy, examine target mission fields for the community chaplain, and cover the practical aspects of the myriad of ministry opportunities encountered by a chaplain. In its pragmatism, the goal of *The Complete Community Chaplain's Handbook* is to equip men and women for the work of chaplaincy where God has "planted" them. Interspersed throughout the text will be a combination of practical exercises and case studies designed to engage the chaplaincy student in the equipping process.

The handbook is organized into four units. The first unit highlights some specific areas in which a community chaplain may serve. Unit 2 lays a foundation for community chaplaincy. The calling to chaplaincy and the biblical basis for chaplaincy is explored, and the challenge of postmodernism and multiculturalism is discussed. Unit 3 details the core principles of community chaplaincy. These principles serve as the guiding force for the care provided by chaplains in a wide spectrum of situations. The book concludes in Unit 4 with practical principles for equipping the chaplain to help individuals in times of crisis.

Community chaplaincy is not a new idea. In fact, a close examination of the Scriptures dates it back to the days of Jesus and the work of the first century church. One does not need to peer far into American history to see how a community chaplain can be effective. Take a look at the community in which God has placed you and claim it for Him. Jeremiah Lanphier, a businessman in New York City, ignited a revival in 1851 through the vehicle of a simple lunchtime prayer meeting. Today, that movement, awakened a century and a half ago, finds its expression through the conduit of more than 1,000 workplace ministries. These ministries function through a variety of methods, including workplace prayer meetings and Bible studies, Christian business mentoring groups like C12, workplace ministry conferences, and chaplaincy. Only God knows how He will use your willingness to be a community chaplain to use your sphere of influence for His glory!

Fig. 1.2 Companies of all shapes and sizes are beginning to provide chaplaincy as a benefit for their employees.

What is a community chaplain?

Chaplaincy enjoys a long history dating back to the man who came to be known as St. Martin of Tours, who is recognized as the initiator of the office of chaplain. While still a soldier, Martin one day encountered a cold beggar. Moved by compassion, he removed the heavy cape from his uniform, sliced it in half with his sword, and shared it with the man. This became the start of his legendary service as a chaplain. The picture this paints of chaplaincy is wonderful. A chaplain is one who comes alongside to share with and help another in distress. Later that night Martin dreamed he saw Christ wearing the half of the cloak he had given away to the beggar. Among Martin's congregations of service, the half cloak he kept became known as a "cappa" and was an object of great respect. The place in which the "cappa" was kept was called "cappella," which through the French word "chappele" became our word "chapel." The priest in charge was called "chappellanus," or "chappelain" in French. The chaplain is the keeper of the cloak or the keeper of compassion.

Simply defined, a chaplain is a spiritual caregiver. Dictionaries usually classify a chaplain as a member of the clergy attached to a chapel who conducts religious services for an institution, such as a prison, a hospital, or for the armed services. With this definition in mind, this text will identify a community chaplain as a personal and spiritual caregiver whose primary job is to serve the emotional, physical, spiritual, and personal needs of people in the community around him.

What is a process-managed approach to community chaplaincy?

Process management is something most people would recognize but may not readily be able to define. Perhaps an example will best describe the term. If I succumb to my children's pleas for a McDonald's cheeseburger on the way to the beach, process management demands that a cheeseburger in another town taste the same as the one I buy them in our hometown of Raleigh, NC. Why? Because McDonald's uses the same ingredients, trains their employees in the same cooking process, and utilizes the same equipment in every location in order to prepare a cheeseburger with consistent taste and consistent quality.

Likewise, a process-managed approach to community chaplaincy stipulates that chaplaincy care look the same in Raleigh, NC as it looks in Grants Pass, OR. Does this mean the chaplains look the same? The simple answer is no. Process management in chaplaincy means that the process of care provided to the community utilizes a consistency that spans culture, age, geography, and uniqueness of circumstances, in order to ensure that chaplains are responding in similar fashion throughout the various communities they serve. Process management is accomplished significantly through a proper training model, extends through the chaplain introduction process, and finds its completion through a consistency of response among chaplain team members to the variety of crises encountered.

Process management can be applied to community chaplaincy in this way: each chaplain has a specific mission field in which he serves. Relationships are built with those in his community, or mission field, over a period of time. This can be accomplished by regularly scheduled, routine visits that we will call "rounds" with those in his community. The purpose of these rounds will be explored later in the text, but the ultimate goal is to build a trusting and caring relationship with each person in the mission field. Being available to those in need is crucial to the success of community chaplaincy. Consider having business cards printed that display your contact information. Distribute these cards to those in the mission field.

As the relationship with each person develops, the chaplain is positioned to serve as a pastoral caregiver to those found in the mission field. In essence, the chaplain is serving as a pastor to people who have no pastor. Care can include hospital visitation, marriage or family caregiving, performance of funeral services, and assistance with a variety of other difficult issues. The care provided is always at the initiation of the individual, and only after permission is granted by them. The community chaplain will act as a conduit of care between the church and those in the community.

The caregiving ministry provided by community chaplains has succeeded because it has utilized a very practical strategy to achieve a very focused goal. The goal is simple - the personal and spiritual care of people. The strategy is to reach people where they are by addressing their point of need during a moment of crisis. According to statistics, people are more likely to be found engaged in community activities than at home or church.

In spite of the stress brought on by the competing demands of family and work responsibilities, people continue to ignore avenues such as counselors, employee assistance programs, and the church as sources of strength and support. Data from the Barna Research Group indicates that 60 percent of people do not attend church on a typical weekend. What this data indicates is that a significant majority of people encountered in the community environment have no pastor or other caregiver to turn to during a time of crisis. Perhaps an even more alarming statistic indicates that adults over age eighteen have only a 6 percent likelihood of accepting Christ as Savior.[1] What this statistic tells us in simple terms is that only 6 percent are likely to discover a long term spiritual solution to the problems they face. It is the remaining majority that Community Chaplains of America seeks to reach with the life-changing Good News of Jesus Christ.

This book is needed for three basic reasons. First, an understanding of the biblical basis for chaplaincy is essential. Secondly, it will serve as a tool to expand the work of community chaplaincy throughout the United States and the world. Finally, those people God is calling into service as community chaplains will see themselves in these pages and be drawn into what He wants them to do.

Matthew 9:35-38 records the teaching of Jesus as He spoke of the need for additional workers for the harvest field. Ephesians 4:11-13 records the apostle Paul providing practical instruction about the responsibility of equipping people for the work of service. It is the desire of the authors that this work provide practical instruction, so that men and women might be equipped for the role of community chaplain.

Some who will read this text and be taught its content will recognize God's call upon their lives into community chaplaincy. As this call is answered, Jesus' request for more workers for the harvest field will be answered. Effectively trained chaplains will be essential for the strong growth of the community chaplaincy movement and its continued success in solidly impacting the culture. The words of Jesus recorded in Matthew 9:36-38 can be very easily applied to today's society.

> *36 He felt great pity for the crowds that came, because their problems were so great and they didn't know where to go for help. They were like sheep without a shepherd. 37 He said to his disciples, 'The harvest is so great, but the workers are so few. 38 So pray to the Lord who is in charge of the harvest; ask him to send out more workers for his fields'* (Matthew 9:36-38 NLT).

The authors' prayer for the readers of this work is that they might discover some practical help for the most pragmatic of callings - the call to community chaplaincy. Thank you for embarking on this journey of discovery and for allowing us the privilege of sharing some lessons learned along the way.

Stories From the Field: #1
"What Is a Community Chaplain?"*

The day had already been busy. Six hours had been invested in the life of one family, and it was only lunch time. Community Chaplain Alana waited patiently in line to place an order for her favorite sub, a turkey and cheese on honey oat bread. As the line snaked slowly forward, she noticed the gray-haired, slightly balding man with the yellow bow tie staring at the logo prominently displayed over the pocket of her shirt. The blue triangle logo and the words "Community Chaplains of America" were always clearly visible from ten feet away. After five years of chaplain service, Alana was familiar with the response and knew the question that was coming before it was even asked. "What is a community chaplain?" Alana thought back to the day she had boarded an elevator to the 5th floor cancer wing of Rich Creek Memorial Hospital and had been asked that question for the first time. Her answer that day had been a rambling description that really failed to communicate anything at all. After many false starts, she was eventually able to explain she was an ordinary person who happened to serve in the community, helping those with the problems that come in life. The bow tie man responded to her answer with a puzzled expression and a response she was to hear many more times over the years: "I've never heard of that. I didn't know there was such a thing."

*Individuals in this story have granted permission for its use.

Questions

1. How would you respond to the question, "What is a community chaplain?"
2. What would be your response to the statement, "I didn't know there were community chaplains"?

Practical Exercise # 1

Conduct an internet search using the words "workplace ministry" or "corporate chaplaincy". Identify the top five ministries, spend time examining their web sites, and develop a half page summary of each ministry.

Endnotes

I. See Barna Research <http://www.barna.org> (Accessed December 27 2000).

Unit One

Mission Fields for the Community Chaplain

The first unit in this text highlights some of the specific areas in which a community chaplain may serve. As these target mission fields are explored, emphasis is placed on identifying an area of ministry, gaining access to the mission field, and assessing vital ministry needs related to the area of the community served.

Chapter One

The Community Chaplain
to School Systems

CHAPTER ONE

The Community Chaplain to School Systems

———————————— Objectives ————————————

During the course of this chapter, we will perform the following tasks:

- Identify the proper steps and channels of approach when establishing a school system chaplaincy.

- Identify the various types of school systems within America.

- Establish approaches for addressing the unique and specific issues within a school district.

S erving a school system as a chaplain can present challenges which are quite unique for a caregiver. Within this academic setting lies a vast array of social and economic platforms. It is important to recognize first that as we discuss school systems, we will be including both the private and public arena in our study. Each of these can present their own individual challenges and oftentimes will require a different approach due to tremendous pressures which can exist from both inside the system and out. Your intimate knowledge of the particular system which you are serving will be a key factor in the choices you make in the caregiving process. But first, we must identify how to approach a school system with the prospect of a community chaplain caregiving service.

The first step in beginning your role as a community chaplain to a school system is to meet with administration. Find out who the decision maker is and schedule a time to meet with him or her. In most cases, the principal of a school may not necessarily have the decision making ability. Do not be surprised if your initial contact will need to be with the school superintendent or even a school board. During the meeting, plan to introduce yourself, explain what services you can offer to the school staff, students, and parents of the students. This is the time when you will need to put forth your best effort to help the decision maker understand that you can be of great benefit to all people within all levels of the system. You may want to gain insight from this person regarding the needs of those within the school system and the unique challenges that these various people face. Always be sure to thank the administrator for his time and follow up with correspondence that recaps what occurred during the meeting to avoid confusion in the future. Some items to include in your communication with the system leader may include times and days that the chaplain will be at the facility, what the chaplain will and will not do, and contact information for the chaplain in the event of an emergency.

It would be wise to be prepared to answer questions that you anticipate before meeting with the decision making person or group. Make a list of questions that you would ask if faced with such a decision. Try to place yourself in the place of a person who may be skeptical or even reluctant to have a chaplain within their school system. It would also be helpful to ask your friends and family members what questions and concerns they would have in this situation. The key is to have a well worded response to as many questions and concerns as possible before entering the process. Being as prepared as possible for questions will accentuate your professionalism and give credence to your desire to care for those people within the school system.

Fig. 1.1 There are various types of schools which operate throughout our country.

Perhaps now would be a good time to identify the various types of schools, in addition to the public school system, that exist in America. Depending upon where you are in our country, you may see one or all of the various types of schools and school systems which operate throughout our country.

- **Charter schools (public):** These autonomous, "alternative" public schools are started by parents, teachers, community organizations, and for-profit companies. They receive tax dollars, but the sponsoring group must also come up with private funding. Charter schools must adhere to the basic curricular requirements of the state but are free from many of the regulations that apply to conventional schools and the day-to-day scrutiny of school boards and government authorities.

- **Magnet schools (public):** These highly competitive, highly selective public schools are renowned for their special programs, superior facilities, and high academic standards. They may specialize in a particular area, such as science or the arts. Students who apply to these schools go through a rigorous testing and application process.

- **Independent schools (private):** These schools are nonprofit and governed by elected boards of trustees. Independent schools draw their funds from tuition payments, charitable contributions, and endowments rather than from taxes or church funds. They may be affiliated with a religious institution but cannot receive funds or governance from them. Independent private day schools generally cost from a few thousand to more than $10,000 per student per year, while an independent boarding school charges each student approximately $20,000 annually.

- **Parochial schools (private):** These church-related schools are most commonly owned and operated by Catholic parishes or dioceses but also by Protestant denominations. Hebrew schools may also be termed parochial. The majority of the private schools in the United States are parochial schools. Their academic curriculum is supplemented with required daily religious instruction and prayer. Teachers may be clergy or laypersons who may or may not be trained educators. Your child doesn't have to be Catholic to attend a parochial school, but he or she will still be required to attend religious education classes and prayer services. Parochial schools generally cost between $1,200 and $2,400 per year for an elementary school student and between $4,600 and $7,500 for a high school student.

- **Proprietary schools (private):** These private schools are run for profit. This is a relatively new category of school. They do not answer to any board of trustees or elected officials. Because of this, they claim to be able to respond quickly to the demands of the market. Tuition is comparable to that of private, non-profit schools.

- **Home schools:** These schools include an educational environment in which a student receives instruction offered in a home, as regulated by state law, for reasons other than health.[1]

If there is anything certain pertaining to school systems in America, it is the variations that exist between them all. These variations are broken down in each system to reflect the multi-cultural and socio-economic diversity within that particular system. As the chaplain for these schools, it is imperative to understand that dealing with school employees, students, and parents will require different approaches as you move from one cultural or economic group to another. For example, if you are involved in a ministry opportunity with the Superintendent of Schools, you will more than likely be dealing with a highly educated person who is probably operating under a Doctorate or Ph.D. educational degree. In most cases this person is earning an income in a six figure range. According to the U.S Department of Education, the average secondary school teacher in America earned in year 1998-1999 an income of $42,459.[2] This can represent a vast difference in lifestyle and even financial stress. The division can become even more complicated when we begin to add the custodial staff, cafeteria staff, ground maintenance crew, and even the employees who are driving school buses. The chaplain's ability to cross over these financial divisions and be accepted and respected by all will be a determining factor in the success of the ministry.

Experience has shown time and time again that the chaplain who easily maneuvers through the differing socio-economic levels represented within a school system or any other ministry situation is the chaplain who has a much better success rate in terms of overall service to people under that particular ministry. The tools required for this success can be many; however, it always comes down to how well the chaplain meets the person "where they are" in life. Showing genuine concern, being a good listener, and offering good practical guidance to each person, regardless of where they stand on the economic ladder of life, will go far to building a successful ministry within any situation.

But what about the financial differences within the population of the school attendees? The table below comes from the U.S. Department of Education, National Center

Fig. 1.2 Many students receive federally funded free or reduced price lunches.

for Education Statistics, and reveals that a large number of students within the public school systems of America qualify for and receive federally funded free or reduced price lunches each school year. This is an important piece of information, because it shows that as a school system chaplain, you must be prepared to be knowledgeable of other local assistance programs in order to help these families find specific help for the problems they face. Oftentimes adults who struggle financially not only carry the stress of the finances with them throughout the day, but also transfer the anxiety forward to the children within the home. This creates a host of issues for the child, as he or she is already struggling to fit in to an increasingly difficult peer pressure situation at school. As the table reveals, regardless of the reason, a large number of American families have difficulty meeting the price of school lunches within the public school arena.

Public school students receiving federally funded free or reduced price lunches, by selected school characteristics: School year 1993-94:

School characteristics	Percent of students participating in program			
	Total	Elementary	Secondary	Combined
1	2	3	4	5
Total	33.2 (0.5)	38.8 (0.7)	22.0 (0.4)	39.1 (1.7)
Community type				
Central city.	44.9 (1.0)	52.1 (1.3)	28.9 (0.9)	52.2 (3.0)
Urban fringe/large town. . .	23.5 (0.9)	28.3 (1.4)	14.6 (0.6)	23.9 (3.8)
Rural/small town	32.2 (0.6)	36.3 (0.8)	23.0 (0.4)	39.9 (1.9)
School size (students)				
Less than 150	38.6 (1.3)	38.4 (1.9)	35.8 (1.5)	50.2 (2.4)
150-299.	38.1 (0.9)	39.5 (1.2)	28.4 (1.1)	51.8 (4.9)
300-499.	37.0 (0.9)	38.8 (1.0)	26.2 (1.1)	37.3 (2.6)
500-749.	33.5 (0.9)	36.0 (1.0)	22.3 (0.7)	34.7 (2.2)
750 or more	29.7 (0.9)	42.5 (1.8)	20.6 (0.5)	34.3 (3.2)
Minority students				
Less than 5%.	22.0 (0.5)	24.4 (0.7)	17.0 (0.6)	28.6 (1.6)
5 to 19%	18.9 (0.5)	22.2 (0.8)	11.7 (0.4)	30.6 (2.3)
20 to 49%.	32.0 (0.7)	38.1 (1.0)	20.1 (0.4)	38.6 (5.0)
50% or more.	57.3 (1.1)	65.5 (1.2)	38.9 (1.0)	60.6 (3.2)

NOTE: Combined schools include schools beginning with grade 6 or below and ending with grade 9 or above. Standard errors appear in parentheses.[3]

Families who are receiving federally funded lunches within the public school system are not likely to be able to afford the cost of professional counseling services when the need for in-depth counseling is required. They also often face struggles with transportation issues, problems that high debt causes, paying utility bills, and many other daily needs of life with which others may not be faced due to the difference in income levels. Because of these financial struggles, the school system chaplain will be faced with questions and issues surrounding financial needs on a regular basis and must be prepared to assist when called upon. It is highly recommended that you keep a listing of all of the funded assistance programs within your area, as well as debt reduction and debt counseling services.

Caring For Children, Adolescents, and Teens

As you step into a school system as "the caregiver", you will undoubtedly be faced with opportunities to minister to and care for the students within the system. This can present an array of scenarios that many ministers with years of experience would find difficult to process. Unless you have had extensive experience dealing with youth and the many crises they face, you may find yourself being treated as an "outsider". Young students can be highly selective concerning whom they trust and allow into their lives. It is important to remember that you owe the same commitment of confidentiality to the students as you would to an adult. There may be many times when your best avenue of ministry is to offer your presence and support with the student as they share something with an adult or a parent. But breaching the confidentiality of a student will be a guaranteed way of ending your trust with the students and ultimately ending the success of your chaplaincy in the school system.

When looking within the context of youth and family counseling, we can quickly find a vast array of topics that are regularly addressed. Below are listed just a few of the topics and needs that face our youth and the family environments from which they come.

- Family Therapy
- Parenting Skills
- Marital or Couples Therapy
- Depression
- Anxiety Disorders
- Conduct Disorders
- Adolescent Development Issues

- Single Parent Issues
- Family of Origin Issues
- Blended and Family Issues
- Grief Therapy
- Job Related Stress
- Substance or Alcohol Abuse Recovery[4]

One of the disorders with which you will undoubtedly be faced is Attention Deficit Disorder (ADD) and/or Attention Deficit Hyperactivity Disorder (ADHD). "Attention Deficit Hyperactivity Disorder affects about 5% of students in school. ADHD in all six of its types impacts about two students in every classroom, in every school, in every state, across America."[5] Being familiar with and knowledgeable of the symptoms and treatments is important before you enter a conversation on the subject.

As you look over these topics, you may come to realize that without a counseling certification, a person is most likely not qualified to handle these in-depth topics. A wise chaplain knows when to refer a person or a family to a professional counselor. As a well-intending chaplain with a heart for caring for families, you can find yourself in a real legal battle to save and maintain your ministry due to overstepping your boundaries by offering counseling advice that you are not qualified to give. Know your limitations! A chaplain can find just as much satisfaction in pointing a person or family in the right direction for help as actually providing the in-depth counseling service. Remember, you have the answer to life; the answer is a relationship with Jesus Christ. If you can get a person or family to understand and complete that need in their life, then all of the other questions will eventually come together as Jesus Christ opens the doors and begins to lead them through a Spirit-filled life.

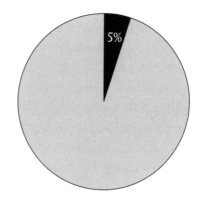

5%

◤= Percentage of Students with ADHD

Fig. 1.3 ADHD impacts about 2 students in every classroom.

26

Endnotes

1. See Connect with Kids <http://www.connectwithkids.com/tipsheet/2003/II5_marI2/school.html (Accessed I9 June 2006).
2. See National Center for Education Statistics <http://www.nces.ed.gov/programs/digest/d00/dt079.asp> (Accessed I9 June 2006).
3. Cited by National Center for Education Statistics <http://nces.ed.gov/programs/digest/d0I/dt375.asp> (Accessed I9 June 2006).
4. See Youth and Family Counseling <http://www.youthandfamilycounseling.com> (Accessed I9 June 2006).
5. See <http://www.addinschool.com/> (Accessed 20 June 2006).

Chapter Two

The Community Chaplain
to Public Servants

CHAPTER TWO

The Community Chaplain to Public Servants

Objectives

During the course of this chapter, we will perform the following tasks:

■ Determine who comprises the population group called public servants

■ Lay out a plan to establish a ministry to public servants

■ Understand the characteristics specific to the mission field of public service

■ Examine the specific processes for ministering to public servants

---

W e come into contact on a daily basis with those who are considered public servants. As a society, we tend to take them for granted. The services they offer to the public at large are often seen as entitlements by the general population. So, then, we must first consider who is the population group that works in public service? All levels of government include public servants. Congressmen, judges, police officers, fire and rescue personnel, hospital workers, correctional officers, and local county and city officials all have areas of responsibility that affect our daily lives. These jobs and the duties associated with them are often "thankless" and require placing oneself in danger.

With all of the negative aspects of public perception and the stress of physical and emotional danger, why would someone choose to enter this line of work? A study conducted by Mark Prebble

Fig. 2.1 As a society, we tend to take public servants for granted.

of public service workers reveals some insight. The 2005 Career Progression and Development Public Service Report is the only survey to span across all Public Service Offices that asks staff about their perceptions and career aspirations, training and development, and their work environment.[1] Take a look at some of the findings:

- Public servants are committed to their work and take pride in what they do.

- There is a need to improve the management in the public service field of work.

- Public servants would like to have great work-life balance, and they expect their employers to help provide this balance.

- Public servants are more likely to have a growing sense of ambition than in the past.

- A feeling of accomplishment, challenging work, effective management, and pay and benefits were highly important to most public servants.

- Opportunities for advancement have become highly important for public servants, especially those under the age of 30.

- There is an increasing sense of job security and satisfaction in recent years.

- Nearly a third of public service workers reported that a concern that they would not be able to balance work and family responsibilities had stopped them from applying for a higher level position.

Because much of the public service sector faces staffing shortages and funding cuts, the workload placed on the existing public servants is greater than it has been in recent years. Budgets are spread over more agencies; Homeland Security, for example. Remaining staff members are required to cover for vacancies due to budgeting or personnel issues and to train new staff members. The mission field that is occupied by public servants is ready for a chaplain. In addition to seeking to reach those employed, either on a vocational basis or voluntary, the public that is served is also in need of a chaplain. For this reason, we will explore the ministry needs of those employed in the public service industry and those who are being served.

The chaplain must first establish a presence in the mission field of the public servant. Because this type of population has many layers of bureaucracy, it is important to discover who has the authority to allow a community chaplain to minister to the needs of those in the mission field. This means that the community chaplain may need to do a little research on the hierarchy of the organization. The local Animal Control manager may be in favor of implementing the services of a community chaplain but may lack the authority to allow such a program to be present in the building. Someone at a higher level of that organization may need to make the decision. One person may not be able to make the decision; it may need to be made by a review board of some sort. Examine the following ideas:

- **Hospital:** Director of Chaplain Program (also called Pastoral Care) or Hospital Administrator

- **Jail:** Sheriff or Chief of Police

- **Court System:** District Attorney or State Supreme Court Justice

- **Fire Station:** Fire Chief or Director of Chaplain Program

- **Police Station:** Chief of Police or Director of Chaplain Program

Once you have discovered who the decision maker is at a particular public service organization, schedule a time to meet with him or her. While you are together, introduce yourself to the decision making person or entity. This is a great time for the community chaplain to gain insight into the needs of the population group in the mission field. Continue the meeting by explaining the services that you can offer to the public servants, ultimately leading the person(s) to the understanding that you can be of great benefit to the organization. At the conclusion of the meeting, thank each person involved for his or her time. Follow up with a communication that again offers gratitude and reviews the events of the meeting so that everyone is on the same page. This letter, e-mail, or phone call may be a great time to suggest times and days that the community chaplain is available, what the chaplain will and will not do, and contact information for the chaplain in the event of an emergency.

After an affirmative response has been given by the decision maker, it is important for the community chaplain ministering to the needs of those working in the public service organizations to be aware of the specific issues that face public servants. While some were mentioned at the beginning of this chapter, we will examine the needs of the mission field in detail at this point. There are two major issues that are faced by many working in the public service arena. The schedule that they are required to work is not traditional, leading to difficulty with family life and other activities that take place when ←— many people have leisure time. Church services may be a challenge to attend with the work schedule of many police officers, fire and rescue officials, and the like. The second major challenge of public servants is the type of work that they do, as well as the type of things that they see and experience as a result of their work. Many public servants perform the type of work that many "ordinary people" find difficult, not for the faint of heart, and emotionally taxing. For example, most of us reading this text do not encounter a bloody car crash or pull a burn victim from a building on a daily basis, if ever. The public servant is not put off by these events; he or she feels a calling to this work.

Because many of those working in the public service area see humanity and the community around them at its worst, they can be distrustful and building a relationship may be challenging. There is an isolating barrier that many police officers, hospital and rescue workers, correctional officials, and other public servants place around themselves so that they can separate themselves from the work that they perform. This compartmentalization bleeds over into other areas of life, including relationships with those most important to them. Public servants have a unique character, and not just anyone can reach them. A feeling of invincibility and often a morbid sense of humor are common traits. A community chaplain can be effective with those in the public service community by reaching out in the following ways:

- Give care to public service personnel such as firefighters, police officers, correctional officers, EMS personnel, ER staff, etc.
- Offer care to family members of those working in public service
- Visit sick and injured public servants at home and in the hospital
- Provide services to the family of an injured public servant
- Make death notifications
- Provide assistance to victims of crisis situations
- Teach those in public service about stress management, ethics, family life, and victim response
- Serve as part of the Critical Incident Stress Management Team

- Assist at an emergency scene
- Serve as a liaison between clergy and the community
- Offer prayers at special occasions such as recruit graduations, awards ceremonies, dedications of buildings, and retirements
- Serve on review boards, awards committees, and the like
- Furnish responses to spiritual questions commonly asked by those who encounter death on a daily basis[2]

The ministry needs of those in public service are very different than the needs of those in any other community because of the nature of the environment in which they work and live. The often graphic nature of the chosen profession can harden them to a relationship with Christ and cause them to ask questions of a spiritual nature that most of us would not consider. The chaplain must be careful and skilled in building relationships. These relationships can be built through one on one time with individuals or in group related activities. Because many public servants spend part of their time actually living at the place of work, group dynamics must be considered when building relationships. Time spent with those working in public service will be a large part of connecting with them. Because of the work schedule of many public servants, many leisure time activities, such as church services and family functions like birthday parties, cannot be attended. A typical work schedule for a public servant could range from a normal 8 hour shift during the day to being at work for 36 hours straight, including nights and weekends. It then becomes important to bring some of those leisure time events that happen when public servants are working to where they are: at work. The community chaplain can show that the public servant is valued when he or she brings those things that are usually inaccessible:

- **Worship Services:** The chaplain can lead a weekly service. There should be consistency regarding the time and day of the week. Because most of the population in public service is men, they may not be as willing to sing or speak out loud at such a service. Be prepared for interruptions such as emergencies that require public servants to leave the service for a rescue or to give medical care to others.

- **Holidays:** The public servant misses many holidays because they are at work. Bring the holiday to the fire station, police headquarters, or hospital. Keep these events light-hearted and fun. Most public servants like to have fun and enjoy playing practical jokes on each other. The community chaplain may even have a few embarrassing moments planned by the public servants. Do not take offense when they include the community chaplain in the practical joking. It is one way that they bond with you.

■ **Hospital visits:** The risk for a public servant to be injured is great. When an injury does occur, immediately go to the hospital. You will find the waiting room filled with friends and coworkers of the public service official who all want to know what is happening. The community chaplain can be an effective conduit of information. Also, these public service workers are used to "fixing" a problem and being the hero. All they can do in this situation is to wait. It is very uncomfortable for a results oriented hero to have to let someone else fix the problem. The feeling of helplessness is perplexing for the public servant. Although this will be a time intensive ministry opportunity, the community chaplain can build strong relationships with public servants through this process.

■ **Funeral Services:** Because of the line of work that public service entails, there is inherent danger. On occasion, this danger is fatal. The community chaplain should always make special effort to pay homage to the fallen public servant, especially one who gave his life in the line of duty. The community chaplain may also be needed to help communicate the news to the rest of the public service community. Additionally, the chaplain may be a vital resource in dealing with the funeral home. If the family does not have a pastor, the chaplain may be asked to officiate the funeral service. The background and faith experiences of the family and the deceased should be taken into consideration by the chaplain.

Fig. 2.2 Birthdays can be lonely for public servants.

■ **Birthdays or other special days:** It may be a good idea for the chaplain to plan a weekly or monthly birthday party to celebrate the birthday of the public servants. Because families can live far away or not make the effort to be with them at work, these days can be lonely for them. Be sure to take into account special days, such as Veteran's Day or Memorial Day, as many of those in public service are former active duty military veterans.

■ **Library:** As mentioned earlier, many public servants can not participate in church services, but they may have a great deal of time on their hands waiting for a call to come in. This is a great opportunity to leave something at the fire station or jailhouse that is nourishing to the mind, emotions, and spirit. Tapes of sermons from your church can be a treasured commodity. The Bible on tape, books on tape, and even some wholesome DVDs may be used to pour spiritual truths into the mission field of those in public service.

■ **Public Service Day at church:** Set aside a special day at your church to honor and recognize public servants in your community. Talk to your church staff about inviting all public servants to a special worship service, where they are recognized for their service to the community. This would be a great kickoff to the community chaplain program.

There are many people who place the needs of the community and individuals around them at a greater priority than their own personal safety or comfort. We call these people public servants. They work in EMS and paramedic rescue squads, hospital emergency rooms, 911 dispatch centers, jails, fire stations, and police cruisers. The ministry opportunity to public servants is great. Without the public servant, the quality of life for everyone in our society would diminish. Will you accept the challenge to reach out and serve a group that is usually serving you?

Fig. 2.3 Public servants place the needs of others ahead of their own.

Endnotes

1. See State Services Commission <http://www.ssc.govt.nz/career-progression-survey05> (Accessed 14 June 2006).

2. This list is a compilation of information found at Federation of Fire Chaplains <http://www.firechaplains.org>, International Conference of Police Chaplains <http://www.icpc4cops.org>, and American Correctional Chaplains Association <http://www.correctionalchaplains.org/articles/role_of_jail_chaplains.html> (Accessed 25 June 2006).

Chapter Three

The Community Chaplain

to the Elderly

CHAPTER THREE

The Community Chaplain to the Elderly

Objectives

During the course of this chapter, we will perform the following tasks:

- Plot a course on how to begin a ministry to the elderly

- Examine the unique characteristics of the mission field of the elderly

- Explore the specific processes for ministering to the elderly

---

I t is a fact that the largest population group in the United States, the "baby boomers", is getting closer to retirement. As this segment of society moves out of the work force and into the golden years of life, ministry needs will change as well. Because there will be a growing need for chaplains skilled to minister to the aged, it is important to understand how to meet the needs of the elderly.

While the elderly are sprinkled throughout communities all across the nation, there are clusters of the aging found in a few different settings. Because home builders understand the law of supply and demand, many new communities are being built specifically as "over 55" neighborhoods. These developments have age restrictions placed in the declarative covenants that allow residents only over the age of fifty-five to reside in the community. Ministry to the elderly can also be effective when done in a seniors' community center, an assisted living facility, a graduated medical center, or

Fig. 3.1 There is a growing need for chaplains skilled to minister to the aged.

a nursing home.

To establish yourself as the community chaplain to an elderly population living in a "55 and over" neighborhood, please refer to the chapter focused on neighborhood chaplaincy for more details. At this time, we will look at strategies to minister to the elderly in the facilities that are mentioned above. Nursing facilities, assisted living centers, and other institutions like them have staff that is focused on providing physical and medical care for residents. The goal of the chaplain in the elder living facility will be to act as a bridge between the church and those who often are not physically able to participate in church related activities.

The first step in beginning your role as a community chaplain to the elderly in a nursing facility is to meet with administration. Find out who the decision maker is and schedule a time to meet with him or her. During the meeting, plan to introduce yourself, explain what services you can offer to the residents, and help the administrator understand that you can be of great benefit in the facility. You may want to gain insight from the administrator regarding the needs of the facility and its residents. Always be sure to thank the administrator for his time and follow up with correspondence that recaps what occurred during the meeting to avoid confusion in the future. Some items to include in your communication with the institution leader may include times and days that the chaplain will be at the facility, what the chaplain will and will not do, and contact information for the chaplain in the event of an emergency.

Once the mission field has been cleared for the chaplain, it is important for the community chaplain ministering to the needs of the elderly to be aware of the specific issues that face the aging. There are certain biological changes that take place as we age. Patho-physiological alterations in the form and function of cells, organs, and systems of our physical bodies occur with aging.[1] These changes affect our senses:

- Eyesight diminishes
- Hearing deteriorates
- Sense of smell is altered
- Taste is affected
- Touch is lessened

In addition, bones may become less dense, leading to a light and brittle skeletal system. Muscles lose strength and atrophy from lack of use. All other systems, including our digestive, cardiovascular, glandular, and central nervous, take on various changes. Often a change in one system causes change in another. All of these changes, when happening together, can cause us to be less resistant to illness. This means that the community chaplain should be especially sensitive to the reduced immunity of those in his mission field.

Psycho-social changes also take place with increasing age. James Weisz, a chaplain caring for the aged, states that "the senior population allows me to meet and accept others at their highest level of vulnerability: most have no homes, few possessions, and limited resources. No longer able to care for themselves, they are powerless. All they want is to maintain their dignity, their self-esteem, and their faith."[2] With age there is typically a reduction in activity, overall productivity, and sense of worth. This can lead to financial insecurity, social constraint, and a reduction in employment and leisure activities. Because many losses occur, both through increased dependence on others and through a loss of control, depression may be present. Many familiar things and people are gone. This diminished status can often result in a focus on death for the elderly.

In addition to the changes mentioned above, spiritual changes take place as we grow older. With physical ability declining, there is typically an inability to participate in formal religious institutions and practices. Attendance of church services and organized worship is reduced. As a result, there is often an increase in personal spiritual activity. Personal prayer, meditation, private Scripture intake through reading or listening to the Bible on tape/CD, and listening to religious programs on radio and television often take the place of organized worship services as they can be done in the privacy of one's room and a time that is convenient for the participant. Often, because the elderly person has more time due to retirement, there can be an increase in time spent in caring for others. Dr. David Skelton, a geriatrician and minister, conducted a survey on his patients that came into the office regarding spiritual activity. Here are the results:[3]

- 72% of them did Bible reading or study, either individually or in group settings
- 68% of them had a self described "significant" prayer life, often including interceding for others
- 7% of them considered themselves to have "distinct personal ministry" as advisors, counselors, intercessors to family and circle of friends
- 4% of them had participation in formal religious activities (church)

In addition, Dr. Skelton asked his patients about how they felt about the church and its response to their needs. The issues stated included poor transportation to church, a need for large print books, a need for improved outreach by telephone, mailings, or visits, improved acoustics in church so the message could be heard, better access to church buildings and to the altar, improved access in restrooms, better temperature control in the buildings, and worship style that is not so modern.

So it can be seen that there is a mission field for the elderly. They are desirous of ← interaction with spiritual matters, but often lack the ability to interact in an organized fashion. So what are the nuts and bolts of ministry to the elderly? Once you have established yourself with the nursing facility and understand that the elderly have a specific set of needs, steps must be taken to meet those needs.

Remember that the ministry of presence, covered in a later chapter in detail, is important with the elderly. Because of some of the changes that take place physically, the elderly can feel shunned by America's youth obsessed culture. We must also examine why we may avoid the elderly. Is it that we do not want to look at our own mortality? Perhaps. Focus on the overall mission. The community chaplain is here to meet residents at their point of need. They need someone to value them, to care for them, to listen to them, something that nurses, doctors, and administrative staff are all too busy to do. When the community chaplain takes time to listen to a complaint, to pray for a physical pain, to answer a question about faith, or share a memory of life, he is expressing value to the resident. A variety of ministries can take place with the community chaplain who is focusing his efforts on the elderly. Let's take a look at a few of them now.

■ **Worship Services:** the chaplain can lead a weekly service. There should be consistency regarding the time and day of the week. Because more traditional music, worship styles, and style of sermon are preferred by the elderly, this should be noted when planning the service. Be-

Fig. 3.2 Chaplains can minister to the elderly by leading a worship service.

cause many elderly cannot stand or sit up for extended periods of time, the duration of the service and activity required during the service should accommodate physical limitations. Be prepared for distractions from patients who may suffer from dementia or other mental impairments.

■ **Funeral Services:** because the elderly residents are dealing with life threatening illnesses, death is inevitable. In this event, the community chaplain can offer to assist the family in communicating the news to friends at the facility. Additionally, the chaplain may be a vital resource in dealing with the funeral home. If the family does not have a pastor, the chaplain may be asked to officiate the funeral service. The chaplain should take the background and faith experiences of the family and the deceased into consideration.

■ **Birthdays or other special days:** it may be a good idea for the chaplain to plan a weekly or monthly birthday party to celebrate the birthdays of the residents. Because families can live far away or not make the effort to be with the elderly, these days can be lonely for them. Be sure to take into account special health and diet concerns when planning for a cake or other treats. Involving others in entertainment or planning to have children or even canine companions present can make the occasion special for all.

■ **Library:** as mentioned earlier, many elderly cannot participate in church services. Tapes or CDs of sermons from your church can be a treasured commodity. The Bible on tape, books on tape, and even some Braille books can be used to help keep the minds of the elderly sharp. Make sure that the tape/CD players in the library are easy to operate, having large buttons and clear markings.

Besides the residents that are in the elder care facilities, there are the family members of the elderly who will also need the care of the community chaplain. It may be beneficial to hold family support groups. Placing a parent in a nursing facility is a difficult time for most children. They may experience guilt, helplessness, and fear. Knowing that they are not alone and gaining insight on dealing with these feelings may be of great help to the family. Meetings can take place in the nursing facility or at a nearby location. In addition to support groups, more formal education by the chaplain may take place. The chaplain can hold classes that offer practical information about what to expect when a loved one is placed in a nursing facility. The chaplain may lead classes where he has some experience and expertise. However, the chaplain should be careful to recruit others to speak to areas where he has no knowledge.[4]

When planning for elder ministry, there are certain points to keep in mind. First, count the cost involved in making the commitment to establish a community chaplain with the elderly. The elderly may have faced rejection from family and other members of society due to age. Another rejection is the last thing that they need. Once the decision has been made, visit regularly. Be consistent with the day of the week and the time of the day. Be friendly and respectful to the residents. Smile, and provide appropriate cues for what is happening to help compensate for loss of senses. For example, hold out your hand when you want someone to shake your hand. Coach children and others who may not be familiar with the elderly on how to interact. For an elder with hearing loss, speak in a natural voice, slowly and distinctly, separating each word. Try to speak in a low voice, especially if you are a female. Higher pitched voices are harder to hear for the elderly. Those with vision problems will be more at ease if the chaplain wears the same color shirt each time he visits, making the chaplain easier to recognize. For numerous reasons, the speech of the elderly may be difficult to understand. Do not pretend that you understood what an elder said if you did not. Simply ask him to repeat himself. A family member may be available who has a better understanding of the elderly person's speech.

Fig. 3.3 Higher pitched voices are harder to hear for the elderly.

Engage the elderly person in conversation. Ask about mementos they have displayed in their living space. Ask questions that require more than a "yes" or "no" answer. Look for things to ask about and draw them out with follow up questions. Some topics that have been proven to extend conversation without being offensive include the following:

- Current events
- Local events
- National events
- Worldwide events
- The weather, now and in recent past
- Things related to the current season, like flowers in bloom, holidays, etc.
- News from their church
- Things related to nature, like birds, squirrels, etc.
- Pets, both present and past[5]

While you may wish to bring gifts, this practice should be limited to small amounts of food. Otherwise, the elderly will feel obligated to return the gesture. Spending time reading to the elderly can be enjoyable, as reduced visual acuity may have limited the ability to read. They love to have the Bible, newspapers, magazines, or short stories read to them. Check to make sure that they can hear you. Stop periodically and interact with the elderly about the story that you are reading.

Because many elderly are not mobile enough to physically go to church, it may be up to the community chaplain to bring the church to the elderly. This can be accomplished by organizing a worship service in the facility. Most people in this age category enjoy singing hymns and will know them by heart, making song books unnecessary. Consider using a devotion book and spend time discussing the text of Scripture that is written about in the devotional. Use a regular routine or format for familiarity and comfort. Have a prayer time together. Be prepared to hear about physical ailments during prayer time.

There are some aspects of elder care that can be upsetting, intimidating, and even discouraging. These things make us uncomfortable and can cause us to cease elder care. How do we combat these aspects? First, recognize that there will be new and possibly unpleasant odors and sights experienced in the ministry of elders. Often this discomfort lessens with exposure and time. Remember that we are all just "clay pots" that hold us during our time here on earth. We all have dignity and worth because we are created in God's image. Secondly, it is important to know that many elderly are negative. Physical deterioration, loss of independence, and even certain medicines can have the effect of depression. Affirm and reaffirm the elderly. Be positive and upbeat. If you suspect that someone is depressed and you have a concern for them, be sure to respect the bounds of confidentiality, but inform proper personnel when there is a concern for the safety of the individual. Finally, mental capacity will often diminish during the aging process. Dementia, Alzheimer's disease, strokes, and other illnesses can impair memory and mental stability. These medical issues can cause the elderly to become easily agitated. Your presence, consistently, can

Fig. 3.4 Remember that we are all just "clay pots".

actually serve as a calming factor. Even if the person is not able to recognize you, emotional level responses can take place. Your love and attention gives a sense of normalcy and worth to their existence. As both short and long term memory can be impacted, patients may forget that a loved one has died. When the elderly ask about someone who is deceased, it may be best to avoid the direct answer as this may trigger a new grief response as if the person is hearing it for the first time.

As it can be seen, there are several important aspects to keep in mind when ministering to the elderly. Strategies to establish the ministry to the elderly are crucial. Additionally, the specific needs of the population of your mission field should be ever in front of you. These needs will result in shaping the ministry to the elderly. Finally, the fact that worth and dignity is important to God's creation is exemplified when we meet the needs of the elderly.

Endnotes

1. Rev. David Skelton, "Ministry and the Elderly," <http://www.zeuter.com/~accc/sermons/min-elder.htm> (Accessed 25 May 2006).

2. James M. Weisz "Why I am a Chaplain," <http://www.gbhem.org/chaplains/whyiamItem.asp?item_id=13> (Accessed 25 May 2006).

3. Rev. David Skelton, "Ministry and the Elderly," <http://www.zeuter.com/~accc/sermons/min-elder.htm> (Accessed 25 May 2006).

4. Chaplain Fellowship Ministries, "Nursing Home Chaplaincy," <http://www.chaplain-ministries.com/certifi.html> (Accessed 25 May 2006).

5. Peg Hoekstra, "Resources for Senior Adult Ministry PART XII Suggestions for Visiting Home or Facility-Bound Elderly," <http://www.rca.org/disciples/senioradults/visitations.html> (Accessed 25, May 2006).

Chapter Four

The Community Chaplain

to Children

CHAPTER FOUR

The Community Chaplain to Children

───────────────── Objectives ─────────────────

During the course of this chapter, we will perform the following tasks:

- Identify indicators of potential children at risk

- Examine methods for caring for children of broken homes

- Observe causes and solutions for children who are incarcerated

- Explore the specific processes for evangelism for children and teens

───

T here will be a wide variety of situations that you might encounter as a community chaplain as you begin to care for your mission field. Spiritual care will be your main focus; but in order to maximize your ministry opportunities, it is important to have some guidelines to help you successfully accomplish your mission. While we all have needs, there are specific situations that will be faced by children. The next few pages will address methods of meeting these needs as a community chaplain.

In this chapter we will cover topics that include, but are not limited to, how to care for children in divorce, children with serious illnesses, and youth in detention centers, as well as what to be aware of in these particular circumstances. Additionally, in order to be adequately equipped, each community chaplain must be open to the guidance of the Holy Spirit. He is the one who will guide you into sharing the life-changing good news of Jesus Christ in a fashion that these children and parents will understand and openly receive. The truth of God's Word is what people need in any crisis they are experiencing, and the same is true when it comes to caring for children. The Word of God brings hope for the future and healing for the emotional and spiritual aspects of each child.

Although not all problems or crises are spiritual, they are fundamentally related to a fallen human condition. This means that complete healing—spiritually and emotionally—are impossible apart from a relationship with God and obedience to His Word. In helping any child, it is important to recognize signs that identify a potential problem emerging. Such signs may include changes in behaviors, eating habits, or routines, and the emergence of sudden fears. Changes in dress, personal hygiene habits, and daily activities may also be present.

In addition to physical changes, emotional changes may be recognized by parents, friends, teachers, and church leaders. While many of these problems are outside of the scope of the community chaplain, gathering valuable resources, such as qualified counselors specializing in the care of children, can prove to be a tangible way to show God's love to the child who is hurting. This can be a way to minister to the needs of the entire family.

Caring For Children in Divorce

Caring for children who are faced with the possibility of divorce, are in the middle of divorcing parents, or have been through the pain of divorce can be problematic for the community chaplain. What does one say to a child? The effective community chaplain will not ignore this issue due to discomfort. Every year in the United States, more than a million children watch their parents go through divorce.[1] This can be very painful, especially during the first twelve to eighteen months following the divorce and especially for children under six and older than fourteen or fifteen. Confused, afraid, and in-

Fig. 4.1 Every year in the US more than a million children watch their parents go through divorce.

secure, these young people often express their frustrations in truancy, fighting with siblings, running away, school problems, absences, nightmares, or regression to more childish behavior.[2] The problems are greater when the child doesn't get along with the custodial parent or when contact with the father is significantly reduced.[3]

When caring for children and even parents who are going through divorce, it is critical that the caregiver's own attitude be brought under the control of the Holy Spirit in order to properly care for the victims of this crisis. The effective helper must take time for personal reflection on his or her attitudes toward divorce, divorced persons, and people who are going through divorce.[4]

There are certain realities that we want to communicate to children in divorce. First, inform the children that both parents genuinely love them. Next, communicate in a way that the children will understand that their parents will provide for them. Third, it is crucial that the children understand that this circumstance is not their fault. Emphasize that you are there for all parties involved to care in a nonjudgmental manner to the level and degree with which they are comfortable.

As a caregiver seeking to meet the needs of children and families that are facing the crisis of divorce, there are certain measures that should be common practice. Confidentiality is a cornerstone for the effective community chaplain. Parents of children who are dealing with divorce must understand that chaplains must keep information that the child tells them in confidence. There are, however, instances when a community chaplain should breach confidentiality. When a child gives signals that he is in danger of hurting himself or others, this should be investigated as outlined in another chapter dealing with confidentiality and promptly reported, if circumstances warrant such behavior.

Fig. 4.2 The effective community chaplain should be aware of the many different kinds of losses that a child of divorce experiences.

The effective community chaplain should be aware of the many different kinds of losses that a child of divorce experiences. Children lose the daily presence of one parent, and often the remaining parent is overwhelmed with financial and emotional worries. However, unlike the case of a death in the family, in which church and community members surround the family with care, the opposite frequently happens in the case of divorce. When a divorce occurs, people flee. Children often feel abandoned by their parents and the church during a divorce. There is a feeling of emptiness and vacancy. Children of divorce require much time and attention. If one does not have the time to invest for a divorce case, it may be a good idea to partner with another community chaplain or the church in order to properly care for this family, especially the children. This is not a situation in which you can serve half-heartedly.

It is not unusual for children of divorce to also experience anger. This stems from the feeling of abandonment and fear associated with it. These feelings often surface when financial security changes due to divorce. As a community chaplain, being familiar with state and local programs targeting "dead beat dads", or those who neglect to pay child support, can be helpful. Such programs leverage governmental authorities and the court system to step in and hold fathers accountable for providing for their children. While many successes can be attributed to these programs, they are far from meeting the needs of each family that has been impacted through divorce.

In one story, a mother and four children were left by the father, ultimately resulting in divorce. One consequence was a growing need for financial help. With the mother working three jobs with little extra to go around, it was not uncommon for her to come home from work or the children to come home from school and find the electricity turned off or the water turned off. In this situation, the parents of the mother stepped up to help when things got tight. Obviously, the children were adversely affected in various ways. The oldest turned to drugs and alcohol, only to find herself in legal difficulties, pregnant, and unmarried. The other children were affected in less obvious ways. The second oldest became a man too early for his years and developed an anger problem. The two youngest children developed serious insecurity issues. This kind of situation is not all that unusual; but as a community chaplain, these are the types of challenges you could uncover as you begin to invest your life in broken families.

Child Care Providers and Family Caregivers Provide Stability

Sports, youth activities, and positive role models at school have all been used to care for youth suffering from a divorced home. A person who genuinely cares for the child is what is significant. As Cindy Strasheim points out, "The bond with a caregiver may be the most stable relationship for the child during a divorce. No one likes to feel like they are in unfamiliar territory. Changes during divorce can feel very uncomfortable. A sensitive care provider can establish a safe, secure, and familiar place for the child to rest and regain perspective on family life-although they may not be able to understand the meaning of divorce in a family."[5] Strasheim lists some good caregiving skills that we must possess and practice if we are to give the care children need in this area:

How to be a Caregiver Band-Aid

Listen

Love

Laugh

Let them solve problems

Let them go when they are ready

Know if they need more help than you can give

In sessions of *Kids Talk About Divorce*, children reported that they want someone to listen to them, hold them, tell them they love them, and assure them that everything will be okay. Class participants responded to the opportunities to be creative. They gained from acting out their emotions in serious and silly ways. Laughter helped them feel better. They wanted to learn to solve problems at the appropriate kid level- not copying what they see parents say and do.

When they were ready to move on and do things normally and on their own, they wanted encouragement and permission. They liked encouragement to seek new experiences that will continue to build character. They yearned to get through the divorce.[6]

We, as community caregivers, are called to listen carefully, love unconditionally, and laugh easily. We need to lead them to problem solving, launch them when they are confident, and release them to capable hands when we have seen that our time with them is done.

In Romans 8:28, the Apostle Paul is teaching the church at Rome in one of the most quoted verses in all of Scripture: "And we know that God causes all things to work together for good to those who love God, to those who are called according to His purpose" (NASB).

This verse allows any of us to take a position of hope when difficult times come into our lives. Divorce is no different. Strasheim also lists five positive outcomes that children can experience when they have good caregivers and are given good direction:

Positives for Children of Divorce:
- Divorce can be a time for personal growth.
- Divorce can be the start of a better life for children.
- Divorce can teach resilience to kids better than any other experience.
- Divorce can teach children responsibility.
- Divorce can teach children respect for different ways of thinking and acting.[7]

We, as community chaplains, are challenged to encourage children of divorce to stay connected, not only with both parents, but with those who are reaching out to help them and encourage them. Sometimes this will be outside the boundaries of a community chaplain's ministry, so it is important that you know the local resources that you can recommend to families to help care for them along with your continued support. This will include getting the family connected with a local church. Elizabeth Marquardt states that:

The churches are now beginning to address the consequences of divorce, as well as the needs of divorcing adults and there is much more to be done in that area. At the same time, chaplains and churches need to understand and include the distinctive experience of the children. In our society, adults tend to get more attention than children because they are bigger, louder, and speak in a language that other adults understand. The churches must continue widening their embrace of divorcing adults, but they must do so by reaching around them and including the children in their grasp as well.[8]

Caring For Terminally Ill Children

Unfortunately, we live in a world that contains illness. Children are not immune to the effects of living in a fallen world. We now turn our attention to children with life ending illnesses. When examining how to care for children who are terminally ill, we must begin to talk honestly and openly about the reality of the child's circumstances. The role of the community chaplain may be to coach parents on how to have a conversation about these facts with the child. There are times that the com-

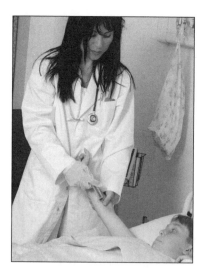

Fig. 4.3 Most critically ill children already suspect or know that they are dying.

munity chaplain may be called on by the family to assist in delivering negative news. How and when to speak with a child about death and dying is a very personal decision, made only in conjunction with and having the permission of the family for which you are caring. Certainly those administering the medical treatment must be part of the decision about when the time is appropriate. If a child's illness is progressing slowly, parents may have more time to decide when and what to tell the child. If a child's illness is progressing more rapidly, parents may decide to talk with their child right away. Nobody knows the child better than the parents, so they are the best judge of what to tell their child and when.

Many parents believe they can protect their child by not telling him or her the truth. However, most children already know or suspect that they are dying. They sense the truth from listening to and watching the adults around them, as well as from experiencing the changes inside their body. It is important to be honest and open; allow your child to discuss his or her fears and questions. Children will feel less anxious and alone if he or she knows what to expect and can count on you for support and love. If your child senses he or she cannot talk with you, he or she may feel isolated, lonely, and more afraid. Not talking about your child's death also prevents both the parents and the child from bringing closure to his or her life—by sharing memories, expressing love, and saying good-bye.[9]

You as a community chaplain may find some of the questions children ask about death upsetting. Knowing how children view death will help you understand and respond to these questions. A major factor influencing a child's understanding of death is his or her developmental level.

Preschool-age children are too young to understand the concept of death, but they do fear separation. They need extra reassurance with frequent touches and hugs. School-age children are just beginning to understand death, but their understanding is not well developed. They may view death as a separation or as a person, such as a ghost or an angel. Teenagers have a more adult understanding of death, but this understanding directly challenges their feelings of immortality and their growing need for independence.

Your child's understanding of death is also influenced by cultural norms, your family's religious beliefs, and things he or she has seen on television or read in books. Different cultures and religions have different beliefs about the meaning of death and what happens after death. These beliefs influence how your child understands and feels about death and dying. For example, a belief that you and your child will see each other again after death can be comforting.[10]

In this particular situation, sharing with permission the love of Christ and how Jesus Christ paid for the sin of man, allowing for forgiveness and the promise of eternal life, will provide much hope.

As a community chaplain, you may be called upon to speak to the family and even the child about death and what one can expect. Consider the following guidelines from the organization "People Living with Cancer":

- Ask **open-ended questions** that give your child the chance to answer in his or her own way. For example, ask, "How did you feel when Grandma died?" rather than a "yes-no" question, like "Were you sad when Grandma died?"

- **Look for hidden meanings in the child's questions** or comments. For example, if your child asks, "What do you think happened to Grandma after she died?" your child may also be asking what will happen to him or her.

- Look for "teachable moments"—everyday moments that are opportunities to talk about what your child is thinking and feeling. Teachable moments could be an animal dying or the illness of a character in a book or a movie.

- **Look for signals from your child that he or she is ready to talk,** such as asking you questions or bringing up the subject of death, even if it is the death of an animal or an imaginary person.

■ **Look for signals that your child is done talking for the moment,** such as changing the subject, looking away, fidgeting, or playing with toys rather than listening to you. It is important to respect your child's need to drop the conversation.

■ **Use simple, direct language** that they can understand. Use the words, death and dying, rather than misleading or confusing terms, such as passing away or going to sleep.

■ **Have as many conversations as the child may want about death and dying** to let him or her know that you or someone else is always available to talk. Encourage, but don't force your child to express emotions—positive and negative.

■ **Reassure them that he or she will not be alone.** It is critical that children know their parents will be with them when they die and that parental love and support will continue.

■ **Reassure your child that after death, any pain and suffering go away and never come back.**[11]

Children need to know that they made a difference in the lives of others. Take this opportunity to encourage the parents to remind their child of the special things he or she has done and the teachers, friends, nurses, and others who will always

remember him or her. Reassure him or her that the special feelings and love will continue forever.

Discuss the family's religious or spiritual beliefs about death and what happens after death. Many dying children feel guilty for leaving their parents and worry about what will happen to their family without them. You may need to guide the parents in giving their child "permission" to die, so he or she can do so peacefully and with-

Fig. 4.4 Parents need to allow their child to be a child as long as possible.

out guilt.

Although parents often feel powerless caring for a child with an advanced illness, there are many things parents can do to help meet their child's psychosocial and physical needs. As a child's illness progresses, his or her needs will change. Paying close attention to the child's behavior will help you adjust to these changing needs. It is important to help parents allow their child to be a child as long as possible. Here are more suggestions for parents from "People Living With Cancer":

- Give your child time to play and engage in other age-appropriate activities, such as watching television, reading, or playing outside.

- Encourage your child to continue attending school, even if he or she cannot attend full time. If your child must miss school for long periods, ask the teacher to have the class write letters, draw pictures, or make videotapes.

- Encourage your child to maintain friendships and other meaningful relationships.

- Encourage your child to continue setting goals. Short-term goals, such as learning to read or taking a special trip, help children gain a sense of achievement and give meaning to their lives.

- Continue to set limits on your child's behavior and practice normal parenting. Without limits, your child will feel overwhelmed and out of control.

- Advocate for your child to help ensure that pain and other symptoms are quickly and effectively treated.

- Give your child as much privacy and independence as possible, in his or her personal care, decision-making, and the desire to be alone.

- Encourage your child's end-of-life wishes, such as giving away special belongings or writing letters to friends.

- Give your child time to say good-bye to family, friends, teachers, and other special people. This can be done in person, with letters, or through a parent.

- Stick to comfortable routines. If possible, try to keep the same caregivers.

- Continue to make caregivers and medical staff aware of your child's physical needs, especially the need for pain management.

- Without using graphic or frightening descriptions, talk about the physical symptoms and changes your child can expect as his or her cancer progresses. Knowing what to expect will make him or her less anxious and afraid.[12]

Finally, it goes without saying that parents are not supposed to outlive their children and that nothing can erase the anguish and distress that parents experience caring for a child with an advanced illness. It is normal for a parent in this situation to experience emotions such as anger, guilt, and frustration. Encourage them to talk with their spouse, family members, or friends about their feelings and fears. Be supportive by putting in place certain resources that will help this family begin to heal. Realize that limitations of time and ability may require a professional counselor to assist in this situation.

Adults face a challenging position when caring for a sick child. The dual role of parent and caregiver can be physically and emotionally exhausting. Take advantage of those who would want to show their support for the grieving family by helping organize their church, neighbors, and friends. Offer to be with the family as they make decisions about limitations on medical treatments. These are legal instruments, commonly known as a living will or advanced directives, that are designed to outline specific instructions about medical procedures or treatments concerning the care for dying patients. These instructions can be verbal or written, although there is a strong preference for them to be in writing. Helping the family make funeral arrangements in advance will be helpful once death has occurred. This will keep the family from making emotional decisions that may harm them after the funeral. Take these final days to reassure the family that you will be around as often as they need you to be, all the while being sensitive not to hover or be a distraction.

Caring For Children in Juvenile Detention Centers

Just as children may deal with things that are outside of their control, like a disease that has no cure, many children and youth will face circumstances that are a direct result of choices that have been made. Here are some facts:

Fact: There are more than seven million children in the U.S. who have a parent under some form of correctional supervision.

Fact: One in seven children will, before reaching the age of 18, have an incarcerated father, according to Wade F. Horn, PH.D., of the U.S. Department of Health and Human Services.

Fact: Children of prisoners are six times more likely than other children to be incarcerated at some point in their lives, according to U.S. Senate Report 06-404, September 8, 2000.

Without effective intervention strategies, as many as 70 percent of these children will become involved with the criminal justice system.[13]

When young people are in these circumstances, it could be for numerous reasons. Many times, those who are in open rebellion are seeking to have a need met. Gary Collins, in his book *Christian Counseling, A Comprehensive Guide*, lists a few reasons youth may come in conflict with the law:

■ **Some unmet need has surfaced**, such as security, acceptance, discipline, or encouragement;

■ **Neglect or abuse of the spiritual** - Psalm 78 emphasizes that children should receive spiritual instruction so they will put their faith in God, remember His faithfulness, and not become unruly, stubborn, or rebellious.

■ **Instability in the home** - When parents cannot cope with their stresses or when they don't get along with each other, children can feel anxious, guilty, and angry. They may be threatened with feeling left out, forgotten, and even manipulated by one spouse or the other. There is the fear of abandonment, physically and emotionally.[14]

Taking the opportunity to attend special events in the lives of these youths, being available for one-on-one spiritual caregiving, and coordinating a support group to assist those who need help will only draw you closer to the opportunity to share Jesus Christ with young people. We want to make a difference in the lives of youth at risk,

Fig. 4.5 What many incarcerated youths are lacking is a meaningful relationship with someone.

but ministry does not stop there. Our opportunity to care for the youth is magnified when we are allowed to reach out to the families of the youths in juvenile correction facilities. It is important to remember that incarceration does not impact only those held in custody, but also their entire family.

One fundamental element in being a productive community chaplain will depend on one's "Countability". The Encarta definition of this word is "able to be counted".[15] It can be further inferred that it is "the ability to be counted on". If we want to be counted on, we need to make sure that we are always on time and on task. This should be the backdrop to any community chaplain's ministry. It is critical to those for whom we are caring that we are available and responsive in times of need.

As seen in the earlier discussion, what many incarcerated youths are lacking is a meaningful relationship with someone. The good news is that as a community chaplain, you can be that person. Terrie M. Williams, in an article written for *Essence Magazine*, 1999, gives some suggestions on how to engage the young person for whom you are caring:

■ Talk to your new young friend and learn about their interests and developing talents. Take them to a family gathering, your office, or a cultural event.

■ Help them learn to set small goals and take action to achieve them. Regularly send them a book, a magazine, or some affordable artwork that will inspire and encourage them.

■ Help them celebrate birthdays and other milestones in their life with cards, notes, or a phone call.[16]

These are excellent ways to build a relationship with these young people. The effective community chaplain will engage the youth in spiritual aspects of life as well, for it is in this arena that the ultimate healing of the young man or woman will rest. It is critical for the community chaplain to begin to invite the individual to church to ⟵ launch them on the road to what God has for their future. This invitation must be for the young person as well as for the parent(s).

As stated earlier, incarceration impacts the entire family. Let's turn our attention to ministry to the family. The goal of these efforts is prevention. The community chaplain can stop cycles of crime, incarceration, drug use, welfare, and poverty by building meaningful relationships with all members of the family.

Parents need care. Much of the time parents blame themselves for the problems their children are going through. Be there to support and encourage them. Help parents realize that their adolescent is a not just a teenager, but a person who seeks to be understood. Also, help the parents seek God's guidance as they care for and guide their teenager. Encourage the parents to seek professional help as needed. This help should apply to all family members, not just to the teens at risk. If any one person in the family has a problem, the whole family has a problem.

For the teenager or adolescent, the community chaplain must be willing to build a rapport based on honesty and respect. This, when mixed with grace and compassion, builds a level of trust in which relationships thrive. As a follower of Christ and His instrument in crisis situations, we must remember that not all problems or crises are spiritual. They are, however, basically related to a fallen human condition, making complete wholeness—spiritually and emotionally—impossible apart from a relationship with God and obedience to His Word.

The community chaplain can foster relationships that encourage trust in God as well as provide nurturing support in times of need. Your life and lessons should help students develop a healthy view of God—His unconditional love and ultimate power. Remind them that Christ's suffering paid the complete price for forgiveness (theirs and others') and freedom from guilt and pain. Encourage teens that neither they, nor their circumstances, are beyond God's reach and ability to repair. With God, the best is never in the past. He has an ultimately fulfilling plan for each life and can, at any time, take a person from anywhere and put them where He wants them to be.

Certain aspects of ministry to children and teens with a history of incarceration should be noted. Consult beforehand with your pastor and/or youth pastor, keeping them apprised of the situation as it progresses, being careful not to breach confidenti-

Fig. 4.6 Know how and when to make a counseling referral for students.

ality at any time, unless there is the intent to harm themselves or someone else. Help students communicate with parents if they have had difficulty doing so. Never offer care to anyone behind closed doors. Don't make promises that you cannot morally or legally keep. Admit your limitations, knowing how and when to make a counseling referral for students who willingly admit the need for further help or whose situation or behavior is potentially harmful to themselves or others. Give appropriate personal attention to individual students—actively listening with an open mind and heart. If you suspect a problem, ask questions. Before responding, make sure you have a clear understanding of what has been communicated. Confront the student's own failures, inconsistencies, or harmful attitudes in a loving, gentle, nonjudgmental manner, directing them to answers in God's Word. Give them information that is relevant to their immediate concerns and encourage students to take stock in the spiritual resources available. Above all, rely on God for wisdom and discernment. Since students will not always convey the whole story, you must ultimately rely on the perception of the Holy Spirit to expose the root of a problem.

Learn what resources are available in your community and prayerfully consider what best fits a struggling student's needs. Ask questions and get a feel for the personal and spiritual qualifications of a potential counselor. Help the student and family understand the need for the referral, and let them take initiative in the final decision. Offer continued support and encouragement to the family throughout the process.

Evangelism of Children and Teens

While a crisis is often the time that an adult will first realize his need for Christ, this is not necessarily the case with children and teens. Why place such an emphasis on evangelism when discussing young people? This question is answered by Massimo Lorenzini:

Why this subject matters: for the honor of Christ, the truth of the gospel, the eternal souls of children, the happiness of parents, the purity of the church, and the sake of those outside the church who are repelled from Christ because of the hypocrisy of false Christians. A lot is at stake![17]

There is no doubt there is much to lose if we are not fervent about seeing children come to Christ.

Here are some facts concerning people coming to a saving knowledge of Jesus Christ:

■ Nearly half of all Americans who accept Jesus Christ as their Savior do so before reaching the age of 13.

■ Thirty percent of the world's population is under 15 years of age.

■ Seventy percent of children are born into non-Christian homes.[18]

The truth of God's Word is the remedy for hurting people, and caring teachers with helping skills, as well as scriptural knowledge, can be the instruments through which the Word brings healing and hope. This is also true for community chaplains. Whatever the crisis—family problems, torn relationships, addiction, abuse, sexual misconduct, tragedy, depression, suicidal thoughts, or attempts—the greatest gift you can bring a child is the unchanging truth of God's Word. Our Lord wants us to teach children about Him and encourage them to believe in Him. He made this very clear to His disciples.

[13] And they were bringing children to Him so that He might touch them; but the disciples rebuked them. [14] But when Jesus saw this, He was indignant and said to them, 'Permit the children to come to Me; do not hinder them; for the kingdom of God belongs to such as these. [15] Truly I say to you, whoever does not receive the kingdom of God like a child will not enter it at all.' [16] And He took them in His arms and began blessing them, laying His hands on them. (Mark 10:13-16 NASB).

Lorenzini further states, "A child's thinking is undeveloped, simple, and naïve. We should be reluctant to place too much expectation on a verbal commitment to Christ just as we would any commitment a child makes."[19] The Apostle Paul wrote to the church at Corinth: "When I was a child, I used to speak like a child, think like a child, reason like a child; when I became a man, I did away with childish things" (I Corinthians 13:11 NASB).

However, when it comes to teenagers and adolescents, we need to be proactive when sharing the gospel. We need to remember that just like adults, the students' greatest problem is their total depravity. The prophet Jeremiah was clear when he said, "The heart is more deceitful than all else and is desperately sick, Who can understand it?" (Jeremiah 17:9 NASB)

It's important to remember that their greatest need is regeneration. As a community chaplain, you cannot affect the depraved heart, in that you did not cause it nor can you change it. But we can introduce the adolescent to the one Person that can impact, affect, and eventually change their heart and that is Christ Jesus. There's only one remedy for the child's inborn depravity: the new birth or regeneration (see John 3:3-7; Romans 8:7-8; Ephesians 2:1-3).

What is our top priority as a community chaplain? It is to build relationships through caring opportunity, in order to gain permission to share Christ with the youth and all those who surround them. We need to do the work of an evangelist, as Paul told Timothy. We as community chaplains do not have the luxury the parents have to make evangelism a lifestyle and not an event. Many times you will find that the opportunity to share the gospel will be thrust upon you and within hours or minutes you may have to share Christ with a young person. So we must be equipped and ready.

> *but sanctify Christ as Lord in your hearts, always being ready to make a defense to everyone who asks you to give an account for the hope that is in you, yet with gentleness and reverence* (I Peter 3:15 NASB).

It is spiritual malpractice for a chaplain to apply pressure on a child to make a profession of faith rather than patiently waiting for God to bring about faith in the child's heart. If the adult does apply that pressure, the child is not able to emotionally bear it and makes a profession simply to satisfy the adult.

As community chaplains, what should we teach? What does the Bible say that children need to hear? Very simply the message should be about the cross of Christ.

Children need to know why the cross was necessary - to make remedy for our sin. We also need to explain that sin is the breaking of God's law (I John 3:4) and that God is the loving, sovereign Creator of all. Remember, we must help a person understand that he is lost before we can help them understand how they may be saved. The program entitled "Sharing Jesus Without Fear" is a particularly helpful way to share the Gospel. It is consistent, does not cause the chaplain to feel the need to save anyone, and is totally dependent on what the Scripture says. This simply allows the community chaplain to be a witness and allow God's Word and the work of the Holy Spirit do the rest.

We know that no one can enter the kingdom of God on the credit of their parents' religion. They must eat the bread of life for themselves and have the witness of the Spirit in their own heart. They must have repentance of their own and faith of their own. When that occurs, they will have sanctification of their own.

Identifying Marks of Child Salvation

- *Conviction* - of sin that is exposed by God's law (John 16:8; Rom 3:19-20; 7:7)

- *Revelation* - of the truth of God and Christ (Matt 11:25-27; 16:17)

- *Regeneration* - bearing the marks of the new birth (Ezek 36:26-27; John 3:3)
  - *Repentance* - confessing and forsaking sin (Ps 32:5; I John 1:8-10; I Thess 1:9)
  - *Trust* - in Christ's atonement alone as basis of salvation (Rom 3:19-28). No mixture of trust in self or works or religion, but only Christ and what He has done and will do
  - *Affection* - love for Christ (I Cor 16:22). What will love for Christ look like in a child? A longing to please Him, a stronger allegiance to Him than to any thing or anyone else, a disdain for anything that dishonors Him.
  - *Obedience* - love expressed in obedience from the heart (John 15:15; 15:10; I John 2:4)
  - *Association* - The child has an aversion to the world and gravitates to other Christians for fellowship (Jas 4:4; I John 2:15; 3:14; 4:20).
  - *Determination* - to follow Christ no matter the cost (Luke 14:27; Matt 16:24)

What To Do When a Child Makes a Profession of Faith

Encourage them—Encourage every sign of faith and have them tell their parents of their new decision.

Provide for them - materials to help them grow in their new faith. Give them a copy of *The Compass*. This and other resources for new believers are available from Lanphier Press at www.lanphierpress.com.

Invite them to your church - A Bible teaching church will guide them into believer's baptism and help them grow in their new walk with Christ.[20]

As chaplains to our communities, our desire needs to be to see the lives of people in our sphere of influence transformed, helping them to discover their God-given purpose and to live productive lives. We can accomplish this aspiration by being a person of influence, living a life that impacts our community. With the guidance of the Holy Spirit and the course of action laid out for you as a community chaplain, you will be sure to honor Christ as you serve in the greatest mission field, the one right around you.

Endnotes

1. Gary R. Collins, Ph.d., *Christian Counseling, A Comprehensive Guide Rvd Ed.* (Dallas: Word, 1988), 462.

2. Ibid.

3. Ibid.

4. Ibid., 458.

5. Cindy Strasheim, "Supporting Children of Divorce: Guidelines for Caregivers," NebFact <http://www.ianrpubs.unl.edu/epublic/pages/publicationD.jsp?publicationId=272> (Accessed 3 August 2006).

6. Ibid.

7. Ibid.

8. Elizabeth Marquardt, "Ministering to Children of Divorce Through their Lives," *Circuit Rider*, May/June 2002, cited by AmericanValues.org <http://www.americanvalues.org/html/3_ministering_to_cod.html> (Accessed 3 August 2006).

9. "Caring for a Terminally Ill Child: A Guide for Parents," *People Living with Cancer (PLWC)* May 2006 <http://www.plwc.org/portal/site/PLWC/menuitem.034b98abc65a8f566343 ccl0ee37a0ld/?vgnextoid=e24903e8448d90l0VgnVCMl00000f2730adlRCRD>(Accessed 3 August 2006).

10. Ibid.

11. Adapted from "Caring for a Terminally Ill Child: A Guide for Parents," *People Living with Cancer (PLWC)* May 2006 <http://www.plwc.org/portal/site/PLWC/menuitem.034b98 abc65a8f566343ccl0ee37a0ld/?vgnextoid=e24903e8448d90l0Vgn VCMl00000f2730adlRCRD> (Accessed 3 August 2006).

12. Ibid.

13. Cited by Child Evangelism Fellowship (CEF) <http://www.cefonline.com/ministries/prison. php> (Accessed 3 August 2006).

14. Collins, *Christian Counseling, A Comprehensive Guide Rvd Ed.*, 153-154.

15. See Encarta < http://encarta.msn.com/> (Accessed 3 August 2006).

16. Terrie M. Williams, "Investing Time in Our Troubled Children - caring for problem children," *Essence*, April 1999, cited by Find Articles <http://www.findarticles.com/p/articles/mi_ ml264/is_l2_29/ai_54256699> (Accessed 3 August 2006).

17. Massimo Lorenzini, "Child Evangelism: *A God-Centered Approach for Genuine Conversion*," Frontline Ministries <http://www.frontlinemin.org/childevangelism.asp> (Accessed 3 August 2006).

18. Cited by Child Evangelism Fellowship (CEF) <http://www.cefonline.com> (Accessed 5 August 2006).

19. Massimo Lorenzini, "Child Evangelism: *A God-Centered Approach for Genuine Conversion*,"

Frontline Ministries <http://www.frontlinemin.org/childevangelism.asp> (Accessed 3 August 2006).

20. Adapted from Massimo Lorenzini, "Child Evangelism: *A God-Centered Approach for Genuine Conversion*," Frontline Ministries <http://www.frontlinemin.org/childevangelism.asp> (Accessed 3 August 2006).

_____

_____

_____

_____

_____

_____

_____

_____

_____

_____

_____

_____

_____

_____

_____

Chapter Five

The Community Chaplain
to Sports Leagues

CHAPTER FIVE

The Community Chaplain to Sports Leagues

———————————— Objectives ————————————

During the course of this chapter, we will perform the following tasks:

■ Identify the various sports team opportunities in your area

■ Identify who is included in your specific mission field

■ Explore the intricacies of sports team chaplaincy care

A ll across America sports teams take the field, hit the court, and flock to the track every day. Sports programs of varying kinds and of varying levels are active in virtually every town. If you are interested in serving as a sports team chaplain, chances are you will not have to look very far. From kids playing T-Ball to school teams to adults in AAA leagues, the opportunity to provide spiritual care for these athletes is certainly available.

The first task in serving as a sports chaplain is finding a team to serve. Your community probably has a Parks and Recreation Department. Teams that are involved in the community recreation system will be registered with this department. These leagues will generally consist of Little League baseball, basketball, soccer, and T-Ball teams. The teams sponsored through the Parks and Recreation Department will most likely provide the greatest opportunity for evangelism because of the great mix of participants representing your community. You may contact the Parks and Recreation office in your area to request the names and phone numbers of the various coaches.

Another area to consider for chaplaincy is church league athletic teams. Each season church leagues from all denominations fill the softball fields, basketball courts, and soccer fields. The participants range in age from the very young to the very old, but the needs are the same. This could possibly be the most challenging area to serve, as most churches will consider themselves already available and doing the type of care service you are offering. Your response should be that you will offer to them a designated caregiver. If a crisis arises during a game, there will be no confusion over who is to step into that official role. There is also the issue of confidentiality, which would be difficult for general laypersons of the church to understand and offer.

This is by no means an exhaustive list of the sports team opportunities available for chaplaincy service. The opportunities in your area of the country may be greater and more extensive. If you feel the calling or desire to serve as a sports team chaplain, the opportunities are varied and readily available in most communities.

Who is your mission field as a sports team chaplain? The most obvious answer to that question is the team members who are actually involved in the sport. However, as a sports chaplain, the scope of your mission field will reach far beyond the team roster. A general rule of thumb when caring for a specific people group is, "*If they are important to you, they are important to me.*" Following this simple rule will multiply your mission field exponentially and open opportunities for service that will impact large numbers of people.

Fig. 5.1 If you are interested in serving as a sports team chaplain, chances are you will not have to look very far.

But what exactly does this mean? It means that the team members you will be serving have family, friends, and neighbors for which they have deep care and concern. Fully investing yourself in the life of the team members is where you will find the greatest fulfillment and reward as a team chaplain.

In what other ways can you fulfill your role as a sports team chaplain?

- by contacting all head coaches to identify needs
- by identifying Volunteer Team Chaplains to connect with each of the teams
- by making regular contacts to interact and build relationships of trust and friendship

- by being available for crisis intervention or other team needs
- by developing relationships with immediate family in order to provide support
- by networking and coordinating the volunteer chaplains into a unified effort
- by valuing biblical principles for relationships and life
- by helping them take an honest look at themselves and what they believe
- by building relationships that will last a lifetime
- by planning ongoing Bible studies
- by working with head coaches to coordinate chapel services
- by coordinating opportunities for student athletes to serve and speak
- by creating a safe environment for difficult questions to be discussed[1]

Each of these areas will broaden your mission field and establish you as a quality community chaplain in your local sports programs.

The foundations of chaplaincy apply to a sports team chaplain as with any mission field. Experience has shown time and time again that the chaplain who easily maneuvers through the differing socioeconomic levels represented within a ministry situation is the chaplain who has a much better success rate in terms of overall service to people under that particular ministry. The tools required for this success can be many; however, it always comes down to how well the chaplain meets the person "where they are" in life. Showing genuine concern, being a good listener, and offering good practical guidance to each person, regardless of where they stand on the economic ladder of life, will go far to building a successful ministry within any situation.

Ministering to the needs of a sports team is different than most other kinds of ministry experiences. Simply transferring pastoral skills from past ministry opportunities can be a detriment to the mission of the community chaplain seeking to serve a sports team. This type of ministry will present its own unique set of circumstances. Approaching a sports team in the same manner as one would approach many traditional ministry situations will result in an adverse reaction. There are unique circumstances involved when dealing with individuals outside of a church setting. In the discussion that follows, we will address various methods that will allow the community chaplain to enjoy a successful and enriching ministry to those who are particularly interested in sports.

It is essential that the community chaplain gain the trust of those in his mission field. This trust is built through absolute confidentiality. Once violated, the community chaplain will find it extremely difficult to repair the loss of trust and damaged relationship. It only takes one breach of confidentiality to destroy months or even years of relationship building.

It is essential that the team chaplain attend all games and practice sessions. Oftentimes a team member will wait to speak to a chaplain at the game or practice session. If the chaplain is sporadic on visitation, the team members cannot plan towards speaking with him or her. Establishing and adhering to a set day and even a set time will greatly increase the chance that someone will use your service.

Your sports team ministry will live and die by your communication skills. Availability is paramount for success. A chaplain who cannot be reached is a chaplain who cannot care for the needs of those he serves. When a chaplain develops the reputation for returning calls promptly, those in his care come to realize the seriousness with which he addresses his mission field.

Most of the players that a sports team chaplain serves will not be churched, generally speaking. Because they have no frame of reference for things of the church, they may even have a negative view of ministers and the church. The community chaplain will do well to avoid any behavior that helps to reinforce negative stereotypes. It is imperative that the community chaplain to the sports team be held to the highest standard of ethical behavior. For instance, under no circumstances should a community chaplain either accept money from or charge a team member for services rendered,

While all of the above items are important for effective chaplaincy to a sports team, the most essential part of your ministry is an active prayer life. A lack of prayer will have devastating results on the effectiveness of your ministry. Once you have been equipped with this vital part of ministry in the sports world, you can serve with power and success.

It is certainly understandable that while serving as a sports team chaplain you will be more accepted if you are wearing sportswear. However, if it is not done so in a clean and crisp way, you will lose the respect of those with whom you are trying desperately to gain trust. Remember, you are a professional caregiver and you are wearing a logo

Fig. 5.2 The Community Chaplains of America logo serves as your badge.

that reflects the name of God (*I AM*). For those reasons alone, you should present yourself in a clean and neat manner. There are, however, some basic rules that you will need to follow in order to be as successful as possible. So that you are easily identified across the sports venue, always wear a Community Chaplains of America logo shirt. This will be helpful in identifying you as a caregiver and allow access to normally restricted areas in times of crises.

Your mission as a sports team chaplain can be one of the most exciting and rewarding services in which you are ever involved, as well as the most fun. Make the most of the opportunity which God has presented to you by performing your mission in a loving, caring, and professional manner.

Endnotes

I. Dr. Byron Weathersbee, "Sports Chaplaincy," *Baylor University* <http://www.baylor.edu/um/index.php?id=22011> (Accessed 8 August 2006).

_____

_____

_____

_____

_____

_____

_____

_____

_____

_____

_____

_____

_____

_____

_____

_____

Chapter Six

The Community Chaplain
to the Small Business

CHAPTER SIX

The Community Chaplain to the Small Business

---------- Objectives ----------

During the course of this chapter, we will perform the following tasks:

- Review the history of chaplaincy
- Examine the strengths and weaknesses of different workplace chaplaincy models
- Explore the legality of a chaplaincy program
- Explore the views of company leadership and employees of the idea of workplace chaplaincy
- Establish the five essentials of workplace chaplaincy

As you begin to look at serving as a chaplain in a workplace environment, it is important that you come to realize that you are facing the largest mission field inside the borders of the United States. It has been estimated that as much as 80% of the average workforce in America has no church affiliation. Perhaps that estimate is not quite as high where you live or are looking to serve, but it still gives us a compelling reason to continue to look for opportunities to bring hope and comfort to the employees and business owners within our communities.

Let's begin by examining exactly where the role of chaplain care began. Chaplaincy enjoys a long history dating back to the man who came to be known as St. Martin of Tours, who is recognized as the initia-

Fig. 6.1 A chaplain is one who comes alongside to share with and help another in distress.

tor of the office of chaplain. While still a soldier, Martin one day encountered a cold beggar. Moved by compassion, he removed the heavy cape from his uniform, sliced it in half with his sword, and shared it with the man. This became the start of his legendary service as a chaplain. The picture this paints of chaplaincy is wonderful. A chaplain is one who comes alongside to share with and help another in distress. Later that night Martin dreamed he saw Christ wearing the half of the cloak he had given away to the beggar. Among Martin's congregations of service, the half cloak he kept became known as a "cappa" and was an object of great respect. The place in which the "cappa" was kept was called "cappella," which through the French word "chappele" became our word "chapel." The priest in charge was called "chappellanus," or "chappe-lain" in French. The chaplain is the keeper of the cloak or the keeper of compassion.

Staff Chaplain Model

While chaplaincy dates back several centuries, the documented history of work-place chaplaincy spans but a few short decades. Two early models of corporate chap-laincy reach back to the 1940s and 1960s, respectively. The first found its origins in the R.J. Reynolds Tobacco Company in Winston-Salem, North Carolina, operated under the title "Industrial Chaplain". The second and longest continuous chaplaincy program was instituted at Allied Holdings, a company based in Georgia. This company has em-ployed chaplains since the mid-1960s and has continued to maintain the program even after going public in 1993. Today they employ 77 part-time chaplains (representing 17 denominations), at 97 locations in 35 states and 9 Canadian provinces.

The model developed and utilized successfully by R.J. Reynolds and Allied Hold-ings is one that remains in a vast number of companies today. These companies range in size from as large as Tyson Foods with 114,000 employees, to Interstate Batteries with more than 1,400 employees, to companies as small as Joe Gibbs Racing with 300 employees. The model utilized by these companies has one primary characteristic: all chaplains are staff employees of the companies they serve, receiving full salary and benefits from the company just as the employees they serve do.

The model of full time staff chaplaincy has an inherent strength, contrasted with several weaknesses. The strength of a staff chaplaincy model is that it allows company leadership to take a more hands on approach to the management and organization of the program. The leadership of an organization should be most closely in tune with the culture of the company and thus able to impart the company's unique makeup onto and through the chaplain's functions.

There are challenges when utilizing the model of staff chaplain. First, as employees, staff chaplains have a fiduciary responsibility to the company as their employer and must serve the needs of other employees through this paradigm. This fiduciary responsibility impacts the tenet of confidentiality, which is a cornerstone of great chaplain care. Chaplains working in staff positions acknowledge this conflict.

A second weakness is one faced by any company attempting an endeavor outside its primary mission. Interstate Batteries, for instance, clearly identifies its mission. The mission of Interstate Batteries is: "To glorify God as we supply our customers worldwide with top quality, value-priced batteries, related electrical power-source products, and distribution services. Further, our mission is to provide our partners and Interstate Batteries System of America, Inc. (IBSA) with opportunities which are profitable, rewarding, and growth-oriented."[1] Interstate Batteries is in business to make batteries. The core of their business is not corporate chaplaincy. While the case may be made that every company has tasks necessary to the operation of the business that fall under the category of support functions, chaplaincy is unique in that there is typically no one on staff with the training and experience specific to the task of implementing and managing a chaplain care program within a large organization. Even those trained for ministry positions typically have no experience or training for such a task. The process, at best, is an on-the-job learning experience and is one where companies are forced to learn lessons from other likeminded companies or learn lessons through the trial and error process of experimentation.

A third weakness for a staff chaplaincy model is found in those companies large enough to employ a full time chaplain but too small to need the services of a multi-chaplain staff. In this situation the corporate chaplain functions in a lone ranger fashion, and the benefit of a team concept of chaplaincy is absent.

When a workplace chaplain is functioning in a lone ranger capacity, as a single chaplain without a support system, many things are missing. First, the presence of on-going continuing education training specific to the acquisition of chaplain skills is not readily available. Second, the workplace chaplain in such an environment lacks the camaraderie present when functioning as a team. This missing support can be particularly acute for both chaplain and company when the chaplain is facing a major crisis, such as an on-the-job injury or employee fatality. In such cases the needs of the employees may be more than can be met by one person, and the solo corporate chaplain may find themselves overwhelmed and unable to properly care for the employees or even for themselves. Instances such as these bring a tremendous amount of stress into the life of the chaplain and make it essential for them to be able to debrief with someone who understands the caregiving pressures they are facing.

A final challenge facing a staff chaplain model focuses on the employees. Often, employees are uncomfortable seeking the help of a workplace chaplain that they simply view as a fellow employee. This discomfort may come from questions regarding the confidentiality of the program or even questions regarding the motivations of the company's leadership in providing a benefit such as corporate chaplaincy. Skepticism among employees is initially present toward any chaplaincy program, but perhaps even more so when the chaplain is a fellow employee. Questions raised in the minds of employees are many. Is the chaplain simply a company spy hired to aid management in keeping track of employees in their jobs and even in their personal lives? Will the things I share with the chaplain really be held in confidence? Is the chaplain's real role a preventive measure on the part of the company to stave off unionization? These fears can be dispelled through time, but the initial barriers can be quite steep to over-

Fig. 6.2 Some employees fear the chaplain is simply a company spy.

come. Utilizing the skills learned in this training will help overcome these obstacles.

Tyson Foods, Inc.[2]

While there are weaknesses in staff model corporate chaplaincy, success is still being achieved. The list of staff chaplain models is impressive, and good employee care is being provided. Take Tyson Foods, Inc. for example.

In 2000 John Tyson, the grandson of the founder of Tyson Foods, Inc., became the CEO and Chairman of the Board. When Tyson Foods acquired Iowa Beef Packers (IBP)

Fig. 6.3 Tyson Foods, Inc. is an example of a Staff Chaplain Model.

in August 2001, they became the world's largest processor and marketer of chicken, beef, and pork, the second-largest food company in the Fortune 500, and a member of the S&P 500. The corporate headquarters is located in Springdale, Arkansas, and their Fresh Meats Division is located in Dakota Dunes, South Dakota. The company has approximately 114,000 team members employed at more than 300 facilities and offices in the United States and around the world. Through its Core Values, Code of Conduct, and Team Member Bill of Rights, Tyson strives to operate with integrity and trust and is committed to creating value for its shareholders, customers, and team members. The company also strives to be faith-friendly, provide a safe work environment, and serve as stewards of the animals, land, and environment entrusted to it.

John Tyson's spiritual journey led him to a deep conviction that he wanted chaplain services as an alternative team member benefit. This would be alternative in the sense that team members could choose to use or not use the service and alternative in that it was a choice left up to each complex or plant manager as to whether they wanted the program at their location. His support and backing of the program has been essential to its success.

In October 2000 Alan Tyson, not related to the owner, was hired as Tyson's Director of Chaplain Services. Alan is a retired US Army chaplain with 23 years active duty and experience as a health care and corporate chaplain. As of May 2006 there are 130 chaplains that serve 242 Tyson facilities in the USA, Canada, and Mexico. The facility chaplain positions are all part time and are filled with pastors from the community. It is an interfaith program with chaplains from 32 different faith affiliations to include a Muslim Imam. Approximately 40% of the chaplains are bilingual.

The facility chaplains are expected to make weekly visits on

Fig. 6.4 Chaplain Alan Tyson of Tyson Foods was hired as Director of Chaplain Services in 2000.

all shifts in the workplace. They minister by wandering around the production areas, break rooms, hallways, and offices. Through this ministry of presence and availability, the chaplains get to know the people and the chaplain becomes a known person. The chaplains also respond in times of crisis and make hospital, home, and jail visits.

The chaplains meet annually for a two and a half day training conference in Springdale, Arkansas. The training is focused on enhancing their pastoral care skills, networking, and sharing best practices. Chaplains are supervised through a combination of site visits, monthly reports, and telephone or video conferencing.

Outsource Model

The outsource approach to corporate chaplaincy differs from the staff chaplain model by having the chaplain serve the company as an agent for the company rather than an employee of the company. In the outsource model, the chaplain is an employee of the providing agency and may serve only one company or may serve multiple companies.

The strengths of the outsource approach are many. First, the outsource model allows the employees served a greater level of trust in the confidentiality of the relationship with the chaplain. The employee will know they are talking with a chaplain that is not an employee of the company but instead is an outside confidant. Second, the outsource model provides a greater level of on-going training and support. Because the chaplains are serving as part of a larger organization, they are part of a team of chaplains who receive the support of a team around them. For this reason, chaplains are able to serve in small company situations normally served by a single chaplain, while at the same time benefitting from the continuing education training and ongoing support system. Finally, the outsource model provides a stronger level of service to the company. A chaplain organization can bring a multi-chaplain response to a major crisis, providing a greater level of assurance that the needs of employees are being met.

These strengths and many others will be highlighted through a closer look at the two largest outsource providers of corporate chaplaincy: Corporate Chaplains of America and Marketplace Ministries.

Corporate Chaplains of America

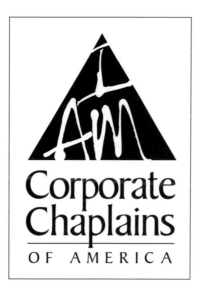

Fig. 6.5 Corporate Chaplains of America was the first to implement a process managed approach to corporate chaplaincy.

Corporate Chaplains of America was founded in Raleigh, North Carolina in 1996 as a non-profit 501(c)3 corporate chaplaincy organization dedicated to ministering to the needs of employees in the workplace. Founder and President Mark Cress relied on his business management education and his experience as a successful entrepreneur to develop a clear business model and the first process managed approach to corporate chaplaincy. This model was developed with a clear mission in mind. The mission of Corporate Chaplains of America is to "build relationships with employees with the hope of gaining permission to share the life-changing Good News of Jesus Christ, in a non-threatening manner."

Media stories have routinely reported on the motivation behind the founding and development of Corporate Chaplains of America. However, after having a personal conversation with Cress, the story is best summed up in saying that the service of Corporate Chaplains of America developed in response to a calling from God.

He feels that this calling grew out of his concern for his employees during his days as a successful entrepreneur and business owner. In the early 1990s, Cress owned a TV production company that was considered one of the country's fastest-growing private companies. As an owner, Cress never felt fully equipped to meet the vast array of needs affecting his employees. However, he always knew that God was in control and was there to meet the needs of his people.[3]

Cress' sense of call to ministry, coupled with his entrepreneurial instinct to see and meet a need, led him to make some major lifestyle changes in 1993. He sold the

Fig. 6.6 Mark Cress, President Corporate Chaplains of America

majority of the stake he had in his company and relocated his family to Wake Forest, North Carolina, where he enrolled in seminary. In February 1996, just prior to completing a master's degree in divinity, Cress launched what is now Corporate Chaplains of America with himself as the lone chaplain and a vision to build the organization to the glory of God with a future staff of over 1,000 full time chaplains serving more than one million employees.

The corporate chaplaincy program provided by Corporate Chaplains of America is offered as a benefit by client companies free of charge to their employees. The chaplains are full time employees on staff with Corporate Chaplains of America, with each chaplain serving between one and eight companies and from 650 to 750 employees. With the development of this model, Corporate Chaplains of America was the first chaplain organization dedicated to the provision of full time career corporate chaplains. The reasoning behind this concept is simple. Employees

Fig. 6.7 The goal set for Corporate Chaplains of America chaplains is to see every employee once each week.

are busy living full time lives and therefore need access to a full time chaplain who is available to serve them 24 hours per day, 7 days per week, free of other vocational responsibilities. The concept of the full time chaplain is also believed to enhance the quality of life for the chaplain, as well as that of their family.

The service of one to eight companies per chaplain allows companies of any industry and any size to utilize the services of the chaplain program. Companies with as few as six employees can count on a chaplain to be available to care for their employees on a 24/7 basis. Companies with as many as 10,000 to 30,000 employees can expect to be served by a team of chaplains serving in multiple locations under the direction of a trained and committed managing chaplain.

The ministry works in simple fashion. A chaplain is provided to serve each company and their employees. The chaplain then makes rounds at the client companies at regularly appointed hours to see if anyone wants or needs to talk. Each chaplain has the established goal of seeing every employee once each week. The purpose of this goal is simply to build a trusting and caring relationship with each employee. Employees served are also given a business card that bears the name of their chaplain. In addition, the card contains the slogan "Caring in the Workplace" and is accompanied by a toll free telephone number that gives employees 24-hour, seven day per week access to their chaplain.

As the relationships develop, the chaplain is positioned to serve as a pastoral care-giver to each employee and their family. The care given can include hospital visitation, marriage or family care giving, help with planning or performance of funeral services, and assistance with a variety of other problem or crisis issues. The care provided is always at the initiation of the employee and only by permission granted by the employee. Confidentiality is the hallmark of the relationship between the employee and the chaplain.

Marketplace Ministries[4]

Fig. 6.8 Marketplace Ministries is an example of an Outsource Model for chaplaincy.

Founded in 1984 in Dallas, Texas, Marketplace Ministries was one of the first outsource approach models for corporate chaplaincy. Founder Gil Stricklin brought a varied background and more than 20 years of military experience to bear as he pioneered the concept of businesses outsourcing their chaplain care programs to a third party provider. Marketplace Ministries is the first and longest continuing operational outsourced chaplaincy model in the United States today. The study and review of the chaplaincy model developed by Stricklin and Marketplace Ministries is essential for a proper understanding of the corporate chaplaincy movement in the United States and its growth.

Operating today under the name Marketplace Chaplains USA, their mission is simple and focused. "Marketplace Chaplains USA exists to share God's love through chaplains in the workplace by an on-site Employee Care Program for client companies." This simple mission has propelled Marketplace Chaplains USA to grow to become an organization of 1400 chaplains caring for 300,000 employees and family members in 38 states and 400 cities.

Working from his background as a military chaplain, Stricklin sought to apply the military model of chaplaincy to the American workplace. Relying on a team of full-time, part-time, and on-call chaplains, Marketplace Chaplains USA speaks of providing an "umbrella of compassion and concern" through on-site, regular workplace visits of a chaplain care team. Marketplace Chaplains USA describes themselves as a proactive and personalized employee care provider. Client companies are assigned a team of male, female, and ethnically diverse chaplains who visit the work site regularly and are available for crisis care, any needed help, and confidential discussions 24 hours a day, 365 days a year nationwide. On behalf of company leaders, Marketplace Chaplains USA utilizes Chaplain Care Teams to help meet the variety of needs of employees and family members coming from a variety of backgrounds.

Fig. 6.9 Gil Stricklin, Founder of Marketplace Ministries

The recruitment of professionally trained and experienced chaplains is a key element necessary to providing over 1,000 part-time, on-call, and full time chaplains for the workplace. Each chaplain is expected to bring extensive experience in caring for people, have a clear understanding of business, and have significant workplace experience. Every applicant undergoes criminal and financial background checks, along with extensive personal reference checks to verify character and personal history. Technical training, significant caregiving experience, and mature and proven character are essential qualities needed for chaplains to provide exceptional service to the employees and families of their client companies.

Each chaplain on a chaplain team is supported and supervised by a veteran in chaplaincy and administration. The chain of accountability is vital to Marketplace Chaplains USA's decades of successfully caring for workers at work. Chaplains also benefit from working within the framework of policies and procedures developed over their 20 year history of successfully caring for employees and families in companies of all types and sizes.

Motivation for Chaplaincy

But the question remains, what motivates a company to obtain the assistance of a workplace chaplain in caring for their most valuable of assets - their employees? The motivations for such a decision and the views toward a chaplaincy program are many, and they differ according to the position the person holds within the company.

Research conducted by the U.S. Chamber of Commerce dating back nearly two decades points to differences in understanding between management and employees, as to what employees genuinely desire and what can really make a difference in the company's culture. Asking the question, "What do employees want?" produced three key needs identified by employees. In order of importance, employees stated that they desired from their employer:

1) Appreciation	2) Feeling "in" on things	3) Help with personal problems

Conversely, management rated these three topics toward the bottom in order of importance. Management rated employees' need for appreciation as eighth on the list, while feeling "in" on things scored tenth, and help on personal problems came in ninth. Management's order of importance as to what employees wanted had an entirely different top three. Management thought employees wanted:

1) Good wages	2) Job security	3) Promotions[5]

This disparity points to the significant role that can be played by the corporate chaplain in helping any company to create a more caring culture. Specifically, the role of the chaplain can help companies meet the third greatest desire identified by employees: help with personal problems. A simple survey of many companies that utilize a corporate chaplain program often cites the creation of a caring family atmosphere for the company as one of the driving forces. A survey of the landscape of today's business climate highlights this need as well.

The issues faced in the American workplace are numerous and provide ample opportunity for making a difference not only in the lives of employees, but also a huge difference in the life of a company. In fact, many executives will state emphatically that the chaplain program has done more than make a difference in their company culture; chaplaincy has helped to shape a different culture. An employee told one owner who utilizes a chaplaincy program that they would rather have the company cancel their health insurance benefits than take away the chaplain program. The value to the employee and to the company is obvious through such a statement.

Before exploring the reaction to workplace chaplaincy by company leadership and by the employees, let us begin with the human resource profession. While many may be initially skeptical of the concept and approach chaplaincy with more questions than support, it is interesting to note the response of the human resource leader following successful implementation of a chaplaincy program.

The initial questions generally focus on the human resource fiduciary responsibility to abide by employer laws, policies, and procedures. Is chaplaincy legal? How will the employees respond? Will the company be inviting trouble through a chaplaincy program? The questions reflect the human resource responsibility to ensure compliance and limit legal liability to the company. While these are valid goals, the ultimate goal of human resource professionals should always be to maximize the human resource potential found in every company. Because of this goal, the chaplain can quickly become an extra set of hands for the human re-

Fig. 6.10 The chaplain can quickly become an extra set of hands for the human resource department.

source department and should, in the best of circumstances, become a most valuable asset to the human resource director.

Human resource professionals are in constant search for solutions and methods to improve problem areas. The search for solutions has not neglected the part spirituality can play in addressing workplace needs. In a feature article on workplace chaplaincy, *HR Magazine* posed the question, "Can chaplains help boost employee morale, retention, and productivity?"[6] The conclusion of the article was a strong "yes". Chaplains can serve as employee sounding boards, offer counseling, guide employees to other counselors, and assist in situations ranging from office closures to employee arrests. The bottom line is an improvement in both morale and employee retention.

A recent study cited in *Workspan* magazine indicated the struggle to maintain a satisfying work/life balance is one of the top two sources of job-related stress faced by employees.[7] A myriad of responsibilities and demands can wreak great havoc with achieving a healthy balance between life in the workplace and life outside the employment field. At any given time, employees may be facing the challenges of child care issues, decisions concerning aging family members, the stress of a hospitalized family member, the imprisonment of a family member, or even death of a family member.

However, when these challenges come, the responsibilities at work do not cease. In facing these difficulties, employees need the support of someone who cares about them as a person. A quick scan of the "What's New" feature in *HR Magazine*, which highlights new products and services, shows that human resource professionals recognize the importance of caring for employees by helping them achieve a healthy work/life balance. One resource highlighted is a web site called "Working Lifescape". Employees can get answers to a wide range of personal questions or conduct research on topics such as anxiety, substance abuse, parenting, child care, and elder care. Still another source providing answers to similar issues is a series of guidebooks and videos provided by Resource Pathways, a Washington state based firm.[8] The challenge to human resource professionals is clear. There is a need to care for the needs of employees that go beyond simply providing basic employment and a paycheck.

Recent articles appearing in the *Washington Post* and *Fortune Magazine* highlight a growing trend on the part of business to go beyond the basics. The *Washington Post* article ran under the headline, "Good for the Soul - and the Bottom Line", with a subtitle, "Firms Promote Spirituality in Workplace and Find It Pays".[9] *Fortune Magazine* pointed out the changing attitude toward a traditional view of keeping religion and business separate. They write, "Bringing spirituality into the workplace violates the old idea that faith and fortune don't mix. But a groundswell of believers is breaching the last taboo in corporate America."[10]

Employee Religious Rights

Given the multicultural nature of the American workplace, concerns could be raised over the rights of Christians seeking to live out their faith in the workplace. While the concerns may be valid, each employee has the freedom of religious expression. The White House Office of the Press Secretary issued guidelines on religious exercise and religious expression in the federal workplace on August 14, 1997. The nine pages of guidelines state in clear and unambiguous language the rights and freedom of religious expression afforded to federal employees. The guidelines state, "As a general rule, agencies may not regulate employees' personal religious expression on the basis of its content or viewpoint."[11]

While these guidelines were specifically issued for the federal workplace, the guidelines speak to the issue of constitutional protection. Thus, they have application to anyone seeking to live out their faith in the workplace and lead others to saving faith in Christ. The guidelines state:

> Employees are permitted to engage in religious expression directed at fellow employees, and may even attempt to persuade fellow employees of the correctness of their religious views, to the same extent as those employees may engage in comparable speech not involving religion. Some religions encourage adherents to spread the faith at every opportunity, a duty that can encompass the adherent's workplace. As a general matter, proselytizing is as entitled to constitutional protection as any other form of speech - as long as a reasonable observer would not interpret the expression as government endorsement of religion.[12]

In addition to the clarity of the statements, numerous examples of acceptable expression are provided. Given the evangelistic focus of this project, one example deserves special note. The guidelines state, "During a coffee break, one employee engages another in a polite discussion of why his faith should be embraced. The other employee disagrees with the first employee's religious exhortations but does not ask that the conversation stop. Under these circumstances, agencies should not restrict or interfere with such speech."[13] The example provided is clear; evangelism is permitted.

While the *Washington Post* article did focus on a few of the concerns, the tone of the article, as well as that of the *Fortune Magazine* article, was favorable toward spirituality in the workplace. In addition, the federal guidelines provide clear support to the person who desires to actively share his or her faith at work. The *Washington Post* article pointed out the use of a phrase to describe the workplace goal of many. "I don't want to park my soul at the door." The conclusion is

Fig. 6.11 Coffee break discussions of religion are permitted, if certain criteria are met.

clear. Employees need not park their souls at the door but can instead enjoy the freedom of living out their faith in the workplace.[14]

What Are My Rights as an Employee?

Fig. 6.12 Actual page from the official White House website, August 14, 1997

From The White House, Office of the Press Secretary, August 14, 1997:

"As a general rule, agencies **may not regulate** employees' personal religious expression on the basis of its **content or viewpoint**" (p. 1).

"In informal settings, such as cafeterias and hallways, employees **are entitled** to discuss their religious views with one another, subject only to the same rules of order as apply to other employee expression" (p. 2).

"Employees are permitted to engage in religious expression directed at fellow employees, and **may even attempt to persuade** fellow employees of the correctness of their religious views, to the same extent as those employees may engage in comparable speech not involving religion. **Some religions encourage adherents to spread the faith at every opportunity, a duty that can encompass the adherent's workplace.** As a general matter, proselytizing **is as entitled to constitutional protection** as any other form of speech – as long as a reasonable observer would not interpret the expression as government endorsement of religion" (p. 2).

"Many religions strongly encourage their adherents to **spread the faith by persuasion and example at every opportunity, a duty that can extend to the adherents' workplace.** As a general matter, proselytizing is entitled to the same constitutional protection as any other form of speech. Therefore, in the governmental workplace, proselytizing should not be singled out because of its content for harsher treatment than nonreligious expression" (p. 7).

"But employees must refrain from such expression **when a fellow employee asks that it stop** or otherwise demonstrates that it is unwelcome" (p. 2).

"During a coffee break, one employee engages another in a polite discussion of why his faith should be embraced. The other employee disagrees with the first employee's religious exhortations, but does not ask that the conversation stop. Under these circumstances, **agencies should not restrict or interfere** with such speech" (pp. 2-3).

"During lunch, certain employees gather on their own time for **prayer and Bible study** in an empty conference room that employees are generally free to use on a first-come, first-served basis. Such a gathering does not constitute religious harassment even if other employees with different views on how to pray might feel excluded or ask that the group be disbanded" (p. 5).[15]

With all of this in mind, how does a company president respond when first introduced to the concept of chaplaincy? How do they view the benefits, opportunities, and challenges of chaplaincy? First and foremost, company presidents who respond positively to the concept of chaplaincy do so for two primary reasons.

First, they provide leadership to offer a chaplain to their employees because of eternal benefits. Second, they provide leadership to offer a chaplain because of economic benefits. Let us explore together what is meant by these two thoughts.

First, a company president is motivated to provide a chaplain who will have an eternal impact in the lives of his or her employees. The company leader has discovered what it means to have God as Leader and know that his or her eternal destiny is secure.

Through this personal discovery, they have come to understand the responsibility placed on them by God to offer impact in the lives of their employees that goes beyond providing them with secure employment, a paycheck, fringe benefits, and the ability to provide for material needs. They understand that the people in their employment have been entrusted to them by God and that the provision of a chaplain is but one means by which they can impact more than just the material needs of employees. A chaplain can bring impact spiritually. They recognize that every physical, emotional, material, and personal need in the lives of their employees pales in comparison to their need for a personal relationship with God through Jesus Christ. Eternal motivation is first and foremost the greatest contributing factor in prompting a company president

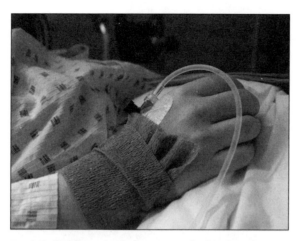

Fig. 6.13 Chaplains can help to ease the burden of worry carried by those they serve.

to provide a chaplain to his or her company.

Second, a company president is motivated to offer a workplace chaplain because of the economic benefit brought to the life of the company. The impact of a workplace chaplain in helping employees through personal crises has a direct impact on company issues such as turnover rate, employee retention, and productivity. When a chaplain cares for an employee struggling with marital difficulties, that time spent *outside of* working hours pays dividends *during* working hours by allowing the employee to receive help, but in a way and at a time that does not take them away from the work they are hired to do. When a workplace chaplain visits the hospitalized parent of an employee and then encourages the worried employee with a brief phone call, the chaplain improves the productivity of the employee by easing the burden of worry the employee carries with them to work.

A chaplain will find a varied response among the employees in a company to the introduction of a chaplaincy program. Following initial introduction of a company chaplain, employees will generally fall into one of three categories in their receptivity to the chaplain and the idea of a chaplaincy program.

The first group can best be described as the attitude-of-gratitude category. Employees in this group will approach the company president or other leadership team members and express appreciation for the provision of a benefit like a chaplain assistance program. Their enthusiasm for virtually everything the company does is unmatched. They see the chaplain program as one more reason why they work for such a great company and typically cannot imagine working anywhere else.

The second category might best be described as the no-big-deal group. The attitude displayed by these employees could be labeled as ambivalence. They believe it might be a help to others going through crises but do not see themselves as ever really benefiting from the chaplain. They do not see the chaplain as a bad thing for the company, but their real focus is on other matters. The tendency is to not see any real value in how the chaplain might be able to benefit them personally.

The final group might best be described as the anti-chaplain-crowd. The attitude of this group is one of hostility. In some cases they will verbally state they want nothing to do with the chaplain and believe it is wrong for a company to have a chaplain. In other instances, their closed communication and avoidance of the chaplain sends the clear, if unspoken, message that they do not want a relationship or interaction with the company chaplain.

Acquiring the Mission Field

Perhaps you already know exactly where you are going to serve as a community chaplain. Maybe you have a friend who owns a small company and the number of employees is just perfect for you to handle in a part time ministry basis. However, many community chaplain candidates are just realizing their call into a workplace ministry and are searching for that perfect opportunity. How is that done? This is where the experience of those who have gone before you in an organized workplace chaplain ministry can be an enormous value. There are certain do's and don'ts that will help you to identify the company who may be interested in a workplace chaplain. But just as important is your presentation of the service to the decision maker.

First, you should target companies with Christian owners. These are the individuals who will be more receptive to your mission. This is not to say that companies who are owned and operated by non-Christians will not be interested, but your chances of serving in the role of chaplain are greater when the owner of the company shares the same desire to see his/her employees cared for by a faith based organization as you have.

Next, your goal in presenting employee chaplain care should *always be* to get before the company decision maker. This will generally be the owner of the company. No one can make the presentation to the owner better than you. You are the only one who has knowledge of the training and support system of Community Chaplains of America. Many opportunities to serve employees with chaplain care are squelched because a well meaning supervisor or Human Resource Manager made the decision that the program would not work before the decision maker ever had the opportunity to see and hear the benefits such a program could offer. For example; Bob is a community chaplain. Bob's neighbor Tim is a lead supervisor for a twenty-five employee company. The only thing Bob should be getting from Tim is the number for the telephone that the owner of the company will answer. Bob explaining employee chaplain care to Tim and expecting Tim to sell the deal does not work! Again, your goal is to get before the decision maker.

The best time to call a company owner, as a general rule, is between 7:15 and 8:00am, or between 5:15 and 7:00pm. The company owner will usually arrive early to his/her office and take the auto attendant off so as to receive calls. In the evening, the auto attendant is usually not yet set. Be very specific to identify yourself and never request an appointment for more than fifteen minutes of their time. The outline below shows how to best utilize the fifteen minutes you have to present Community Chaplains of America to a company owner.

1. Opening (5 minutes)

- Give a business card and ask for a business card.
- Ask, "Do your friends call you _____?"
- "Where would you like me to sit?"

2. Probe: Transitional Phrase

- "Let me tell you what I'd love to accomplish."
- "I want to quickly learn a little about your business."
- I want to quickly tell you about workplace chaplaincy."
- "Then, I want to answer any of your questions."

Allow the owner to tell you about their business, i.e. when and how it started, etc.

3. About Us: Transitional Phrase

- "Thank you. You've helped me learn a lot about your business. Let me take a minute and explain how chaplaincy works. Is that o.k.?"

4. Close

- "Does that sound like something that you think would help your company?"

This simple sales outline is a proven technique for presenting the benefits of workplace chaplaincy to owners in a professional manner. As a member of Community Chaplains of America, the companies you approach will generally employ a small number of employees. Larger companies will be best served through a full time corporate chaplaincy approach. Remember, you requested fifteen minutes, so your presentation must be concise and to the point. If you go over the fifteen minutes, make sure that you acknowledge that and be confident that the owner is aware of the overage and agrees to it. What your mother told you is true; "You only have one chance to make a good first impression."

The Essentials of Workplace Chaplaincy

Serving as a chaplain for a business or industry cannot be compared to any other ministry experience. Workplace chaplains who have tried to transfer pastoral or other previous ministry experiences into the workplace environment more often than not have been met with adverse reactions. There are unique circumstances involved when dealing with the employees of a business. When fully understood and applied to the ministry, the chaplain can enjoy a successful, enriching ministry opportunity. Without these unique and important approaches, the ministry will most likely flounder and fail.

1. First, *confidentiality* must be the absolute cornerstone of your ministry in a workplace environment. If an employee ever feels that you have violated their trust by breaking this basic rule, the trust you have worked hard to earn with all of the employees will be tainted. If there is one absolute in workplace chaplaincy, it remains to be confidentiality.

2. Secondly, regular scheduled visitations to the company or office are essential. Oftentimes an employee will wait and even expect to speak to a chaplain on the regular day that he or she is scheduled to arrive. If the chaplain is sporadic on visitation, then the employees cannot plan towards speaking with him/her. Establishing and adhering to a set day and even a set time will greatly increase the chance that someone will use your service.

3. The promptness in which you return pager or cell phone calls will speak volumes to the sincerity of your mission to your employees. A chaplain who cannot be reached is a chaplain who cannot care for the needs of his or her mission field. Your workplace ministry will live and die by your communication skills.

4. Never, under any circumstances, accept or ask an employee for money. Generally speaking, most of the employees of a company are unchurched. Thanks to the approaches of some ministries, many of the employees have already established a negative attitude concerning *"preachers"* and money. Deserved or not, there remains a perception in many people's minds that you are in their workplace strictly for financial reasons. Accepting or asking for money will only work to enhance this attitude.

5. The final essential to workplace ministry is prayer. If you do not pray regularly for the company you serve and their employees, your ministry there is destined for failure. The failure will come by either the company stopping your service or your ministry there being ineffective and dull.

Equipped with these five essentials of workplace ministry, a chaplain can serve within a business environment with power and success.

There remain some basic rules to follow to ensure that your workplace ministry is as successful as it can possibly be. Remember, there are eternal consequences involved with the work you do as a Community Chaplain.

■ Always wear a Community Chaplains of America logo shirt when entering the company or representing the company in any way. The CCA logo is your *badge* to gain access to all areas of the company and to identify yourself as a professional caregiver in emergency situations. Dress as a professional. Make sure your pants are clean and pressed and your shirt is clean and "crisp".

■ The appearance of your vehicle should always reflect the same professional cleanliness.

How does the prospective chaplain apply the insights of this chapter? On the one hand, he or she recognizes the motivations of the different constituent groups within a company. The motivations of a leader are different from that of a human resource professional or front line manager and from that of the employees. On the other hand, the needs of each group should be served on the terms of their motivations. A relationship of trust, respect, and value must be developed on terms established by those being served and not by the chaplain.

Endnotes

1. "About Us: Mission Statement," *Interstate Batteries* <http://www.ibsa.com/www_2001/content/about_us/mission.asp> (Accessed 18 May 2005).

2. Information on Tyson Foods, Inc. Chaplaincy Services Program provided by Tyson Foods, Inc. (May 2006)

3. Personal Conversation with Mark Cress, President and Founder of CCA, by Dwayne Reece, Raleigh, NC, 5 June 2000.1.

4. See Marketplace Ministries <http://www.marketplaceministries.com/> (Accessed 24 April 2005).

5. Rob Lebow, *A Journey into the Heroic Environment* (np: Prima, 1997), 76.

6. Lin Grensing-Pophal, "Workplace Chaplains," *HR Magazine* (August 2000): 54-62.

7. Stephen LoJacono, "Back-Up Care," *Workspan* (January 2001), 16.

8. Lynn Miller, "What's New: Products and Services," *HR Magazine* (April 2000), 173.

9. Bill Broadway, "Good for the Soul - and the Bottom Line," *The Washington Post* 18 August 2001 <http://www.washingtonpost.com/wp-dyn/articles/A30944-2001Aug18.html> (Accessed 21 August 2001).

10. See Fortune Magazine's electronic archives, Marc Gunther, "God and Business," *Fortune Magazine* 9 July 2001 <http://www.fortune.com> (Accessed 21 August 2001).

11. The White House Office of the Press Secretary, "Guidelines On Religious Exercise and Religious Expression In The Federal Workplace," <http://www.whitehouse.gov/WH/New/html/19970819-3275.html> (Accessed 14 August 1997).

12. Ibid.

13. Ibid.

14. Bill Broadway, "Good for the Soul - and the Bottom Line," *The Washington Post* 18 August 2001 <http://www.washingtonpost.com/wp-dyn/articles/A30944-2001Aug18.html> (Accessed 21 August 2001).

15. The White House Office of the Press Secretary, "Guidelines On Religious Exercise and Religious Expression In The Federal Workplace," <http://www.whitehouse.gov/WH/New/html/19970819-3275.html> (Accessed 14 August 1997).

Chapter Seven

The Community Chaplain
to the Neighborhood

CHAPTER SEVEN

The Community Chaplain to the Neighborhood

———————————————— Objectives ————————————————

During the course of this chapter, we will perform the following tasks:

- Identify neighbors

- Examine reasons for neighborhood chaplaincy

- Describe how to establish a community chaplain in a neighborhood

T hey are all around us. Great ones can make the quality of our lives really wonderful, and horrible ones have a great impact on how we live our daily lives as well. Of course, I am speaking of our neighbors. Over the past few decades, the population has become more concentrated into metro urban and suburban centers. As the late 1990's saw a collapse of the tech sector for investing, many people turned to real estate for rental, refurbishment, resale, or development purposes. Because of this trend, housing prices have risen drastically during this century. A byproduct of this trend is more tightly clustered homes on smaller tracts of land. The type of neighbor living next door and down the block has had an increasing impact. The balance of interaction and privacy has been tricky at times. All this is to say that there has never been a time that community chaplaincy in a developed neighborhood, condo association, or rural community was more relevant.

The Bible has much to say about our neighbor. In Matthew 19, Jesus teaches us to "love your neighbor as yourself". The New Testament meaning of "neighbor" was clearly more expansive than our current definition. When used in Scripture, the term has even been extended to include "the least of these". Clearly, this would not just include the people who live in the homes on either side of us. According to authors Robert Banks and R. Paul Stevens, much of the earthly ministry of Jesus took place as He wandered from village to village, ministering in houses and streets. Examine a quote from *The Complete Book of Everyday Christianity*:

"Many of His parables were drawn from aspects of neighborhood life, illustrating the presence and challenge of God 'in our own back yard'. Elsewhere in the New Testament the command to 'love your neighbor as yourself' is restated no less than nine times. When crises happen at home, neighbors are more often the only ones close enough to call for help, and if we do not know them this is more difficult to do."[1]

But why claim your neighborhood as a mission field? People are increasingly living in areas that are off limits to traditional kinds of outreach from the church. Homes that are built in gated communities are on the rise. It has long been a practice of mission sending agencies to rent or purchase apartments in exclusive buildings to gain access to the residents. The most sobering reason is this: George Barna's study in 2004 states that "there has been a 92% increase in the number of unchurched Americans in the last thirteen years. In 1991 there were 39 million unchurched Americans compared with 75 million currently (2004)."[2]

Fig. 7.1 People are increasingly living in areas that are off limits to traditional kinds of outreach from the church.

The chaplain wishing to serve his neighborhood must look for the ways that information is communicated and accepted specific to the community. For some, it may mean writing a column in a monthly neighborhood newsletter. This can take any form. Maybe an inspirational writing, a devotional for the month, a biblical insight in dealing with an everyday problem or the like could be offered. There is really no right or wrong format to introduce your chaplain services through the newsletter. The neighborhood may have a website, where the chaplain information may be posted. Infiltrate the ranks by volunteering to be a part of the homeowners association. Once you have gotten to the person of influence in the neighborhood, take the opportunity to introduce yourself and explain what a chaplain can do for the community. Many people who work in volunteer positions within the homeowners association (HOA) only hear complaints from the community. The community chaplain seeking to serve his neighborhood will help to assuage this trend. Because the HOA officers may know of problems within the community, this may be a great time for the community chaplain to gain insight into the needs of the population group in the mission field. At the conclusion of the conversation, be sure to thank the HOA officers for the time offered to you. Follow up with a communication that again offers gratitude and reviews the events of the meeting so that everyone is on the same page. This letter, e-mail, or phone call may be a great time to suggest times and days that the community chaplain is available, what the chaplain will and will not do, and contact information for the chaplain in the event of an emergency.

Another type of community ministry can take place in apartments. Since these tend to be more transient than a community of houses, special ministry opportunities are available. The majority of unreached people in the United States live in

Fig. 7.2 The children are the future!

multi-housing units such as garden and high rise apartments, duplexes, and mobile home parks. In these densely populated areas, block parties can be held to reach out to families or singles. These are often urban areas, with problems of poverty, lack of education, language barriers, and little or no health insurance. Beginning programs that benefit those in this situation will have long term impact and open the door to share the life-changing Good News of Jesus Christ. Consider opening a food and clothing bank. Many restaurants and grocery stores will donate food that is close to its expiration date or will otherwise be wasted. The food and clothing bank is a good way to build relationships, as people will return often for more supplies. This can be a good way to show the love of Christ on a consistent basis.

One of the most significant ways to stop the cycle of poverty, despair, and create lasting change is to reach out to the children of a community. The children are the future. Because children of the poor are frequently transient, there is little stability in their lives. They may live with a number of relatives, foster parents, or child welfare caretakers in a short period of time. These children are craving a positive and intense relationship with someone who cares for them. Develop relationships with local government agencies to build infrastructure necessary to provide consistent care. Programs that reach the entire child should be developed. This can include spiritual teaching at age appropriate levels, homework assistance and after school tutoring, cultural enrichment activities such as arts and crafts, and even a game or movie night. For school age children, Backyard Bible Clubs can be effective. Gain permission from parents and any property manager to hold the event. These can be comprised of a simple Bible story, a snack, a craft, some games and a memory verse. This can be done one time, weekly, or monthly. Finally, for most children, there are a few times throughout the year that mean the most to them. Children love to feel special on the first day of school, their birthday, and on Christmas Day. Take advantage of these opportunities to have influence in the lives of these children by providing them with school supplies at the beginning of the school year, a small remembrance of their birthdays, and a gift at Christmas.

In addition to the preschool and elementary years, the teenage years can be a tremendous time of influence. The teen years are among the highest for death by accident, homicide, and suicide. Teenage pregnancy is on the rise, causing more poverty. The neighborhood chaplain can help to reverse some of these trends by offering the hope of glory, Christ. Helping teens see a way to a better life can have wonderful outcomes. A combination of spiritual training with practical problem solving will help teens navigate through the potential crises of gang involvement, pregnancy, homelessness, educational importance, and family problems. Summer can be a time of temptation for teens. With too much time and not enough to do, many teens make choices with disastrous consequences. Providing activity based programs can change the summer, and eventually the direction of a young life. These programs can include fun worship times, Bible teaching, crafts, sports, field trips to interesting places, teaching on abstinence, life skills, and job skills. The goal is to build memories with the teens while teaching them about the things of God.

In addition to providing for spiritual, educational, nutritional, shelter, and clothing needs, many neighborhood chaplains see positive changes through medical care. Disadvantaged families are more likely to experience health problems. A medical clinic in the neighborhood can prove to be a valuable resource. Gathering doctors and nurses who are willing to volunteer time and some medical knowledge can provide a strong

Christian presence at a time of need.

As it can be seen, the goal is to reach out to the community with the message of hope in a method that will be well received by the neighborhood. This goal will not be achieved without a long term commitment to building relationships. These relationships should seek to prevent people from making destructive lifestyle choices and intervening when such choices have already been made. Seek to meet the needs of the entire person: physical, emotional, mental, and spiritual, all the while offering love, hope, and biblically based care. As a member of the neighborhood that you chaplain, seek to help fellow residents define the needs of the community and enlist help to design culturally relevant, sustainable solutions. Seek to network and partner with existing community organizations. Search out others in the neighborhood that have a common mindset. Identify them, train them, and provide opportunities for them to serve their communities. In this way, you nurture individuals in the development and wise use of the gifts that God has given to them. Involve the neighborhood and the church with each other. This is a tangible expression of the church's call to serve the poor, orphaned, widowed, and lost. Create synergy whenever possible by involving many. Build cross cultural relationships through which Christians can celebrate the diversity of the many different kinds of people that God has created.

A ministry to the neighborhood should begin with a firm foundation: a calling to do this type of ministry. Secondly, pray for the neighborhood to which you will be ministering. As written about Jabez in the Old Testament, pray for your influence to increase so that you may be a blessing to all that you encounter. Take a look at the steps to begin a community chaplaincy program by Leslie Doyle:

■ **Form a relationship with your neighbors.** Find a way to serve and meet their need. Offer to feed their pets or get their mail and newspapers while they are away. Demonstrate the spirit of Christ and truly love them, unselfishly.

■ **Find areas of compatibility.** Paul said in I Corinthians 9:22 to "be all things to all people." Find common ground to build a relationship. There are "relational neighborhoods", i.e., sports teams, offices, schools, local parks, and grocery stores that can be the cornerstone to inviting someone to your home.

■ **Be available.** One great way is to be outside in the good weather, sitting out, gardening, or walking the dog. All provide good opportunities to meet and build relationships. Once the relationship is established, it opens the door to movie nights, horseshoe game nights, Easter egg hunts, and cookouts. All these functions create the closeness that brings people to the foot of the Cross.

Fig. 7.3 Be authentic. The world hungers for honesty and truth.

■ **Be authentic.** The world hungers for honesty and truth. Admit your failings or struggles, against the backdrop of the light and help of Christ. Ask the Lord if there is anything blocking your pathway to your neighbor, such as unrepented or unforgiven sin on your part. If there has been a strained relationship in the past, ask for forgiveness. Treat your neighbors with "Golden Rule Evangelism". This means that you would relate to your neighbors in a way that you would want to be treated if you were the unsaved neighbor.[3]

The most important thing is to look around and seek to see others through the eyes of Christ. The leadership of Vineyard Christian Fellowship have found the following to be valuable in establishing strong neighborhood chaplains:

■ **Follow God's lead in loving and serving others.** Depend on God to guide and sustain you with wisdom, discernment, compassion, grace, mercy, and the Holy Spirit. In addition, seek to know God's heart through Scripture. Not only does the Bible help us to understand God's concern for our neighbors - those who are poor, marginalized, and in need - but the Bible also provides a lot of guidance on how to proactively engage in service, compassion, and justice.

■ **Be committed to relationship and affirm the dignity of others.** Make a commitment of time that you can honor as much as possible. Developing a relationship takes time and consistency in order to build trust and friendship. Ultimately, as you develop friendships, you'll avoid objectifying people and discover a ton of blessing as you learn to give to each other with humility and to receive from each other with dignity.

■ **Be generous with your time and resources.** Many of us have fears of being hurt, manipulated, under resourced, or over burdened. And many of us are disillusioned in our ability to make a difference. But Jesus tells us that we will do far more than he ever did and that whatever we give in his name will be returned to us a hundred times! Giving generously can be a means of experiencing this as it helps to transform our fear and indifference into faith and passion.

■ **Educate and equip yourself.** As you come up against the physical and spiritual strongholds of poverty, oppression, and suffering, you'll want to properly equip your heart, mind, and soul. One of the first obstacles you'll likely face is overcoming your own stereotypes and expectations. Learning from the more experienced and reading relevant books and magazines will greatly enhance your understanding, passion, effectiveness, and longevity in loving and serving others. For example, in better understanding the issues, you may find yourself becoming more interested in helping people to move out of poverty and not just to manage their poverty. In fact, that's also a pretty good definition of justice right there.

■ **Do it in community.** Support and pray with each other as you process all that is happening. As in any spiritual battle, loving others and coming up against issues of poverty, oppression, and suffering can be extremely taxing. Community support and debriefing is always helpful in making sense of your difficult experiences and in preventing any seeds of bitterness or apathy from being planted in your heart.[4]

We can have an impact for Christ without leaving our neighborhoods. Regardless of where you live, from Spokane, Washington to Miami, Florida, we all live in a community. Sure, the architecture, culture, leisure activities, and climate may be different, but one thing is the same. The community around you needs to hear about the life-changing Good News of Jesus Christ. Will you answer the call to reach the neighborhood around you with the message of hope?

Endnotes

1. Cited by Intervarsity Ministry in Daily Life <http://www.ivmdl.org/cbec.cfm?study=133> (Accessed 1 June 2006).

2. Leslie Doyle, "Having a Neighborhood Ministry," <http://www.christianactivities.com/articles/story.asp?id=4921> (Accessed 1 June 2006).

3. Ibid.

4. See Vineyard Christian Fellowship of Cambridge <http://www.cambridgevineyard.org/serving/NeighborhoodOutreach.htm> (Accessed 1 June 2006).

1. Gain Permission
2. Point people to Christ
3. Genuine Care.
4. Wait for the right time to share
5. Pray, 3 ~~trust to~~ minister for the Holy Spirit
6. Meet people at their point of need.
7. Be prepared for rejection

Unit Two

Foundations of Community Chaplaincy

Like everything in life, chaplaincy must be built on a firm foundation. Unit 2 seeks to lay this firm footing by exploring the biblical and historical basis for community chaplaincy.

Chapter Eight

Calling to Community Chaplaincy

CHAPTER EIGHT

Calling to Community Chaplaincy

―――――――――――― Objectives ――――――――――――

During the course of this chapter, we will perform the following tasks:

■ Examine the four-fold calling to community chaplaincy

■ Explore the benefits that calling can bring to the life of a community chaplain

■ Apply the concepts of calling to assist the prospective chaplain in examining God's call on his or her life

―――――――――――――――――――――――――――――

If you are reading the words on this page as a believer in Jesus Christ, then God has called you to live out your faith in your community. In fact, God has called you to live out your faith in every place. This is the essence of calling we must first understand before we plunge into examining God's specific call to community chaplaincy. A statement made by the Apostle Paul, and recorded for us by the physician Luke in the book of Acts, is one we would all do well to emulate. "But my life is worth nothing unless I use it for doing the work assigned me by the Lord Jesus - the work of telling others the Good News about God's wonderful kindness and love." (Acts 20:24)[1]

This passage demands the asking and answering of a key question. What work has God assigned to me? Some might argue that it is presumptuous to think there is specific work to be assigned. However, is it too much to expect that the God Who intricately designed our universe is equally interested in forming, shaping, and fashioning us for a unique assignment in the world He worked so diligently to create?

The calling of a community chaplain is essential for excellent service in the care of those in his or her charge. Without calling, chaplaincy is just another activity. With calling, the community chaplain is empowered as the servant of God with the opportunity to impact the lives of individuals in office cubicles, the school playground, the dugout at the ball field, the local children's shelter, or the gym.

The questions that must be asked are basic. What has God called me to do? Does

God have a specific plan for each of us? Has he uniquely molded and fashioned me for service in my community? How does God want to use the bundle of aspirations, ambitions, hurts, frustrations, disappointments, successes, and even failures I have experienced in life to build His kingdom? Perhaps a question one would not expect to find in a textbook on chaplaincy should be asked. Does God call some to be presidents of companies? This last question is one to be revisited later in this chapter.

As we begin examining the concept of calling, many misconceptions must be addressed. Ed Silvoso, in his book *Anointed for Business*, provides an excellent description of what he labels "four lethal misbeliefs." He writes:

"The combination of four major misbeliefs usually neutralizes God's calling on those anointed for marketplace [read "community"] ministry:

1. There is a God-ordained division between clergy and laity.
2. The Church is called to operate primarily inside a building often referred to as the temple.
3. People involved in business cannot be as spiritual as those serving in traditional Church ministry.
4. The primary role of marketplace Christians is to make money to support the vision of those 'in the ministry.'"[2]

In countering these misconceptions, Silvoso makes the case that believers can indeed be called and anointed for service in the workplace, no matter what type of workplace it may be: the school system, a sports league, or a nursing home. Speaking to men and women involved in occupations ranging from stockbrokers to receptionists to plumbers to police officers, Silvoso makes a compelling defense saying:

It is imperative that they realize that not only is it *OK* to do ministry in the marketplace, [read "sphere of influence"] but that God has explicitly *called* them and *anointed* them for it. By 'anointed' I mean that they have been chosen and empowered by the Holy Spirit for a divinely sanctioned assignment. By 'ministry' I mean that they can do more than just witness; they can bring transformation to their jobs and then to their cities - as happened in the first century.[3]

The call to community chaplaincy is an anointed call. In fact, it is really a four-fold call. First, there is a call to ministry itself. To state it plainly, every believer is called to

Fig. 8.1 You can be an effective workplace minister no matter what your occupation.

ministry. Perhaps this call could best be described as an avocational calling. Secondly, some are called to vocational ministry. In other words, their calling is one from which they earn their livelihood. Some in this group might also minister bivocationally in their ability to hold employment in a paid ministry position, in addition to some other type of employment. Thirdly, some called to vocational ministry may be called specifically to community ministry. Finally, some called to community ministry may be called in particular to community chaplaincy. Perhaps the key question to be asked is this: What is God's highest and best use for my life? This is an individual question demanding an individual answer.

Let us examine this four-fold call one step at a time. First, every believer is called to ministry. Scripture teaches this principle and believers will often affirm its truth verbally, but sadly there is often a failure to implement the concept practically.

Utilizing the analogy of a body and its parts, Paul writes of how every person making up the community of believers has a part to play. Ephesians 4:16 states, "Under His direction, the whole body is fitted together perfectly. As each part does its own special work, it helps the other parts grow, so that the whole body is healthy and growing and full of love."

It is an awesome thought to know that the God of the universe has a perfect place for you to fit for service to Him. It is both encouraging and comforting to know that He wants you to be in that perfect place even more than you want to be there. Reflect on that thought for a moment. Paul begins this verse reminding his reader that the work of ministry that all believers are called to is under the direction of God. Ministry is God's idea, not man's. In I Corinthians 12:4-7 Paul writes:

> *⁴ Now there are different kinds of spiritual gifts, but it is the same Holy Spirit who is the source of them all. ⁵ There are different kinds of service in the church, but it is the same Lord we are serving. ⁶ There are different ways God works in our lives, but it is the same God who does the work through all of us. ⁷ A spiritual gift is given to each of us as a means of helping the entire church.*

The Scriptural point is clear. We all have gifts. We are all to put those gifts to use in service to others.

Second in this four-fold call is the reality of God's call to vocational ministry service and the requirement placed upon everyone to earn a living. While they compose a small percentage, God does call some to serve vocationally in roles such as pastor, associate pastor, church planters, and missionaries. Those called to this role have a unique and crucial part to play as they seek to equip others for the work of the ministry. Ephesians 4:11-13 highlights the purpose of this God-given call.

> [11] He is the One Who gave these gifts to the church: the apostles, the prophets, the evangelists, and the pastors and teachers. [12] Their responsibility is to equip God's people to do His work and build up the church, the body of Christ, [13] until we come to such unity in our faith and knowledge of God's Son that we will be mature and full grown in the Lord, measuring up to the full stature of Christ.

God's call to vocational service is central to helping believers mature in their faith. In this equipping role, those called to serve are also to be compensated for their service. Paul writing to Timothy details this God-given plan for not only calling, but also compensating those in vocational ministry. I Timothy 5:17-18 states: "17 Elders who do their work well should be paid well, especially those who work hard at both preaching and teaching. 18 For the Scripture says, 'Do not keep an ox from eating as it treads out the grain.' And in another place, 'Those who work deserve their pay!'"

Elsewhere, Paul wrote to the church at Corinth and gave them clear instruction for those called to serve the organized church in Corinth. I Corinthians 9:10 states, "... Just as farm workers who plow fields and thresh the grain expect a share of the harvest, Christian workers should be paid by those they serve."

While the New Testament certainly provides guidance for the concept of what has come to be called full time ministry, we need look no further than the example of Jesus Himself to recognize there is much more. The spectrum of roles necessary for God to accomplish His purposes in our world today is much wider than just those serving as full time staff members of organized churches. Jesus himself was a business leader who called other people in the workplace. It is interesting to note the derision towards Jesus' workplace background in response to one of his earliest recorded acts of ministry.

> *² The next Sabbath he began teaching in the synagogue, and many who heard Him were astonished. They asked, 'Where did He get all His wisdom and the power to perform such miracles? ³ He's just the carpenter, the son of Mary and brother of James, Joseph, Judas, and Simon. And His sisters live right here among us.' They were deeply offended and refused to believe in Him.* (Mark 6:2-3)

Notice the contemptuous phrase, "He's just a carpenter." Today, we hear many speak self-condemning words of criticism when they say things like, "I'm just a salesman." "I'm just a computer programmer." "I'm only a school teacher." We will have achieved a biblical perspective on calling when we routinely hear people answer the question, "What is your ministry?" with answers like, "My ministry is a firefighter," or "My ministry is a surgical technician." We will have achieved a correct biblical perspective on calling when the owner of a company can confidently affirm God's call upon his or her life as the president of a company. I have heard of some people who have truly grasped this concept of calling, who answer the oft-asked question, "What kind of work do you do?" with very clever answers. One said, "I am a minister of Jesus Christ masquerading as a dentist." Another said, "I am a servant of God masquerading as a registered nurse." Still another said, "I am a workplace pastor masquerading as an auto mechanic." These are people who truly understand the instruction of the apostle Paul found in his letter to the church at Colossae. Colossians 3:23 states, "Work hard and cheerfully at whatever you do, as though you were working for the Lord rather than for people."

God's call for every believer is found clearly here in Colossians 3:23. We are called to view the work we do in this world as work done for God. This call is modeled for us as Jesus called his earliest followers in the workplace to make a difference in the lives of their co-workers. The clearest example is Jesus' call of Matthew as recorded in Matthew's Gospel:

> *⁹ As Jesus was going down the road, he saw Matthew sitting at his tax-collection booth. 'Come, be my disciple,' Jesus said to him. So Matthew got up and followed Him. ¹⁰ That night Matthew invited Jesus and His disciples to be His dinner guests, along with his fellow tax collectors and many other notorious sinners. ¹¹ The Pharisees were indignant. 'Why does your teacher eat with such scum?' they asked His*

> disciples. *[12] When He heard this, Jesus replied, 'Healthy people don't need a doctor – sick people do.' [13] Then He added, 'Now go and learn the meaning of this Scripture: 'I want you to be merciful; I don't want your sacrifices.' For I have come to call sinners, not those who think they are already good enough.'* (Matthew 9:9-13)

A simple examination of this passage reveals that perhaps Matthew filled the role of the first community chaplain. He clearly sought to build a relationship with those he was closest to - his co-workers. Matthew's co-workers were his fellow tax collectors, and they clearly joined Matthew for dinner with Jesus with many needs, problems, and issues evident in their lives. The needs of Matthew and his fellow tax collectors were so obvious that they attracted the indignation and scorn of the Pharisees, the religious leaders of the day. In fact, they question Jesus' disciples about His willingness to associate with such a group, even referring to them as "scum." Jesus responds to this indignation with a very fitting statement that perhaps penetrates to the heart of the calling to be a community chaplain. Jesus states, "Healthy people don't need a doctor - sick people do." Then He adds, "I want you to be merciful."

Fig. 8.2 Do you look upon those who are hurting with indignation or with mercy?

Do you look at the needs of people in your sphere of influence and recognize that the words of Jesus apply? Just as sick people need a doctor, so hurting people need someone who will help. Do you look upon those who are hurting with indignation or with mercy? If your answer is mercy, then perhaps your response is an indicator of a heart that God is preparing for service as a community chaplain. Do the needs that you see around you prompt you toward indignation, or do they prompt you to want to make a difference - to do something about them? The words of Jesus in Matthew 9:36-38 apply as much to the culture of today as they did to I[st] century Jewish society.

> [36] *He felt great pity for the crowds that came, because their problems were so great and they didn't know where to go for help. They were like sheep without a shepherd.* [37] *He said to His disciples, 'The harvest is so great, but the workers are so few.* [38] *So pray to the Lord who is in charge of the harvest; ask him to send out more workers for his fields.'*

The calling to community chaplaincy is a tremendous call to go where there are hurting people and to help in every way possible.

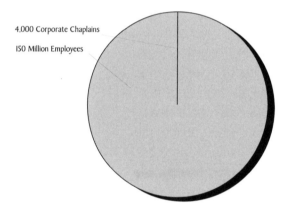

4,000 Corporate Chaplains

150 Million Employees

Fig. 8.3 Ratio of Chaplains to Employees in America

The Benefits Calling Can Bring

Calling brings two primary benefits to the life of the chaplain. The first benefit is energy for the journey. Secondly, calling provides clarity during the challenges.

Caring for those with whom one comes into contact on a daily basis is the call of the community chaplain. When a person says "yes" to this call, they are saying "yes" to a task that will demand a tremendous amount of energy. He or she is agreeing to be ready and "on call" to serve the needs of others 24 hours per day, 7 days per week. The needs of others do not end when the business day ends at 5 p.m. The acceptance of God's call to community chaplaincy must be accompanied by a lifestyle of dependence upon God for energy for the journey. In John 15:5 the apostle John quotes the words of Jesus pointing out our relationship of dependence. Jesus spoke and John

John 15:5

wrote, "I am the vine; you are the branches. If a man remains in me, and I in him, he will bear much fruit; apart from me you can do nothing" (NIV). Jesus' words are clear and emphatic. The accomplishments we can make on our own are nothing.

The second benefit of calling is the provision of clarity during the challenges. Challenges in chaplaincy will come, and they bring with them the potential to create confusion. Confusion can serve to plant seeds of doubt in the mind of God's servant. Questions may arise. Do I really know what I am doing? Am I really doing what I am supposed to be doing? When the confusion comes or the questions arise, the community chaplain can stand in his or her calling with the recognition possessed by the apostle Paul and recorded for us in Ephesians 3:7: "By God's special favor and mighty power, I have been given the wonderful privilege of serving him by spreading this Good News."

What made the apostle Paul so mightily effective as a servant of God? That is a big question with a very simple answer. For Paul, his service to God was much more than a responsibility; it was a privilege! The service he provided to others in the strength and power of God was service provided out of desire, not obligation. For the effective chaplain, service is offered to others because we want to and not simply because we have to. When one finds they are doing something out of desire ("want-to") instead of obligation (a "have-to" mindset), it is then that one can recognize a discovery of God's will. As one reads through Paul's many letters to the various churches he helped start, many insights become obvious about the man responsible for writing much of the New Testament. One thing is very clear. Paul never got over the greatness of God's plan or the greatness of God's work in his own life. He looked at his own life and recognized God's special favor toward him. Paul realized it was God's mighty power that was at work in him and through him. Instead of focusing on the problems or praise of people, Paul chose instead to focus on God's power and recognize his own privilege as God's servant. When the challenges come, we as community chaplains need to remind ourselves of a simple truth provided to us by Paul. Serving God is a wonderful privilege!

Stories From the Field: #2
"Give Me A Pick-me-up"*

Brian had been serving the same group in his community for the past 18 months. Every Thursday at 4 p.m. he found himself easing his way toward the end of a day that usually began at 5:30 a.m. on the loading dock of a trucking company. As the afternoon wore on, he would often find himself searching for a Mountain Dew or a cup of coffee to provide that little pick-me-up he needed to get through the afternoon. The fatigue of a long Thursday would often be accompanied by the dread of interacting with his neighbors at the weekly Bunco games. He would often find himself praying a prayer, "Lord, help change my 'have-to' attitude to a 'want-to' and 'get-to' attitude."

*Individuals in this story have granted permission for its use.

Questions

1. How do you respond to fatigue?
2. What role does fatigue play in ministry effectiveness?
3. How can a calling to the task provide sufficient energy to overcome fatigue?

Practical Exercise

Imagine you are interviewing for your first chaplaincy position. How would you respond to the following questions?
1. Why do you want to be a community chaplain?
2. Describe your calling. What could change your calling?
3. What do you love the most about ministry?

Stories From the Field: #3
"The Kid"*

Rick was right where he had always envisioned he would be. Sitting at gate C1 in the Atlanta airport enjoying his favorite Ben and Jerry's flavor, Chunky Monkey in a waffle cone, and awaiting his flight for home gave him the opportunity to reflect on how far he had come. At 29 years of age, he was earning a six figure income, had a company car, and was privileged to visit new cities on almost a weekly basis. He was the top sales producer for the third consecutive year with his company Medtronics, the top producer of pacemakers and heart monitoring equipment in the world. He was often referred to by others in the company by nicknames like "The Kid" and "Boy Wonder", nicknames he cherished and that even his wife Brittany had taken to calling him.

Every time he heard the nickname "The Kid", he was reminded of the most incredible of blessings he and Brittany had received from God during the past year – the birth of their first child, Rick, Jr. – or "Rickster" as Rick liked to refer to him. Rickster's birth ranked up in the top three of life moments, along with his wedding day and the day of his spiritual birth. As he continued savoring his Chunky Monkey, he found it hard to fathom that he had only been a believer in Christ for what seemed to be a short five years. The church he and Brittany had joined shortly after their wedding had been tremendous in helping him grow and understand how faith is applied to all that he was involved in, including work. He enjoyed Pastor Chuck's messages each Sunday, but often sat confused and struggling as his pastor would speak so passionately about finding God's purpose. The confusion would always find its culmination in Rick asking himself the same three questions. If I am doing what God wants me to do, why do I feel so empty? What is God's purpose for my life? Is God calling me "into ministry"?

*Individuals in this story have granted permission for its use.

Questions

1. If Rick came to you for advice on discovering God's purpose for his life, what words of wisdom would you offer to him?
2. What does it mean to be "called into ministry"?
3. Study the call of Jesus to his earliest followers in Matthew 4:18-22 and 9:9-13. What principles can we discover from Jesus' call?

Stories From the Field: #4
"Looking to the Future"*

Frank had made the transition a success. He had begun as an 18-year-old kid working in the mail room of the family company and was now just six months into his current role as the 42-year-old president. By surviving 50 years and into a third generation of *private ownership, the company had been able to do what few other businesses in U.S. history have been able to accomplish. With a strong market share and annual revenues approaching $1 billion annually, the company's privately held status always made it an attractive acquisition target for much larger companies, who aimed to enter the company's lucrative niche. When these offers were presented, Frank would often ponder his future and wonder privately what it would be like to be free of the demands of running a company. What would it be like to be free to pursue full time his love for mission and ministry that he had discovered while on a short term mission trip with his church to Mexico? When these thoughts would come, God would quickly remind him of ideas he had learned from reading Ed Silvoso's book, Anointed for Business. The reminder was simple. God had called him to be president of the family business and had entrusted the company to him as his platform for ministry.*

*Individuals in this story have granted permission for its use.

Questions

1. Does God's call include the call to be a business owner?
2. Describe what it means to view a company as a platform for ministry.
3. Read Mark 6:1-6. Is it surprising to learn Jesus Himself was president of his family's carpentry business? How would you describe this calling of Jesus to run the family business to someone exploring God's call on his or her life?

4/21/08

Endnotes

Handwritten margin notes: CNA Certified Nurse Assistant "Simply Chuin can send Marcapes to those around you."

1. All scripture quotations are from The New Living Translation (NLT), unless otherwise specified.
2. Ed Silvoso, *Anointed for Business* (Ventura: Regal, 2002), 23.
3. Ibid., 18.

+ Be my witness - Command / Mandate to share Salvation to the world -
+ Build Bridges to relationships
+ ½ Christians except Christ before Age 13
+ Edward Kimball 1800's - Sunday School teacher
+ D.L. Moody - ~~Evangelism~~ Evangelism in 1800s
+ Billy Graham - Has infected the world / 1934 w/ the witness of DL Moody
+ 2 Cor 5:21 - God made him who had NO Sin to take on the Sin of the world.
+ Matt 4:19 - Make you fishers of man
+ Be good News before you share the good News
+ St. Francis of CC - There is No use in walking anywhere to preach - unless our walking is our preaching

God made

Chapter Nine

Biblical Basis for Community Chaplaincy

CHAPTER NINE

Biblical Basis for Community Chaplaincy

——————————— Objectives ———————————

During the course of this chapter, we will perform the following tasks:

- Examine the biblical basis for community chaplaincy

- Develop a biblical model that can serve as a "role model" for the community chaplain

- Apply the doctrine of the incarnation to caring for others via the community chaplain

I n the Introduction, the concept of community chaplaincy from the Christian perspective was explained. The definition of and job description for the community chaplain were also established. This chapter will expand on the job description by providing a basis for, and biblical model of, community chaplaincy.

The central claim of Christianity is that one God revealed Himself personally in the Person of Jesus Christ, Whose death and resurrection made available a relationship with God for all who would trust in Him and His work. The mission of every Christian is to make known this essential message.[1] The divine plan of God to reveal Himself in a person can serve as a model for chaplains to allow Christ to be revealed in them.

This chapter will explain the doctrine of the incarnation and explore several examples of relationship-based caregiving from the life of Christ and from the lives of his earliest followers. This doctrine and these examples will be utilized to provide workable principles every chaplain can use in caring for others in a way that has a practical and eternal impact on those they serve.

The central premise of this chapter was born out of personal involvement as chaplains. Upon reflection, we have concluded that the great effectiveness we see in personal caregiving can be traced to the relationship-based approach that allows our chaplains to incarnate the Good News to the people we serve.

In *The Word of the Cross*, Lewis Drummond highlights the essence of the incarnation. "As startling as the phrase *God becoming a man* may be, such is what the incarnation means. That is positive and constitutes the primary truth of the incarnation. God truly did incarnate Himself."[2] The most basic definition of the incarnation is simply that God became a man in the person of Jesus Christ.

While Christians cannot become God, they are called to be like Christ. As chaplains live Christ-like lives in their respective cultures, they can embody the message of the gospel to those around them. The apostle John penned the words found in I John 2:6, "Whoever claims to live in him must walk as Jesus did" (NIV). Chaplains living as Jesus did can be a powerful influence on factory floors, office cubicles, loading docks, schoolyards, city parks, neighborhood pools, jails, and anywhere else that a community chaplain is called to serve. They can serve as role models for a

Fig. 9.1 We can follow Jesus' example by building relationships with people in order to impact their lives.

value based approach to living. Chaplains can be encouragers to those they encounter in the community. They can develop trust and earn the right to have an impact in the lives of those around them. As John Maxwell states, "You can *impress* people at a distance but you can *impact* them only up close."[3] In Jesus, God was able to move beyond impressing us from a distance and move into the realm of impacting each of us up close.

With the task of chaplaincy being the primary focus of this text, the truth of the incarnation raises many questions concerning the relationship between chaplaincy and the doctrine of the incarnation. Why did God choose to reveal Himself in such a personal way? What can be learned about the job of caring for others from an examination of the incarnation? How can chaplains today apply its lessons in serving the needs of those around them? Ultimately, how can chaplains build relationships with those in their sphere of influence with the hope of gaining permission to share the life-changing Good News of Jesus Christ, in a non-threatening manner? These questions and other issues will be addressed in this chapter.

John Stott details the significance of the incarnation to both our chaplaincy and evangelistic efforts in tremendous fashion in his book *The Cross of Christ*. Stott writes:

In all evangelism there is also a cultural gulf to bridge. This is obvious when Christian people move as messengers of the gospel from one country or continent to another. But even if we remain in our own country, Christians and non-Christians are often widely separated from one another by social sub-cultures and lifestyles as well as by different values, beliefs and moral standards. Only an incarnation can span these divides, for an incarnation means entering other people's worlds, their thought-world, and the worlds of their alienation, loneliness and pain. Moreover, the incarnation led to the cross. Jesus first took our flesh, then bore our sin. This was a depth of penetration into our world in order to reach us, in comparison with which our little attempts to reach people seem amateur and shallow. The cross calls us to a much more radical and costly kind of evangelism than most churches have begun to consider, let alone experience.[4]

Many people who work together on a daily basis are separated, as Stott writes, by different values, beliefs, and moral standards. The activities in which they participate, their goals in life, and their sense of right and wrong differ in many noticeable ways. The goal of community chaplaincy is to span the divide of culture, lifestyle, values, and belief systems in order to help people in times of need. It is work aimed at achieving radical identification with and penetration of the world in which individuals reside, the world in which they spend the bulk of their time – this could be a business environment, a neighborhood, or a school. The specific means of this penetration is the provision of a well-trained chaplain, equipped with the practices and motives to enter the thought life, alienation, loneliness, and pain of those they serve. As the doctrine of the incarnation is developed and explained, let us remember the focus of this work is to equip chaplains to be a genuine caring presence in the community and to help them build relationships with those in their mission field, with the hope of gaining permission to share the life-changing Good News of Jesus Christ, in a non-threatening manner.

The most important lesson to learn from a study of the incarnation is one that can be incorporated in the chaplain's daily work from day one. It is also one the chaplain can spend a lifetime learning and adapting. The primary principle for every community chaplain to apply is to be like Christ in everything we do. Jesus is our model for ministry and mission in our current society. Jesus Christ is the model chaplain. This conclusion will be further developed through an investigation of the incarnation and its significance for how we carry out the task of chaplaincy.

The Incarnation Explained

Before the relationship between chaplaincy and the incarnation can be more fully addressed, the incarnation itself must be explained. The New Testament contains four primary passages that form the foundation for this doctrine. The passages of importance include Colossians 1-2, Hebrews 1-2, John 1, and Philippians 2. The focus of this work limits an exhaustive study of the incarnation; therefore this study will focus on the basics of the doctrine and the implications for the task of community chaplaincy.

Charles Ryrie provides an excellent description of the incarnation. He writes, "More concisely one may describe the person of Christ incarnate as being full Deity and perfect humanity united without mixture, change, division, or separation in one Person forever."[5] The two key components of this description are first, full Deity, and second, perfect humanity. When we see Jesus in the Gospels, we are seeing both full Deity and perfect humanity.

Two passages in particular help focus attention on this basic teaching of the incarnation. Of special importance is Colossians 2:9, which is perhaps the clearest and most concise statement in the New Testament that holds the two components of full Deity and perfect humanity together. Paul writes, "For in Christ all the fullness of the Deity lives in bodily form" (Colossians 2:9 NIV). Every word in this verse has significance for the doctrine of the incarnation. The word "fullness" translates the word *pleroma*, which is then defined by the addition of *tes theotetos*, which means "of the Deity."[6] Richard Melick writes, "The fullness of deity was Paul's way of stating that Jesus is every bit God."[7] Paul's emphasis here is on the fullness of the powers and attributes of God. Where is this fullness found? Paul identifies the location of the fullness as being "in bodily form." The fullness is found "in Christ" and "in bodily form." The word Paul uses is the word *somatikos*, which is a word used to describe a real, physical body.[8] In essence, Christ is regarded as containing and representing, in bodily form, all that God is.[9] The word "incarnation" comes from the combination of Latin terms, *in* and *carnis*, meaning "in flesh." It is the state of being clothed or invested with flesh.[10] John writes in John 1:14, "The Word became flesh and made his dwelling among us ..." (NIV). The word John uses here is *sarx*, which affirms real human flesh. Jesus did not simply seem to be human; he was truly human. A second significant word in this verse is "dwelling," which translates from *skenoun*.[11] In coming to this world, Jesus came as a person to live among people. Jesus was truly human living in the midst of other humans. In

Jesus we have the picture of perfect humanity. In Jesus, we have God living among us.

What is the significance of this truth in regards to the task of chaplaincy? The significance is simple - Jesus entered our world. The application of this truth is that we too can enter the world of those we are trying to reach as we seek to live out our faith in the community. While it is impossible for a chaplain to contain and represent in bodily form all that God is, it is very possible, even necessary, for chaplains to represent in bodily form the nature and character of Christ. Chaplains, like all Christians, hold in common with Jesus the characteristic of being in flesh. As followers of Christ, we do not have to become flesh. We already are flesh! However, as chaplains, and as believers in Christ, we do need to become like Christ. Christ made his dwelling among people in the flesh that they might be able to see what God is like. The task of living out our faith in the workplace is the assignment of living as a changed person among other people. It is the task of living a truly human, yet Christ-like life in the midst of other humans. It is the task of modeling Christ in the flesh to individuals around us.

While much work and attention is often given to explaining the incarnation, the issue of "why" helps clarify the importance of the incarnation to the task of evangelism.

Fig. 9.2 Why did God send His Son in the likeness of sinful flesh?

Why did God send His Son in the likeness of sinful flesh? In response to this question, Charles Ryrie enumerates seven reasons for the incarnation. Three of Ryrie's reasons hold particular importance for the task of community chaplaincy. First, through the incarnation God provides an example for our lives. Secondly, through the incarnation Christ came to be an effective sacrifice for sin, in order to redeem humanity and reconcile us to God. Finally, through the incarnation God reveals Himself to us.[12] Each of these three reasons will be examined in detail and will serve as practical principles for chaplains seeking to live out their faith in their respective mission fields.

The Incarnation as Example

Perhaps most important to a solid caregiving strategy is that through the incarnation God provides an example for our lives. Ryrie writes, "The earthly life of our Lord is held up to us as a pattern for our living today. Without the incarnation we would not have that example."[13]

The Christological passage placing the greatest emphasis upon Christ's example for believers is Philippians 2:1-11. Paul writes in the fifth verse, "Your attitude should be the same as that of Christ Jesus" (Philippians 2:5 NIV). In the verses that follow, Paul describes the attitude of Christ. Homer Kent writes, "The great example of humility is Christ Jesus. Although verses 5 to 11 contain one of the outstanding Christologies in the New Testament, they were written to illustrate the point of humility and selflessness."[14] While chaplains cannot duplicate the exact ministry of Jesus, they can display the same attitude of humility and selflessness.

The key verse that holds the Philippians 2 passage together is verse 5. This verse acts as the hinge that connects the instruction of verses 1-4 with the theology of verses 6-11. Danny Akin contends that the primary intent of the passage is ethical. The exhortation to have a proper attitude is given in verses 1-4. The example of the type of attitude to have is found in Jesus and detailed in verses 6-11. Akin writes, "Interestingly, therefore, the hymn of 2:6-11 actually serves as an illustration (a divine one at that!) of the mind of Christ; the mind the believer should seek after and cultivate."[15]

Essentially, the illustration teaches us a model of humility and servanthood. When we possess humility, we have the ability to carry out the instruction of verse 3 to consider others better than ourselves. We can willingly wear the title of servant. Being a servant calls us to carry out the instruction of verse 4 to put the interests of others ahead of self-interests. Elsewhere in Paul's writings we are instructed to follow the example of Christ. Paul writes to the church at Corinth a clear instruction, "Follow my example, as I follow the example of Christ" (1 Corinthians 11:1 NIV). To the church at Ephesus he writes, "Be imitators of God, therefore, as dearly loved children" (Ephesians 5:1 NIV).

Paul is not alone in his challenge to Christians to follow the example of Christ. One of Jesus' earliest followers, the apostle Peter, writes, "To this you were called, because Christ suffered for you, leaving you an example, that you should follow in his steps" (1 Peter 2:21 NIV). Peter knew well what he was writing about. He had heard Jesus speak the words recorded in the Gospel of John. Jesus himself said, "I have set you an example that you should do as I have done for you" (John 13:15 NIV). In Jesus, God set an example for us.

The application to the life of the chaplain is clear. A chaplain is called to the role of servant and to carry it out clothed in humility. When this position is clearly understood, the community chaplain can with humility put the interests of others ahead of self-interests. With the 24 hour, 7 day per week demands of chaplaincy, this understanding is essential to effective service.

Assuming the role of servant can by itself have tremendous impact on the response of those being served. The world is not accustomed to the person willing to put the interests of others ahead of self-interests. Our society encourages and often even applauds a self-centered, me-first attitude. We use words and phrases like "dog-eat-dog" and "survival of the fittest".

Robert Coleman provides excellent insight into the evangelistic influence of the selfless example provided by Jesus. He writes:

> The good news is that God has acted to save a people for Himself. To know what this means, we have only to look at Jesus. He is the Evangel incarnate - the gospel alive. For a few brief years He took upon Himself our identity and demonstrated in our midst who God is and how much He cares.[16]

The principles we could learn from Christ's example are numerous; this work will focus on but a few that apply specifically to carrying out ministry and mission in the various mission fields that exist today. The following description of these principles is influenced by Coleman's work in *The Master's Way of Personal Evangelism.* [17]

First, Jesus was a servant to people. Philippians 2:7 states that He took the very nature of a servant. Jesus Himself said He did not come to be served but instead to serve. It is striking to note how accessible Jesus was to people looking for help. He responded to people on an individual basis wherever He happened to be. In addition, He often went to extraordinary lengths to meet people at their point of need. Jesus ministered to people from all walks of life. He recognized that everyone needed help from time to time, and He was able to show people that He cared.

The ninth chapter of Matthew's Gospel gives a clear picture of Jesus' approach to people and to ministry. In this chapter He is found meeting the needs of a paralyzed man, a synagogue leader, a sick woman, two blind men, and a demon possessed man. He is found spending time with people of poor reputation, as well as people with spiritual interest. Matthew 9:35 provides an excellent summary of Jesus' approach. Matthew writes, "Jesus traveled through all the cities and villages of that area, teaching in the synagogues and announcing the Good News about the Kingdom. And wherever He went, He healed people of every sort of disease and illness" (Matthew 9:35 NLT). Verse 36 perhaps

Fig. 9.3 A chaplain is called to the role of servant.

provides the motivation for such wide-ranging activities in ministry. Matthew writes, "He felt great pity for the crowds that came, because their problems were so great and they didn't know where to go for help. They were like sheep without a shepherd" (Matthew 9:36 NLT).

How does this apply to carrying out chaplaincy in your community? Very simply, a chaplain is called to be a servant to people. The approach of Jesus that worked over two thousand years ago is an approach that will still work today. People need people who care. They need chaplains who care enough to become servants to those around them. They need chaplains who are willing to go to extraordinary lengths to meet them at their individual point of need. That need could arise when they are in the hospital, when their marriage faces difficulty, or when their teenager rebels. Whatever the need, people will respond to those willing to serve and put the needs of others ahead of their own.

Secondly, Jesus focused on those with spiritual desire. Jesus would respond to those expressing an interest in spiritual things. Often He would seek to draw out that interest by making spiritual statements or by asking probing questions. Jesus made a very direct spiritual statement to Matthew in a workplace setting when He said, "Come, be My disciple." In Matthew, Jesus found someone with spiritual desire, because Scripture records that Matthew became Jesus' follower.

The lesson here is simple. Community chaplains should take a patient approach, build relationships for the long term, and be ready and available when people begin asking questions about spiritual matters. The conversation about spiritual things will be more valuable and have greater impact when the other initiates it. It will also serve as a comfort to those in your mission field, knowing that they can have control over when the matter of faith is discussed.

As chaplains seek to incarnate the gospel in their world, it is important to follow the model of Jesus and focus on those with spiritual desire. Not everyone encountered by the chaplain will have spiritual interest. It is crucial, however, to be sensitive to those who do. Many times their spiritual interest will come in the form of their own spiritual statements or questions. Jesus' interaction with Nicodemus is an excellent example, as Jesus simply responds to Nicodemus' questions and thoughts.

Nicodemus, a leader certainly looked up to by many, approached Jesus with far more questions than answers. He surrendered his pride and his position for a singular pursuit – a personal encounter with Jesus Christ. Perhaps you are serving people who possess the same attitude Nicodemus had when he approached Jesus. Nicodemus recognized Jesus as a great leader and came to Him with words of praise for His wonderful works. He said, "Rabbi, we know you are a teacher who has come from God. For no one could perform the miraculous signs you are doing if God were not with him" (John 3:2 NIV).

While Nicodemus' words were true, they missed the real mark. Jesus' response to Nicodemus was a pointed change of subject. The New Testament records, "In reply Jesus declared, 'I tell you the truth, no one can see the kingdom of God unless he is born again'" (John 3:3 NIV). Jesus brings the real mark into clear focus with a very direct and challenging statement sure to capture the attention of a mover and shaker like Nicodemus. No one goes to heaven unless he is born again. No one "gets in good with God" unless he is born again. No one fixes what is broken about his life unless he is born again. But what do these words "born again" really mean?

The Bible records this supernatural truth to his very natural response:

> [3] In reply Jesus declared, 'I tell you the truth, no one can see the kingdom of God unless he is born again.' [4] 'How can a man be born again when he is old?' Nicodemus asked. 'Surely he cannot enter a second time into his mother's womb to be born!' [5] Jesus answered, 'I tell you the truth, no one can enter the kingdom of God unless he is born of water and the Spirit. [6] Flesh gives birth to flesh, but the Spirit gives birth to spirit' (John 3:3-6 NIV).

As a chaplain stands ready to address the questions of those with spiritual interest, they can do so recognizing the spirit of God stands with them to provide spiritual birth in the life of the interested individual.

Jesus also reached out to people wherever He happened to find them. As we think of following the example of Christ, it is interesting to note that at least five of the twelve followers Jesus designated as apostles were reached in workplace settings. While the call of Matthew at his tax collection booth has been examined previously, Mark records the call of Peter, Andrew, James, and John. He writes,

16 One day as Jesus was walking along the shores of the Sea of Galilee, he saw Simon and his brother, Andrew, fishing with a net, for they were commercial fisherman. 17 Jesus called out to them, 'Come, be my disciples, and I will show you how to fish for people!' 18 And they left their nets at once and went with him. 19 A little farther up the shore Jesus saw Zebedee's sons, James and John, in a boat mending their nets. 20 He called to them, too, and immediately they left their father, Zebedee, in the boat with the hired men and went with him (Mark 1:16-20 NLT).

Fig. 9.4 Jesus teaches us how to fish for people.

Not only did Jesus reach out to these four in a setting that was part of their everyday lives, He indicated a desire to teach them how to reach out to people as well. He said, "I will show you how to fish for people.'" How did Jesus reach out to people? Jesus served the needs of people. Jesus looked for those with spiritual interest. Jesus reached out to individuals wherever he happened to find them.

Finally, Jesus sought to bring about life change. Jesus communicated the truth about Himself and about the Scriptures in a way that called for a decision. Luke 18:18-29 records Jesus' interaction with a rich man. This story is a great example of Jesus' willingness to point out that which might be holding a person back from a significant life change. In this particular case, the man's focus on material concerns outweighed his interest in spiritual matters. How can chaplains bring about life change in the lives of those they serve? In order to answer that question, this work must now turn to two other significant reasons for the incarnation: reconciliation and revelation.

The Incarnation and Reconciliation

Because evangelism is central in the task of community chaplaincy, attention must be given to the ultimate reason for the incarnation. The ultimate reason for Jesus to leave heaven and come to earth was that He might redeem humanity and reconcile people with the God Who gave them life. The reconciling of people with God is the ultimate solution the chaplain has to offer for the life struggles faced by each and every person, no matter their position or place in life. Erickson writes, "He became incarnate, however, because of the task that He had to accomplish - saving us from our sin."[18] Jesus was sent from heaven to earth on a rescue mission to bring us back into a proper relationship with God. Jesus Himself spoke of this purposeful rescue mission. Luke 19:10 records His words, "For the Son of Man came to seek and to save what was lost" (NIV).

The Christological passage that most clearly details Christ's rescue work is Colossians 1:13-22. Paul writes in verses 13-14, "[13] For he has rescued us from the dominion of darkness and brought us into the kingdom of the Son he loves, [14] in Whom we have redemption, the forgiveness of sins" (NIV). The word translated "rescue" is *errusato*, a word that means to liberate, save, or deliver someone from something or someone.[19] Paul teaches that Christians have been rescued from the dominion of darkness. Paul is not content to stop with simply describing the rescue; he continues by teaching that we were rescued from one kingdom in order to be brought into another kingdom. Describing the significance of the word "brought," Curtis Vaughn writes, "'Brought' translates *metestesen*, a word that was used in secular literature in reference to removing persons from one country and settling them as colonists and citizens in another country."[20] The kingdom Christians have been settled in is the kingdom of God's Son.

In referencing the kingdom of God's Son, the apostle turns attention to the One Who provides redemption and reconciliation and the means by which it was provided. Redemption is described in verse 14 as being found in God's Son, Jesus. Richard Melick writes, "The word 'redemption' belongs to the slave market. It involves the payment of a price to secure freedom, and Paul clearly identified that price as the death of Christ."[21] The term speaks of a release brought about by the payment of a price. The release the redeemed person receives is forgiveness. What Paul is teaching is that forgiveness comes through the redemption provided by God's Son.

Many people feel enslaved to the problems they face. They have accepted the troubles and the resulting entanglement as a normal part of life. What they need is redemption and its accompanying forgiveness.

The concept of reconciliation surfaces in verses 19-22. Melick writes, "In using the term 'reconciliation,' Paul assumed that something had gone wrong. All of creation was touched by sin. The world was out of order and needed a correction. This was provided by Christ."[22] Paul writes,

Fig. 9.5 Many employees feel enslaved to the problems they face. They are in need of redemption and forgiveness,

> [19] *For God was pleased to have all his fullness dwell in him,* [20] *and through him to reconcile to himself all things, whether things on earth or things in heaven, by making peace through his blood, shed on the cross.* [21] *Once you were alienated from God and were enemies in your minds because of your evil behavior.* [22] *But now he has reconciled you by Christ's physical body through death to present you holy in his sight, without blemish and free from accusation* (Colossians 1:19-22 NIV).

Elsewhere, Paul focused attention on the issue of reconciliation and relationship. In 2 Corinthians 5:18-20, he writes:

> [18] *All this is from God, who reconciled us to himself through Christ and gave us the ministry of reconciliation:* [19] *that God was reconciling the world to himself in Christ, not counting men's sins against them. And he has committed to us the message of reconciliation.* [20] *We are therefore Christ's ambassadors, as though God were making his appeal through us. We implore you on Christ's behalf: Be reconciled to God* (NIV).

In this passage, Paul tells us the significance of Christ's entry into the world. The specific purpose for which Christ came was the purpose of reconciling the world to

God. In Jesus, God reconciled us to Himself.

Jesus has called His followers to this same mission. Robert Coleman writes, "Perishing humans who come to Jesus and feel His saving grip are no longer their own. We belong to Him who holds us by His grace. And in His ownership, we participate in His mission."[23] As chaplains seek to carry out ministry and mission in the world, they cannot lose sight of the ultimate mission: the task of reconciling people to God. All ministry to others must ultimately lead to carrying out the ministry of reconciliation.

This mission is a charge highlighted by Paul. He teaches that those who have been reconciled to God have been given a ministry, as well as a message, of reconciliation. The job title he selects for the reconciled is "ambassador". Paul saw himself as Christ's spokesman and representative. As a spokesman, the ambassador does not act on his own authority but under the commission of the greater power and authority who sent him. David Garland writes, "An ambassador makes the case for the one who sent him."[24]

The commissioning for this ministry and the delivery of this message of reconciliation is a directive from the lips of Jesus Christ. Immediately following His crucifixion and resurrection, Jesus appears to His closest followers with clear words of direction. John records those words for us in John 20:21: "... As the Father has sent me, I am sending you" (NIV). The Gospel writer Mark elaborates further on the purpose for which those earliest followers were sent. He writes, "And then he told them, 'Go into all the world and preach the Good News to everyone, everywhere" (Mark 16:15 NLT). The remarkable stories of the expansion of the church found in the book of Acts bear witness that Jesus' earliest followers clearly understood the task to which they were called, the ministry they had been given, and the privilege that was theirs as Christ's followers and representatives.

Returning to Paul's teaching on reconciliation in 2 Corinthians 5, we find the essence of the message of reconciliation we have been given. The message we are to deliver is that because of Christ's death, God will not hold our sin against us. Paul writes in verse 21, "God made him who had no sin to be sin for us, so that in him we might become the righteousness of God" (2 Corinthians 5:21 NIV). The message we are given is a message of life change. Lives can be changed as they are restored to a proper relationship with God. This is made possible because God allowed Jesus to be made sin for us.

One cannot overlook the significant truth of Paul's teaching on reconciliation. The truth is simple - only the reconciled can represent Christ and carry out the ministry of reconciliation. Only a follower of Jesus Christ can help another become a follower of Jesus Christ. That is the greatness of God's plan. Those whose lives have been changed are called and commissioned by God to be used in changing other lives. The first step in being used of God to incarnate the gospel and build relationships with others is being reconciled with God. Joe Aldrich writes, "Christians are to be good news before they share the good news. The words of the gospel are to be incarnated before they are verbalized."[25] A person must first be reconciled before he or she can be used of God in the ministry of reconciliation.

The principle for every chaplain is that he or she must be, in reality, what he or she appears to be. To be used of God in the task of reconciliation, it is essential that a person first be reconciled with God. The chaplain must be a genuine follower of Jesus Christ. This principle seems obvious, yet can easily be overlooked. Jesus spoke clear words to those He called. Matthew writes, "'Come, follow me,' Jesus said, 'and I will make you fishers of men'" (Matthew 4:19 NIV). A person must be reconciled with God and growing as a follower of Jesus Christ. Bill Hybels writes, "Inauthenticity among the ranks of those claiming to be Christians can become an almost insurmountable barrier to belief."[26] Chaplains must be, in reality, what they appear to be - genuine followers of Jesus Christ.

Children can easily spot authenticity. So can adults. They get to see the chaplain on a routine basis. They get to see him or her when the pressure is on. Enough time is available to observe if a person's actions match what he says he believes. They know when real life change has occurred. Conversely, they know when real life change has not occurred. Seekers will not be interested in committing their lives to Christ, unless they see genuine change and growth in the lives of those who claim to be followers of Jesus Christ. Becky Pippert writes, "If our lives do not give testimony to the radical difference that knowing Christ makes, our evangelism will ultimately be ineffective and hollow."[27]

Fig. 9.6 Children and adults can easily spot authenticity.

To be effective in chaplaincy, people must begin with their own personal relationship with God. The relationship must be established through reconciliation and be growing. This idea raises a few questions. First, how can a person know if the relationship has been established? Secondly, how can people begin growing in their relationship with God? Finally, what impact does spiritual growth have on effectiveness as a community chaplain?

To answer the first question requires a return to the reconciliation chapter of 2 Corinthians 5. In verse 17, Paul writes, "What this means is that those who become Christians become new persons. They are not the same anymore, for the old life is gone. A new life has begun!" (2 Corinthians 5:17 NLT) It is easy for a person to claim to be a Christian. However, Paul indicates that a changed life is the evidence supporting the claim. Each individual must evaluate his or her life. A few questions can help in this evaluation process. Is my life new and different? Does my life give evidence of the changes brought by faith in Christ? Has my thought life changed? Am I becoming more like Jesus Christ?

Oftentimes one can look at the lives of those who claim the name of Christ, and yet see them living far from a Christ-like life. It is easy in such instances to conclude that there is simply a problem with behaviors matching belief. In effect, the conclusion often reached is that a person is a believer simply because he claims to be a believer. A more accurate conclusion might be the recognition that behaviors are an indicator of what a person really believes, and not simply what he claims to believe. There is a difference! Jesus spoke of this distinction. Matthew writes:

> *20 Yes, the way to identify a tree or a person is by the kind of fruit that is produced. 21 Not all people who sound religious are really godly. They may refer to me as 'Lord,' but they still won't enter the Kingdom of Heaven. The decisive issue is whether they obey my Father in heaven* (Matthew 7:20-21 NLT).

People can tell a difference! An individual can recognize the evidence of a personal relationship with God. The book of Acts demonstrates how easily identifiable the early Christians were. Luke writes, "When they saw the courage of Peter and John and realized that they were unschooled, ordinary men, they were astonished and they took note that these men had been with Jesus" (Acts 4:13 NIV). Any observer should be able to recognize when a person has been with Jesus. This identification will occur as believers take steps to grow in their relationship with God. Growth in a relationship with God can only come when a person spends time with Jesus and with His followers. Growth comes from reading and feeding on the truths of the Bible. It comes from talking with God every day in prayer. Growth also comes from spending time with other

Christ followers in a biblically functioning church. People can tell when reconciliation has occurred. In Jesus, God reconciled us to Himself. Chaplains are called to be His representatives in this ministry of reconciliation.

The Incarnation as Revelation

Finally, important to the task of chaplaincy is that the incarnation teaches us how God chose to reveal Himself to sinful man. Erickson writes, "The most complete modality of revelation is the incarnation. The contention here is that Jesus' life and speech were a special revelation of God."[28] The writer of Hebrews teaches this truth and places emphasis on the superiority of the revelation found in Jesus Christ. Hebrews 1:1-3 states:

> [1] *In the past God spoke to our forefathers through the prophets at many times and in various ways,* [2] *but in these last days he has spoken to us by his Son, whom he appointed heir of all things, and through whom he made the universe.* [3] *The Son is the radiance of God's glory and the exact representation of his being, sustaining all things by His powerful word. After he had provided purification for sins, he sat down at the right hand of the Majesty in heaven* (NIV).

God's revelation of Himself through His Son is the climax of the revelatory process, because Jesus is the exact representation of God. The phrase "exact representation" translates *character*, which was used to describe the impression of an image made on coins. The word "being" translates the word hypostaseos. A better rendering might be the use of the word "substance." Leon Morris writes, "The Son is such a revelation of the Father that when we see Jesus, we see what God's real being is."[29]

As chaplains seek to live out their faith in the community, the goal is clear. The goal is for others to be able to look at the life of a believer and see what Jesus is really like. The character of a chaplain should be becoming like the character of Christ. This does not mean the chaplain is perfect; however, it does mean the chaplain is different. The life of a chaplain can and should be a revelation of Christ.

A second passage that describes God's revelation of Himself through Christ is found in Colossians 1:15. Speaking of Jesus, Paul writes, "He is the image of the invisible God, the firstborn over all creation" (NIV). The word "image" translates the word *eikon*. One element in the meaning of the word is that of manifestation, meaning that the symbol was more than a symbol, because it brought with it the actual presence of the object. In explaining the significance of this word choice, Melick writes:

> The point is that in Christ the invisible God became visible. He shared the same substance as God and made God's character known in this earthly sphere of existence. The revelation of God in Christ is such that we can actually see Him, even with all of our limitations.[30]

What is the lesson to be learned for chaplains seeking to live out their faith in the community? The lesson is simple. God is invisible; the chaplain is not. In a chaplain the invisible God can become visible. In spite of all the limitations of humanity, chaplains can be a model of Christ and impact the lives of those around them.

Finally, the revelation of God in Christ is taught in the Gospel of John. John 1:18 states, "No one has ever seen God, but God the One and Only, who is at the Father's side, has made him known" (NIV). The word translated "known" is the Greek word *exegesato*. D.A. Carson writes, "From this Greek term we derive 'exegesis': we might almost say that Jesus is the exegesis of God."[31] The emphasis is clear. The arrival of Jesus is God's ultimate self-disclosure. Later in John's Gospel, Jesus Himself would state, "... Anyone who has seen Me has seen the Father..." (John 14:9 NIV). When we see Jesus, we are seeing God.

The questions must be asked. Why did God choose to reveal Himself in such a personal way? Perhaps more importantly, what does this teach us about how we are to reveal the Good News to those around us? Erickson provides great insight into this question in his thoughts on special revelation. He stresses that the primary result of special revelation is knowledge of God. The primary goal of chaplaincy is knowledge of God. It is all about bringing God into the equation of people's lives - their work life, home life, married life, every aspect of life. Knowledge of God includes knowledge of His nature, attributes, and actions.

What better way could we get to know God than by actually being able to see Him? Erickson writes, "When the prophets spoke, they were bearers of a message from God and about God. When Jesus spoke, it was God Himself speaking. There was a directness about His message."[32] Erickson continues by describing the disciples as people who found in Jesus a revelation of the Father. In Jesus, we find revelation as act and word coming together. Erickson concludes, "Jesus both spoke the Father's word and demonstrated the Father's attributes. He was the most complete revelation of God, because He is God."[33] In Jesus, God spoke to us. The challenge to the chaplain is to reveal the Good News in both action and word. We are to speak God's Word and demonstrate God's attributes. The two must be brought together as we live our lives before an unbelieving world. The words of our mouths must consistently match the actions of our lives.

Speaking God's Word

While much attention has been given to Christians demonstrating God's attributes, attention must also be given to the speaking of God's word and the communication of the message of reconciliation. The heart of chaplaincy is the sharing of how a person can have new life through the death and resurrection of Jesus Christ. Romans 10:17 teaches of this importance. Paul writes, "Consequently, faith comes from hearing the message, and the message is heard through the word of Christ" (Romans 10:17 NIV). The Bible teaches that true faith comes by the sharing and hearing of the Word of God. Three areas will be addressed. First, a principle for sharing God's Word in casual conversation will be shared. Secondly, principles for the development of testimony will be provided. Finally, ideas for a clear explanation of the gospel message will be offered.

The most important step a chaplain can take in seeking to share God's Word in a casual conversation is the step of being in God's Word on a daily basis. As the chaplain spends time daily meditating upon God's truth, the truth is easily available for sharing in the normal course of a day. Jesus spoke some very important words in John 15:4-5. John writes:

> [4] *Remain in me, and I will remain in you. For a branch cannot produce fruit if it is severed from the vine, and you cannot be fruitful apart from me.* [5] *'Yes, I am the vine; you are the branches. Those who remain in me, and I in them, will produce much fruit. For apart from me you can do nothing ...'* (NIV).

A very practical way for the chaplain to remain as a branch connected to Jesus as the vine is to remain daily in God's Word.

Paul gave some very practical instructions for this task and for maturing as a believer to the church at Colossae. He writes, "In its place you have clothed yourselves with a brand-new nature that is continually being renewed as you learn more and more about Christ, who created this new nature within you" (Colossians 3:10 NLT). The process of renewal is an on-going process. It is a process that occurs as we learn better Who Christ is and what He has done for us. Paul gives clear instruction as to how this can occur in verse 16. He writes, "Let the words of Christ, in all their richness, live in your hearts and make you wise. Use his words to teach and counsel each other ..." (Colossians 3:16 NLT). Before one is able to use Christ's words in a ministry of teaching and counseling, those words must first live in the heart and mind of the chaplain.

Col 3:16

A second crucial step is for the chaplain to be able to verbalize how he or she was reconciled to God. The sharing of how reconciliation occurred is what is often referred to as giving testimony. The chaplain must be able to share his or her own story of reconciliation through Jesus Christ. The word testimony is a word often associated with a courtroom as a witness is called on to testify or give testimony. Likewise, followers of Christ are called on to testify to the change that has occurred in their lives, and more importantly, to give witness to how the change occurred.

The specific instruction of Jesus in Acts 1:8 was an instruction to "be my witnesses" (NIV). The early followers understood this instruction to testify and give witness. Following their arrest, Peter and John boldly proclaimed, "For we cannot help speaking about what we have seen and heard" (Acts 4:20 NIV). Elsewhere John would write, "We proclaim to you what we have seen and heard, so that you also may have fellowship with us. And our fellowship is with the Father and with his Son, Jesus Christ" (I John 1:3 NIV). In sharing his testimony with an angry mob, Paul shared with them the task he had been instructed to carry out. He said, "You will be His witness to all men of what you have seen and heard" (Acts 22:15 NIV).

The sharing of testimony is simply communicating what we have seen and heard. It is passing on what we have seen and heard about the death and resurrection of Jesus Christ. It is talking about what we have seen God do in our lives. Testimony is simply our personal account of how God has changed our life. Perhaps the greatest example of giving testimony is the example of Paul recorded in Acts 26. Verses 4-11 of this passage record Paul sharing what he used to be like prior to the changes God made in his life. He conveys what he believed, what he thought, and the actions that resulted. In verses 12-18 Paul provides a vivid description of the things that occurred as God changed his life. In verses 19-23 Paul shows the result of the life change brought about by his encounter with Jesus Christ on the Damascus road.

Finally, the chaplain must be able to communicate the basic teaching of what Christ accomplished through His death and resurrection. Becky Pippert summarizes well the task being carried out. She writes, "Therefore, our task is to tell 'His' story and 'our' story in the hope that it may one day be 'their' story."[34] The communication of the basic teaching of the gospel message is the telling of Jesus' story. Many methods have been developed for the sharing of the Good News; however, this work will focus on two.

Perhaps the easiest way of sharing the basic teaching of the gospel is by using a simple tract, developed by Billy Graham, called "Steps to Peace with God." This tract utilizes sixteen verses from God's Word and communicates in a systematic way how a person can be reconciled to God. The tract begins by focusing on God's purposeful desire to give life to every person. It addresses the problem of sin faced by each and every person who has ever lived. The tract communicates God's solution for the sin problem that is found in Christ's death and resurrection. Finally, the tract calls for a response. The use of a tract relieves the chaplain of the task of turning to different places in the Bible. In addition, it removes the fear that many people have of memorizing an outline and accompanying Scripture.

Finally, an alternative method for sharing the gospel is One Verse Evangelism, developed by Randy Raysbrook.[35] One Verse Evangelism utilizes the teaching of Romans 6:23. There Paul writes, "For the wages of sin is death, but the gift of God is eternal life in Christ Jesus our Lord" (Romans 6:23 NIV). Utilizing this verse allows the chaplain to communicate in simple fashion the basic teaching of the gospel: that Jesus Christ came to this earth to be the atoning sacrifice for the sin of mankind, paid the penalty, and offered, to all people who would receive it, the free gift of eternal life.

Helping people discover this Good News is the ultimate goal of community chaplaincy. Equipping chaplains to help others discover this truth is the ultimate goal of this work. The words of Jim Petersen serve as words of challenge to every chaplain. He writes:

Change is hard to face, especially in areas of behavior. Going into the world requires change. It implies participation in people's lives. It means to think, to feel, to understand, and to take seriously the values of those we seek to win. The incarnation is our prototype.[36]

As chaplains allow the incarnation to be their prototype for ministry in the community, real life change can be the result.

Endnotes

1. Michael Green, *Evangelism in the Early Church* (Guildford, UK: Eagle, 1970), 214-15.

2. Lewis Drummond, *The Word of the Cross* (Nashville: Broadman, 1992), 121.

3. John Maxwell, *Developing the Leader Within You* (Nashville: Thomas Nelson, 1993), 128.

4. John Stott, *The Cross of Christ* (Downers Grove: Intervarsity, 1986), 291.

5. Charles Ryrie, *Basic Theology* (Colorado Springs: Chariot Victor, 1982), 247.

6. Curtis Vaughn, *Colossians*, The Expositor's Bible Commentary, vol. 8 (Grand Rapids: Zondervan, 1978), 199.

7. Richard Melick, *Philippians Colossians Philemon*, The New American Commentary, vol. 32 (Nashville: Broadman, 1991), 255.

8. Ibid.

9. The Wycliffe Bible Commentary, Electronic Database. Copyright (c) 1962 by Moody Press.

10. Danny Akin, *Systematic Theology II Class Notes, Book I: Christology* (Wake Forest: Southeastern Baptist Theological Seminary, 1994), 36.

11. Gerald Borchert, *John 1-11*, The New American Commentary, vol. 25A (Nashville: Broadman & Holman, 1996), 119.

12. Ryrie, *Basic Theology*, 244-45.

13. Ibid., 244.

14. Homer Kent, Jr., *Philippians*, The Expositor's Bible Commentary, vol. 11 (Grand Rapids: Zondervan, 1978), 122.

15. Danny Akin, *Systematic Theology II Class Notes, Book I: Christology* (Wake Forest: Southeastern Baptist Theological Seminary, 1994), 35-36.

16. Robert Coleman, *The Master's Way of Personal Evangelism* (Wheaton: Crossway, 1997), 11.

17. Ibid., 143-58.

18. Millard Erickson, *Christian Theology* (Grand Rapids: Baker, 1983), 761.

19. Vaughn, *Colossians*, 179.

20. Ibid., 180.

21. Melick, *Philippians Colossians Philemon*, 208.

22. Ibid., 225.

23. Coleman, *The Master's Way of Personal Evangelism*, 11.

24. David Garland, *2 Corinthians*, The New American Commentary, vol. 29 (Nashville: Broadman & Holman, 1999), 295, 298.

25. Joe Aldrich, *Lifestyle Evangelism* (Sisters, OR: Multnomah, 1993), 19-20.

26. Bill Hybels, *Becoming a Contagious Christian* (Grand Rapids: Zondervan, 1994), 54.

27. Becky Pippert, *Out of the Saltshaker & into the World* (Downers Grove: InterVarsity,

1949
2008/
59

1999), 73.

28. Erickson, *Christian Theology*, 190.

29. Leon Morris, *Hebrews*, The Expositor's Bible Commentary, vol. 12 (Grand Rapids: Zondervan, 1981), 14.

30. Melick, *Philippians Colossians Philemon*, 214-15.

31. D.A. Carson, *The Gospel According to John* (Grand Rapids: Eerdmans, 1991), 135.

32. Erickson, *Christian Theology*, 190.

33. Ibid., 191.

34. Pippert, *Out of the Saltshaker & into the World*, 135.

35. Randy Raysbrook, "One Verse Evangelism," *Discipleship Journal* (1986): 94-99.

36. Jim Petersen, *Living Proof* (Colorado Springs: Navpress, 1989), 118.

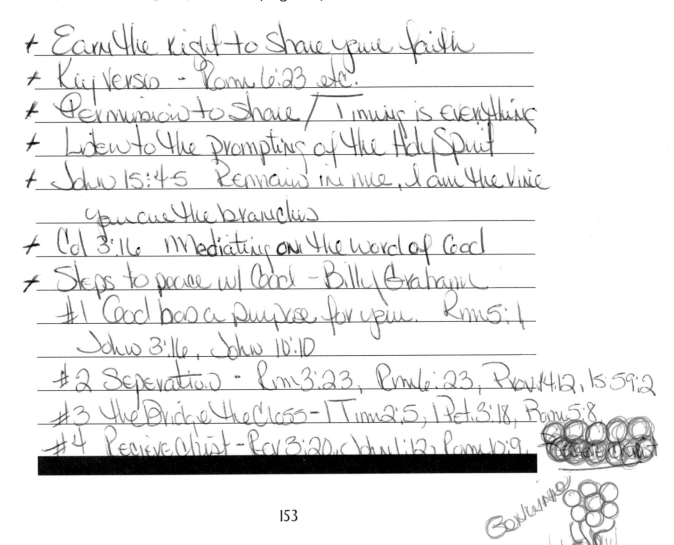

+ Earn the right to share your faith
+ Key Verses - Rom 6:23 etc.
+ Permission to share / Timing is everything
+ Listen to the prompting of the Holy Spirit
+ John 15:4-5 Remain in me, I am the vine
   you are the branches
+ Col 3:16 Mediating on the word of God
+ Steps to peace w/ God - Billy Graham
   #1 God has a purpose for you. Rms 5:1
   John 3:16, John 10:10
   #2 Seperation - Rm 3:23, Rm 6:23, Prov 14:12, Is 59:2
   #3 the Bridge the Cross - 1 Tim 2:5, 1 Pet 3:18, Rom 5:8
   #4 Recieve Christ - Rev 3:20, John 1:12, Rom 10:9

Chapter Ten

Community Chaplaincy in a Postmodern Culture

CHAPTER TEN

Community Chaplaincy in a Postmodern Culture

—————————————— Objectives ——————————————

During the course of this chapter, we will perform the following tasks:

■ Define and explore postmodernism

■ Examine models for engaging the truth claims of a multicultural world

■ Examine findings from various focus groups used to learn more about ministry in a postmodern world

■ Discover principles of ministry for serving in a multicultural world

T his chapter will focus on the rapidly changing postmodern world in which we operate today and will explore the implications for quality, defect free community chaplaincy service. The world we live in is clearly changing. The changes are rapid and can sometimes leave a chaplain grappling with the challenges of the postmodern and multicultural mission field he or she is serving. This chapter will seek to define postmodernism and explore multiculturalism, with the hope of providing valuable insight which will enable chaplains to serve in a respectful manner, free of complaint or criticism.

The question facing providers of chaplaincy services and churches desiring to provide a chaplain is this: what role may faith play amid the challenges of multiple religious truth claims? This chapter will provide a framework for addressing this issue and guidance to do so in a respectful way. What is the appropriate posture and approach of the chaplain who desires to be faithful to his or her faith, yet is available to serve the needs of those of differing faith backgrounds?

Keith Eitel, who was a teacher in the Corporate Chaplains Institute, presented an excellent summary of three models for engaging the variety of truth claims encountered in the workplace and throughout the world in which we live, breathe, and play. The models are: 1) pluralism, 2) inclusivism, and 3) engagement.

Let us explore each of these approaches.

First, *pluralism* is an approach advocated by John Hick, which states that all exclusive truth claims are equally false. His model demands a rejection of the exclusive truth claims of Christianity, as well as any modern efforts to appease the current culture with a form of inclusivistic or universal salvation. With all exclusive truth claims being equally false, Hick would open the door for the potential of all religions to lead a person to full personal actualization. Further, through a rejection of exclusive truth, Hick annihilates the uniqueness found in the different world religions. His view ultimately leads down a road of relativism, where each and every truth claim is as valid, or invalid, as any other and each individual is the author of his or her own religion. Hick's view might be best summarized by the contemporary words of singer Alanis Morissette: "So what it all boils down to is that no one's really got it all figured out just yet."[1]

The second model for approaching multiculturalism is Karl Rahner's *inclusivism*. Rather than ruling out truth claims like Hick, Rahner attempts to tame the exclusive claims of Christ by affirming that all religions are really acknowledging the same Christ. Rahner invents the concept of the "anonymous Christian," which asserts that all devout adherents of all religious traditions affirm a type of "cosmic" Christ and, in so doing, are Christians whether they are conscious of it or not.[2]

Rahner's model is an attempt to hold hands with two different people groups and, in fact, force them to hold hands with one another. The first group would be those who hold to the exclusive truth claims of ancient Church tradition. For this group he affirms Christ is the answer. The second group is a modern group that hungers for both relativism and exclusivism simultaneously. Rahner's model seeks to appease this group by affirming Christ is the answer even for those who do not realize Christ as the answer.

Rahner's balancing act is tenuous at best. In the final analysis, it commits more of an exclusivistic blunder than it aims at resolving. He plants the Christian flag on the face of any and all religious traditions, declaring them to be followers of Christ in ignorance. At its best, this is an insult to those adhering to the exclusive truth claims found in other world religions. At its worst, this approach would serve to alienate those who might otherwise enjoy a respectful difference of opinion in regards to differing exclusive truth claims. Traditional biblical exclusivism at least requires conscious examination of Christ's claims and a personal act of faith transitioning into the Christian tradition. Rahner's approach ignores this essential ingredient.

Let us finally turn our attention to the model of *engagement*, the model affirmed by

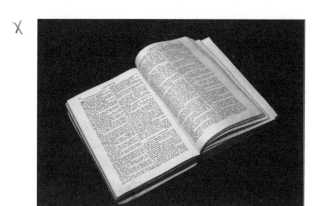

Fig. 10.1 Evangelicals affirm the finality of Christ as the supreme form of God's revelation and the infallibility of the Bible as the interpretive grid for knowing and interpreting the meaning of Christ as revelation.

this work. Evangelicals affirm the finality of Christ as the supreme form of God's revelation and the infallibility of the Bible as the interpretive grid for knowing and interpreting the meaning of Christ as revelation. With this in view, Christ's attitude and that of any biblical examples toward other religions would seem paramount in our quest. Paul's engagement of the learned Greeks in Acts 17:16-34 provides a working model for faith amid competing and contrasting mixes of religious ideas.

> *[16] While Paul was waiting for them in Athens, he was deeply troubled by all the idols he saw everywhere in the city. [17] He went to the synagogue to debate with the Jews and the God-fearing Gentiles, and he spoke daily in the public square to all who happened to be there. [18] He also had a debate with some of the Epicurean and Stoic philosophers. When he told them about Jesus and his resurrection, they said, 'This babbler has picked up some strange ideas.' Others said, 'He's pushing some foreign religion.'*
>
> *[32] When they heard Paul speak of the resurrection of a person who had been dead, some laughed, but others said, 'We want to hear more about this later.' [33] That ended Paul's discussion with them, [34] but some joined him and became believers. Among them were Dionysius, a member of the Council, a woman named Damaris, and others* (Acts 17:16-18, 32-34 NLT).[3]

Knowing and accepting the uniquely true claims of Christ must not lead to intolerance or any sense of arrogance. Rather it has only one reasonable outlet, to engage respectfully in accomplishing the Great Commission. Paul uses a common ground point of departure, but it is apparent his desire is to engage in dialogue that seeks understanding and asserts a positive witness of Christ. He next moves to address the root of their idolatry from the standpoint of unique truth, exhibited through the resurrection of Christ, although the name of Christ is not introduced before the meeting ends. Luke's account of Paul's message notes that he stirred up the crowd with mention of the resurrection, but some believed.

Let us conclude with some applicable insights that we as community chaplains can learn from Paul's approach of engagement. First, he was deeply troubled by what he saw. The trouble we feel as we look around the places we serve can provide motivation for us as it did for Paul, and it can move us to our second point of application - action. Second, Paul took initiative to speak with those who were interested. What we learn here is simple. Not every person under our care will be equally interested in the care and help we offer. This is not a problem. We can take special initiative with those who are. Third, Paul received a mixed response. Once again, the reminder is obvious; not everyone responds the same way. This too can be overcome, because the final application idea is clear. Finally, he helped some become believers. Paul provides an excellent summary of his approach in his letter to the church at Colossae. Colossians 4:5-6 states, "[5] Live wisely among those who are not Christians, and make the most of every opportunity. [6] Let your conversation be gracious and effective so that you will have the right answer for everyone."

In examining these three models, what are the concluding lessons for the chaplain? Hick's model rejects the idea of dialogue that affirms or bears witness to Christian truth, because he contends that the only possible results are conversion or alienation. Yet, Leslie Newbigin and others raise the possibility of a third outcome, namely understanding and respect. As chaplains serving in the community, it is not necessary to yield the exclusive truth of Christ, either historical and objective, or experiential and subjective. Instead, the call of chaplaincy is to engage in dialogue that bears witness of these truths without acting or reacting in ways that would undermine the gospel itself. Even in a community setting, we can and should affirm a positive, polite witness as the free exercise of our faith, while affirming tolerance, in varying degrees and kinds, of other faith traditions. Grace and truth will go a long way in achieving either conversion or mutual understanding, while avoiding alienation.

Many articles and even books have been written that speak of ministry to postmodern people, referring to it as "ministry to postmoderns". While acknowledging that some are more postmodern in their thinking than others, the focus here will be to point out that everyone living today is affected at some level with a thought process influenced by postmodernism.

To define postmodernism is a large undertaking in itself. Stanley Grenz writes, "Whatever else it might be, as the name suggests, postmodernism signifies the quest to move beyond modernism. Specifically, it involves a rejection of the modern mind-set, but launched under the conditions of modernity."[4] In essence, postmodernism is a rejection of the key tenets of modernism.

Tracing its intellectual roots to the Renaissance and the Enlightenment, the modern mind held knowledge to be certain, objective, good, and accessible to the human mind through rational inquiry and investigation. These tenets led to an optimistic outlook, because it was believed that continual inquiry would lead to greater understanding and that greater understanding would lead to inevitable progress.

Grenz writes, "Postmodernism represents a rejection of the Enlightenment project and the foundational assumptions upon which it was built."[5] First, the postmodern mind rejects the human intellect as the final arbiter of truth. In its place are other valid paths to knowledge, including the emotions and intuition. In effect, postmodernism rejects that truth is certain and thus rational. Second, postmodernism rejects the belief that knowledge is inherently good. Grenz writes, "Postmodernism replaces the optimism of the last century with a gnawing pessimism. Gone is the belief that every day, in every way, we are getting better and better."[6] Finally, the postmodern mind rejects that knowledge is objective. The world is not simply an objective entity that is "out there," but is rather an historical, relational, and personal reality we participate in.

Francis Shaeffer selected what has proven to be a very prophetic title for his 1968 analysis of the trends of modern thought. He titled his work *Escape from Reason*. Today, the message of the gospel is being communicated to people who have made the escape. Explaining the reason for the despair of modern man, Schaeffer writes, "[Despair] arises from the abandonment of the hope of a unified answer for knowledge and life. Modern man continues to hang on to his rationalism and his autonomous revolt even though to do so he has to abandon any rational hope of a unified answer."[7] The postmodern conclusion is that there is no answer. Community chaplains are seeking to provide answers to the questions for which postmodern individuals in the community have conclusively determined as having no answers.

The Use of Focus Groups

While a proper contextual understanding of multiculturalism and postmodernism is essential, it can be equally helpful to understand what practitioners and people today have to say. With this in mind, focus groups were utilized in an effort to inform a proper model of care.

In order to gain first hand insight for the impact of chaplaincy care in a postmodern culture, two focus groups were conducted. In preparation for the focus groups, research was conducted on the nature, composition, and purpose of focus groups. One market research firm noted the purpose of conducting a focus group. They stated, "[The purpose is] to gain insights by listening to a group of people from the appropriate target market talk about issues of interest to the researcher."[8] In this instance, chaplaincy care in a postmodern culture was the issue of interest to the researcher, and two primary groups were the targets for needed insights.

The first focus group sought to obtain practical insights from full time corporate chaplains currently serving on staff with Corporate Chaplains of America. The second group focused on obtaining insights from unchurched people.

Chaplain Focus Group

The corporate chaplain focus group involved five full time corporate chaplains who were selected based on two criteria. First, the chaplain had to have completed a minimum of one year of full time service with Corporate Chaplains of America (CCA). Second, the chaplain had to have received the "Soul Winner of the Quarter" award at least once during his or her service with CCA. The "Soul Winner of the Quarter" award is given to the chaplain reporting the most salvation decisions for a given quarter. These criteria were utilized to insure insight was being obtained from individuals who were experienced and consistent in carrying out the mission of building relationships with employees, with the hope of gaining permission to share the life-changing Good News of Jesus Christ, in a non-threatening manner.

As the focus group was conducted, it was begun with the goal of delving into the thoughts of the chaplains to discover why Corporate Chaplains of

Focus Group Criteria

Corporate Chaplains:

- 1 year full time service with CCA
- Received "Soul Winner of the Quarter" award

Unchurched Group:

- Not active in any church

America has had such evangelistic effectiveness in the workplace. Many valuable insights were gained from the responses of the chaplains that ultimately helped inform the practical principles developed for serving employees in a multicultural work environment.

The general consensus among the chaplains was that CCA was experiencing ministry effectiveness free from complaint for several reasons. First, the work of corporate chaplaincy is to go where people are and not wait for them to come to us. In effect, we are not asking people to change their behavior patterns to meet us where we are; we instead are changing our behavior patterns to meet them where they are. CCA is attempting to meet people where they are, both in a physical and spiritual sense.

A second reason for ministry effectiveness is due to the strength of building ongoing relationships with the employees. One chaplain stated:

> In the workplace where you are going to see them repeatedly, the pressure is not to share the gospel with them. The pressure is to know when to share the gospel with them and how to show them you really care. Because now it's not a matter of if I'm going to share, but when will they be most receptive. You learn to recognize when people are ready to hear the gospel.

The building of a caring and trusting relationship is the key that opens the door for the communication of the Good News. Another chaplain added, "When we've taken the time to build a relationship and get to know them on their terms, and then wait for the crisis time to occur, we will see about eighty to ninety percent make a positive decision for Christ because the time is ripe and we've earned the right to share."

The statement above leads to a third reason for the care-giving effectiveness of chaplaincy. Chaplaincy takes a servant approach to minister to people in moments of crisis. One chaplain pointed out that a servant approach was his most significant ministry discovery since becoming a corporate chaplain. He stated, "People are ready to hear the gospel when they're in a time of crisis." The sentiment among the chaplains was clear; the ministry of presence, of simply being there for someone else serves as a powerful bridge for the communication of the gospel.

Finally, focus was given to internal attitude as an important reason for effectiveness. One chaplain raised a very significant rhetorical question. He asked, "Are we soul winners because we're corporate chaplains, or are we corporate chaplains because we're soul winners?" He continued by answering his own question, "Every one of us had a burden; our attitude was a sense of calling. God has called us to ministry, and the burden on our heart is to see lives changed and to share the Good News." This burning desire and single-minded focus is perhaps the key that motivates the entire approach toward evangelism. It is what moves the chaplain forward in his or her mission to build relationships with the hope of gaining permission to share the life-changing Good News of Jesus Christ, in a non-threatening manner.

Fig. 10.2 Chaplains are effective due, partially, to relationship building.

Unchurched Focus Group

The focus group of unchurched people was conducted with very simple criteria. Participants in this group had only one criterion to meet; they could not be active in any church. This group involved five individuals: two females and three males ranging in age from 22 to 40.

The spiritual beliefs, as well as the past spiritual involvement of this unchurched group, were very wide-ranging. Pluralism is the defining description of their religious involvement, while skepticism toward all things religious would be the defining description of their personal beliefs. One participant had a religious heritage that included Presbyterian Church attendance with his grandmother, alongside involvement with the Catholic Church. A second participant was involved in a Southern Baptist youth group while being reared by a mother who was Catholic. Still another participant had a spiritual background that included Methodist baptism at birth, Baptist baptism by immersion at age four, Lutheran communion at age eight, and adult study with Jehovah's Witnesses and Mormon missionaries. One other participant had a spiritual background that included Protestant military church involvement and involvement in Jewish synagogue worship. Only one participant affirmed any on-going church involvement as an adult. Interestingly, this person was the only participant indicating any type of faith commitment to Jesus Christ.

The current beliefs of the group were as varied as their spiritual backgrounds. One person was a self-described atheist. He stated, "I tried to find a religion I believed and concluded I didn't believe any." He continued with his opinion, "God is mankind's desire for limitations. We look at the world around us and ask questions that are difficult to answer, and the answer we give is, 'It's got to be God'. We turn to God to avoid really answering the questions."

Outside of the one participant to affirm belief in Jesus Christ, one other participant's belief description provides a good example of the overall belief state of the group. She stated, "I believe there is something out there; I don't know if it's God or not. I have trouble believing in the kind of Southern Baptist God. I believe there is some type of higher power, no matter what it is. I grew up in church, but I don't believe you have to go to church to know God." If something resembling consensus could be found among this group, it was that something bigger than them did exist, even if they did not fully understand it or were unable to explain it.

In an examination of their thoughts about people who attempt to discuss religion, there was unanimous agreement in their aversion to such attempts. The question posed was simple. Has anyone ever attempted to share his or her faith and/or religious beliefs with you? Every participant had experienced such efforts made toward him or her by others. These attempts were described as intrusive, presumptuous, and offensive. One participant described the experience as bringing the same feeling he gets when approached by a used car salesman. He told of an experience at an airport where a guy tried to shove a tract in his pocket. He stated, "The guy reminded me of the people at the mall who try to shove a sample of teriyaki chicken in your face."

While most of the experiences described were negative, the overall consensus was one of a willingness to discuss religious beliefs with others. One participant spoke of being friends with a young minister. She said, "I have a good friend who is a minister, and we disagree on lots of things; but we sit down and discuss our beliefs, and we still remain good friends." Still another participant stated, "I've had good conversations about faith, unless a person came at me with the Bible in their hand and they were using it for their own means."

The consensus opinion of the group toward people involved in church was strongly averse as well. Given the opportunity to describe people who are actively involved in church, one word rang through loudly and clearly – "hypocrite." One participant even borrowed from the words of Jesus and described churchgoers as "whited sepulchers."

The lesson to be learned from this focus group is simple, yet invaluable. While the unchurched are deeply skeptical of religion and religious people, they are open to discussions about spiritual matters with people who will demonstrate respect and have a willingness to invest the time.

Focus Group Conclusion

In reflecting on the ideas discovered from each of the focus groups, one key insight emerged:

> The key insight is the contrast between the enthusiasm for spiritual dialogue and caregiving of the chaplains and the aversion of the unchurched to talking about matters of faith and to anyone seen as religious.

The attitude of the chaplains was an attitude of excitement and enthusiasm. The desire to share the Good News and the expectation that lives would be changed shown through in the responses of the participants. The unchurched attitude was one that sought to avoid anyone who might go overboard in his or her evangelistic efforts. Their attitude could be described in one word: resentful. They were bitter toward the churched for their aggressive approach, the perceived hypocrisy, and the assumptions they believe others make about their spiritual condition.

Practical Approach

So how does a community chaplain approach service and attempt to communicate the truth claims of Christianity in this postmodern culture? The apostle Peter, writing over 2,000 years ago, gave great chaplaincy advice. He writes in I Peter 3:15: "But in your hearts, set apart Christ as Lord. Always be prepared to give an answer to everyone who asks you to give the reason for the hope that you have. But do this with gentleness and respect" (NIV). Peter's inspired advice is perhaps more valuable now than ever. It is essential that we think clearly on how to communicate answers and grounds for hope in what may often appear to an individual to be a hopeless situation. We must share the reasons; however, we must be aware that reason itself is no longer adequate in communicating truth based answers to the postmodern mind.

So what will work? How does a chaplain proceed to do more than simply make a difference in the life of a person in his care? Is it possible to go beyond simply making a difference and instead seek to make a different situation? The concepts to great care are really quite basic.

- Relationship
- Practical help and practical answers (provide them something that works)
- Authenticity

So what is the most adequate means of communicating the truth claims of Christianity? Very simply, people need to see the reasons for our hope, in order that we might earn the right to share the reason for the hope we have. Leonard Sweet writes, "Christians are people who show others how to 'get a life,' whose lifestyle evangelizes: what and how we wear, drink, play, drive, and read can communicate our values and faith."[9]

Acknowledging the confusion one can have in attempting to evangelize and, in fact, even understand postmodernism, Susan Hecht writes, "Despite all that is unclear concerning postmodernism, what is clear is that people long for connection with others."[10] She concludes, "Although rational, logical arguments alone have lost the strength of persuasion they once had, relational connection, authenticity, and pragmatic answers to life's problems are key elements that can help open the door for the gospel."[11] Each of these elements is central to unlocking the door for people seeking to live out their faith in the community. The purpose of this work bears repeating here. The purpose is to equip and mobilize chaplains to build relationships with their co-workers, their neighbors, their teammates, their classmates, and their public servants, with the hope of gaining permission to share the life-changing Good News of Jesus Christ, in a non-threatening manner.

Hecht uses the word "authenticity" as a key element that can help open the door for the gospel. Perhaps more than anything else, people in today's world are looking for that which is real. One need not look far for evidence that this is true. A quick scan of recent hit TV shows will reveal the growing interest in reality TV. People are more likely to ask, "Is it real?" before asking "Is it true?" People will look at Christians and ask, "Are they real?" before examining Christianity and asking, "Is it true?" The great author Ralph Waldo Emerson once stated, "What you are shouts so loudly I cannot hear what you say."

In addition to authenticity, Hecht emphasizes the importance of relational connection. Because of the vast amount of fractured relationships, many people are left with no one to turn to during the crisis times of life. Not only do people look for that which is real, they also look for someone who cares. Picking up on Hecht's last point, they look for someone who cares enough to help and who cares enough to provide them with practical answers to life's problems.

The American culture is the ideal setting for people to be real, to show they care, and to provide others with practical answers to life's problems. Perhaps more than any other location, the community, the setting in which the chaplain already interacts with those who are seeking, provides an opportunity for people to be able to see what others are really like. They can see how people respond to pressure, how they react when they have been wronged, and how they act when they are having a bad day. If what people see in the lives of those who claim the name of Christ matches what they say they believe, then doors for the communication of the gospel can be opened. Hecht writes, "In a postmodern culture that is leery of truth-claims and that looks for practical answers to life issues, what people see in our lives will communicate to them as much as, and probably more than, what we communicate to them verbally."[12]

Not only does the unbeliever get to see the believer in action, the opposite is also true. The American culture provides a perfect setting for the believer to observe the lives of their co-workers. A believer can see the stress or perhaps hear the complaints a neighbor might share about his or her home life. He or she can observe the struggles of dealing with a sick family member or of facing some other crisis.

However, more than merely observing these crises, believers can place themselves in a position to help, as they simply demonstrate care for those with whom they work or live.

Fig. 10.3 A believer should always observe the lives of their co-workers in order to get insights about issues they may be facing.

Robert Coleman stresses that part of the incarnation is becoming a servant and loving people where they hurt. Citing the example of Jesus, he points out how readily people will listen when they know someone cares. Coleman writes:

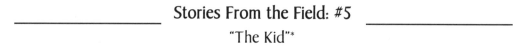

The same holds true of skeptics today. To reach them, we must take the servant's mantle. When they know they are loved, we have their attention. In a generation like ours that has lost a sense of objective truth, living by their feelings rather than by faith, this may be the only way to make sense to them initially.[13]

It is the business of every chaplain to simply look around their place of service and see how they can meet a need. As needs are identified, the chaplain can be the one to step forward and try to help. Coleman concludes, "Unassuming as it may be, this is how our witness becomes credible."[14]

Coleman's use of the word "credible" returns us to the previous idea: people are looking for that which is real. As a chaplain reaches out to an unbelieving individual in genuine ministry, that person will discover someone who cares and is real. Once this discovery is made, the door is opened for sharing the practical answer of the gospel to life's greatest difficulty - the problem of sin. This is an approach that engenders trust, confidence, and friendship and is best summarized by Proverbs 16:7: "When the ways of people please the LORD, he makes even their enemies live at peace with them."

Stories From the Field: #5
"The Kid"*

Ron had been on rounds for an hour. The time was 9:30 am; the day was Thursday, one week before Thanksgiving. Conversations so far that morning had been focused on holiday plans, travel itineraries, and general excitement over the upcoming long weekend, now less than a week away. Because of his sales background, Ron always enjoyed his rounds in the marketing department and his ability to truly understand the demands faced by his co-workers..

As he approached Frances' cubicle, he paused as she completed a call and removed her headset. She acknowledged him with a smile and a quick greeting. "I'm glad you're here today. We're going to see family next week, and I need to ask you a question." She continued, "You know I grew up as a Jehovah's Witness, and my mom still stays after me to remain faithful. Did I ever mention that my husband grew up in a Mormon family?" Ron paused, thoughts racing forward in anticipation and curiosity at the question that was about to follow. "No, I didn't know your husband was Mormon," he replied. "Is he still active or has he become a Jehovah's Witness?" "He's not active in any faith," Frances replied. "I know the question is going to come up over Thanksgiving, and I wanted your opinion." Glancing at a picture of a beautiful little girl sitting in a nice frame on her desk, she continued. "Gracie is almost three now, and I was wondering what we should do about celebrating Christmas?" Ron paused, searching for the right words and response to a question with no easy answer. "That's a big question." Wanting to respect her time and the company's time, Ron continued. "What time is your break?" Glancing at her watch, Frances replied, "15 minutes." "How about we meet in the 3rd floor conference room at 10 a.m.?" Ron responded.

*Individuals in this story have granted permission for its use.

Questions

1. When the time comes for the meeting, how would you open the caregiving session?
2. What advice would you offer to Frances in answer to her question?

Practical Exercise

Take a few minutes to reflect on some crisis moments or moments of joy experienced by your co-workers. What was their faith background? How did they respond to the event? Was their faith commitment strengthened or weakened? Were they more or less responsive to discussing matters of faith?

_____

_____

_____

_____

_____

_____

Endnotes

1. Leonard Sweet, *SoulTsunami: Sink or Swim in New Millennium Culture* (Grand Rapids: Zondervan, 1999), 310.

2. Rahner gives the most clear definition of the anonymous believer indicating: "Therefore no matter what a man states in his conceptual, theoretical and religious reflection, anyone who does not say in his *heart*, 'there is no God' (like the 'fool' in the psalm) but testifies to him by the radical acceptance of his being, is a believer. But if in this way he believes in deed and in truth in the holy mystery of God, if he does not suppress this truth but leaves it free play, then the grace of this truth by which he allows himself to be led is always already the grace of the Father in his Son. And anyone who has let himself be taken hold of by this grace can be called with every right an 'anonymous Christian.'" Karl Rahner, *Theological Investigations*, trans. Karl and Boniface Kruger (Baltimore: Helicon, 1969), 6:395.

3. All scripture quotations are from The New Living Translation (NLT), unless otherwise specified.

4. Stanley Grenz, *A Primer on Postmodernism* (Grand Rapids: Eerdmans, 1996), 2.

5. Ibid, 3-5.

6. Ibid, 7.

7. Francis Shaeffer, *Escape from Reason* (Downers Grove: InterVarsity, 1968), 45.

8. See "View Finders Market Research," <http://www.view-finders.com/client/services/focusgroups.html> (Accessed 7 February 2001).

9. Leonard Sweet, *SoulTsunami: Sink or Swim in New Millennium Culture* (Grand Rapids: Zondervan, 1999), 54.

10. Susan Hecht, "Faithfully Relating to Unbelievers in a Relational Age" in *Telling the Truth*, ed. D.A. Carson (Grand Rapids: Zondervan, 2000), 246.

11. Ibid.

12. Ibid, 252.

13. Robert Coleman, "The Lifestyle of the Great Commission," in *Telling the Truth*, 256.

14. Ibid., 257.

Unit Three

Core Principles of Community Chaplaincy

Unit 3 details the core principles that serve as the guiding force for the care provided by community chaplains.

Chapter Eleven

The Role of Relationships in Community Chaplaincy

CHAPTER ELEVEN

The Role of Relationships in Community Chaplaincy

———————————— Objectives ————————————

During the course of this chapter, we will perform the following tasks:

■ Define Relationship

■ Explore Scripture and the need for human relationships

■ List boundaries necessary for relationships in community chaplaincy

■ Describe reasons for developing relationships in the community

■ List goals for relationships in the community

■ Describe the process for developing effective relationships in order to have a greater impact as a chaplain

*R*elationship: What does the word mean to you? For some, it means a spouse. Still others immediately think of a son or a daughter, maybe a pet, a significant other, an abusive father, or a good friend. How we define the term *relationship* is based largely on our past experience. The *Oxford American Dictionary* states the meaning as follows:

> **Relationship:** (noun) 1. the way in which one thing is related to another, a similarity or correspondence or contrast between people or things or events. 2. being related. 3. a person who is a relative. 4. dealings with others.[1]

Spend a few moments and reflect on the significant events in your life. Use the space on the next page to write them down.

_____

_____

_____

_____

_____

_____

_____

_____

_____

_____

_____

_____

As you think about those major life happenings, do you focus more on the actual event itself or on the people that are involved in that life event? People are generally either task-oriented or relationship-oriented. If you tend to focus on the task more than on the people involved in the task, you are most likely task-oriented. If the people that you get to work with, or the people in your life take priority over a task, then you are probably more relationship-oriented. While we all have to balance both people and tasks, we usually favor one or the other. Some of this depends on our basic personality style and our life experiences, while other influencing factors include the type of work that is performed and the structure of any industry.

When examining the definition of *relationship* in terms of community chaplaincy, one must look beyond the "dealings with others" that is suggested above. Relationships are the core of a healthy and flourishing society. It is essential that the truth about relationships be recognized and shared with others. Healthy interaction between individuals is paramount if life is to be lived to the fullest. The effective community chaplain will have a sense of intentionality about the relationship between himself and those in his mission field. This means that the relationship is not just developed for the sake of relationship. The relationship has a purpose, a goal, and an accompanying action plan. The ultimate goal in the relationship building process is to introduce them to the One with whom human beings were created to commune: Jesus Christ. In his book *Understanding People*, Larry Crabb states that

God is an independent person with the capacity to long, think, choose, and feel. A human being is a dependent person with the same four capacities. Our beginning framework for understanding people can now be presented simply. Each of us is a personal being who longs deeply, a rational being who thinks, a volitional being who chooses, and an emotional being who feels.[2]

Relationships: A Mandate From Scripture

Scripture clearly gives the chaplain his mandate for building relationships so that those in the community, the chaplain's mission field, can be exposed to the life-changing Good News of Jesus Christ. In fact, Jesus Christ became a sacrifice so that redemption could occur, all out of a desire for a relationship with those He created. Therefore, if Scripture is interpreted correctly, relationships built for the purpose of sharing the gospel in the community are simply an outflow of the mission. Ephesians 2:10 states that "For we are God's workmanship, created in Christ Jesus to do good works, which God prepared in advance for us to do" (NIV). The *Handbook of Bible Application* clearly summarizes this idea:

We are God's workmanship. Our salvation is something only God can do. It is his powerful, creative work in us. If God considers us his works of art, we dare not treat ourselves or others with disrespect or as inferior work. We become Christians

176

through God's unmerited grace, not as a result of any effort, ability, intelligent choice, or act of service on our part. However, out of gratitude for this gift, we will seek to help and serve others with kindness, charity, and goodness, and not merely to please ourselves. While no action or work we do can help us obtain salvation, God's intention is that our salvation will result in works of service. We are not saved merely for our own benefit, but to serve Him and build up the church.[3]

Set Up Boundaries For Safe Relationships

When meeting others for ministry in the community, it is crucial to understand that all will not greet the chaplain enthusiastically. The traditional "bell curve" applies in this situation as well. The majority of the population found in your mission field, about eighty percent, will welcome the community chaplain warmly but feel that there will most likely not be a need for the chaplain. This segment of the population feels that they are immune to the struggles to which the rest of the world may be subject. This majority will not be openly hostile to the community minister. On the contrary, they will be friendly, cordial, and, from a safe distance, receptive to the idea. That leaves twenty percent of the population. Half of that twenty percent, ten percent, will be the cheerleaders of the chaplain. This group will be ecstatic that the chaplain is on site.

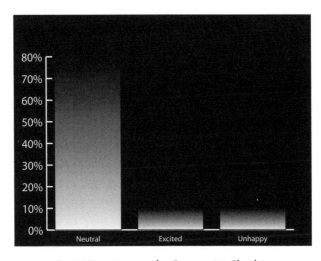

Fig. II.I Reactions to the Community Chaplain

However, be on guard not to show favoritism toward any particular group of people.

Additionally, avoid conversations that can be theological "hot potatoes" and potentially cause division among the company you keep. Redirecting conversation away from lightening rod issues is a skill that the effective community chaplain must have in his toolbox. Finally, the remaining ten percent of the population base may not be amenable to the idea that a chaplain is present. This segment of the population commonly believes that the world at large and religion should be kept apart. These people may even attempt to get the chaplain program removed from the mission field. It is important for the chaplain to know where the legal boundaries are for ministry in his mission field and to remain inside those boundaries. (See the legal section of this text for more information regarding the legalities of faith in the different communities.) In the pages that follow, establishing a safe environment for relationships to flourish will be discussed. It may seem like overkill and extreme, but it is important to remember that this ministry is taking place in the culture we call America, not the local church.

First, be sure to treat all people with dignity and respect. Because people come to the mission field with various backgrounds and life experiences, actions that actively seek to avoid the appearance of all evil can eliminate potential problem areas before they arise. Again, all individuals are to be treated with honor, respect, and dignity; remember that they are created in God's image. Sexual harassment, or harassment for any reason, should not be a practice for the chaplain and should not be tolerated under any circumstance. While most community ministers will not seek to be offensive, knowing the boundaries can avoid any confusion. Sexual harassment includes soliciting sexual favors from an unwilling subordinate or co-worker in return for promotions, increased wages, continuance of the job, and the like. Please be advised that any reported incident of harassment should be investigated by appropriate authorities and suitable action should be taken. Every chaplain should be committed to providing an environment free of harassment. In keeping with this commitment, the effective community chaplain will maintain a strict policy prohibiting unlawful harassment, including sexual harassment. It is important for everyone to understand that jokes, cartoons, nicknames, stories, and comments about appearance may be offensive to others. For this reason, it is best to avoid conversation about the physical appearance of those found in the mission field to which the community chaplain ministers.

As caregivers in the community, we should always strive to provide an environment that is free from unlawful and immoral sexual harassment. Any involvement in sexual harassment will not be tolerated. This extends beyond the parameters where we serve to include any form of sexual harassment. This conduct includes, but is not limited to:

- Deliberate and repeated offensive and/or suggestive comments or gestures of a sexual nature.
- Physical actions and/or threats of a sexual nature.
- Continual or repeated verbal abuse of a sexual nature.
- Graphic verbal commentaries about an individual's body.
- Sexually degrading words used to describe an individual.
- The display or possession of sexually suggestive objects or pictures.
- Differential treatment in any personnel action as a result of submission to, or rejection of, sexual requests or demands.

If you feel that any action on your part may be construed to be sexual harassment, report this situation to your ministry contact within the church that endorsed you immediately. If you ever feel that you have been compromised by a suggestive comment by a person of the opposite sex, you must immediately contact your ministry contact and report the incident. This will work to prove due-diligence on your part should the incident come up later. Remember Potiphar's wife.

When caring for others while in the mission field, remember that it is recommended that the community chaplain NEVER meet with an individual of the opposite sex in a closed-door atmosphere. Develop a policy that strictly prohibits you, as a minister, from ever being alone with a person of the opposite sex. This policy should extend to automobiles, homes, offices, and other environments. While this can be a very inconvenient policy, it should be enforced to protect the community minister, the population he serves, and the church that endorsed the community chaplain. This is an inconvenient policy, to be sure. In some cases, it will require some education on the part of those who are being served, as most do not have a policy like this in place for themselves. In a kind and gentle way, it can be explained that this policy is for the protection of all involved: the individuals in the mission field, the church endorsing the community chaplain, and the community chaplain. This policy should never have an exception. It should extend to the worksite, the hospital, a home, a car, or any other place you may find yourself for ministry.

In addition to safety from harassment of any type, most people want and are attracted to a company with a drug-free work environment. They also want to live in a community that is free from drugs and the problems that they bring. A chaplain should be committed to providing a safe environment and to fostering the well being and health of others. This commitment is jeopardized when any associate illegally uses drugs on the job, comes to work under their influence, or possesses, distributes, or sells illegal drugs in the workplace. Crime rates increase in neighborhoods that are overrun with drugs. The community minister is an example of a strong commitment to maintain a high moral standard that will be pleasing to God. To that end, a chaplain will conduct himself in a manner that is above reproach and that reveals an attitude of worship towards our Savior and brings glory to His name. He will abstain from any activity that does not reflect the purity and holiness of the Lord Jesus Christ.

Since a great segment of society perceives alcohol as a vice, Romans 14:13-14 clearly instructs us:

> *13 Therefore let us not judge one another anymore, but rather determine this—not to put an obstacle or a stumbling block in a brother's way. 14 I know and am convinced in the Lord Jesus that nothing is unclean in itself; but to him who thinks anything to be unclean, to him it is unclean* (NASB).

The use of illicit drugs, to any extent and in any manner, is to be considered a practice that makes it unsafe for an individual to have confidence in the community chaplain. This also includes the misuse of prescription substances, tobacco, and alcohol.

While taking measures that include providing an environment free of harassment and avoiding stumbling block issues is critical, there are other aspects that must be put in place for the people in the mission field of the chaplain to feel safe and free to share the innermost part of who they are. An atmosphere that is free from condemnation is crucial for the community chaplain program to be successful. A fear that is held by some individuals in the community is that the chaplain will "judge" him for the choices made in life. There is some confusion between examining the fruit of someone's life and judging him. Being so-called "judgmental" is quite politically incorrect today. It runs against the moral relativity of the culture. On the surface, not being "judgmental" appears exceptionally civil, kind, and compassionate. That is why many so-called religious persons are interested in being politically correct. These people are most often theologically liberal, not biblically sound individuals. Theological liberals will buy into whatever is politically correct in a particular time and place. Theological conservatives are moored in divine revelation. "Being judgmental" today is interpreted by liberals as expressing in an unkind way some practice or belief to be right or wrong. However, what the liberals do not understand is that conservatives are not being judgmental, but rightly analytical. Because the theologically conservative individual uses Scripture for formulating his moral code, he takes, for instance, the statements of Jesus most seriously.

When it comes to judging others, Jesus said, "Judge not, that you be not judged" (Matthew 7:1 NKJV). By that, Jesus meant that no mortal has the divine right to pronounce an eternal judgment of heaven or hell upon another mortal's eternal destiny. There are no reasonable theological conservatives who would dare that. They know that the same Scripture states that only God sees a person's heart; God alone then can judge a soul to its eternal state. However, Jesus did state that His followers can analyze another's lifestyle to discern whether its practices are right or wrong, good or bad, righteous or evil. Jesus told His disciples that they could look upon another's life tree to discern whether the fruit was proper or unfit. So the goal of caring for the population in the mission field becomes facilitating the intersection of the individual's life with truth, that is, the Scripture. This must be done in a kind and compassionate manner for the environment to be considered safe by the population found in the mission field.

One more crucial element that must be present for someone to perceive the environment as safe for open communication with the chaplain, is confidentiality. If the chaplain goes to the efforts required to accommodate the other "safety" issues that have been discussed thus far but fails to provide confidentiality, all of these efforts have been in vain. The individual must know that everything said to the community minister will remain

Fig. 11.2 Chaplains must keep conversations confidential in order to create open communication.

between the two parties mentioned, and only the two parties mentioned. This means that there is information that will be obtained while caring for those in the community that must be protected. Because meeting with the community chaplain may be the first time that the person has ever spoken with anyone regarding how to deal with life's struggles and a strategy to negotiate them successfully, it is important to make the individual aware of the ground rules. He or she has the right to tell you or not to tell you anything desired. They must also understand what will happen with the information that is given. The chaplain may wish to take notes during the caregiving session so that important details can be remembered for later use. The confidentiality also extends to these records. In the United States, many laws are written that impact how much the community chaplain is legally allowed to share and when. For the protection of all parties involved, we will explore these general ideas.

Privilege, or confidentiality, is actually viewed as a "thing" that the person who is being cared for owns. This means that the information about his or her life (the privilege) is something that only he or she can share, because it is theirs to own and distribute. Since you do not own the information about an associate's life, you cannot share or disseminate it. One of the basic laws regarding confidentiality is stated below:

> They may create, and to the extent the records are under their control, maintain, disseminate, store, retain, and dispose of records and data relating to their professional and scientific work in order to (1) facilitate provision of services later by them or by other professionals, (2) allow for replication of research design and analyses, (3) meet institutional requirements, (4) ensure accuracy of billing and payments, and (5) ensure compliance with law.[4]

Interestingly enough, the person sharing technically owns the information that is printed on the paper regarding him, while the community chaplain technically owns the paper on which the information is written. As a caregiver in the community, you will know a great deal about the people in your mission field. Even the fact that an individual is speaking with you about a life issue is held in strict confidence. As the chaplain, you must maintain confidentiality of much information. Realize that this confidentiality extends even after the relationship or caregiving has ceased. Even if a person dies, the caregiver cannot share any information about him. An individual may come to meet with the community chaplain and ask, "What if I have committed a crime?" Well, even criminal activity is protected by the shield of confidentiality. So you can instruct the person to relax, if that happens to be his particular concern—*unless*, of course, he is still engaged in criminal activity which jeopardizes the life or safety of others, and he reveals the details of this activity to the chaplain. Such a case could fall under one of the *exceptions to confidentiality*, which we will discuss in great detail later. For now, understand that there are a few basic instances under which the caregiver may breach confidentiality. All of these exceptions concern harm to self or others.

- Where there is a reasonable suspicion of child abuse or elder adult physical abuse;
- Where there is a reasonable suspicion that the client may present a danger of violence to others;
- When there is a reasonable suspicion that the person is likely to harm himself unless protective measures are taken.

In all of the above cases, the caregiver is either allowed by law or required by law to break confidentiality in order to protect the individual or someone he may endanger from harm.[5] The rule of thumb is when in doubt, do not break the confidential relationship that has been established with someone.

Getting To Know The People

As a caregiver in the community, you have gone to great lengths to establish a safe environment, where individuals will be able to share without fear of judgment, condemnation, harassment, or stumbling blocks in a confidential manner. Once the environment is safe, the relationship may begin. In essence, the relationship between a chaplain and his mission field is like dating. You are both trying to make a good impression on each other, you are on your best behavior, and there is still much unknown about the other. So how do we break the ice? Prepare yourself first.

As with all types of work, there are certain items that are required to do the job adequately. Community chaplaincy is no different. A mechanic is always in possession of certain tools needed to perform work on an automobile. A surgeon would never consider conducting a medical procedure on a patient without the necessary instruments in a sterilized environment. Likewise, the effective chaplain will utilize specific pieces of equipment to reach individuals for Christ.

Some of these tools should be kept on the actual person of the chaplain. Other items need to be stored in the mobile "office" of the community minister, his automobile. It can therefore be understood that a chaplain should have the following suggested items on his person to realize his fullest potential while performing rounds in his community.[6]

Items Carried By the Community Chaplain On His Person

■ **The Business Card of the Community Chaplain:** This item is invaluable. A community chaplain cannot be successful in accomplishing his mission if he is not available to his mission field. A business card should include information on how you prefer for those in your care to reach you. For example, you may wish to incorporate your e-mail address, your street address at home or at an office location, a mobile phone/Nextel number, a home phone number, or an alpha-numeric pager number into your business card. Be sure to generously distribute these business cards to the people in your care.

■ **The Business Card Holder:** While the obvious feature of this item is that it enables you to keep a supply of business cards in your pocket, it also serves in other capacities. When using a business card holder, cards can be stored in clothing pockets without fear of bending or otherwise damaging them. In daily interactions with others, you will both distribute and receive many business cards.

By having a business card holder that has two pockets in it and folds in the middle, you can maintain a mini-filing cabinet in your pocket. In one side of the holder, keep a stack of your own cards to give away to those that you presently chaplain, those you meet in the community that are potential chaplaincy candidates, and others with whom you wish to network.

In the opposite side of the card holder, you may keep business cards of others that you collect during the day. In this pocket you may also wish to keep business cards with notes made to yourself, reminding you of certain actions that you need to take with a particular individual, messages from voice mail sources, or notes taken on the back of a business card while conducting a caregiving session.

Finally, a business card holder lends to the professional image that a chaplain wishes to portray to the community.

■ **The Personal Data Manager:** This is probably the most important item to keep with you while performing rounds. When choosing a personal data manager, be sure to keep several things in mind. The system of information management should fit your "style" of chaplaincy.

If you prefer pen and paper only, select a system that incorporates all of the functions that you deem appropriate. There are several on the market. Brands like Daytimer, DayRunner, and Rolodex all have features that make them unique from others. Spend some time deciding what features in a pen and paper system that you must have, and purchase the one that comes closest to your desires.

Conversely, some prefer to go more technical or computerized when searching for a personal data manager. Again, there are many choices on the market. Research the market for the system that has the features that you like. Most personal data manager systems either come with a cover of some type or can be used with a generic cover.

A cover is necessary for a couple of reasons. First, it protects the personal data manager from damage, should it be dropped. Further, harmful effects of weather and moisture are minimized by utilizing a cover. More importantly, however, a cover usually has many pockets inside. This allows the personal data manager to play an even greater role in your chaplaincy.

When performing rounds, it is crucial that the chaplain build relationships with others. An organized personal data manager will assist him in this function. Inside the cover of the personal data manager, the chaplain can include tracts that can be used to explain the plan of salvation to an individual, a computerized or pen and paper calendar/memo system to mark important dates and appointments, and pen and paper to leave notes when necessary. Another useful item to include in this personal data manager is sticky notes. These can be used to leave reminders for yourself or an encouraging note for someone.

One of the most useful items that can be stored in the

Fig. II.3 Personal Data Managers are important in the life of an effective chaplain.

personal data manager cover is a personal item that aids in building a bridge to the mission field. For example, my wife and I have a very young daughter. Sharing pictures of her growth and progress over time helps to bond other individuals to my entire family. This makes me more of a "real" person to the groups that I chaplain. This lends credibility to any parenting strategies that I may share with an individual, but more importantly, it opens conversations with those that otherwise may not have happened. Through these conversations, the relationship is built, leading to the goal of sharing the gospel with those who need to hear it.

The personal data manager can also be used to make note of prayer requests or important happenings in an individual's life. For example, if someone shares with me that his wife is expecting a child, I will make a note of the due date in my personal data manager. As the delivery of the child approaches, I can keep an accurate count of how far along in the pregnancy the couple may be. The impact of this simple notation is seen when the individual perceives that you "remember" the due date for several months. In reality, you are utilizing the personal data manager effectively.

Personal information on those in your mission field can also be kept in this tool. Addresses, phone numbers, dates of birth, employment anniversaries, and anniversaries of the death of a loved one are all pieces of information that prove to be invaluable to a caregiver in the community.

■ **Breath Mints and/or Gum:** Items used to freshen breath are vital to a chaplain. Studies reveal that a lack of moisture in the mouth results in bad breath. Since a chaplain speaks with people in the process of relationship building, his mouth is likely to become dry. Utilizing breath mints or gum will help abate this potential problem. Further, the proximity in which a chaplain stands in relation to his population group can be small. Speaking with an individual in need over a small table at a coffee shop or in a discreet environment at the place of business means that he or she will be able to determine the freshness of your breath.

Certainly, halitosis should not distract the person from hearing the full impact of the message of the gospel. Lastly, fresh breath is a professional courtesy. It is part of an image of professionalism that the chaplain must portray.

■ **A small amount of cash/pocket change:** Carrying a small amount of cash and possibly even some spare change in your pocket can have a large impact in the life of an individual in need. This money can be utilized to purchase a cup of coffee or a soft drink while discussing a problem he or she is experiencing. This will aid in putting the person at ease.

At times, having a small cup to hold in their hands brings security to an uncomfortable situation. Also, when the individual needs a break from sharing, possibly due to high emotions or even tears, taking a sip from a cup gives them an "excuse" or reason to stop talking and regain composure in a way that is more comfortable for them.

This cash may also be used for refreshments or a meal at a hospital. Many surgical procedures take hours and the chaplain can provide ministry to those waiting by purchasing items from a vending machine or cafeteria. Parking fees at hospitals, courthouses, and parking decks, as well as tolls for roads and bridges, can be handled from this fund also.

■ **Gospel Presentation Tracts:** Gospel tracts should be in the possession of a chaplain at all times. Regardless of the specific tract that is chosen, be sure that it is always available when needed. Tracts can be kept in the personal data manager or in clothing pockets.

These booklets containing information on how to enter into a personal relationship with Jesus Christ as Savior and Lord should be reviewed with the person seeking. In this way, questions that the individual may have are answered on the spot.

Another method that can be utilized in distributing tracts is to give the tract to the person to

Fig. II.4 Even spare change can impact an associate in need.

read. Then, at a later time, ask what he thought about what he read. Answer questions and present the gospel to the individual at this time.

■ **The Pocket-Size Bible:** Carrying a Bible while performing rounds is extremely useful. There are several types on the market today. Select one that most suits your needs. The version is important. A Bible written in modern day language is appealing to a variety of people groups. Unchurched individuals will be able to understand it easier and churchgoers will most likely not be opposed to this type of translation. A thinline pocket Bible will prove to be handy.

A Bible marked with the gospel presentation, especially when coordinated to a gospel tract that you use, can be beneficial. Certain evangelical groups, such as "Share Jesus Without Fear" provide Bibles that fit nicely into pockets and contain several different gospel presentations within them.

Another alternative is to purchase software that contains Scripture to download to your computerized personal data manager. Software containing the Bible is available at Christian bookstores, software outlets, and online via the Internet. In addition, many software providers have developed animated gospel presentations specifically meant for a palm-sized computer. This type of software can really bring the plan of salvation to life for those who prefer a more concrete approach to evangelism. Also, the novelty of this type of presentation is alluring to many.

■ **At Least One Handkerchief:** An effective chaplain should have a handkerchief in his pocket. At various times throughout the day, he will encounter those with painful

circumstances in their lives. When he shares these problems and hurts with the chaplain, tears may accompany the story.

A very simple way to minister to a person in need is to be able to give him a handkerchief when he needs it most. Not only will this meet an immediate need, but it will also have future ministry potential.

Each time that the individual touches, sees, or thinks about that handkerchief, it will again remind them how much the chaplain cares for them and, even

Fig. II.5 An effective chaplain should have a handkerchief in his pocket.

more important, how much God cares about them. Be sure that the handkerchief is clean and smells fresh. When purchasing new handkerchiefs, be sure to run them through the laundry to soften them up and then fold them neatly for later distribution.

■ **Communication Device:** Accessibility and availability are crucial to the success of a chaplain. For this reason, he should always carry some type of communication device(s) while performing rounds.

The most common types of technology that serve this purpose include cellular telephones, numeric pagers, voice data pagers, and mobile e-mail paging systems. Evaluate the features, benefits, and cost of many options to determine which system would be best for your ministry needs. Whatever method or methods of communication you select, dependability and portability are qualities to be considered.

■ **Comfortable Shoes:** Since a chaplain is always on the move, shoes that provide comfort are crucial. Shoe style is also a factor to consider when purchasing this item. Since blue-collar workers can often be distrusting of those wearing shoes with a highly buffed shine, select a shoe that has a low or medium shine. In this way, mechanics as well as executives will be accepting of the community chaplain. Remember, the goal is to dress so that you are not offensive to anyone in your mission field, regardless of their station in life.

Several shoe manufacturers have realized the need for comfortable yet stylish and businesslike footwear. Brands that have included a comfort system of some sort into their product line include Bass, Bostonian, Johnston and Murphy, and Rockport, among others.

■ **Yourself, The Community Chaplain:** While all of the above mentioned items are important to carry on your person, the manner in which you conduct yourself is of utmost importance. For this reason, a chaplain must conduct himself in such a way that conveys the image and message intended. An understated sense of confidence, stability, friendliness, acceptance, and approachability help to ensure that the population of your mission field will utilize the chaplain in a time of need.

The face of the community chaplain must carry a smile, when appropriate. Part of the task of rounds is to encourage and uplift those under your care. A warm and welcoming smile may be just what an individual needs to see during a stressful day. Further, the chaplain knows the answer to the question that most of those in his mission field are asking deep in their hearts. He knows that the secret to fulfillment is found in a relationship with Christ.

The community chaplain should be a walking billboard for his Lord and Savior. This does not mean, however, that he should be fake or phony in his happiness. Instead, true joy and freedom found in the abundant life will flow out of the relationship that a Christian has with his Lord, Jesus Christ.

Good posture is another way to send the message that the chaplain is confident in what he does and in the skills that he possesses. Individuals will be drawn to this subtle clue that the chaplain is secure, someone to rely on in a time of crisis.

Closely related to good posture is eye contact. When the chaplain is engaged in conversation with someone, eye contact is essential. This will inform the individual that he is important, valued, and special. Further, eye contact reassures the individual that the chaplain is someone who can be trusted. Constant eye contact, however, is discouraged. Occasional glances to the side or to the floor are appropriate. These glances will convey that the chaplain is listening and thinking about what is being said. In addition, uninterrupted eye contact may give people the feeling that he is being interrogated.

The effective chaplain will also be sure to listen carefully when conversing. This can have a lasting impact on the relationship between a chaplain and his population. It may

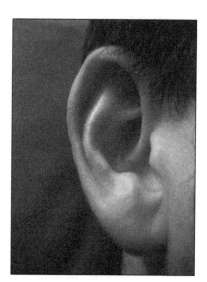

Fig. II.6 Learning truly to listen is an important skill for the corporate chaplain.

be something as simple as the individual's name, the number of children he has, or what he does for fun that can be used later in conversation to convey that what he has to say is important. He now knows that he is valued and that the chaplain can be trusted with more intimate matters in the future.

The community chaplain needs a keen sensitivity to the Holy Spirit. Only by listening to and obeying the Holy Spirit can he be used most effectively to impact the community. People will then be drawn to the Christ that is seen in the chaplain, not simply to the personality of the community caregiver.

Next, for the sake of practicality, an effective chaplain will be sure to use some type of visible identification or marker that conveys who he is to the people in his care. Some constant identifier, be it a logo or a specific uniform, will help distinguish the chaplain. This is also a good public relations and marketing tool to expand the ministry of chaplaincy.

Finally, the chaplain will be sure to wear a watch. Time is money, as the saying goes. Businesses need their associates to be productive during the working hours. Families need time together to bond, and sports teams need time for practice. For this reason, the chaplain is sensitive to the time constraints of life's demands and utilizes a watch to make sure that he does not invade too heavily on someone's time. In closing, a watch will also assist the chaplain in maximizing his own time usage and management.

Items Stored by Community Chaplain in the Automobile

In the above section, many items were listed that an effective chaplain will carry on his person. There are also items that should be stored in the automobile of a chaplain.

As a result, this "office on wheels" should be a pleasant place. Some of the items on this list assist in making the automobile of a chaplain an enjoyable place to be, while others are supplies that the effective community minister will need from time to time during the day.

■ **Encouraging and Uplifting Christian Music:** Keeping a constant and ever-changing stock of Christian music is essential to the chaplain. The effective community caregiver must first allow God to minister to him before he can even consider attempting to minister to others. Praise and worship music is but one method to have an encounter with God throughout the day.

Because the chaplain is giving of himself all day long, commuting time between business appointments can be used to recharge the ministry "batteries" necessary to serve others in need. The source of this encouragement may take many forms: Christian tapes and CDs, Christian books on audio tape, tapes of favorite encouraging or challenging sermons, and a favorite Christian radio station. The style of music is not as important as the message contained within.

■ **Outerwear:** While the above information is useful for spiritual comfort and encouragement, this category is essential for the physical comfort of the chaplain. Because no two days are exactly the same, it can prove handy to keep a selection of these objects in the car.

Depending on the time of year and the geography of ministry, items such as a light jacket, a heavy coat, a pair of gloves, a raincoat, a tube of lip balm, and an umbrella are within reach when needed. God honors a plan, so plan to be ready for any climate situation that you may encounter.

■ **Items Used For Correspondence:** During the course of the ministry day, events will present themselves for caregiving in the community. At times, however, care may need to be given long distance or in numerous formats. It is for this reason that various specific and generic correspondence items should be placed in the automobile.

Specific items used to communicate with an associate will vary, but things found to be useful include thank you notes, sympathy cards, get well cards, and congratulatory notes. Additionally, generic stationery, possibly including the ministry logo, will be beneficial for many occasions. Keeping a small sample of various cards, along with postage stamps on hand will allow the chaplain to write a short letter appropriate to the ministry situation on the spot. The individual feels truly valued because the correspondence will reach him quickly, conveying a message that he is important to you and to God. Further, the chaplain can be assured that he will not forget to send the appropriate note to the person in his mission field.

■ **Antibacterial Hand Sanitizer or Waterless Soap:** Since the community chaplain comes in contact with many people every day, germs can become a problem. Industry realized the need for such a product and developed antibacterial cleansers that require no water. These gels come in small containers, perfect for the glove box or console of a car.

By utilizing such a product, several desired outcomes are achieved. The chaplain is less likely to become ill, sickness is not easily passed from one person to another, and the condition of currently ill individuals, especially those with autoimmune disorders, is not worsened. Further, recent studies have revealed that as many as 65% of all men and 37% of all women do not wash their hands after using the lavatory. These are the people with which the chaplain is shaking hands. The message is clear: keep your hands clean, because most likely others are not.

■ **Baby Gifts:** There are many times that a chaplain will visit someone in the hospital at the birth of a child.

Using a standard baby gift eliminates many potential problems. Since all people will receive the exact same baby gift, there is no chance of favoritism or the appearance thereof. Additionally, purchasing many of the same item can lead to bulk purchasing, saving on the per item cost. When considering what item to give as a baby gift, think about storing and packaging/gift wrapping. For example, a gift that can be placed in a collapsible, decorative gift bag can be advantageous. In this way, gifts may be stored in the trunk of a car, along with gift bags and colored tissue paper. When someone has a baby, all the community minister has to do is place the gift in the bag and finish with the appropriate colored tissue paper; blue for the boys, pink for the girls, and a mixture of the two colors if limited information is given.

Be sure to write a personalized message on a general purpose note card, a card of congratulations, or a computer generated card. Finally, place a business card down into the gift bag. This reinforces the fact that the chaplain is always on duty and can be reached for any reason.

■ **Phone Books:** There are times when the chaplain will need to have access to phone numbers, making phone books necessary. However, with the widespread use of cellular communication, phone booths, especially those containing phone books, are diminishing in number. In order to save the time and prevent the hassle of looking for a phone book, keep one in the automobile. Some cities have cellular phone books in addition to land line phone books. Keeping a set of phone books in the car can streamline locating in-

Fig. II.7 There are times when a phone book is necessary.

formation needed and reduce the cost of "411" information calls.

Throughout the day a chaplain will travel to many locations. Some of these places will be familiar and others may be new and foreign. The wise minister will purchase an atlas or a map of the region in which he serves. This will help to ensure that no matter where and when God decides to work, logistics will not be an issue. It is especially helpful to mark the location of frequently visited hospitals, funeral homes, and cemeteries on the map.

■ **Mini-Cassette/Digital Recorder:** Another item that can be kept in the car is the mini cassette recorder or mini digital recorder. Because a chaplain does spend much time on the road, a mini recorder will assist in multi-tasking. While driving from one location to another, the chaplain may speak into the mini recorder for various reasons. Personal notes can be recorded regarding an individual, various tasks that need to be completed may be listed, and helpful resources, phone numbers, or websites mentioned on Christian radio stations while commuting may also be recorded.

■ **Administrative Items:** A chaplain must maintain a certain amount of administrative information for many purposes. An administrative item that is useful to keep in the automobile of the community chaplain is the variety of passes or security badges needed. Many businesses now require associates, and therefore the workplace minister, to display identification badges of some type. At times, these identification devices are necessary to even enter the building. Further, hospitals, jails, and other entities are now requiring similar identification. This emblem with a photo identification may be needed to have complete access to all areas of the facility, such as the ICU, CCU, or ER section of the hospital.

Many local and state detention centers call for a minister of any capacity to register with the authority prior to visiting any inmate. During this process, a photo identification card may be required. Along with this identification badge, proof of licensure or ordination to the clergy may also be requested by the commanding officer. Many of the local hospitals and/or jails may charge a nominal fee to generate one of these identification badges. The fee usually ranges from $4.00 to $10.00. However, over time the fee will be recovered, as many of the hospitals will allow either free or reduced rate parking with such a badge.

■ **Miscellaneous Items:** There are several items that should be kept on hand in the automobile of the community chaplain for distribution throughout the day. The community minister can then replenish the item on his person to offer to another associate later the same day. Below is such a list:

1) Handkerchiefs	3) Business Cards	5) Gospel Tracts
2) Breath Mints/Gum	4) Discipleship Materials	6) Bibles

Other items that will prove beneficial for the chaplain to keep on hand in the car include a cigarette lighter cellular phone charger kit, a hands-free cellular communication device, batteries of various sizes to replace in handheld items or paging devices, a sports coat and tie for trips to the funeral home, and an assortment of compact discs for encouragement throughout the ministry day.

Finally, a word concerning the vehicle driven by the minister: In all that a chaplain does, he is setting an example for others and sending a message of the utmost importance. Physical grooming is crucial for the minister for obvious reasons. However, the manner in which the chaplain maintains his vehicle is also important.

It is clear in Scripture that God expects us to be good stewards of the material items that he has placed in our care. Further, the effective minister can even use the care and maintenance of his vehicle as an evangelistic tool.

After you have gotten yourself prepared to meet your new mission field, it is important to think about those to whom you will minister. In building a relationship, there are some personality styles which mesh more easily together than others. This is why we are drawn to certain individuals, have more in common with them, and have less conflict with them than with other personalities in the community. Knowing your personality type and being able to evaluate the basic personalities of those around you will help to enhance communication for the chaplain. While there are several personality inventories that can be used, most all agree that there are four basic personality styles. Some clinicians call them by a letter, such as the DISC profile or the Myers-Briggs. Others refer to them as animals, colors, or even types of publications. Below, you will see an amalgam of such information along with a brief description of the four major personality types.

The Population Groups Found In Rounds

The Four Major Personality Types:

There are four basic types of population groups that will be encountered over the course of performing rounds. We will discuss in detail how to relate most effectively to these people groups. In addition, we will address the overarching principles that apply to all types of people encountered in the community. According to Gary Smalley and John Trent, there are four basic personality types, one of which can describe all of us. By identifying and understanding what personality type an associate may be, the chaplain will be better equipped to minister to him.[7]

The Lion Personality

■ **Representative color:** His favorite color is probably red, because his personality type is fiery and dominant.

■ **Representative careers:** The Lion likes to be in control of all situations and, therefore, will most likely be the President or Chief Executive Officer of an organization.

■ **Personality Traits:** He likes to focus on the task at hand rather than the people who will be performing the task. A Lion prefers to use few words to convey a message. Instead he leaves the details of how to get the job done to those who will be performing the task. A Lion can tend to be harsh, especially with his words, without really meaning to be. A Lion that trains himself to capitalize on his strengths will be a very effective leader. However, a Lion that does not tame his weaknesses will be a leader with no followers.

■ **Percentage of Total Population:** Lion personalities make up about twenty percent of our population.

The Golden Retriever Personality

■ **Representative color:** A Golden Retriever's favorite color is blue, because he is true blue to the very end.

■ **Representative careers:** Many teachers, ministers, and nurses tend to be Golden Retrievers because of their ability to sympathize with others.

■ **Personality Traits:** Loyalty is his middle name. If a Golden Retriever has a leader he can believe in and follow, he will almost follow him off of a cliff. However, if the leader ever does anything to destroy the trust that a Golden Retriever has placed in him, beware. Once the Golden Retriever loses respect for his leader, it is very difficult for him to ever follow or trust that leader again. A Golden Retriever may tend to take on the emotions of those around him. However, this people group needs to learn to toughen up a little and not wear their feelings on their sleeves or take everything so personally. Further, Golden Retrievers also need to be more task-oriented, and not so relationship-oriented.

■ **Percentage of Total Population:** This personality type is the most popular. More than half of all American workers are Golden Retrievers.

The Otter Personality

■ **Representative Color:** The Otter can be portrayed by the color yellow, because it is sunny and bright, like the outlook of the Otter.

■ **Representative Careers:** This personality type lends itself to sales positions, marketing and advertising jobs, artists, and chefs.

■ **Personality Traits:** Smalley and Trent describe this personality type as the life of the party. Creativity and spontaneity are crucial to the Otter. He lives in the present. This can, at times, lead to his demise. Otters are often late to meetings and miss deadlines because they just get caught up in the work or whatever else got their attention. All people types tend to be drawn to Otters because of their positive, and often carefree, approach to life. Otters tend to hurt the feelings of others because they are seen as insensitive and uncaring. This insensitivity is most likely unintentional. Instead, Otters just think about the present and will often overcommit themselves, leaving someone to be disappointed. If an Otter can ever harness his charisma and charm into a disciplined lifestyle, he can accomplish much.

■ **Percentage of Total Population:** Otters make up about ten percent of our corporate culture.

The Beaver Personality

■ **Representative Color:** Beavers can be represented by the color green or white. These colors have been chosen because they are calm, soothing and neutral, much like a Beaver.

■ **Representative Careers:** This personality type tends to hold jobs in accounting, data entry, computer science, and anything else that requires tremendous attention to detail and accuracy.

■ **Personality Traits:** Without Beavers, we would not have such high quality products or services. A Beaver is very task focused and can sometimes be seen as withdrawn and shy because of this. The Beaver can accomplish great tasks with minimal supervision and guidance. However, he tends to miss deadlines much like the Otter, because he gets so caught up in the details of what he is doing.

■ **Percentage of Total Population:** This is the smallest segment of our society, accounting for about five percent of workers.

No matter what your personality style may be, it is important to have this information so that you may be able to relate most effectively to those in the community. God has created us all with different nuances and gifts that are specific to each individual. Trying to be someone that you are not will not only be uncomfortable, but those in your mission field will detect it. Have confidence in who you are in Christ, and then pass the Christ that is in you along to those in your care.

Cultural Experiences and The Workplace

Once the chaplain is aware of his basic personality and is cognizant of the interaction with other personality types in the mission field, he must be astute to the differences in culture. These cultural differences can occur because of background, life experiences, ethnicity, type of work environment, and the like. The effective minister will study the cultures that are present in the community in which he serves so he may be, as Scripture instructs, as wise as a serpent, but as harmless as a dove. As Americans, we assume that most of the world operates like we do. This is an incorrect assumption. Even common business practices in the United States can be offensive to those of other cultures. Take a look at the following examples of business courtesy that could be potentially offensive. Most Latin American and Hispanic cultures find it offensive to monopolize the conversation, to speak excessively, especially if you are younger than many of those engaged in the conversation. Many cultures, predominately Asian, find it offensive to call someone by his first name or to talk about family matters in a business setting. Some cultures are offended when business cards are not exchanged. Other cultural dictates to be studied include beliefs regarding punctuality, proximity for conversations, the amount of physical touch that is tolerated, table manners, gift giving and receiving etiquette, and gender expectations.

When examining the intricacies of building relationships with those in the workplace, one must look in depth at the differences between white collar and blue collar environments. Several key areas of distinction can be made regarding white collar versus blue collar associates. While this does not claim to be a complete list, it is a good overview. There are exceptions to every generalization. In the following discussion of employee types, there will be associates that stand in contrast to the information presented. However, most of the profiling detailed in this section will apply to general population groups found in the workplace.

The chaplain ministering to white collar workers will likely spend more time developing relationships with associates before he is given permission to share the Good News of Jesus Christ. Compared to a blue collar employee, the white collar associate is more guarded about sharing his innermost thoughts. Because the white collar environment may be more competitive and cutthroat than the blue collar world, the chaplain must work hard to establish and enforce a sense of trust.

More "pre-encounter" work must be done to build relationships with white collar associates than their blue collar counterparts. For example, white collar workers are more likely to desire conversations that require a working knowledge of current pop culture events, political happenings, the arts, and important events that will impact industry, business, and the stock market. To be adequately prepared to have these conversations, the chaplain must spend some time studying such items from a variety of sources. Magazines, industry newsletters, news websites, hard copy newspapers, and a home page tailored to these interests can all be helpful in this pursuit.

Likewise, a white collar associate will be more likely to involve the chaplain in some type of social activity prior to sharing his problems. Often a white collar associate will ask the minister to his home for a meal, to a restaurant for a luncheon, or a golf course for a round to get a "feel" for the chaplain to be sure that he can be trusted with the dilemma that the associate is facing.

White collar associates will prefer a higher degree of confidentiality than their blue collar counterparts. This means that a white collar employee will often schedule meetings off the work site to be sure that coworkers do not know about private matters. Further, because a white collar worker is more inclined to be stressed about job security, he will not want to take a large amount of time away from his work day to discuss personal problems. He will more likely set an appointment with the workplace minister at a time that is mutually acceptable.

Physical contact is another area that differs among white collar and blue collar associates. White collar associates will tend to limit physical contact to a handshake. Both types of employees respect personal space, but blue collar workers tend to stand closer and make physical contact more often than white collar workers.

While it is crucial to build relationships with all types of people, the strategy used to do so may vary. It is important to "see" those in the mission field, those to whom the chaplain will minister, through the eyes of the Creator. No matter what personality style, socio-economic strata, cultural background, worldview, or type of work environment a person possesses, each is in need of a relationship with the hope of Glory, Jesus Christ. This is the entire reason that the relationship is built. In chapters to come, we will discuss how to develop the relationship to the point of evangelism. For now, simply understand that the relationship must be established before permission can be gained to share the life-changing Good News of Jesus Christ.

Stories From the Field: #6
"Someone Is Always Waiting To See The Chaplain"*

Her name was Carrie, and she wanted to speak to the chaplain after the orientation session. After we had concluded the orientation for her son's swim team, Carrie approached me and in a soft voice she said, "Chaplain, can I talk to you?" She began by sharing how she felt empty, and that life was a day-to-day drudgery. She felt there had to be more to life than simply going to work every day and then going home. Carrie was in her fifties, unmarried, and took care of her elderly mom and pre-adolescent son. This is what she did after she left work. She admitted she was tired and depressed about the health of her mother. She said she felt alone. She said our coming and speaking about the things we had, had given her, in her words, "a shot in the arm." I listened to her talk for about 30 minutes until she had told her story. Then I asked if I had her permission to share with her some good news. I told her it was the best news in the world, and I was not exaggerating. I then proceeded to share the good news of Jesus Christ with Carrie. She listened as I shared the gospel. I asked Carrie, "Does this make sense to you?" She said yes, and then I asked her, "Would you like to receive this gift of eternal life?" She said yes, and right there we bowed our heads and prayed the sinner's prayer. After that I prayed for her and then began to explain the things she needed to know now that she had made this decision. As I explained, her eyes began to swell with tears and she began to sob. I told her there was no need to cry, "This is good news!" She said her tears were tears of joy. "I just now realized that I will never have to be alone ever again." I agreed and explained to her how Jesus promised never to leave us nor forsake us. Praise God, for He meets us at the point of our need. This day Carrie's needs were met. She was just waiting to see the chaplain.

– Submitted by Henry S.
Ft. Lauderdale, FL

*Individuals in this story have granted permission for its use.

Stories From the Field: #7
"A Soda For Tina"*

I had just begun working with a new company. I was still figuring out who was who and the role that each played in the organization. I knew of one important figure, since I had seen her in many of the meetings that led to chaplaincy being established in the company. I learned that Tina had been with the mortgage company for 14 years, and she had seen many changes over those years. She was determined and effective in her work, respected by many.

It happened one Friday afternoon that Tina received a call that her sister had been murdered in another state. It was the time of the year for company reviews. Tina was busy performing these associate reviews. Tina's assistant called me and told me about what had happened. I immediately dropped what I was doing and went to Tina's office. Some-

thing that I had noticed about Tina is that every time she left to go to a meeting, to an off-site event, or to go home, she took a Diet Coke with her. I went to Tina and explained that several associates within the company had already paged me, and that they were all very concerned about her. I knew that it was important to gain permission from these associates to share with Tina that they were concerned for her.

Tina was resistant to leaving work to take care of her intense family situation. I spoke with her for a while and instructed that I would be there to care for her as closely or as distantly as she would like. I then went to the break area, put 60 cents into the vending machine, and selected a Diet Coke. After requesting permission from her supervisor, I took the soda back into Tina's office and let her know that it would be all right for her to go home. I also instructed her that I would be available for her and the family, eventually assisting in the funeral preparation and officiating in the service.

Through those few days of ministry, 21 people came to profess Christ as their Lord and Savior. Relationships are crucial. Even something as simple as noticing what pref-erence of soda a person drinks can make an impact, conveying that they are of worth, possessing value and dignity because they are created in the image of God.

– Submitted By Chris H.
Atlanta, GA

*Individuals in this story have granted permission for its use.

Questions

Reflect on the Stories From the Field found in this chapter and answer the following questions:

1. How would you handle the situation that was described?
2. What information found in the story is confidential?
3. What information found in the story can be shared with others? With whom may this information be shared? Under what circumstances may this information be shared?
4. How does the information found in this chapter pertain to the story?

Endnotes

1. Eugene H. Ehrlich, ed., *Oxford American Dictionary* (New York: Oxford University Press, 1980), 569.

2. Lawrence J. Crab, *Understanding People: Deep Longings for Relationships* (Grand Rapids: Zondervan, 1987), 96.

3. Neil S. Wilson, and Bruce B. Barton, eds., *The Handbook of Bible Application* (Wheaton: Tyndale, 1992), 128.

4. "Ethical Principles of Psychologists and Code of Conduct: Record Keeping and Fees (6.01)," *American Psychological Association (APA)* <http://www.apa.org/ethics/code2002.html #4_05> (Accessed 25 April 2005).

5. "Ethical Principles of Psychologists and Code of Conduct: Privacy and Confidentiality (4.05)," *American Psychological Association (APA)* <http://www.apa.org/ethics/code2002.html#4_01> (Accessed 25 April 2005).

6. *CCA Training Manual* (7/27/05 edition).

7. See the *CCA Training Manual* (7/27/05 edition). This research is an amalgam of other sources that includes, but is not limited to, Richard Nelson Bolles, *What Color Is Your Parachute? A Practical Manual for Job-Hunters & Career Changes* (Berkeley: Ten Speed, 1992); *Know Your Animal*; a seminar presented by AWANA Clubs of America; and internet research.

Chapter Twelve

The Role of Permission in Community Chaplaincy

5/4/08

CHAPTER TWELVE

The Role of Permission in Community Chaplaincy

———————————— Objectives ————————————

During the course of this chapter, we will perform the following tasks:

- Discover the relationship between trust and personal satisfaction

- Discuss the importance of trust and success with people

- Explore the significance of trust and chaplain ministry

- Apply the concept of respecting boundaries to the goal of gaining permission to share the life-changing Good News of Jesus Christ in the mission field

- Develop strategies for building relationships to gain permission to talk about spiritual matters

- List effective methods for bridging conversation from the trivial to the spiritual

A s a community chaplain, you will serve God, the area in which you minister, and many people of varied and different backgrounds. The chaplain has the task of ministering to people of different faiths, while being true to his own. Praying publicly in a manner that preserves one's own spiritual integrity, while at the same time not offending others, requires the utmost discretion and diplomacy. Yet one of the features that distinguish the community minister from other types of clergy persons is precisely this ability to be both a careful respecter and supporter of the religious needs of others, as well as a faithful representative of their own religious group. All chaplains, lay or professional, are ministers, but not all ministers are chaplains. Believing that God is the answer to all of people's dilemmas, chaplains stand ready to bear witness to the forgiving love and redeeming power of God through Jesus Christ to all people, especially those in crisis. Ministers in the community, school, sports league, or marketplace pray that God will guide their thoughts, words, and actions. They seek to be a channel of God's presence and love, to have a ministry of presence, to represent God to the people that are in the mission field, and provide guidance, care, and comfort in times of crisis or need. All of the care is accomplished on a "by permission" basis only. This chapter will examine the boundaries that exist in healthy relationships, how to gain the trust of the individuals in the mission field, and how to gain permission to share the life-changing Good News of Jesus Christ.

The permission that we seek as community chaplains, the permission to share the gospel, cannot be obtained without trust. Each time that we have interaction with an employee, a neighbor, or a little leaguer, we have the opportunity to build and/or deepen the trust that exists between that person and us. Many people do not realize the importance of this trust. In the wake of the myriad of layoffs over the last few years, as well as the debacles at Enron and WorldCom, it is fair to say that employees are a little wary, and in some cases downright suspicious, of our corporate leaders. Although most companies and their leaders are honest and treat their employees fairly, gaining and keeping trust takes more than the absence of lies and scandals. Each time a leader creates an expectation and does not carry through on it, trust is broken. It is important to recognize that a community chaplain is a leader. Many will admire, respect, and listen carefully to your words.

Building Trust

Captain D. Michael Abrashoff, author of *It's Your Ship! Management Techniques from the Best Damn Ship in the Navy* and speaker at leadership conferences, has said, "Leadership is not rocket science, rather it is a collection of minor things that, when taken as a whole, create a climate where people feel honored and valued." There are a number of areas that leaders can focus on to improve trust.[1]

Perhaps the single most important trust building exercise is to open the channels of communication. This includes sharing the bad news as well as the good. Attempting to shield people from bad news only makes things worse. When presented with a void of information, they will attempt to fill it. They will speculate, refer to the rumor mill, and finally when the news comes out at the last moment, they will be angry and frustrated. Being up front and explaining the rationale behind certain decisions will help them to understand the various factors affecting their situation and give them a sense that they are being dealt with fairly and honestly.

In addition to communication, leadership can build trust through increased individual responsibility. By giving others more challenging responsibilities, leaders are demonstrating trust and belief in others.

Accountability is just as important as responsibility. If a child is consistently breaking curfew, it is essential that leadership (in this case, parents) take action. Leaders must reflect on the situation to determine whether the duties and responsibilities were appropriately assigned. If leadership chooses to ignore poor performance or policy violations, poor performance will spread as those reporting to the leader lose respect for leadership.

One of the most important traits needed for community chaplaincy to work is credibility with those in the mission field. Credibility will help produce outstanding results for the mission field. Be honest. You owe it to those in your charge to be honest. This must be balanced with tact and the leading of the Holy Spirit. Remember to speak the truth in love. Be positive, yet do not sugar coat it. Secondly, be consistent. Be consistent with your communication among your people groups. You will lose credibility if they see you communicate differently with different people concerning the same situations.

Fig. 12.1 One of the hardest times for a community chaplain to build trust is when there is bad news.

One of the hardest times for a community chaplain to build trust with a group of people, or individually, is when there is bad news. This could be the news that the tests came back confirming cancer, a loss of employment, or an unfaithful action by a spouse. It is crucial that the chaplain is sympathetic with the distressed in this time of sad news.

Trust can be built when someone has a problem of some sort. People want to succeed. They want to make a difference. This can happen when the community minister involves them in the creation of a solution. When the chaplain develops a solution without the help of the individual, he is in essence making the person dependent on the community chaplain, not on God. This is very dangerous. We should be there to facilitate the application of God's Word to the situation at hand, but ultimately it is the choice of the individual to implement the solution. If given the opportunity, those in your mission field will come up with solutions that are innovative, proactive, and in some cases better than any solution we can ever develop.

"Trust is probably the most basic human value," stated Fred Rogers, better known as Mr. Rogers from the children's show, *Mister Rogers' Neighborhood.* Nothing is harder to regain than lost trust. I believe people do business with people they trust, be it a chaplain, a car dealership, or a home builder. I believe people do business with people who are knowledgeable, efficient, and will deliver what they promise. The chaplain must earn the trust of those to whom he will minister. This trust means that the chaplain has delivered some major principles that are intended to build and maintain trust. Take a look at the following acronym for trust that was developed by Anne Obarski but amended for our discussion on community chaplaincy:

T- **Truth:** Trust and solid relationships are built on telling the truth.

R- **Responsibility:** Trust is built when everyone within an organization realizes what their responsibilities are and that they are held accountable for them.

U- **Unselfishness:** Trust is built when people give of their time and talent and do it unselfishly.

S- **Security:** Trust is built on a feeling of security.

T- **Teamwork:** Trust is built when everyone within the organization feels a sense of ownership.[2]

We are at a time when gaining an individual's trust is critical. It is a daily process, on purpose. It is a time to maximize potential ethically and to deal with conflict and problems with credibility.

While these principles are usually written to the business community, they can easily be applied to the chaplain and the relationships that he wishes to develop. There is a certain amount of permission that has been granted to take the gospel to your mission field. It can be noted that several more traditional ministries, such as the Billy Graham Evangelistic Association (BGEA), are taking notice of the increased receptivity of the business and other communities to faith matters.

The Future of the Workplace[3]

Almost 300 workplace leaders, workplace ministries representatives, and pastors were in attendance at a conference aimed at teaching business leaders how to impact others in their sphere of influence with their faith. Among the many exciting initiatives and visions to come out of this historic meeting, the following list of what we can expect to see in the next five years as a result of God's movement among believers in the workplace also developed:

- We will see intentional training in the local church to help men and women conceptualize their work as ministry, with practical application.
- We will begin to view churches as equipping centers that will support Christians in their workplace calling.
- We will begin to see a movement similar to Promise Keepers, with major events around the faith at work theme.
- We will see the men's movement integrate this message into its focus.
- We will begin to see corporations take a more proactive acceptance of faith at work issues.
- We will see prayer impact the workplace even more.
- We will see our first cities transformed because those in authority will become active and passionate about their faith where they work.
- We will begin to see more faith expressed in government agencies, in the entertainment industries, in educational institutions, and in corporate workplaces.
- We will see many people come to Christ as more major ministries embrace this move of God and integrate it into their operations.
- We will hear of miracles in the marketplace because of new wineskin Christians who are willing to move, in faith and obedience, into arenas that the religious leaders have believed heretofore taboo.
- Pastors will be the last to embrace the movement but will ultimately be responsible for the greatest influence, once they do embrace it. It will be the breakthrough for which many pastors have been looking.

There is a revival coming, revival that is returning us to our roots to understand what the early church understood—that work is a holy calling in which God moves to transform lives, cities, and nations. 'Someone recently said that the 'First' Reformation took the Word of God to the common man and woman; the 'Second' Reformation is taking the *work* of God to the common man and woman,' notes Tom Phillips, vice-president of training for the BGEA. 'That time is now. The greatest potential ministry in the world today is the marketplace. Christ's greatest labor force is those men and women already in that environment.' This line of thought can be applied to many different situations: schools, sports leagues, nursing homes, jails, neighborhoods, and any other environment where people spend time.

Clearly, there is receptivity to faith in new places. Let us spend some time learning how to approach this subject without offending; gaining permission to share the life-changing Good News.

Boundaries

NASCAR drivers win races by staying within the lines around the track and meeting rules regarding the car. Musicians in a band play according to a common key, rhythm, and tempo. Both acknowledge boundaries set up to govern their behavior.

Boundaries may appear harsh or controlling. In actuality, they provide the framework for you to become your personal best. It is important for the effective community chaplain to respect boundaries in his relationships, whether the boundaries are dealing with time, emotions, information, or physical activity.

Fig. 12.2 Boundaries provide the framework for you to become your personal best.

Violating boundaries is a problem for exactly this reason—God made you as a human being. "In the beginning," you are reminded, "... God created man in his own image, in the image of God created he him; male and female created he them" (Genesis 1:27 KJV). You are created in the image and likeness of a wonderful Creator Who knows that you are good. Because of this, you have immeasurable value. Whenever you encounter another person, you should see a hint about God to be found in him or her, this "image and likeness of the Creator." God sees the value and good in each person and challenges you to find that good as well.

All relationships require work. We are still human and not perfect, so student/teacher, coach/player, boyfriend/girlfriend, youth minister/youth group member, parent/child relationships are never too easy, but instead demand effort and trust. Boundaries provide the promise of having relationships where both people are committed to preserving trust and upholding the value and worth of each other. Boundaries are best understood when they are clear. Anyone who has played soccer in a backyard knows that it is easier to violate an out-of-bounds that is defined between two landmarks than one where a thick chalk line has been clearly laid down. Boundaries are a good thing. If you have observed them well, your efforts can be acknowledged as real achievements. No points are given when you are out of bounds for a shot after the whistle; no standing ovation comes for a monologue that ignores the script. Boundaries also help protect the players. In hockey, a strong elbow check is a foul; the penalty is a shot or time in the box.

Boundaries related to time should be put in place. Besides limiting time, boundaries are also necessary with respect to emotions. Anger, happiness, frustration, contentment, pleasure, pain, grief, and excitement are all emotions. Being in a relationship, even with someone in the mission field, promises scores of emotional experiences, both positive and negative.

Emotions might confuse or overwhelm you at times. New emotions can sometimes be difficult to understand. Often, they provide a distraction to other things going on in your life. Emotions, however, offer a choice. You can control your emotions and rule them, rather than allowing them to rule you. Even emotions need boundaries. It is a matter of taking charge of your own life. This responsibility is an important task of your teenage years, and it continues to be important, no matter how old you are. This discipline offers challenges. You want to make sure that you have a language for your emotions, that you are able to identify and describe them. Know who among your family, friends, and significant adults might be able to discuss your emotions with you. You can control your emotions with different methods, possibly meditation, exercise, or prayer. Find out which ones work best for you. However, techniques such as denial or addiction only *mask* emotions temporarily, and do not assist you in getting a handle on them.

You can discover many details about a person simply by surfing the Internet. Bloggers post personal diaries online daily. Perhaps you have had a picture of yourself placed on the Web for a school or church activity. It is nice to consider that faraway relatives might be able to download this information. Yet, the Internet poses security concerns. Be cautious about sharing personal details, and protect your passwords. What is true of virtual relationships is true with actual relationships. You hold the password to the details of your life. Take care in building relationships of trust over long periods of time. Trust strongly built cannot be rushed.

Information sharing is important to relationships. You will want to share facets of your life with people you meet. Many of your feelings will need to be processed with others. If someone wrote the story of your life right now, the author would tell all of your geeky, first-grade mistakes. They would share about when your pet died, when you moved to a new town, and new friendships. It would be a great story—a best-seller! It would be so popular that someone would surely offer to write a revision about your life after you graduated from high school. Would the book be the same length? Of course not! It would be expanded with more tales, more experiences, and more feelings. You are a work in progress. Allow yourself to be a fascinating read for others by having your story slowly reveal itself before them. You do not have to race to share the whole story, because you are not done yet. You also can set limits when other people begin to share too much of their story with you. You do not have to be your friends' emotional bellhop, carrying their baggage for them. It is important to be loving and helpful; but sometimes "too much" can become harmful to you, your emotions, and your attitude.

You know that you have value, worth, and dignity as a person made by God. It makes sense, then, to consider the following possibility: It is a moonlit night. A couple sits in a car on a hillside overlooking the city. Romantic music is coming from the CD player. Jude makes the classic "scratch the back of the head, and then reach out and put my arm over her shoulders" move. Teresa shifts closer to him. She looks into his eyes. He looks into her eyes. And you know exactly what they are thinking at that moment....*How wonderful that this person is created in God's image and likeness!* (That was not what you *thought* they were thinking, was it?) Why not? How wonderful physical intimacy could and should be: an embrace, holding hands, a kiss and, yes, even sex! Each of these acts is one "image and likeness of God" coming into contact with another. It should be a sacred and holy moment.

I once was with a group of other adults, delightedly listening to an 82-year-old

Fig. 12.3 All aspects of physical intimacy should be treated as sacred and holy.

man recall his first kiss 65 years earlier. He remembered the way she wore her hair, her dress, the scent of her perfume, and his surprise at the taste and texture of her lipstick. This moment was very special and precious. Physical intimacy is meant to help bond and unite people. If you ignore its power, you disregard the wonderful opportunity it provides. One of the biggest lies ever told is, "Hey, that kiss (or any other intimate act) didn't mean anything!" This intimate physical contact between two images and likenesses of God is so holy that a sacrament, marriage, is attached to sexual intercourse. Because sex is holy, the church and society are upset about sexual violence. Sex involves dignity, respect, and total self-giving, not selfishness and brutality.

You should plan and consider the most appropriate boundaries for you within relationships. What is acceptable for you, not only within your comfort level, but also within your faith level? Discussing these boundaries with a very trusted person can hold you accountable to the standards you set.

Cultural boundaries are also essential to consider when working with a diverse mission field. Do you know that Asian workers never call each other by the first name in a business setting? It is a sign of disrespect. Asians also place a great deal of emphasis on the business card. Use care when introducing yourself to someone of this ethnicity and the exchange of business cards that will follow. Punctuality and formality are appreciated by the Russian and German cultures. In many Latin American cultures, it is offensive to give certain gifts. Giving a knife, for example, represents the desire to "cut off" the relationship. Understanding the intricacies of the people groups in your community can really help to establish trust, mutual respect, and healthy boundaries.

How Am I Perceived?

One of the most important questions to ask yourself as a community chaplain is, "How do those in my mission field perceive me?" When considering this answer, there are a few areas that the effective chaplain will reflect upon. First, take a long look at your body language. There are different distances that should be thought of as personal space, depending on the situation. For example, in social situations such as a dinner party or a picnic, there are appropriate distances for the community chaplain to respect. Keep in mind that these are culturally specific to the United States. Those born in other countries who have migrated to this country may have differing acceptable spatial boundaries. Two distances exist in spatial relationships. The first is called far distance. People that are in "far" distance do not need to be acknowledged. We feel no obligation to have conversation with someone who is in far distance. The typical far distance is considered 7 to 12 feet. Anything closer than 7 feet, but not closer than 4 feet, is considered "near" social distance. If you get closer than this to someone in a social setting, the signal that can be perceived is that the relationship should take on an intimate aspect.

Spatial relationships are important. If you do not think so, consider what happens when you sit down in an airport at a table for two. The restaurant area is crowded, so someone asks to share the table with you. Being a considerate person, you are quick to share. What happens when the other person starts to place his belongings on "your" part of the table? In our minds, we feel like half of the table belongs to us and the other half would be the space of the other person. Intimate distances are widely accepted to be near intimate 0 to 6 inches and far intimate 6 to 18 inches. Remember that those zones change with disposition. For example, studies reveal that a violent person needs about two to four times the distance than those who do not have violent tendencies. This means that a person with a history of violence should be given a wide berth, so that the violent person does not perceive that you are intruding on his personal space. There are some clear signals that you have invaded someone's personal space. These include, but are not limited to, swinging the leg, tapping, rocking, closing the eyes, withdrawal of the chin into the chest, hunching of the shoulders, and bodily removing themselves. As it can be seen, these signals are subtle attempts to "close" or remove the invasion of personal space.

In addition to spatial relationships, eye contact is another means through which we can communicate using body language. But how much eye contact is appropriate? Too little seems cold and uninterested; too much is threatening and judgmental. When you are less than 7 feet from an individual, eye contact is less important. When greater than 7 feet apart, eye contact takes on more importance. Much can be conveyed through eye contact. Making eye contact is acknowledging that the person is present. Be careful to avoid staring at someone. Staring carries the connotation that someone is an object. We should only stare, gaze for a long time at, or study an object. This means that art, an animal, or a car is acceptable for a long stare, but another person is not. A good example of this kind of interaction is the interaction between a waiter and a diner, or a busy executive and the janitor emptying his trash can. Watching someone's eyes when in conversation is important. When a person is questioning, his eyes open wider. This will help you know when someone is really seeking, perhaps even giving you permission to bridge the conversation into spiritual matters. The percentage of time that the chaplain listens to the individual is very important. It is suggested that the chaplain speak only about 20 percent of the time, and listen about 80 percent of the interaction time. Studies reveal that the more we speak, the less we really look at the other person. By listening to those in our in the mission field, we are communicating that we value what they have to say. This leads to more developed relationships in a shorter amount of time.

If handled correctly, physical interaction is another method with which we can gain permission to delve deeper into the life of a person. When speaking with an individual, your body position should convey that the other person is valued. Be sure that your body language is inclusive of those around your immediate area. This means that you should not, unless you are attempting to be discreet and communicate privacy to those in the area, turn your back on others that are in listening range. Your body orientation should parallel the other person in the conversation in most cases. If the other person is sitting, they would most likely prefer that you sit as well. If you stand during a conversation that lasts more than 5 minutes, you are communicating through body language that you are superior to the other participants in the conversation. Body language should be congruent with the message that you are speaking. In other words, you have to believe what you are saying, or the listener will be able to decipher this disparity. You will be able to pick up on this incongruence as the listener, too. There are times when you talk with an individual who is resistant to the community chaplain. Often this happens when meeting a couple in a caregiving session. Possibly one spouse wants to solve an issue in the marriage, and the other is simply not interested. This can be overcome, to some degree, through the use of body language. When dealing with someone who is sending defensive body language signals, respond with the opposite body language. When the other defensive person is crossing his arms and legs, conveying the message that he is closed to you, be sure to keep an open posture.

Fig. 12.4 Your body language needs to be inclusive to those around you.

Physical appearance conveys messages to those in the mission field in which the chaplain seeks to gain permission to share the life-changing Good News of Jesus Christ. The effective community minister must realize that appearance and physical beauty is not the measuring device for us; we know that God looks on the heart. However, grooming and the way that you carry yourself communicate to those in the culture called America. Do you reflect the Christ that is in you, the hope of glory? Your appearance and demeanor should convey this hope. How is your posture? Are you standing erect, confident in who you are in Christ, avoiding arrogance? The effective chaplain will dress appropriate to the mission field in which he is serving, being careful to avoid overdressing. When the chaplain overdresses, he can come across as arrogant to those who feel underdressed. Grooming habits and cleanliness seem like issues that would not need to be addressed in a text on community ministry, but care and attention should be given to these areas. Lastly, when thinking about your appearance to those found in your mission field, reflect on the appearance of neediness that is conveyed. It must be ever present on the mind of the chaplain that he is in the community to serve, not to be served. He is in the environment to encourage and reflect Christ, not to drain energy from others by fishing for compliments or pretending to be a martyr.

Personality Styles

When seeking to gain permission from those found in your mission field to share with them, measures should be taken to make each feel as special as God has created them to be. The proficient chaplain will spend time understanding what personality style each person possesses. He will also seek to find methods to interact in an effective way with each of them. Investing the time to discover the interests of each person conveys value. Calling everyone by name is crucial. All of these efforts are to gain acceptance, not for you, but for Christ.

One type of person who can be challenging to build a relationship with is the person who always likes to be in charge. There are some strong personality types, as discussed earlier. A leader can have a strong personality that can, even unintentionally, be intimidating. Be sure to care for everyone, even those who appear not to have any needs at all.

Permission must be gained from all people found in the mission field. As an open minded person, some ministers will understand the functions and role of the chaplain. Other clergy will not fully grasp the importance of ministry through the community. Regardless of what role you may serve as a minister, be that as a church Pastor, a support staff member of a church, a minister that reaches out through recreation, a missionary among foreign nations, or a community chaplain, all are members of the same body. Building bridges to other clergy in your area of influence should be a priority. Respect for others in ministry should be shown. Efforts should be made to instill a sense of camaraderie among the ministers of various backgrounds in your city. The effective chaplain will devise creative ways to encourage teamwork to accomplish the goals of his ministry, the ministry of others, and the command to share the life-changing Good News with the entire world.

First Impressions

We have mentioned that there are four main tasks that can be accomplished when performing functions surrounding the building of relationships with those in your mission field. These functions are used to establish relationships with individuals, to then build and strengthen those relationships, to minister in a time of crisis, and to evangelize. All of these different levels of relationship are contingent upon the permission being granted by the person to the chaplain. It is, therefore, important that the chaplain make a good impression on the first visit. A chaplain can make a great first impression by dressing attractively, but comfortably. He will be aware of his posture, appearing open, alert, and confident by sitting and standing correctly. He will give the appearance of sincerity by truly being genuine in his care for those entrusted to him. It is important that the chaplain not tell others how wonderful he is; he should instead show people how wonderful Christ really is. Be interested and interesting. Listen to what people say, and ask appropriate questions. Care should be taken to avoid interrupting someone else who is speaking. Exceptional manners cover a multitude of faux pas. Notice body language of the other person. Palm position, slouching, leaning, eyes, arms, mouth, and nodding are all things of which to be particularly aware. Receptivity will increase in direct proportion to the permission that is granted by the individual. The goal of the community minister is to build a long term relationship for evangelistic purposes. This is accomplished through the mindset that this is a marathon, not a sprint. Rushing through formulaic, canned gospel presentations will sour them to future evangelism efforts.

As it can be gathered, listening to people will go a long way toward gaining permission. The chaplain, remember, should spend about 80% of his time listening, and the remaining 20% of his workday speaking. This means that becoming a good listener is critical. First, position yourself to look into the eyes of the person who is speaking.

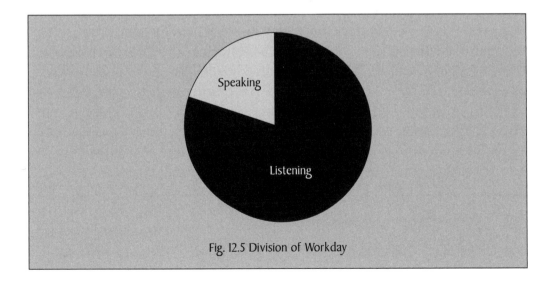

Fig. 12.5 Division of Workday

Minimize distractions, and do not look over the shoulder of the speaker to see what else is going on around you. The natural tendency of a listener is to think about what he will say when the speaker is finished. This practice should be avoided. Pay special attention to non-verbal cues, such as body language and environmental issues. Make an attempt to rid yourself of bias and listen to what the other person has to say. Asking open-ended questions and listening to the complete answer without interruption can go a long way to convey value to the other person. Statements that contain the word "I," or sharing stories of an experience that you had that was similar to the narrative that associate just shared, should be avoided. This can only end up in a "one-upsman" type of relationship, where no one is the winner.

There are some people who just seem to be naturally able to build intimacy with almost anyone. These people have accomplished this by exercising the abilities that God has gifted them with to strengthen their relationship building skills. In order to become more natural and proficient, practice conversing with everyone that you can: cashiers, waiters, people you know, and neighbors. Make attempts to chat with folks who are unlike you. Additionally, you should read everything. Cookbooks, newspapers, magazines, and the like are great for finding discussion starters. Keep a journal, practice telling stories, and talk to yourself in the mirror, being sure to smile appropriately. Try new things that are not in your comfort zone. These can be experiences to share in caregiving times. Take the necessary steps to be a better listener. Be confident in who you are in Christ, remembering to never put yourself or anyone else down. Sensitivity to spatial needs and body language will help you understand how well things are going. No matter who you are, there are some topics that are statistically a favorite: movie stars, houses, pets, and food. Likewise, some topics that are statistically not a hit: salaries, politics, and computers. It is generally a good idea to stay away from these areas of conversation.

Sometimes the hardest part of starting a conversation with someone is the first sentence. As the saying goes, "There is only one time to make a first impression." Some easy conversation starters that are great for putting the associate at ease include topics like a favorite teacher in school, favorite subject in school, places that they have been, favorite dessert, movies that they have recently seen, what they like most about this city or this company, favorite season, vacation spot, and type of music. Other topics that are great for allowing people the opportunity to share about themselves include leisure activities, a favorite celebrity, favorite childhood toy, favorite superhero, or pet. Remember to listen carefully and fully when someone is sharing with you. Stay in touch with people, especially when you do not need something from them. Talk to people everywhere you go. Strive to become a better listener and practice presentation of your own skills. A conversation with a good community chaplain will come across with comfort, sincerity, and interest.

These conversations are intended to lead the relationship in a general direction: towards the life-changing Good News of Jesus Christ. There are two reasons that most people do not share their faith in their community, or anywhere for that matter. One reason is because of the fear of rejection. It is crucial to understand that the other person is not rejecting you; he may, however, be rejecting Christ. The second reason is simply not knowing what to say. It is very important to understand how permission and confidentiality are intermingled, especially when it comes to discussing matters of faith. Easy methods to gain permission from someone include phrases like, "May I share with you what I have found to be helpful?"; "Would you like to hear what the Bible says about that?"; or "Do you know what many people believe about...?" The person with whom you are speaking may have given you permission to talk about spiritual matters, but those who may also be in hearing range have not granted you permission. For this reason, witnessing should not take place in front of groups of people. It should be done privately. **Always, always, always** ask permission before you begin to share the gospel with an individual. If you are going to give them a tract, ask permission. "You know, I have something here that you might want to read." If you witness to a co-worker, and she comes to faith in Christ, obtain permission from her to share the news with the employer. You might ask your co-worker to share this personally. Next, it is great to present them with a Bible and inscribe the Bible with their spiritual birthday. If at all possible, present this Bible to the individual the day of their profession of faith. For this reason, it is good to keep a couple in the trunk of your vehicle.

Transitions to the Spiritual

How do you know when a person is ready to make the transition from trivial conversation to that of spiritual things? Determine the readiness of the individual by reflecting on what you know about the person's religious background. Think about opportunities that you have had to plant seeds and the response that he had to those conversations. Do you sense that this person enjoys being with you or the Christ that is in you? What needs have you discovered that relate to the gospel solution? Consider

221

how much of your personal testimony you have had a chance to share, and look for clues that the person is open to evangelism. Some pretty clear "buying" signals for evangelism include the asking of questions, the willingness to read books that answer these questions, a willingness to attend events where the gospel would be presented, willingness to explore reasons for belief, and freedom from defensive attitudes.

There are some standard transitional statements that most Christians have heard taught through an evangelism seminar or other learning opportunity. These include some of the following:

- Why should such a holy God let you into Heaven?
- The assurance transition: On a scale of 1 to 10, how sure are you that if you were to die tonight you would go to heaven?
- The spiritual pilgrimage transition: Where are you in the process?
- The marriage transition: Imagine your relationship with God as a marriage...
- The house transition: Is God allowed in all rooms of your home?

However, there are many more bridges that can be built that carry the conversation from the mundane to eternal matters. Some of the following are less traditional in nature, but can be perceived as more natural and less "canned" to the listener.

- People invest time and energy into developing their career, their bodies, and relationships but often neglect the spiritual dimension of their lives. How do you actively pursue spiritual growth?
- Do you think much about spiritual things? (This usually leads to conversation about what "spiritual" means--i.e. religion vs. relationship.)
- How has this experience affected the way you look at God?
- I'd like to tell you how I established a personal relationship with God. (Tell your personal testimony of how you became a Christian. Keep it to three minutes, using the following outline: Before--What characterized my life before I trusted Christ. During--How I came to trust Christ. After--How I am different now.)
- What is your concept of God? Do you view Him positively or negatively?
- Have you ever come to a point in your life where you trusted Jesus Christ as your personal Savior and Lord, or do you think that is something you're still moving toward? May I share with you how I came to that point?
- Do you find that faith and spiritual values play a role in your work / day / marriage /

perspective on life?

- If you could be sure there is a God, would you want to know Him? Or, if you could know God personally, would you want to?
- Invite an employee to your church or a Christian event, then ask:
  - What did you think of it?
  - Did it make sense to you?
  - Have you made the wonderful discovery of knowing God personally?
  - Would you like to?
- Do you go to church? I know that you have a reason for not going. Do you mind if I ask what that reason is? Do not ask "why or why not"; questions like these place people in the defensive mode.
- I'd hate for you to come to my church and not understand what it's all about. Would you want to get together and discuss our basic beliefs?
- We've been friends for quite some time now, and I've never really talked to you about the most important thing in my life. May I take a few moments and do so?
- Is church something that has had an influence in your life? Are you at a point now that you want church to be a bigger part of your life? What prompted this? Would you want to hear our basic beliefs so you'll know if that fits in with what you're looking for?
- How do you think someone becomes a Christian?
- Can I share the thing I've found most important to me as a dad / mom / boss?
- What do you think about when you go to sleep at night? (If anxiety or guilt robs them of sleep, introduce the peace found in a relationship with Christ.)
- Most people in America say they believe in God. What does believing in God mean to you?
- Before I came to know Christ personally, God was a vague concept that I could not relate to or grasp. How would you describe your view of God? Jesus? Is He a reality to you or more of a vague concept?

Whatever approach you use, never argue or condemn the other person's beliefs. Focus on God's love for the person, Jesus' death on the cross for our sins, His resurrection, and the person's need to make a commitment to follow Christ. Invite the person to actually pray with you and commit his or her life to Christ.

Once the person has given permission, try to lead them to a decision. Begin to set up the opportunity to share and lead them to make the same decision that you have made, to have a life radically transformed by the power of God. Remember, you have set up the opportunity to share, followed up with questions, and gathered and remembered good illustrations from the discussion to use to make abstract principles clear to them. It is then up to the listener to make the commitment. Celebrate the decision to surrender, but do not chastise the one who is not ready to make the decision for Christ. If handled correctly, this has been a time that will lead to permission to share in the future.

Stories From the Field: #8
"Permission To Speak Freely"*

*A few months ago a truck driver who lives near me pulled me aside. He said he had wanted to talk to me for months but had not had the courage. He was having a problem with depression and did not know what to do. A Christian friend had given him a copy of **The Purpose Driven Life**, but he did not really understand it. After explaining to him for several minutes why he did not, I asked permission to share Christ with him. As he prayed to receive Christ, he hesitated; and I looked up and saw the tears streaming from his face and literally hitting the floor. I gave him a Bible and a copy of **The Third Awakening**. Within the next few days, I got on the internet and searched for some good churches in our part of town. I called a few and interviewed the pastors and came up with a church for him to attend. I keep in contact with him for accountability and to see how things are going. The world would have put him on some kind of medication for his depression; but our God is so big, he saved this man and is caring for him. When he starts to feel depressed, he reads God's Word. That is the way it should be.*

– Submitted By Troy
Harrisburg, PA

*Individuals in this story have granted permission for its use.

Stories From the Field: #9
"Removing The Red Eye"*

I had just finished work on a Wednesday afternoon, when my pager began beeping for my attention. It was a guy I knew from one of my business contacts that wanted to know if I could meet with him the following Saturday morning at a local McDonald's. He would not share with me his name or any details as to why he wanted to meet with me. I felt in my heart the Holy Spirit prompting me to meet with this construction worker, so I agreed that this coming Saturday I would meet with him.

I will not forget the long drive (approximately 35 miles) that early Saturday morning. I prayed that the Holy Spirit would give me wisdom, knowledge, and discernment to help this man with whatever problem he may be going through. I also prayed that the Holy Spirit would draw him to Calvary and open his heart for the life-changing good news of Jesus Christ.

Upon arriving at McDonald's, I could see this lonely looking young man wearing dark sunglasses and a long sleeve shirt sitting outside near the playground area. After a brief introduction and reminding him that whatever he shared with me would be confidential, Tom began to share with me about how miserable a life he led. He shared with me that he was about to lose his wife and children. I will never forget the moment when he took off his sunglasses to show me his bloodshot red eyes, a result of drug abuse. Tom was a cocaine addict. I asked Tom why he decided to contact me about his drug issues. Tom said, "Chaplain, I have only two options left in life." When I asked what those two options were, Tom replied, "I will either be arrested for being a thief and drug addict and end up in prison, or I will overdose and die. Either way I will lose my wife and children." Tom began weeping like a child. I could sense that Tom had hit the bottom of the downward spiral of a life dominated by sin.

I told Tom that I thought he had a third option. He immediately interrupted and shared with me about the many times that he had tried to quit on his own. I told Tom that I believed he was right in his analysis of his future. I also told him that I agreed that trying to quit again would probably result in more failure. I asked Tom if, since his options were so gloomy, he would permit me to share with him a third option that has a guaranteed success rate. I called it "the original option" after all human efforts fail. Of course the option I was referring to was God's plan of salvation and transformation. Tom allowed me to share God's plan for the transformation of his life both now and for eternity. After I shared the life-changing good news of Jesus Christ, Tom asked me to help him pray the sinner's prayer of forgiveness and trust in Jesus Christ. I gave Tom a Bible and a tract, and I wrote in his Bible that on this date Tom was born again. I reminded Tom that he was God's masterpiece (Ephesians 2:10) and that God had a plan for his life, but that any change would be more like a marathon than a sprint. By that I meant that change is a process and that it may take time; however, with God all things are possible. I also stressed that change would only occur if he made Jesus Christ not only Savior, but also Lord of his life. Tom would have to surrender his rights and get on God's agenda if he wished to truly defeat drug addiction. Tom assured me that he was ready to make these changes in his life.

I made it a point to see Tom the very next time I was in his part of town to encourage him. We discussed the need to attend a good church, participate in an accountability group or support group, and begin getting counseling for his addiction problems. I spent hours on the telephone and visiting area counseling centers that I thought could offer him professional help. I put together a resource folder of people and organizations that could help Tom grow in his relationship to Christ and to begin a program to defeat his addiction to drugs.

Upon my next visit to the job site where Tom was supposed to be working, I was told that he was no longer with the company. All my attempts to reach Tom at home or by telephone failed. My heart was greatly saddened, but I knew that God loved him and would be watching over him.

It was nearly a year later that I discovered Tom had been re-hired by the construction company. The company had decided to give him a second chance after he had participated in a live-in drug program at a Christian rescue mission. Tom had finally defeated his addiction to drugs. Today, Tom no longer wears sunglasses to hide his red eyes caused by an addiction to drugs. He now shares with me how many months and days it's been since he was once a drug addict. Tom's eyes today are full of joy and hope. Praise the Lord!

–Submitted By Gary W.
Indianapolis, IN

*Individuals in this story have granted permission for its use.

Questions

Reflect on the Stories From the Field found in this chapter and answer the following questions:

1. How would you handle the situation that was described?
2. What information found in the story is confidential?
3. What information found in the story can be shared with others? With whom may this information be shared? Under what circumstances may this information be shared?
4. How does the information found in this chapter pertain to the story?

End Notes

1. John Maxwell conference presentation, attended on January 2003. See, Michael Abrashoff, *It's Your Ship: Management Techniques from the Best Damn Ship in the Navy* (New York: Warner, 2002).

2. Anne M. Obarski, "Earning Customer Trust," The Sideroad <http://www.sideroad.com/Customer_Service/customer_trust.html> (Accessed April 2005).

3. Reprinted with permission from The 9 to 5 Window: How Faith Can Transform the *Workplace*, by Os Hillman (Ventura, CA: Regal, 2005), 79-89. For some websites researched as a complement to Hillman's work, see Michelle Conlin, "Religion in the Workplace: The Growing Presence of Spirituality in Corporate America," *BusinessWeek* November1,1999<http://www.businessweek.com/1999/99_44/b3653001.htm>(Accessed October 19 2005); and Marc Gunther, "Spirituality: God and Business," *Fortune Magazine* July, 2001 <http://www.fortune.com/fortune/careers/articles/0,15114,371129,00.html> (Accessed 20 October 2005).

[Handwritten notes:]

Drugs & Alcohol

* 9 out of 10 High School Students have tried Alcohol
* An addict cannot function w/out their drug of choice
* Crystal Meth fastest growing recreational Drug in U.S.
* 1/2 of meth users say they are addicted after trying it once

Signs of How Addictive — Loss of Control -

INcrease of use - increase sensation of high
Preoccupation - When can I get the next high
Attempts to Stop -
Continuation of use
Reverse tolerance - Needs less to have a high
w/drawl - Detox
Need to self medicate.

Isolation
moral conduct
Loss of finances

[Handwritten margin notes:] 2004 million users cocaine · Resources · Substanceabuse · christiansforux.com · Alcohol-Anon.com · Addicts.com · Addictions4each.com · AA · Complete addiction w/tobacco · 4,000 yrs death w/tobacco

Chapter Thirteen

The Role of Confidentiality in
Community Chaplaincy

CHAPTER THIRTEEN

The Role of Confidentiality in Community Chaplaincy

————————————— Objectives —————————————

During the course of this chapter, we will perform the following tasks:

- Define confidentiality

- Describe limits of confidentiality

- List circumstances under which confidentiality may be breached

- Examine confidentiality as it relates to Scripture

- Analyze applicable laws regarding confidentiality

- Integrate confidentiality into a variety of caregiving situations

The goal of building relationships with those in your mission field, with the hope of gaining permission to share the life-changing Good News of Jesus Christ, is directly connected to the level of confidentiality presented by the community chaplain. In a world where sensationalism and overexposure is common and rumors and gossip are the norm, the community minister has to offer an alternative - strict confidentiality. Effectiveness will come through the desire to build a relationship with individuals that is based on trust. How the chaplain handles information that appears to be common knowledge about another person has an effect on his mission field. Even if news about someone has been circulating around the community, the manner in which that information is handled impacts how people perceive the chaplain. To increase our effectiveness, to make us more approachable, and to hold a position of trust, we must all practice a strict code of confidentiality.

When asked about someone, refer the inquiry back to the person they are asking about. "I am not at liberty to share that information. You may want to ask him personally."

Avoid any references to individuals and their status when out in the community, even when it appears to be safe or simple to do so. If you are asked how another person may be doing, simply respond, "I am not able to share any information about their status with you. It might easily be construed as a breach in confidentiality. You can be assured that I would never share any information about you with anyone either."

When a friend, family member, or neighbor asks you about someone they may honestly care about, someone whom they told you to seek out because of issues they already know about, respectfully say that you do not have permission to share about that, and it would be a breach of confidentiality.

When you use the "confidentiality factor" with anyone, it will establish your credibility to them as a reliable source for delicate information. Our mission field needs to know that when they finally get up the courage to expose their frailties or failures with you, they will be safe. Trust is critical in creating an open door for everyone.

Laws on exceptions to confidentiality can be a murky and conflicted area of legal doctrine for the community chaplain. There are five general categories under which the duty to maintain confidence may be legally compelled or accepted. Not every state allows or mandates all five of them, and each state has distinct rules, both in statutes and judicial opinion, that define the boundary between confidence and disclosure. Again, it is imperative that the chaplain study the rules of his or her resident state to know the specific duties under the law. Much time will be spent on each of the following areas in this text. A brief description of disclosure guidelines can be found below:

- Consent to disclosure. The most common exception to confidentiality is when the client voluntarily consents to disclose information by written release of information.

- Child abuse reporting. Child abuse reporting requirements serve as a significant statutory exception to the rule of confidentiality and privilege.

- Danger to self or others. A chaplain with a person, who is a danger to himself or to someone else, may be legally compelled to breach therapeutic confidence and take action to protect the threatened person(s).

- Emergencies. Common law tradition, statutes, and courts have defined various emergency exceptions to the rule of confidentiality. These include, but are not limited to, abuse, danger to self or others, or minors who have been the victim of a crime.

■ Judicial order and court action. Courts often compel disclosure by subpoena for a variety of legal actions by individuals in the mission field. While privilege statutes protect penitent and chaplain or patient and therapist in most states, these rules are not absolute. Again, seek information on the specific boundaries of privilege statutes in your state.

Components of Effective Community Ministry

Earlier in this text, building relationships that are safe for those to whom the community chaplain will minister was described. One aspect of the safety that was briefly mentioned was confidentiality. In this chapter, we will explore many aspects of confidentiality. This subject is crucial for the success of chaplaincy in the community. Without the trust that is vital to the effectiveness of the community chaplaincy program, people will not open up to the chaplain.

Christ must be the center of all ministry done in the community. If you were to place a component of effective community ministry on each one of the corners of a square, with Christ in the center of the square, the following would be found: Compassion, Caring, Competence, and Confidentiality. While Christ is the core, impactful ministry cannot take place without **compassion**. In Scripture, Christ was often "moved with compassion" for a crowd. The feelings that He had for the people compelled him to act. Compassion is a passion for people that cannot be ignored. **Caring** is a second ingredient in chaplaincy that must be present. The citizens of this country that we call America may not all have Christ, but they can all discern whether or not they are really cared for. A sincere, profound, and deep care must be present for effectiveness. Reflecting the person of Christ is the function of the chaplain. This means that care must be exuded from the spiritual leader in the mission field, the community chaplain. This care for others must be Holy Spirit empowered. To attempt to do this in the flesh is ludicrous. Next, there must be **competence**. No matter how much the chaplain cares

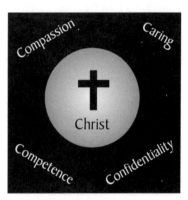

Fig. 13.1 Effective Community Ministry

for his mission field, if he is not skilled, he will not be effective. The chaplain who really wishes to make a difference will seek out initial training and preparedness for the ministry ahead. In addition, seeking out continuing education for the sharpening of current skills and the acquiring of new ones should be practiced. Finally, the characteristic of **confidentiality** needs to be addressed. While briefly pondered in other chapters, the subject of confidentiality will be studied throughout this entire chapter. It is that crucial.

Why is confidentiality one of the cornerstones of a good ministry in and to the community in which you live? First, as stated earlier, it builds trust in the relationship between the chaplain and his mission field. Next, it is a rare commodity. In fact, most people do not believe the chaplain when instructed that everything, with a couple of exceptions we will discuss later, is held in strict confidence, meaning that only the chaplain and the individual speaking with the chaplain will have access to the shared information. In effect, not keeping the innermost thoughts that an individual shares with the chaplain in confidence is breaking a promise. Scripture clearly instructs to "... let your 'Yes' be 'Yes', and your 'No', 'No' ..." so that we can be reflections of Christ in the community (Matthew 5:37 NIV).

Again, the importance of confidentiality cannot be emphasized too strongly. It is one of the elements that must be present for an associate to perceive the environment as safe for open communication with the chaplain. If the chaplain goes to the efforts required to accommodate the other "safety" issues that have been discussed thus far, but fails to provide confidentiality, all of these efforts have been in vain.

Aspects of a Community Chaplain

As mentioned earlier, letting your "yes be yes, and your no be no" is an important part of building trust with your mission field. Confidentiality is really all about trust. How many people do you trust? Really trust. Who would you trust with a key to your home, the Personal Identification Number (PIN) to your checking account, or your deepest innermost thoughts? People are skeptical. They are programmed not to trust. Life experience has taught them that others cannot be trusted. Reality television has taught us not to trust. Our mission field needs to see the reality that we can be trusted and Christ can be trusted. James 1:26-27 and James 3:5-8 speak to this very issue.

> ^{26} *If anyone considers himself religious and yet does not keep a tight rein on his tongue, he deceives himself and his religion is worthless.* ^{27} *Religion that God our Father accepts as pure and faultless is this: to look after orphans and widows in their distress and to keep oneself from being polluted by the world* (James 1:26-27 NIV).
>
> ^{5} *Likewise the tongue is a small part of the body, but it makes great boasts. Consider what a great forest is set on fire by a small spark.* ^{6} *The tongue also is a fire, a world of evil among the parts of the body. It corrupts the whole person, sets the whole course of his life on fire, and is itself set on fire by hell.* ^{7} *All kinds of animals, birds, reptiles and creatures of the sea are being tamed and have been tamed by man,* ^{8} *but no man can tame the tongue. It is a restless evil, full of deadly poison* (James 3:5-8 NIV).

Like a reality TV show, the individuals to whom you will minister view the words that you say as the sound and the life that they see you live as the picture of your reality show. Are the two consistent with one another? These verses describe the picture and sound of an effective community minister.

Three aspects of a chaplain can be found: love, lifestyle, and language. Verse 27 describes the love found in a follower of Christ. It should look and sound like a genuine love, rooted in faith, that defines your compassion for people. The words "look after", found in this verse, describe a burdensome sense of responsibility that cannot be ignored. "Orphan" and "widow" help us to identify helpless or distressed people groups. A vibrant faith will help the helpless.

Secondly, the lifestyle of a community minister will reflect this love for people. It will come through in his code of conduct. Remember, Satan's goal is to stain us so that we will feel paralyzed and incapable of ministry. The coldness of corruption comes through when speaking with a person who has something to hide. The Bible tells us that we have been bought with a price, and that what Christ has made clean cannot be corrupted. Once we put aside the lies of unacceptability that Satan wants us to believe, we can understand that we are saved FOR works. Read carefully: we are not saved BY works, but FOR works. Romans 12:2 speaks to this issue. We accept the call to cleanliness, to stay close to Christ and His Word, and then to change where necessary to live a lifestyle of service that glorifies our Creator.

Finally, the language of a chaplain should be indicative of someone who can be trusted. A common theme of Scripture, a great declaration, is that the tongue should be disciplined. Verses 5-8 of James 3 make this clear. There is also a godly discernment that is empowered by the Holy Spirit. We realize that there is a possibility for deception through the tongue. It has a dual purpose, much like the bridle of a horse. The desire to be liked and feel superior is dangerous, especially when it comes to the temptation to use the tongue for impure motives. The capability that the tongue has to destroy is also very real. It is like a small spark that can start a raging fire. True discipline and restraint come from God. This discipline means that the tongue is under the control of the Holy Spirit. When the chaplain is under the control of the Holy Spirit, his language will reflect this presence in many ways. His language will always show a desire to honor God, it will build others up, it will not harm others, and it will not hinder the lost from seeing God. One of the most telling "tests" to see if your language is passing the screening for these attributes is to think about how you might react if the words that you are saying were printed in the newspaper.

The acronym below, T.R.U.S.T., shows a decision making model for deciding when or if something may be considered confidential.

Use the T.R.U.S.T. model when faced with an issue of confidentiality:

T- **Think:** Think about the situation objectively. Clearly understand the situation. Know the facts and identify the real issues

R- **Recognize:** Recognize and analyze motivations. If the situation troubles you, ask yourself why. Consider the other party's motivations

U- **Understand:** Understand your policies and any applicable laws. Consider all options. Know whom and when to ask for help

S- **Satisfy:** Satisfy the headline test. Ask yourself if you would feel comfortable seeing your action reported in the news. Think about how your family and colleagues would feel about your decision. Consider the consequences of your decision on your ministry, your clients, your family, and yourself.

T- **Take:** Take responsibility for your actions. Make an appropriate choice and act accordingly. Remember, you are accountable for your actions and the outcome of your decisions.

Limits of Confidentiality

The community chaplain will hear many very private issues from those in his care. The population of the mission field must know that everything said to the community chaplain will remain between the two parties mentioned, and only the two parties mentioned. This means that there is information that will be obtained by the chaplain that must be protected. Because meeting with the community chaplain may be the first time that an individual has ever spoken with anyone regarding how to deal with life's struggles and a strategy to negotiate them successfully, it is important to make sure that everyone understands the ground rules.

He or she has the right to tell you or not to tell you anything desired. They must also understand what will happen with the information that is given. The community chaplain may wish to take notes during the caregiving session so that important details can be remembered for later use. The confidentiality also extends to these records. In the United States, many laws are written that impact how much the community chaplain is legally allowed to share and when. For the protection of the community minister, we will explore these general ideas.

Privilege, or confidentiality, is actually viewed as a "thing" that the person who is being cared for owns. This means that the information about his or her life (the privilege) is something that only he or she can share, because it is theirs to own and distribute. Since you do not own the information about an associate's life, you cannot share or disseminate it. One of the basic laws regarding confidentiality is stated below:

> [You may] create, and to the extent the records are under their control, maintain, disseminate, store, retain, and dispose of records and data relating to their professional and scientific work in order to (1) facilitate provision of services later by them or by other professionals, (2) allow for replication of research design and analyses, (3) meet institutional requirements, (4) ensure accuracy of billing and payments, and (5) ensure compliance with law.[i]

Interestingly enough, the "caregivee" technically owns the information that is printed on the paper regarding him, while the community chaplain, or "caregiver", technically owns the paper on which the information is written. As a caregiver in the community, you will know a great deal about the people in your mission field. Even the fact that someone is speaking with you about a life issue is held in strict confidence. As the chaplain, you must maintain confidentiality of much information. Realize that this confidentiality extends even after the relationship or caregiving has ceased. Even if an employee is terminated, a neighbor moves to another state, a student graduates, or the baseball season is over, the caregiver cannot share any information about him. An individual may come to meet with the chaplain and ask, "What if I have committed a crime?" Well, even criminal activity is protected by the shield of confidentiality. So you can instruct the person to relax, if that happens to be his particular concern—*unless*, of course, he is still engaged in criminal activity which jeopardizes the life or safety of others and he reveals the details of this activity to the chaplain. Such a case could fall under one of the *exceptions to confidentiality*, which we will discuss at this point in the text. Strictly speaking, the community minister is bound by law NOT to share anything that an individual discloses during the course of caregiving, unless it is revealed that the person intends to harm himself or someone else. This caveat also includes the mandatory reporting of child abuse. There are many laws that speak to this issue. Collectively, they are called the Tarasoff Laws. Here is what the law specifically says:

Exceptions to Confidentiality include:

- When there is a reasonable suspicion of child abuse or elder adult physical abuse
- When there is a reasonable suspicion that the individual may present a danger of violence to others
- When there is a reasonable suspicion that the person is likely to harm himself unless protective measures are taken.

In all of the above cases, the caregiver is either allowed by law or required by law to break confidentiality in order to protect the individual, or someone he may endanger, from harm.[2]

A Closer Look At The Tarasoff Laws

Note that in all the following cases, the intent of the disclosure, whether mandated or not, is to protect someone from clear and present danger. Once the disclosure is made, the caregiver is bound once more by confidentiality and can say nothing more to anyone without the individual's consent.

Danger to self or others

There is no privilege...if the professional has *reasonable cause to believe* that the patient is in *such mental or emotional condition as to be dangerous to himself or to the person or property of another* and that *disclosure* of the communication *is necessary to prevent the threatened danger* [emphasis added].[3]

Note that there is no *mandate* here; the law simply protects the caregiver from the charge of breach of confidentiality if he decides to break confidentiality to protect someone. Additionally, the laws state that:

There shall be no monetary liability on the part of, and no cause of action shall arise against, any person who is a caregiver as defined in Section 1010 of the Evidence Code in failing to warn of and protect from a patient's threatened violent behavior or failing to predict and warn of and protect from a patient's violent behavior *except where the patient has communicated to the professional a serious threat of physical violence against a reasonably identifiable victim or victims* [emphasis added].[4]

Note that the Tarasoff decision established a duty, but *not* a mandate; it is a court decision about monetary liability and breach of confidentiality. It says that, in general, a chaplain cannot be held liable for not breaking confidentiality about threats of violence made within the caregiving sessions; nor can the caregiver be held liable for failing to predict violent behavior. But, the decision adds, there is one exception to the general rule. *If* the threat is serious, *if* it is communicated directly to the chaplain, and *if* the victim can be reasonably identified, then the community minister *can* be held liable for failing to warn. The decision does not say that, given the proper conditions, the caregiver *has* to do anything; it just says that, under the proper conditions, he is at risk of *getting sued* for not doing anything. So Civil Code 43.92 (a), quoted above, essentially implies that, in warning someone when the highly specific need (duty) arises, the chaplain will *avoid* getting sued for *not* warning anyone, and *cannot* get sued for breaking confidentiality. Civil Code 43.92 (b) adds that, when making one of these warnings, the caregiver should report the impending violence to a law enforcement agency *and* to the threatened victim(s).[5]

There are times that reporting is not merely offered as a judgment call by the caregiver, it is mandated by state and federal statutes. Educate yourself on the laws in your state. Below are some general guidelines on mandatory reporting.

Child Abuse

In respect to minors, a caregiver is mandated to report non-accidental injury inflicted by others; sexual abuse; unjustifiable mental suffering (as in a young child witnessing domestic violence); neglect; cruelty; statutory rape (minor under 16 and other 21 or older, even if consensual); lewd and lascivious conduct (minor under 16 and other 10 years older, even if consensual); consensual sexual contact between minors (where one is 14 years of age and the other is under 14 years of age).[6]

Note that the *mandate* is only in respect to information that arises from within a caregiving situation; it does not apply to something witnessed in a grocery store, for example. Also, the intent of the law is to protect children presently in danger; no report would be made regarding an adult who tells about having been abused as a child—unless this adult tells the chaplain that the abuser (a) has abused someone else who is still a child or (b) has current access to other children.

Elderly and Dependent Adults

In respect to elderly or dependent adults, a community chaplain is mandated to report physical abuse, including sexual assault; misuse of physical or chemical restraint; neglect; fiduciary abuse; neglect; and isolation.

Known Physical Injuries

There are some laws that are applicable to medical doctors that will not apply to chaplains or caregivers of non-medical credentials. These laws do not affect community ministers, because they do not provide medical services for a physical condition, but to avoid any confusion, the law states:

Any health practitioner employed in a health facility, clinic, physician's office, local or state public health department, or a clinic or other type of facility operated by a local or state public health department who, in his or her professional capacity or within the scope of his or her employment, provides *medical services for a physical condition* [emphasis added] to a patient whom he or she knows or reasonably suspects is a person described as follows, shall immediately make a report . . . :
(I) Any person suffering from any wound or other physical injury inflicted by his or her own act or inflicted by another where the injury is by means of a firearm.
(2) Any person suffering from any wound or other physical injury inflicted upon the person where the injury is the result of assault or abusive conduct.[7]

Hospital Patients

The mandated part of this law does not affect community chaplains, unless the chaplain is the hospital administrator. The voluntary part of the law does not mention this type of caregiver specifically, so a chaplain who breaks confidentiality under these conditions could face serious consequences. When in doubt, seek legal counsel. There are some specific and very obscure laws when it comes to mandated reporting in hospital cases. Read the following for some examples.

According to the law, hospital patients who have been transferred from a health or community care facility, or are showing signs of abuse, neglect, or assault injuries require mandated reporting. This is not the case for other injuries.

Every person, firm, or corporation conducting any hospital in the state, or the managing agent thereof, or the person managing or in charge of such hospital, or in charge of any ward or part of such hospital, who receives a patient transferred from a health facility, as defined in Section I250 of the Health and Safety Code or from a community care facility, as defined in Section I502 of the Health and Safety Code, who exhibits a physical injury or condition which, in the opinion of the admitting physician, reasonably appears to be the result of neglect or abuse, *shall report* [emphasis added—this is the mandated part] such fact by telephone and in writing, within 36 hours, to both the local police authority having jurisdiction and the county health department.

"Any registered nurse, licensed vocational nurse, or licensed clinical social worker employed at such hospital *may* [emphasis added—this is the voluntary part] also make a report under this section, if, in the opinion of such person, a patient exhibits a physical injury or condition which reasonably appears to be the result of neglect or abuse.

"Every physician and surgeon who has under his charge or care any such patient who exhibits a physical injury or condition which reasonably appears to be the result of neglect or abuse shall make such report."[8]

Suicide

There are some situations that you are likely to encounter as a community chaplain that could be of concern, related to confidentiality. For example, what happens when someone reveals to the chaplain that he intends to harm himself? This revelation sets into action a course of events for the community caregiver. Remember, an individual may speak of suicide. He may reveal that thoughts of suicide are present. Actually, the issue here is whether there is a *reasonable suspicion* that he is *likely* to kill himself. Just thinking about suicide does not necessarily warrant any extreme action on the part of the chaplain. Experience and the leading of the Holy Spirit will give insight to know how to spot the difference between fantasy and real danger. When an individual does utter the words "I have had enough" or something to that effect, a checklist begins to go through the mind of the caregiver. First of all, understand with whom you are dealing. Does he have the means and motive to follow through with this action? Next, determine what other persons need to be involved in this situation. If this information should be revealed to you over the phone, be sure to find out the location of the person calling you. Always be prepared to hear this information and take notes on the details of the conversation, as you will be under stress while these events unfold. Find out how they are planning on doing this. Be sure to take it seriously. Establish if they have the means and motive for carrying it out. Lead this client to the care of others.

First, directly question the person about the potential for suicide. Sincerely love him through this process. Sensitively listen and seek to understand. Listen for false beliefs, which are making suicide attractive. Begin to counter Satan's deception with God's love. Then, evaluate the potential for actually committing suicide. During this

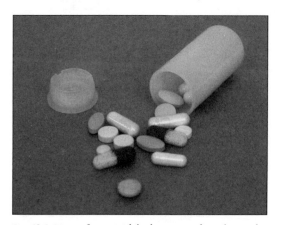

discerning phase, listen for phrases like "I'd never kill myself" due to fear of hell or hurting others, "I occasionally have suicidal thoughts", "I often think suicide is my only hope for peace", or "I already planned how I would do it". These are clues of the thought life. Upon discerning that there is a potential for these thoughts, guide the person to the warning phase. Begin by never encouraging belief in a guaranteed heaven after suicide. Do not be concerned about theological correct-

Fig. 13.2 Listen for suicidal phrases and evaluate the potential for actually committing suicide.

ness of the following statements. The goal is to convince them not to harm themselves. Phrases like "If you are suicidal you may not really know Christ", "You may think you do, but please do not risk eternity on it", or "If you kill yourself, you can't change your mind" can be very persuasive. Utilize techniques to help the suicidal person understand that harming themselves is not the answer.

Next, build hope by helping the individual in crisis to examine other options not yet considered. The effective chaplain will offer himself to walk alongside the hurting person in these new options, explore practical and realistic alternatives, suggest that time often helps to change life circumstances, and encourage a physical exam by a family practice physician to eliminate any physiological causes for these feelings of despair. It is vital to then link the person with an immediate support system. The chaplain will search out friends or relatives of the individual who are supportive. Obtain information needed to contact these supportive persons, and plan to call someone to stay with the person as needed. It is desired to enter into an agreement with the caregivee at this point. Make a covenant-contract for a 12 to 24 hour period. In this contract, the person agrees not to attempt suicide during the contract period. This allows time for the caregiver to provide practical projects toward new alternatives. It is always important to lead the person in a covenant prayer with God. If suicide potential is high, consider referral to a lock down institution. This protection is crucial. The chaplain may try to get the person to voluntarily enter the hospital. If the individual is not willing to do so, then family members may attempt to have the person committed to a lock down facility. If family is unavailable, the coroner can commit someone. Even if the individual is committed, continue to evangelize or disciple as needed. More information about what to do once a person has been committed will be discussed later in the text.

In addition to a potential suicide, there are other times that the questions of if, when, and how much confidential information is required or should be shared become prominent. Some chaplains are licensed counselors and may be listed on a health insurance plan as a medical provider. In that case, the person may have unknowingly waived a great degree of confidentiality. Often, included in the fine print, when an individual signs an insurance form with the provider, he is authorizing any and all medical professionals, with certain credentials. This could require a chaplain to give any information to anyone in the insurance company. This means anyone in the insurance company: a secretary, not necessarily another medical professional, who demands it. In fact, in some cases, failure of the caregiver to provide this information will result in nonpayment by the insurance company. Further, the insurance company is not legally bound, because a waiver has been signed, to maintain the confidentiality of the information. Use extreme care when interacting with insurance providers as a community minister. For this reason, many community chaplains are not licensed caregivers who are on insurance plans.

Court Cases

The effective chaplain will interact with the legal system in his ministry. While the intricacies of how to manage legal issues with an individual will be covered in a future chapter, confidentiality must be addressed when considering the court. There are issues that happen in the lives of those found in your mission field that will have legal implications. Take for example, domestic violence, divorce, alcohol and drug abuse, or child custody issues. While the community minister will support the emotional and spiritual aspects of these cases, very real legal components exist. First of all, it must be stated that the chaplain should NEVER give legal advice. However, at times the attorney representing the persons being charged will want you to testify. Additionally, the court may attempt to compel the chaplain to reveal the details of discussions he has had with those involved in legal proceedings. In such a case, a subpoena may even be served to the community minister. There are a couple of options for such a situation:

- The chaplain has the option of claiming privileged communication and may refuse to disclose the contents of the discussions. In such a case, state and federal laws would most likely protect the confidentiality. Additionally, there is not a precedent for the court system compelling a minister to breach confidentiality with a parishioner.
- If the court compels the testimony of the chaplain, asking him to divulge confidential information through a court order, the minister will have the option of abiding by the court order and releasing the information or seeking his own legal representation to protect the privileged communication. At the time of this writing, a court has not jailed or pressed charges in a situation such as this.
- The person being charged may waive privilege and allow the chaplain to provide the desired information.

Some legal matters involve children. As the chaplain, individuals will inform you of many things that happen in the home. In a case that involves children, as stated earlier, the guardian retains ownership of the privilege surrounding any information that you may discuss. The chaplain merely "holds" the privilege for the client. But if "the client" is more than one person, or a minor without legal rights, then matters become a little more convoluted. In fact, these situations can be so complex that not all states agree on how they should be handled. The chaplain should check with the state in which he lives for clarification. Generally, however, the subject of privilege in regard to children can get very complicated. When a child is a minor without legal rights, the child's parents are often considered to be the legal client. Here are some specific guidelines to keep in mind when a child is involved:

- If a child is a ward of the court, the court holds the privilege unless the court determines that the child is of sufficient age and maturity to hold his or her own privilege.
- If a child has legal counsel, the counsel holds the privilege. However, if the child is of sufficient age and maturity, the child may waive privilege, even if counsel invokes it.

- Some state laws also say that if *anyone*, not just a child, has a legal guardian, then the guardian holds the privilege. But, believe it or not, in legal language parents are not legal guardians.

So where does all this leave children? Well, in one case (In *Re Daniel, C.H.* (1990) 220 Cal.App.3d 814), it was ruled that the child held the privilege. (Mind you, this was case law, not legislative law, but it can set the precedent for future cases.) Common sense, of course, would tell us that in situations that do not involve hostility (such as providing information about a child's private psychotherapy to a school counselor), both the child and the parents should be in agreement. Furthermore, no matter who signs the release, basic human charity should prevail and there should not be any unfortunate consequences. However, when child psychotherapy occurs in the context of a legal proceeding such as divorce, the issue of privilege (that is, the issue of which parent has the right to release information about the child's psychotherapy—usually so that it can be used as a weapon against the other parent) may require legal counsel.

The whole issue can become one more bitter fight in the overall battle between hostile parents—and one more psychological wound for the child to survive. In situations like this, where adults may harm a child to achieve a legal outcome, the chaplain needs to be especially sensitive to maintain confidentiality, in addition to caring for all parties involved. Another concern for community caregivers, when caring for children, is how much to tell well-meaning parents. While the most cautious course is strict confidentiality, it should be discussed prior to beginning to care for the child what may or may not be discussed with parents. Caregiving for children usually includes gaining permission to disclose to parents the progress that the child is making, how the parents may assist in said progress, and that the parents be notified in cases of serious problems such as substance abuse and sexual activity. Again, these matters must be negotiated with all interested parties at the beginning of the caregiving sessions.

Relationship Caregiving

Periodically, a married couple or an entire family may wish to speak to the chaplain to resolve an issue. Confidentiality extends to the participants in different ways, depending on how the issue is discussed. Generally, couples and families hold privilege jointly. Unfortunately, things can get complicated if one individual tells the chaplain a

Fig. 13.3 When counseling couples, discuss possible scenarios regarding confidentiality before the sessions begin.

"secret" in an individual meeting. This possibility should be discussed ahead of time. The most conservative approach is to tell all parties involved that unless the information is shared in a meeting where the others are present, or permission to disclose has been given to the chaplain, the information must remain between the individual and the caregiver. It is very important to have the permission of everyone involved if the caregiver should decide to disclose any information. If he does not obtain permission by all, it is considered a breach in confidentiality, since all parties held the privilege.

If no marriage exists, for example a couple of friends or roommates are speaking with the chaplain, the confidentiality is not as assured. While the chaplain will not disclose without the permission of all involved, the non-married clients are free to discuss the information with anyone. This, again, should be made clear in the first caregiving session.

Deceased Clients

If a person happens to pass away that you have been a caregiver for, either presently or in the past, the privilege then transfers to the legal representative of the deceased. This does not mean that the chaplain should immediately share with a legal representative everything that the decedent had shared before his passing.

Referral To Another Caregiver

At times, because of the complexity of the case, time constraints, or out of need for a different skill set, the chaplain will refer those in his mission field to other caregivers. How is the desired end result then accomplished? Who shares with the new caregiver the information that the chaplain knows to this point? A waiver of privilege should be written out by the person who is bring referred, allowing the community

246

minister to share freely with the new caregiver. If, after you refer the individual to the new caregiver, you become aware of something that would be helpful for the new caregiver to know, it must be accomplished in this manner. Call the new caregiver, identify yourself, state that you understand that the caregiver can not acknowledge that any particular person is a client, but that you want to provide some information if only the caregiver will listen. Most likely, the caregiver will agree. After all, any information can be helpful. It is important not to ask the other caregiver to make any comments about the information. After you are finished, the other caregiver is legally allowed to thank you, nothing further. What the caregiver does with that information then becomes a matter of professional judgment.

In the discussion above, many examples of situations were explored when a chaplain may need to divulge certain information for the protection of an individual in his mission field or others. It is actually rare that a community minister will ever breach confidentiality. The text will now examine the information that cannot be shared by the chaplain. We have already acknowledged the confidentiality of information that is obtained from associates in the mission field. There are two other areas that must be discussed regarding confidentiality.

Do not use confidential information for personal gain or to the detriment of community ministry. Confidential information about your ministry should not be disclosed to unauthorized people, such as reporters. Inquiries from the media should be considered requests for confidential information. All information considered confidential must remain so until it is fully and properly disclosed to the public. Confidential information that is particularly sensitive includes, but is not limited to, records, knowledge of acquisitions and divestitures, new strategies and services, or financial information.

You must use confidential information only in a way that is related to the business activities of your ministry, during or after your ministry activity in the community. Confidential information should not be given to competitors, suppliers, contractors, or any other outside parties unless approved by written agreement.

As it can be seen, confidentiality is one of the main cornerstones of effective ministry. It is vital to protect the information about the individuals served and the inner-workings of the ministry. To do so will help to insure a long and fruitful ministry to the communities in America and around the world. It is equally important for the chaplain to understand when he is allowed to breach confidentiality and the circumstances which mandate a breach. In so doing, effective ministry which honors Christ can be accomplished.

Stories From the Field: #10
"Do You Ever Hear Any Juicy Gossip?"*

*As chaplains, we have to remember that we are in a **marathon** of kindness and patience with our people, not a **wind sprint**. They are the ones who control the boundaries. We respond to their overtures, trusting God to move them our direction. I have a personal example.*

In the first two weeks of making my rounds, I stopped by "Mary's" house. She surprised me by asking directly, "Do you ever hear any juicy gossip?!" I looked cautiously to my left and then to my right and asked, "Can you keep a secret?" She leaned in closer and eagerly and enthusiastically responded, "Yes!!!" I paused, looked at her and said, "...So can I!" We both laughed. As I continued to see her on my weekly rounds, she was friendly; but our conversations were superficial, with her controlling the boundaries and shutting the door to spiritual things.

*About **a year** after the unusual question she had initially posed to me, she presented me with a life issue and qualified it with, "I know I can trust you with this, because you're not going to tell anybody." Although she trusted me with her concern, the circumstance and logistics prevented an opening to a spiritual discussion. I continued to see her on weekly rounds. About **a year after that**, I learned that she had surgery that revealed cancer. She had chosen not to tell me of her pending surgery, but she did tell a neighbor to tell me after the fact. When I contacted her, she was gracious and accepting. She told me that the follow up exams declared her to be cancer free. In the course of my conversation and celebration with her, she exclaimed, "Thank God!"*

*That was the prompting/opening that I had been looking for! I echoed her thanks and asked for permission to look a little closer at what she had just said. Without reservation, she gave me permission. In the course of our discussion, I presented the Gospel and she prayed to receive Jesus! This came after **two years and eight months** of making rounds! This calculated to about **125 contacts** with her! Sometimes in our zeal, we're tempted to attempt to expedite our Mission Statement. We can't create or expedite what God chooses to do in His time. We are just to be ready for the opportunity. It may appear at the 125th contact.*

– Submitted By: Gene R.
Indianapolis, IN

*Individuals in this story have granted permission for its use.

Stories From the Field: #11
"A Cry For Help"*

This past week, I was paged during rounds. It was the sister of one of my co-workers. When I returned the call to the number in the message, my associate's Mom answered. She was crying. When I met with her, I learned that the 12-year-old non-biological daughter, of whom she had custody, had broken into her neighbor's house and had stolen almost all of the clothes in her closet and slipped out the back door. Although Rita, the mother, did not believe she could have done it, when the police officer first confronted her, she felt a nudge from the Holy Spirit that her daughter Celia might be guilty. She looked and looked and finally found the stolen clothes. After being made aware of the family history and her concern that this was not the first time, they asked me to go up and talk with her.

Celia knew me, as I had sat with her in the waiting room of a hospital months earlier when her step-cousin by another marriage was in the hospital for a broken arm. We had built rapport at that time. Her step-mom, my co-worker, was no longer married to her Dad, but she had kept in touch with the biological mother somewhat and had given Celia's address to her biological mother, who was now sending her letters which Rita (Celia's step-non-biological grandmother) just learned about. Although the biological father sees her some, he basically just buys her expensive clothing, like what she stole, and lets her do things she is not allowed to do at home. Obviously, she had many things that needed to be addressed through counseling, but I was able to determine that this appeared to be the first time that she had stolen anything or done something like this.

As we talked, I was able to learn that she had done this for attention because Rita's mother had just passed away, and her mother, who was grieving, had been spending less time with her. While I was talking to her, she started talking about her grandmother that just passed away. With her permission, I asked her if she knew she would go to Heaven if she were to die today. She said yes, but when asked what she would say if she were to die and stand before Jesus, and He were to ask her why He should let her into Heaven, she could not answer. In talking to her, I was able to ascertain that she was not just sorry she got caught, but sorry that she had stolen. That deep-felt remorse made it easy to talk about the consequences of her actions, especially sin. Because of the trouble she was in, I had her undivided attention. I talked to her about how just as it only takes her stealing once to be a thief, it only takes us sinning once to be a sinner, even though we all fall short of the glory of God much, much more than that. I shared The Steps To Peace With God booklet from memory, and she was ready to ask Jesus for forgiveness and to be her Lord and Savior. I then shared what she had given permission for me to share with her mother.

I walked with her and her aunt to the neighbor's house to return the stolen clothes and jewelry and to apologize. They were Christians and were comforted to learn that she was saved as a result of this wake-up call. They were more hurt because she did this than if it had been a stranger, and they didn't want to press charges. I went back the next day to be with the family when she talked to the police officer, who filed a report, to be reviewed by the district attorney since burglary is a felony. She made a written statement. She will likely just be required to go to counseling, which I went ahead and helped arrange with a children's Christian Behavioral Psychologist the next day. I will go with her to court when it is scheduled, but it will likely be four weeks away. She was given a Bible and discipleship material, and Rita was given a book on raising children by Focus On the Family and on grief. Rita and the aunt asked me not to tell my associate. However, they changed their minds several days later, and my co-worker came up and hugged me while I was doing rounds in another part of the building and had her Mom, Rita, on the phone.

– Submitted By: Sherry K.
Charlotte, NC

*Individuals in this story have granted permission for its use.

Questions

Reflect on the Stories From the Field found in this chapter and answer the following questions:
1. How would you handle the situation that was described?
2. What information found in the story is confidential?
3. What information found in the story can be shared with others? With whom may this information be shared? Under what circumstances may this information be shared?
4. How does the information found in this chapter pertain to the story?

---------------------- End Notes ----------------------

1. "Ethical Principles of Psychologists and Code of Conduct: Record Keeping and Fees (6.01),"
    American Psychological Association (APA) <http://www.apa.org/ethics/code2002.html
    #6_01> (Accessed 25 April 2005).

2. "Ethical Principles of Psychologists and Code of Conduct: Privacy and Confidentiality
    (4.05)," *American Psychological Association (APA)* <http://www.apa.org/ethics/code
    2002.html#4_05> (Accessed 25 April 2005).

3. "California Evidence Code: Article 7-Psychotherapist-Patient Privilege (Section 1010-27),"
    Section1024 < http://www.aroundthecapitol.com/code/code.html?sec=evid&code section
    =1010-1027> (Accessed 1 November 2005).

4. "California Civil Code (Section 43-53)," Section 43.92 (a) <http://www.leginfo.ca.gov/
    cgi-bin/displaycode?section=civ&group=00001-01000&file=43-53> (Accessed 1 November
    2005).

5. "California Civil Code (Section 43-53)," Section 43.92 (b) <http://www.leginfo.ca.gov/
    cgi-bin/displaycode?section=civ&group=00001-01000&file=43-53> (Accessed 1 November
    2005).

6. "California Penal Code: Child Abuse and Neglect Reporting Act (Section 11164-11174.3),"
    <http://www.leginfo.ca.gov/cgi-bindisplaycode?section=pen&group=11001-12000&file=
    11164-11174.3> (Accessed November 1 2005).

7. "California Penal Code: Reports of Injuries (Section 11160-11163.6)" <http://www.leginfo.
    ca.gov/cgi-bin/displaycode?section=pen&group=11001-12000&file=11160-11163.6> (Accessed 1
    November 2005).

8. "California Penal Code: Reports of Injuries (Section 11160-11163.6)," Section 11161.8 <http://
    www.leginfo.ca.gov/cgi-bin/displaycode?section=pen&group=11001-12000&file=
    11160-11163.6> (Accessed 1 November 2005).

Chapter Fourteen

The Role of Availability in Community Chaplaincy

CHAPTER FOURTEEN

The Role of Availability in Community Chaplaincy

———————————————— Objectives ————————————————

During the course of this chapter, we will examine the following:

- List the main components of availability in community ministry

- Define availability to God

- Decipher methods to be available to those in the mission field

- Examine ways to be available to yourself and your family

- Determine strategies for preventing over-availability and burnout

A ndrew Carnegie made his fortune in steel manufacturing. He was asked how he had the ability to select and surround himself with good people. He said that finding good people was like digging for gold. "When you dig for gold," he said, "you have to move tons and tons of dirt for a few ounces of gold. But you never go looking for dirt; you only go looking for gold."[1] We have to make ourselves available to God. We may have to move lots of dirt in our lives; but if we look for the gold, we will find it.

We often resist dependence on God. American culture has taught us to be self-reliant; dependence or the need for others is associated with weakness. According to David Seamands, in his book *Healing Grace*, researchers agree that self-reliance is a dominant cultural value in America.[2] Compare an elderly American man who is dependent on his children for support with an elderly Chinese in a similar situation. The Chinese, whose society does not idealize self-reliance, is proud of his children and brags on how good they are to him. The American is ashamed and does not want anyone to know. He wants to boast of his independence from his children. He would rather get a loan from a bank than from a relative. He tends to apologize for bothering his friends when something breaks down. Self-reliance is quite contrary to grace, for grace is free for the asking; it is God-reliant. Extreme self-reliance makes us try to be our own saviors and sustainers. It is hard for Americans to think any good could come out of a dependent relationship, but that is what grace is all about. The ideal of self-sufficiency, deeply ingrained in most Americans, causes many Christians to take the very means of grace and put themselves on the performance treadmill. While they may use the language of grace, at a deep gut level they live as if their salvation and security depend on how much they read or pray or give or work or witness.

Individualism, a highly prized American value, is best expressed in "doing your own thing". We are now seeing ridiculous extremes in the interpretation of the U.S. Constitution because of an excessive emphasis on individualism. Individualism is the theme of many great American novelists, such as Ernest Hemmingway. In the 1985 bestseller, *Habits of the Heart: Individualism and Commitment in American Life*, Robert Bellah and his colleagues glorify various aspects of American individualism that make it possible for a person to get ahead on his own initiative, in the pursuit of wealth or self-expression.[3] Scripture gives attention to the individual. This is balanced by an emphasis on God's actions of both love and judgment upon families, communities, and nations. In the New Testament, saving grace is always relational and is found only in the fellowship of Christ and His people. There are no Lone-Ranger Christians, and the term "saints" is never used in the singular. Grace is received and lived out in the community of faith. Too many people regard religion as one more avenue for self-discovery and self-realization, rather than a vehicle of grace that allows Christ to reign within them for living in a grace relationship with others.

A number of cultural anthropologists have pointed to American activism as an optimistic view of effort. "You can do/be/get anything you really want to if you work hard enough. If at first you don't succeed, try, try again."[4] The demand to make something of yourself through work is a requirement Americans put upon themselves. Doing and obeying, being available to be used by God, are stressed throughout Scripture. We *are* to be "doers" as well as "hearers" of the Word (James 1:22 NASB). All manner of good works are enjoined upon us, but never as a way of winning or earning God's approval. Christ died for us while we were powerless--still sinners--long before we could do anything to achieve our salvation (Romans 5:6-8). Redemption is a pure gift of grace and involves receiving rather than achieving. Good works are the consequence of being accepted, not the cause of it. They are our response to God's unconditional love. Americans regard approval, success, and status as rewards for performing well. When this value system is translated into the Christian life, salvation becomes a matter of our efforts. A cartoon picturing modern-day Pharisees was captioned, "We get our righteousness the old-fashioned way--we *earn* it!"[5] Americans have difficulty with grace!

How does the church play into this mindset? American activism has clearly infected the church's idea of success. The size and design of facilities, the amount of the annual budget, steady growth in membership, and numbers in attendance--these define a successful church or ministry. The health-and-wealth gospel proclaimed by many pastors and televangelists is the most extreme example of this. The name-it-and-claim-it variety shows that Christianity can literally be absorbed by the American worldview. No wonder the church is lampooned by secular comedians as promoting a blab-it-and-grab-it religion. To those who have been missionaries among the poor and oppressed, this twisted version of the gospel (health and wealth) is shocking. When you think of thousands of faithful Indian Christians, who own no land and are thus at the economic mercy of unbelieving neighbors, who sacrifice for their faith and struggle just to survive, it is appalling to hear the success-by-achievement gospel that can apply only to the affluent.

Fig. 14.1 The health and wealth gospel is being taught in many churches today.

A sermon based on the New Testament story of the Rich Young Ruler that was given an incredible conclusion is a good example. You recall how the young man refused Jesus' challenge to give away his possessions, take up his cross, and follow Him. The televangelist accurately called him a millionaire and then commented, "The poor fool! He didn't realize it, but if he had only obeyed Jesus and sacrificed his possessions, *Jesus would have made him a billionaire!*"[6] Certainly, most churches do not go to such extremes. But who can deny the emphasis on activity and the pressure of programming which is the accepted routine of the weekly church calendar? Or the minister's regular call for commitment to these activities to prove the depth of our Christian experience? Gradually the inference is that victorious Christian living depends on how well we perform in the church program. It is not hard to understand the average pastor's frustration. His responsibility is to keep things running and to raise the money to pay the bills and meet the denominational apportionments. When he sees this not happening because of the lack of commitment of his people, he tends to make "commitment" the theme of many sermons. As a result, the people think that commitment and performance are what Christianity is all about. A kind of faith-commitment becomes the work by which they can be justified!

All this is a far cry from the true gospel of undeserved and unearnable grace, which alone can put us into a right relationship with God so that we can be called children of God (I John 3:1). God's grace makes us worthwhile and valuable for who we are, and not because of what we successfully accomplish. The church's distorted gospel of activism and self-effort contributes greatly to the self-belittling and low sense of self-worth so many people feel. It is also a main source of guilt and shame. People are somehow made to feel guilty if they have not succeeded in every area of life--church activities, job, marriage, parenthood--or in trying to relate to someone with whom hardly anyone can get along. This is implied even in those situations that are obviously not our fault or under our control. One example of this is the way many churches look down on divorced persons--regardless of the cause--as if they are moral lepers. With the success-based "oughtness" of so many churches, it is easy to consider oneself a failure. This is as equally true for clergy as for laity.

Another aspect of the church's life which conflicts with biblical grace is an over-emphasis on *the individual Christian life apart from open grace-filled relationships with other people.* The New Testament always presumes that if we *receive* God's unconditional acceptance and grace, then we will always *give* the same kind of grace to other people. This means that the church should provide an atmosphere where this is possible. Most people are hesitant to let people get to know them; in church, we feel we always have to "put our best spiritual foot forward" and "keep our halos on straight". When this is combined with the success emphasis, most people are afraid and ashamed to share problems or weaknesses. Some close up from the sense of, "If I'm a Christian, I ought to be able to handle it myself."

Legalism has always been a problem for the church. The belief that salvation comes through keeping commandments and rules is as old as mankind and is the one basic falsehood behind every religious system in the world--that we can earn God's approval and love by keeping certain moral laws. Evangelical churches and pastors believe in and proclaim a doctrine of salvation by grace through faith and would not intentionally propagate salvation by works. The Sunday school lessons and sermons are sometimes not heard as messages of grace. The hearers filter them through our cultural and religious worldview and distort them into a contradictory gospel--a mixed message of grace and works, unconditional love and performance-based acceptance. Like all mixed messages, this one results in emotional and spiritual problems.

Making ourselves available to God is a choice. It is a choice we make everyday. I believe that each of us would say that we desire to be available to God. We want to be used by Him in the areas of life that we find ourselves. In order to increase our availability, it would be good to identify potential indicators of our unavailability. Revelation 2:4-15 takes a look at three indicators of potentially being unavailable to God. The first is a blurring of priorities. Take a look at verse 4. You have lost your first love. It is easy to lose track of what should be the priority in our life. We must not forsake our first love. We must not forsake our want and need to glorify God and lift Him up in all we do. We must not forsake the priority of keeping Christ central in our lives. Keep your priorities clear. Firmly plant Jesus in the center of your life. You will be available to him. The opportunities will arise.

Indicators of Being Unavailable to God

A compromising of purpose must be avoided. In other chapters, relationships are discussed. These relationships are built in the community for a single purpose: to be a Christ-like example to the population of the culture of America. These verses in Revelation address a group of people whose purpose of being (to glorify God) was compromised. We are to be salt and light. We are to be, ultimately, about bringing people to Jesus and growing them in their faith. A story is told about a man who walked into a Louisiana Circle K Store. He placed a $20 bill on the counter and asked for change. When the clerk opened the cash drawer, the man pulled a gun and demanded all the cash in the drawer. Rightly so, the cashier acted on his demand. The man took the cash from the clerk and fled. In his hurry to get out of the store, he left the original twenty on the counter. What did he get from the cash drawer? Fifteen dollars. It is clear that he forgot his purpose, which was to leave with more than he came. We need to make sure we keep our purpose clear.

A weakening of passion is also shown to be a symptom of being less than fervent for God. Revelation 3:15-16 states that God hates for us to be lukewarm. The church discussed in this passage had lost its passion. We must fight complacency. We must approach every day with a sense of anticipation of what God can do in our own lives and through us to minister to others. We need to be looking around with a "what do you have in store today, God?" attitude. We must fight the want to "settle in" and keep stretching. We must resist getting comfortable at the expense of being courageous.

Andrew Carnegie searched for precious metal. Others have searched for stones that are of great value. It has been said that diamonds are forever. We have the opportunity as community chaplains to live a life of opportunity. Let me reiterate: We are speaking about available living. This availability needs to be where we are. If we think it is someplace else, doing something else, we will miss the opportunities we encounter. There was once the folk story of a South African farmer who dreamed of the day he could spend his time searching for diamonds. He kept putting it off, feeling he needed to take care of his farm and the responsibilities that entailed. Finally, he made the

Fig. 14.2 Our availability to God begins where we are.

choice. He sold his farm. He took the proceeds and used them to fund his diamond hunt. Several years later, the largest diamond mine in the history of South Africa was discovered. This former farmer turned diamond miner did not discover it, but he did have something to do with it. You see, this incredible mine was unearthed on the farmland he had sold. This man who wanted so badly to find his wealth in diamonds never thought about beginning where he was. Our availability to God begins where we are. Let us explore how we can increase our availability immediately.

Increasing Availability

We can increase our availability to God's call to the community around us by living our lives every day for Him. In Acts 3:1-10, Peter and John did not know it, but they were about to be used by God. As they went to the Temple, they passed a man begging for alms. They did not realize that they were going to be used as a result of simply paying attention in the course of their everyday lives. What they were doing was part of their "to do" list. It was routine living. Let us face the facts. Much of life is routine. We find ourselves doing the same things each day. What we have to see is that buried in this routine are the "diamonds" of opportunity. Each one of us is an investment made by God, right where we are. He has intentionally diversified these investments. He has investments in businesses, schools, and even the political offices all around the world. The return on His investment will be dictated by our willingness to make ourselves available to Him where we are, as we are. If we simply look for opportunities to minister, we will see them. As Peter and John entered, the beggar asked them for money. The opportunity presented itself. They may not have recognized it if they had not been looking for it. We know they went to the temple every day. We know the beggar was there every day, but on this day they had an encounter. It is not unlikely that they had passed him before. It would have been easy for him to become "furniture," a fixture in the scene. Peter and John seemed to be opportunity finders; so when it was presented, they acted on it. Each of us has only one day at a time. No day is just another day, another routine twenty-four hours. This day, any day, may contain your golden opportunity, perhaps even the opportunity of a lifetime. You may make a decision today that will affect the rest of your life. Be alert!

As a community caregiver, it is crucial to keep Jesus in the center of everything that you do; or better stated, be in the center of what He would have you do. Peter and John brought Jesus right into the equation. This beggar expected to get something, but the something he expected was not given. However, the unexpected he received overcame all his expectations. He was going to get to walk! Jesus is the genuine difference maker. When he is firmly planted in the center of our lives, we are transformed. Our days are transformed. Our ideas are transformed. Our routines are transformed.

Part of the purpose of being available to Christ is to go where others may not be accepted. A chaplain has access to a group of people with which church pastors will not gain an audience: the people with whom you interact on a daily basis that will never come to a church service. One function of the community minister is to help others reach the potential that they have in Christ. Peter and John helped this beggar to reach his potential, the purpose that God had in mind for him when he was created. He probably never thought walking was an option, but the power of God made this option available to him. This is how God uses us when we are available. We can help many discover unrealized potential. People can have cold hearts warmed. People can have discouraged lives encouraged. People can have the sin in their life eradicated. We can be the bearers of that potentially radical, unleashing power.

Being available to God means investing in other people. Our natural tendency is to invest in our own interests. The only thing that God will save out of this world is people. Nothing else is going to be worth anything. We need to invest in people. Invest in their attitudes, aptitudes, and abilities. Small investments made over an extended period of time will pay huge dividends. Who are you investing in? There are three questions that I periodically ask myself as a chaplain:

- What difference have I made in the life of _____ this week?
- How would each person in my mission field answer the following question: My chaplain has made a difference in my life by _____.
- How would each person in my mission field answer the following question: My chaplain has been a walking advertisement for what it is like to have a relationship with Jesus by_____.

Are you available? Use care so that you do not miss what God has for you, simply because you get caught up in the habit of life. What is God calling you to? There are at least four callings on your life:

- God is calling you to be saved and know the truth. According to I Timothy 2:2-3, this is God's will for you. Jesus said many are called, but few are chosen.
- God's plan for you as an individual, and for the church universal, is to become like Christ in character. He is calling you to a life of purity and holiness. In a passage about marriage, Paul explains this purpose. Jesus died on the cross with the purpose of making believers holy and blameless. He is in the process of cleaning up your mess (Ephesians 5:25-26).
- God has called every one of us to go and make disciples. Make no mistake about it. This is your calling. You may do it in a variety of ways, but that is what you are to be about (Matthew 28:18-20).

■ God is calling you to use your abilities and gifts to serve him in a specific way. You may not know the whole plan, but God has a vocation for you. He is calling you and will supply you with direction at the right time. He is perhaps calling you to be a godly, influential politician. He may be calling you to serve with a Christ-like life in a fast-food restaurant. Several of you may be called to live out your lives in full time Christian ministry in the marketplace. We all have a calling to serve in and through the church in some fashion.

Once we accept the call to be available for God to minister in the community, we must make sure that we remain available to God. This comes through spending time with Him, being close to Him.

The chaplain needs to make himself available to God for several reasons. First, God created you, the mission field, and the world in which you will serve. His very existence commands spending time with Him out of a loving response. Jesus Himself gave the example of the importance of spending time with the Heavenly Father. Time spent with God helps the community minister to produce evidence of eternal life. The more time spent with Christ, the more like Him you will become. This is the task of the chaplain: to be a living example of what it is like to have a relationship with Christ and of the spiritual maturation that follows. There are some common hindrances to maintaining the faith walk of the chaplain. Some of these "distractions" are seemingly noble and ministry-related but still take focus away from spending time with God. Ministry itself can keep the community chaplain so busy that ministry begins to happen in the flesh, because no time is spent with God. Success and ministry experience, if we are not careful, can lead to pride and the belief that we can minister through our own power. Making yourself available to God, first through surrendering to the call to ministry and then through daily surrender to spending time with Him, is crucial to effective ministry.

In addition to being available to God, the successful chaplain will be available to the people in his mission field. This can be a tiring prospect. How can this be accomplished without draining the minister? Let us take a good look at that aspect of community chaplaincy. Chaplains are found in so many locations today that having access to those in need of a relationship with Christ is only limited by the limitations we place in our minds. The growing awareness of spiritual needs in crisis has begun to formalize the response of disaster relief chaplains. National and international disaster relief agencies are beginning to work together to coordinate spiritual care response in disasters of many kinds. With technological advances and the globalization of America, relief agencies have recognized the need to redefine the arena of disasters. It is no longer only the site/location directly impacted by the disaster, but now includes remote locations, institutions, and people groups who are in some way related or impacted by the disaster (e.g., the departure and arrival airports, the out-of-state corporate headquarters, the home church of the children in the bus, the manufacturer and factory of the faulty electrical switch). The need for spiritual and emotional support far exceeds the disaster location, hospital, or disaster shelter. Since crises and disasters happen at all times of the day and night and at any location, the availability of the chaplain is crucial.

One of the methods that a chaplain can use in order to be available to his mission field is pastoral care. The definition of pastoral care is derived from the biblical image of the shepherd who cares for a flock. In a very broad and inclusive way, pastoral care incorporates all pastoral ministries that are concerned with the care and nurturing of people and their relationships within a community. This could include the classic approaches—interpretation, prayer, meditation, presence, listening, and reflection. In disasters, pastoral care is often pictured as providing a calm presence, nonjudgmental listening, and caring interventions.

Availability and Disasters

There are times when a disaster of some sort happens in corporate America. This can take the form of a traffic accident with a fatality, a chemical spill, acts of terrorism, or even the financial collapse of a company that leads to layoffs. The chaplain will need to be available during these times of crisis. The American Red Cross reports that 59 percent of Americans would be likely to seek counsel from a spiritual care provider during a disaster.[7] Pastoral caregiving in the wake of disasters is the integration of spiritual care in the framework

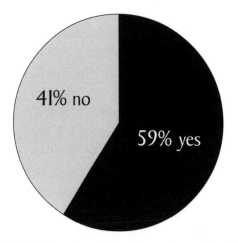

Fig. 14.3 Percentage of Americans who would seek counsel from a spiritual provider during a disaster.

Fig. 14.4 Times of crisis can be a pathway for the gospel.

of established crisis intervention principles. W. E. Vine defines being moved with compassion as being moved in one's inwards (bowels).[8] The *splanchna* are the entrails of the body. Modern vernacular might translate this as having deep feelings in one's "gut". This is the center of one's personal feelings and emotions—love and hate—the feelings that emanate from one's "heart". When the gospels speak of Jesus' compassion, they speak of deep, powerful emotions that far exceed the superficial feelings of regret, distress, or remorse.

The English word "compassion" comes from two Latin words, "cum" and "pati", which form the meaning, "suffer with." It is ". . . a feeling of deep sympathy and sorrow for another who is stricken by suffering or misfortune, accompanied by a strong desire to alleviate the pain or remove its cause".[9] Compassion asks us to go where it hurts, to enter into places of pain, to share in brokenness, fear, confusion, and anguish. Compassion challenges us to cry out with those in misery, to mourn with those who are lonely, to weep with those in tears. Compassion requires us to be weak with the weak, vulnerable with the vulnerable, and powerless with the powerless. Compassion means full immersion in the condition of being human. Compassion enters into the suffering and pain of the one who suffers. It is more honorable than pity and more courageous than sympathy. Complete empathy for the desolation and grief of those who are suffering requires compassion. The effective chaplain must know his or her own biases, needs, and limitations and still deeply desire to identify with the disenfranchised and the wounded, seeking to demonstrate the compassion of Christ as the priority of chaplain ministry. Merely attempting to prevent suffering or trying to not be the cause of suffering will be inadequate.

The effective chaplain must approach ministry from a radically different paradigm. The chaplain must initiate and be an active participant in "being" compassion as a priority and "doing" compassion as a necessity. Recognizing one's own natural instinct to excuse oneself from the crisis, the chaplain must still choose to become engaged in the suffering. The significance of being compassionate may lay in the fact that being compassionate is not an activity one naturally seeks, but an activity that one must intentionally choose, knowing that it "feels" contrary to natural instincts.

The theological foundation for community chaplaincy is supported through the mandate to bear one another's burdens (see Galatians 6:28); and therefore, "You must be compassionate, just as your Father is compassionate" (Luke 6:36 NLT). The cup of cool water and the Good Samaritan also reinforce this imperative. The ministry of pastoral care has often been called "the ministry of presence". A major premise of pastoral care amid crisis is presence. The care of souls first requires being there. A simple, empathic, listening presence is a primary pastoral act, the presupposition of all other pastoral acts. The power of this ministry is in its altruistic service. If chaplains provide compassion by bearing another's burdens, then chaplains choose to "suffer with" those who are suffering. Providing compassion requires stepping out of one's comfort zone and intentionally entering a place of crisis—danger, pain, loss, or grief—during the spiritual and emotional crises of life.

Not only is the chaplain available to God, but God is available to the chaplain. The strength of a caregiving relationship is in the fact that one is never alone. God is present with the chaplain. The presence of God within the ministry situation empowers the pastoral caregiver to provide effective, appropriate spiritual support within the context of crises. It is the compassionate God who chooses to be God-with-us. The chaplain represents the presence of God. The heroes of the faith had one thing in common: They were all ordinary people with no power of their own. The difference is the mighty presence of God. Times may change, but the effect of God's presence remains the same. Chaplains who enter into the suffering and chaos of crisis are empowered by the same presence of God to give them victory over despair, loss, and insufficiency. The chaplain shares God's presence with victims and offers the same words of assurance—"I am with you." The chaplain cannot deny the reality of the crisis, should not minimize the sense of loss it causes, and may not be able to diminish any of the pain. However, the chaplain offers the comfort of God's presence through words of comfort and assurance. Presence may invite a sense of community within the crisis, may lead to healing reconciliation, or may reconnect a disenfranchised person with God.

A chaplain will be available in disasters by demonstrating compassion and by being present in suffering. Sometimes like a "wounded healer", he or she sits among the wounded to bind and unbind his or her own wounds slowly and carefully, so that he will be able to immediately respond to bear the burden of another who is suffering. The chaplain in disasters practices the presence of God through prayer, listening, the spoken word, the Holy Scriptures, and service. In the moment of crisis, many who are suffering desire an advocate who will plead their case before God, and in the prayer, they find comfort and assurance that God hears their plea. During the crisis, victims need to tell their stories and have validation of their feelings and sense of loss. Here the chaplain in disasters practices the presence of God in active listening and the spoken word. Often the crisis requires acts of service. Practicing the presence of God is experienced in feeding the hungry, giving a drink to the thirsty, showing hospitality to strangers, clothing the naked, and visiting the sick (see Matthew 25:35-40). In the aftermath of crisis, worship or remembrance bring healing and closure to the intense suffering and acute pain of loss.

"Presence" is one of the most powerful acts of ministry a chaplain in crisis can provide. Demonstrating compassion by physical and spiritual presence is the beginning of the relationship that brings comfort and healing. In many cultures, establishing and reestablishing the relationship by physical presence is primary to even general conversation. When words have no relevance and actions have no meaning, the Emmanuel—God with us—suffering with the victim may be the most potent act of the chaplain in disasters.

Fig. 14.5 The effective chaplain will be available to people of all cultures.

The effective chaplain will be available to people of all cultures. There is tension in balancing cultural acceptance and uncompromising convictions. With the deteriorating influence of the church in culture and the globalization of society, the tension rises for people of deep faith and convictions. As globalization increases, cultural diversity increases. We live in a multicultural society that is very diverse, but chaplains must not hesitate to demonstrate compassion by ministry action. They must actively search out those in crisis, making no distinction of race, gender, religion, or economic status.

Their actions must speak of kindness and mercy borne out of compassion for all people.

Most of us sense the ability of people to respond to the needs of those less fortunate, but what of the more fortunate—those of higher position, status, or social class? Human diversity includes the rich and famous. Neither political alignment nor religious position must prevent chaplains in disasters from providing compassionate ministry action. Chaplains in disasters may even be called upon to minister to those whose political or religious prominence may be intimidating or abhorrent. Chaplains in disasters, too, may be called upon to offer caring ministry to the outcasts of society—the homeless, the addicted, the incarcerated, the "leper". Sensitivity to human diversity means doing ministry with the disenfranchised of society.

One of the challenges chaplains in disasters will certainly face is a ministry encounter with people who do not come directly under their usual sphere of responsibility, possibly the friends or family members of those in his mission field. The community minister will leverage these opportunities to extend care to those who are valued by those in his area of influence, thereby exponentially increasing his mission field. During a disaster, the chaplain assumes the "anyway" attitude of providing care, crossing the barrier of assumed responsibility, and ministering to victims "anyway".

Doing practical acts of ministry care is perhaps the most obvious demonstration of compassion. Most chaplains who enter the ministry as pastoral caregivers in disasters desire to "help" those in need. "Help" is the active verb which means to give assistance or support, to make more bearable, to give relief, to change for the better, or to serve with food or drink. Often the "help" is presence and encouragement; but equally often it is the action of "helping" by the practical acts of giving something to eat or drink, providing shelter or clothing, looking after, and doing deeds of kindness (see Matthew 25:34-40).

The chaplain who desires to be effective and available in disasters, and who seeks to provide the ministry of care in crisis, must have a servant's heart. The chaplain may be a person of authority, a person of resources, or a person of prominence, but his or her response must grow out of the attitude of a servant. The chaplain must demonstrate compassion in servanthood in the same way Jesus fully identified Himself with humanity in His incarnation, giving up privileged position, heavenly wealth, and divine independence. Robert Greenleaf says that the best test of this servant attitude is: "Do those served grow as people? Do they, while being served, become healthier [has their level of stress been mitigated?], wiser [have the circumstances been clarified?], freer, more autonomous [more able to cope with the crisis or disaster?], more likely themselves to become servants? And, what is the effect on the least privileged in society [the direct victims of disaster]; will they benefit [was there compassion demonstrated in ministry action?], or, at least, not be further deprived?"[10]

During crisis and disaster, people often respond in fear, confusion, or anxiety over such issues as their vulnerability, their grief, and their loss of trust in the natural order of life. A significant demonstration of compassion in the ministry of care in crisis is providing encouragement through words and actions. The chaplain in disasters must be able to convey encouragement to a soul that is despairing by saying, "... Take courage! It is I. Don't be afraid ..." (Mark 6:50 NIV). In the midst of the storms of life—the disasters, the crisis, and the devastation—the chaplain must bring the assurance of hope. Victims may not understand and they may be "astonished", but they will experience the compassionate encouragement of the chaplain.

Victims of disasters "tend to feel anxious and upset because of their apparent helplessness to deal with the situation. A crisis may erupt when a person is faced with a problem that calls on resources or problem-solving abilities that have not been needed before. In other words, they lack experience in dealing with the situation."[11] In situations such as this, the chaplain in disasters provides encouragement by listening, dialoguing, comforting, and clarifying. In the crisis and confusion, the chaplain provides active listening to hear the fears, frustrations, and disappointment. He engages in dialogue as he asks probing questions for self-examination and reflection. He comforts in the silent spaces. He clarifies by examining circumstances and options; then, he releases the victims, empowered to move forward in spiritual and physical healing.

Available chaplains step onto the disaster site, and their reaction is often, "What can I do?" They want to meet the immediate needs of victims. While being present in the suffering of disaster victims and demonstrating sensitivity to human diversity are essential, chaplains also have a deep desire to meet immediate needs. Chaplains often join with disaster relief teams to provide food to the hungry, water to the thirsty, medical care to the injured, shelter for the homeless, and clothing to the exposed. They meet the immediate needs of assistance in searches, rescues, and victim assessments. "There are no atheists in foxholes," reads the bumper sticker. In crisis, even the nonreligious person cries out in desperate prayer, "Oh, God!" In the crisis of disasters and devastation, victims often ask for the ministry of prayer. Christians believe that when

Romans 8:26

"... we do not know how to pray as we should, but the Spirit Himself intercedes for us with groanings too deep for words" (Romans 8:26 NASB). The victim of disaster often sees the chaplain as God's representative and desires "a word of prayer". In anxious moments there is peace in prayer, and chaplains offer the ministry of care through prayer. When chaplains pray for victims, they must remember three things: "First, whenever we long for and pray for the well-being of other people, we are only asking of God what God already longs for far more than we. Second, if we are to be friends of God, we must tell God what we want for others as surely as we must ask God for ourselves, without worrying about the appropriateness of our asking or the probability that what we ask for we will receive. Third, where it is possible, if our prayers are to be true acts of friendship,

Fig. 14.6 The chaplain in disaster will offer the arms of God to those in need.

we must not only pray for others, we must act in accordance with our own prayer." The chaplain in disasters provides caring ministry through prayerful intercession even when fear grips his or her own heart, attending to the victim's perceived need before his or her own.

As the representative of God, the chaplain in disasters ministers to all who are wounded and hurting in crises and emergencies. Unlike the local minister who primarily ministers to his own flock, the disaster chaplain's flock is any who are victimized. As the disaster relief chaplain steps onto the field of disaster, he or she offers the arms of God, hears the cries of distress, and provides informal but personalized prayers that are highly effective and comforting.

The available chaplain will face the task of willingly entering the field of disaster and discomfort to stand with those who have been hurt and suffer losses. Assessing the needs of this "flock" of victims, the chaplain must lead them to resources that will nourish their spirits and calm their trembling hearts. This chaplain must walk alongside, listen to the story, promote a sense of safety and security, and allow the overflow of God's grace in his own life to spill into the emptiness of those in need.

As a minister, the chaplain in disasters may lead religious services or memorial services. These services may occur in makeshift facilities, in the middle of rubble, or standing outside the morgue. Frequently, the ministries are brief and simple—urgent, but meeting the immediate need. The chaplain will be God's voice, healing, reconciling, confronting, and offering hope. Through prayer for the hurt and needy, the chaplain in disasters assumes the role of minister for people of every faith and religious tradition. Invoking God's presence, wisdom, power, and grace, the chaplain intercedes for victims, rescue workers, and concerned people around the world. Individual prayers, formal prayers, corporate prayers—all are utilized and all are appreciated. There are no denominations, no religions, and no sects—only loss.

The ministry of disaster relief is a response to the command: "Bear one another's burdens, and thereby fulfill the law of Christ" (Galatians 6:2 NASB). The word for "burden" (baros) means literally "a heavy weight or stone" someone is required to carry for a long distance. Figuratively it came to mean any oppressive ordeal or hardship that was difficult to bear. Everyone has burdens, but the burdens that result from emergencies and major disasters are often more than one is able to bear alone. Carrying the heavy weight of death, loss of home, or destruction of property is an oppressive ordeal that is difficult to bear alone. God does not intend for us to carry them by ourselves in isolation from our brothers and sisters. The myth of self-sufficiency is not a mark of bravery but rather a sign of pride, strength at the point of exhaustion to those who are weary. The chaplain in disasters demonstrates compassion, for it is a heart of compassion that bears another's burdens (see Colossians 3:12-13).

Differences Between the Pastor and the Chaplain in Disasters

There are differences in making yourself available for chaplaincy, as opposed to the local church pastorate. First of all, the community chaplain is very different in ministry type. Ministering within religious diversity is in sharp contrast to that of one church congregation. The community minister will encounter situations that require specialized and continuous education. A chaplain will be available for many different kinds of needs. A list could include some of the following:

- Hospital visitation
- Stress management
- Problems with wayward children
- Conflict resolution
- Marriage
- Remarriage
- Divorce
- Serious illnesses
- AIDS and related illnesses
- Death and dying
- Spousal and child abuse
- Drug and alcohol dependency
- Psychiatric issues
- Smooth transition of laid off employees
- Financial and budgeting matters
- Assisting supervisors with attraction and retention issues
- Pre-marital counseling
- Ceremony officiating
- Courtroom testimony and support
- Planning and performing funeral services
- Long term grief support
- Fears of national, state, and local terrorist activity

The Ministry of Presence

While many of these areas do require specialized training, many of these issues can receive help through the ministry of presence. Simply being there, being available for the person in crisis has value. It is important for ministers to take the time to listen to those who are grieving. The concept of a "ministry of presence" is vital for those involved in ministering to grief stricken families. A ministry of presence is best described as watching out for those suffering loss of any sort. The minister has to be attentive to the children and adults suffering the loss. All too often, ministers "drive by," offer some official rhetoric, verse of ritual, and then leave. Ministry of presence is about listening, waiting, respecting the silences, and, as the family (or individual) moves with the minister in that journey, to do prayer, communion, confession, rituals, etc. There are times that a person does not need for us to say anything or do anything other than to let them cry on our shoulders. Many people have reported how, in an

271

Fig. 14.7 A visit or letter from the chaplain can make a world of difference in the life of an inmate.

attempt to fill the gap of silence, others have said things that were inappropriate or hurtful and would have been better left unspoken.

If a picture is worth a thousand words, then a pleasant smile and a warm handshake has to be worth at least a million words to a prison inmate before the visitor even opens his or her mouth to say a cheerful "Hi!" Like Jesus hung on the cross, graphically illustrating to the world that God loves all people, so also a visitor's very presence speaks volumes in that the visitor is identifying with the prison inmate, not with the crime. A pleasant smile is visible evidence that someone cares and a warm handshake is tangible evidence that someone cares. To add to that, a cheerful "Hi!" is audible evidence that someone cares. The gift of presence was described by an inmate to a men's prayer breakfast some years ago as follows, "A letter once a week or a visit once a month is as important to a prison inmate as your paycheck once a week or once a month." Even a picture postcard from a vacation trip adds color to the barren cell walls. Know that the gift of presence is a gift that is not free. Consider the example of visiting a person in jail. The visitor not only used fuel out of the tank and put other wear on the car, but also took time out of his or her busy schedule - time from family, hobbies, tinkering in the shop, sports fishing down by the river, quiet time reading a book, or meditating on something inspirational. Although that time can never be returned, it is not lost time. The prison inmate will remember those precious moments together and cherish them, knowing that the visitor cared when it seemed that the entire world was against them. When they feel that family and friends have forgotten, forsaken, and rejected them, they feel like a one-person team against the rest of the world. That is a hard game to play. Prison is a hard place to survive psychologically. Frequently, the news broadcasts the fact that another inmate committed suicide but fails to report that the inmate felt the world had nothing more to offer. A visit or a letter from a friend is priceless, because a positive self-image can no more be purchased than love can be legislated. The visit not only lets an inmate know he is loved; the presence of a dear family member or cheerful friend builds self-esteem, which is difficult to do in a setting that tends to squeeze out love and where forgiveness is almost non-existent. A visitor is a divine gift!

Making Rounds

A specific way to be available to those in your mission field is to build relation-ships with them through prescribed methods. A common term used to describe this method is "rounds". Much like a doctor does rounds in a hospital to visit with patients, check the status of each patient, and prescribe a change in course of treatment as necessary, a chaplain can perform rounds. The chaplain can spend a few minutes with each person as he or she walks through the place of ministry, be it a neighborhood, a place of employment, a jail, a sports field, or a children's home. You can accomplish several objectives while performing rounds. The purposes and procedures for effective rounds can be a valuable study for the community minister. It is imperative that a strict schedule of rounds be maintained. People will note consistency. All of your locations realize that your schedule will change in the event of hospital or court visits. Please remember that you must contact those whom you were scheduled to see if you are not going to be on your regular rounds schedule *for any reason*. Let them know that the rounds will be made up as soon as possible.

There are four major purposes of rounds. The first is to establish a relationship with the people in your community. This is a time of introduction and getting to know each other. The people get to know you and vice versa. The fact that some of the population will not like or react well to chaplains is covered in another chapter. Once the relationships are established, they must then be strengthened and reinforced. This, along with increased credibility, happens with consistency of rounds. Next, rounds enable you to minister to individuals in times of crises. Because of your availability in the physical location of the hurting person, he or she will be more likely to utilize the chaplaincy service. Finally, you will be able to realize the ultimate purpose of rounds, to share the Good News of the gospel. In another chapter, gaining permission to share the gospel will be explored. For now, simply know that evangelism is the purpose of rounds.

As the purpose of rounds is evident, there is a question of how to do this process. The manner in which rounds are performed has a large relationship to the effective-ness and acceptance of the chaplain. Prayer is primary. It must be the first step in an impactful ministry. Pray for those in the mission field, the ones to whom you will be ministering. Pray that you, as a representative of Christ in the community, will be sensitive to the needs of those in the mission field. The leadership in the organizations and in the places that you serve, should be lifted up in prayer. Interceding for the needs of the community itself can be a powerful way to build the relationship with the mission field. As we have seen in recent years, the prayer to expand the boundaries of your ministry can have great meaning for the minister.

After spending time laying the foundation for your ministry through prayer, planning to be effective is the next step for rounds. Taking the time to plan out your day, in addition to setting long-term goals, will help to accomplish more during the ministry day. Measuring the progression in achieving the goals that you have set for your ministry can also be realized through planning.

Finally, it is crucial that people are put in top priority. Alter your day as needed to minister most effectively to the largest amount of people. Vary the way that you do rounds to be sure that different people groups are made to feel important. This will also keep you from getting "bored" with the routine aspects of doing rounds. By varying your routine occasionally, all people will get you at your freshest and best. This communicates value to all of the population in the mission field.

The Costs of Being Available

We have spent a great deal of time discussing the need to be available to everyone in the community, to be available around the clock, meeting others on their timetable, and being available to God for His use and glory. The discussion should now turn to the cost of being available all of the time. This constant availability does take a toll on the chaplain. For this reason, it is crucial that the chaplain take adequate vacation time. This is healthy for you and for your family. We must take steps to alleviate the stress that can come from hearing the concerns of others all day long. Periodically, evaluate the level of stress that you are under as a chaplain. Keep in mind that stress is caused by anything that threatens us, prods us, scares us, worries us, and thrills us. Stress can be defined as the rate of wear and tear on the body or any disruptive influence in a person, whether it be physical, psychological, or spiritual. In other words, stress is anything that upsets the balance in your life. In any extremely stressful situation, we will have the tendency to experience the desire to fight the stressor or to get out of the presence of the stressor. Because we are usually required to remain calm and immobile in our society, our body's response to chronic stress may result in a variety of physical problems if we do not find ways to make the automatic response of the body work for rather than against us. The following list shows some of the physiological changes that take place when we are under stress:

- Tense muscles, cramps, headache, and backache
- Rapid, shallow breathing and hyperventilation
- Increased heart rate and elevated blood pressure
- Impeded digestion and digestion related problems
- Constricted blood flow leading to blackouts
- Increased perspiration
- Decreased saliva
- Irritability
- Inability to concentrate
- General feeling of tension
- Insomnia

There are different types of stress. This is important information for us to know; not only for our own well-being, but also for those to whom we will minister. An injury, a virus, an extreme temperature change, a foreign body, exhaustion, or many other irritants can cause physical stress. Psychological stress is usually from some form of threat to security, self-esteem, way of life, or safety. The threat produces fear, especially fear of loss. Another major threat is uncertainty. The greatest cause of uncertainty is change. Sometimes changes are also losses. The combination of change and of loss contributes enormously to excess stress. Relational stress comes from the relationships in your life. The classic case example of how this works is when "The man gets yelled at while at work, so he goes home and yells at his wife. She gets

Fig. 14.8 A cycle of problems may begin with relational stress.

mad and takes it out on the children, so they kick the dog, who bites the cat, who scratches the furniture, which makes the man angry...and the cycle starts over." Our life involves many relationships, which can produce stress in our lives. Finally, there is spiritual stress, more commonly referred to as spiritual warfare. It is important to realize that none of these types of stress happen in a vacuum. A physical problem has spiritual and emotional responses. A spiritual issue can have emotional and physical implications. Total reliance on God must take place for true stress release to occur. Remember, Jesus knows what it is like to be completely available to people and the stress that can come from this availability.

Healthy Families

A strong support system is one of the ways that stress can be handled. Families are a source of strength that God gives to us. Ministry, especially community ministry, is a family commitment. Commitment is the invisible tie that binds the family together and is perhaps the foundation for the other characteristics. Although many people verbalize a commitment to family, members of healthy families put action behind their words. Persons in healthy families generally are committed to the family above all else. They make a determined effort to invest their time and energy in family activities and to keep jobs and outside demands under control. Family comes first.

At another level, commitment in healthy families involves the commitment of family members to each other. Family members demonstrate respect for each other and report strong bonds of kinship. Both husband and wife (and the children) are willing to change, to lend a helping hand, and to make sacrifices for each other. At the heart of sacrifice and support is the ability to put the best interests of someone else ahead of self—an unselfish attitude.

Commitment to each other also means sexual fidelity. Being faithful to each other is an essential part of honesty and trust in the marital relationship. Members of healthy families describe their love for each other as a steady love which is not subject to mood swings or hard times. It is a love that is conscious and unconditional. Commitment love is a promise to love "because of who you are—not what you do or how I feel".

Members of healthy families report spending large amounts of time together. Most of what they do is commonplace and inexpensive. The value of activities comes from the benefits of being together, such as improved communication, enhanced family identity, and plain old fun. They eat meals together, do house and yard chores, play catch, hike, picnic, walk, attend church, and celebrate special events such as birthdays, holidays, and vacations.

Although members of strong families spend time together, they also allow individuals to have time alone and time outside the family. Too little time together results in a disengaged type of family in which the group lacks cohesion and support for each other, with too few ties that bind them together. On the other hand, too much family time can result in psychological enmeshment where individuals are not free to explore and grow independently; the ties that bind become chains. The answer to whether families need quality time or quantities of time is that they need both—large amounts of high quality time.

The presence of open, effective communication patterns is one of the most frequently reported characteristics of healthy families. Communication in strong families is clear, open, frequent, and honest. Communication in strong families is also a reflection of family members' enjoyment of each other; they enjoy conversing about everything from the trivial to the sublime. This is an important dimension in their communication patterns. Otherwise, if family members talk only about how to solve problems and get things done, the relationship is not much different than the relationship with one's mechanic or dentist. Healthy families' communication patterns promote intimacy. Their intimacy is characterized by closeness, affection, warmth, and self-disclosure. Practicing positive communication habits, such as listening to both words and feelings, being honest and open, and avoiding criticizing, evaluating, or blaming creates the intimacy. There is an absence of manipulation and psychological game playing. Healthy families are not exempt from arguments and conflict. These families resolve conflict situations before they get to extreme levels. One technique they use to attack the problem rather than each other is to clarify the problem, discuss many possible solutions, and select the one that seems best for everyone. Cooperation is emphasized over competition, and attitudes of blaming and hostility are discouraged. Humor is an effective antidote for stress and tension. Members of strong families employ humor to relieve tension and to restore a positive outlook. The humor that they use is kind and non-hurtful.

Persons in strong families not only have a commitment (promise) kind of love for each other, they also genuinely like each other. They express large measures of appreciation to each other. They build each other up psychologically. They tend not to squander emotional energy focusing on each other's faults. Instead, most interactions are pleasant and positive. Persons in dysfunctional relationships tend to focus on negatives and often try to gain energy by feeding off the self-esteem of others. What usually happens is that the positive self-esteem in each is quickly depleted and only destructive feelings are left. When someone appreciates or compliments, it fills a person's self-esteem bucket. But for some reason, the bucket is much easier to empty than to fill; it takes ten or more positive messages to repair (fill) the damage of one negative message. Members of strong families have learned to look for the good in each other and to value it. They realize that it is not necessary to be insincere in expressing appreciation, because each person has many good qualities and accomplishments.

Families that function successfully have clearly defined roles for family members. Research supports the idea that agreement by family members on roles is more critical to harmony than the specific choice of traditional or non-traditional roles. At the same time, members of strong families have an attitude of flexibility about the performance of roles. They often share roles and are egalitarian in fulfilling roles. With a defined yet flexible structure in place, family members are aware of their responsibilities, and the physical and emotional needs of family members are met on a daily basis. The family's ability to adapt is enhanced. Issues of power—who decides what and how decisions are made—are related to the definition of roles. In families where issues of power have not been resolved, conflict and competition may erupt. Families with clearly defined roles that tend to be both flexible and egalitarian are apt to have resolved power issues in a fair and workable manner.

Strong families describe spiritual wellness as: faith in God, faith in humanity, ethical behavior, unity with all living things, religion, and feelings of hope and optimism. This can also include integrity, honesty, loyalty, conscientiousness, virtue, ethics, usefulness, self-esteem, and significance. For many people in healthy families, spiritual wellness is founded in a belief in a higher power. They express their spiritual nature by participation in organized religion—membership in a church or synagogue and attendance at formal worship services, study groups, and fellowship gatherings. One important benefit of spiritual wellness is a feeling of purpose and meaning in life, such as to serve God, to make the world a better place, to become a better person, or to cherish others. This belief enables families to transcend everyday frustration and pettiness, as well as tragedy. Their religious beliefs also help to give them a positive, confident outlook on life. Even though evil and disaster abound in the world, they have faith that their continuous search for goodness and righteousness will bear fruit. The challenges and trials of life are bearable and surmountable because of spiritual resources that can be tapped. Without a spiritual dimension to give lasting meaning, life lacks purpose and direction; people suffer alienation and depression. With it, they feel a part of something bigger than self, and that gives them perspective, hope, and confidence.

Successful families are not isolated from their communities and the wider society. Many are active in improving their neighborhoods by volunteering at school, participating in neighborhood crime watch, leading scout troops, coaching sports, or serving as community chaplains. Many are members of religious communities. This community network provides help when illness, death, birth, natural disasters, and accidents occur. They report drawing a sense of security from living in their particular community. They also seek help when faced with problems, thus improving their ability to cope with life's difficulties. There is a growing conviction that government programs cannot substitute for healthy families. Instead the role of government should be to stabilize families and to increase the family's effectiveness in rearing children.

Healthy families have developed ways of coping with the trials and tribulations of life. A primary factor in the survival of strong families in crises is their ability to see something positive in the situation and to focus on it. In tough situations, members of strong families pull together to help everyone get through. They realize no individual is completely responsible; yet each person, down to the youngest child, can do things to ease the burden. They will also seek help from other groups, like church and friends. Their spiritual beliefs offer support during difficult times. Open communication is another asset to surviving the crisis. Flexibility enables them to weather the storms of life. Family members help each other set realistic limits, especially during hard times.

Families have their own personalities. This personality will come through in the work of the community chaplain. Modeling good family dynamics is crucial for the community minister. Paul Carlisle describes families in terms of personalities. The bonding family is a model of balance between individuality and relationship. This type of family equips its children with a strong sense of identity and security and a capacity to relate to others. This family encourages its individual members to be all that they can be. They are not threatened by differences.[12]

The ruling family has a tendency to be abrasive or insensitive in their relationships.

The parents push their authority. Consequently the kids do not feel cared for, but they do know how to perform tasks. This is in sharp contrast to the protecting family. Children in this family feel cared for, but often the parents do too much for them. The children are not allowed to develop a sense of personal confidence. The parents do not make them endure the consequences of their behavior. The chaotic family is disengaged from each other. Their knowledge of and interest in one another is limited. They are more like roommates than a family, as each individual looks out for number one. Caring for others is considered absurd or stupid, and children are often neglected or abused. Individuals in the symbiotic family find it impossible to be self-directed, because individuality is seen as a lack of allegiance to the family. They are weak as individuals but strong as a group. Children feel smothered in the family and guilty if they want to leave. Survival in the family comes from the ability to conform to the norms: drive the same kind of car, embrace the same political views, and like the same food. The goal is to have a family structure that is a safe place to release and relieve stress but not to overburden other family members with the care of ministry.

Self-Examination: The "Messiah Trap"

A long look at self is necessary from time to time for the chaplain. An examination of the reasons for your availability to God and service to others should be performed periodically. One of the most common reasons for chaplains and other ministers to burn out is called the "Messiah Trap". Carmen Berry, in a book called *When Helping You Is Hurting Me*, addresses this issue.[13] I have to admit that I have at times fallen into the Messiah Trap. If you are a person who spends most of your time helping others while your own needs often get pushed to the side, you also may be caught in the Messiah Trap. Many people are caught in the Messiah Trap - administrators and aunties, mothers and ministers, social workers and secretaries. Messiahs can be found fundraising for important causes, carefully listening to clients, or intensely praying with parishioners. When the children need carpooling to their music lessons, Messiahs are warming up the station wagon. Some Messiahs wear beepers so that patients can call at any hour; some speak before large audiences, motivating them to action; others quietly visit the dying in dark hospital rooms. Messiahs are relied on to stay late at the office to finish up a needed report and to rise early to make sure everyone has a healthy lunch prepared for school. Messiahs try to be helpful wherever they go. Many Messiahs choose professions that focus on the welfare of others, such as the ministry, social work, education, medicine, psychology, or childcare. Others, such as homemakers, students, and senior adults volunteer for a variety of caregiving projects. Wherever Messiahs can be found, you can be sure they will be busy taking care of other people.

Fig. 14.9 Messiahs tend to be the ones who are always busy helping others.

It is easy for Messiahs to become so busy taking care of other people, however, that they do not take care of themselves. In the busyness of the day, Messiahs may not even notice that their needs are going unmet. In fact, it is easy for Messiahs to pretend that they have no needs or inner hurts. Messiahs present themselves to the world as people with answers while ignoring the questions still nagging inside, as people who can give comfort while neglecting the pain throbbing deep within.

Although Messiahs may pretend to feel important, underneath the surface Messiahs often doubt their value. In an effort to earn a sense of worth, Messiahs are motivated to accomplish "worthwhile" goals. They transfer attention from developing an *inner* sense of "specialness" to *external* achievement. They try to excel in such a way as to gain a desired response from those they view as worthwhile - usually parents, teachers, or other authority figures. As children, Messiahs develop skills that are valued by adults, which most often include being "helpful" to those adults on whom the child Messiah depends. Take Elizabeth, as an example. In school, Elizabeth was indirectly taught that she could earn her worth by meeting the expectations of the teachers. She realized that it was the teachers, not the students, who gave out the grades. Consequently, she neglected her need for friends. What mattered to Elizabeth was praise and acceptance from the adults who promised to stay in her life - at least for as long as the school year lasted. When placed in a classroom where the teacher did not reward her overachievement, she became despondent and depressed. Elizabeth swung to the other extreme and traded her extra-good behavior for extra-bad behavior. One way or the other, Elizabeth had to stand out in the crowd. If she were just another child in the room, Elizabeth was afraid that she, like her father, might disappear. Messiahs are adults who were once children, dependent on adults for the meeting of physical and emotional needs. Since most Messiahs grew up believing that good behavior would be rewarded and misbehavior would be punished, pleasing these adults seemed equivalent to securing survival. When in danger or emotionally neglected or abused, Messiah children tend to assume they are being punished because they have been "bad" children. Efforts, then, are focused on being good, which is defined as acting in accordance to the wishes of adults.

Messiah children are usually taught that good people always do good things and say good things. Good people never say mean things. They do not even have mean thoughts. Good people do not get angry and are always cheerful, especially through hardship. Most of all, good people are always thinking of others and they are never, ever selfish. Messiah children are often told things like, "Don't say that. That's not nice. Good children don't say things like that." Messiahs learn that certain feelings are unacceptable. Messiah children are not only forbidden to express certain feelings, but they are told not to feel these feelings at all. Many Messiahs learn to cut themselves off from their emotions, unable as adults to feel parts of their inner selves.

Reflecting back to Elizabeth, she always insisted on an "open door" policy for her office. Whenever a student or teacher needed her, she was available, even when it meant she had to work on Saturdays to meet her own deadlines. Since the Messiah depends on the response of others for a sense of well-being, it is common for the Messiah to allow his or her actions to be determined by others. Messiahs need approval from others to feel special and will therefore behave according to what others dictate. It is very important to recognize that, when you are caught in the Messiah Trap, you give up control over your own life and over your own sense of well-being. Because Messiahs are so busy trying to please others, personal interests are seldom cultivated. What would you like to do if you were not trapped into taking care of others? Do you really know? Most Messiahs do not have a clue. In the desperate search for self-esteem, most Messiahs listen to others, not to themselves. Messiahs become involved in activities that will provide positive feedback from others. Often neglected are those activities that may not be valued by other people but that may address the Messiah's needs and desires. These include the development of peer relationships, personal nurturing skills, and taking time to explore.

Elizabeth always kept her desk cleared of papers and clutter. She never missed a deadline and always came to meetings prepared, a typical overachiever. Messiahs, in the attempt to earn a sense of value, tend to overachieve and over-perform. In order to feel acceptable to others, Messiahs are often enslaved to the pursuit of proving themselves indispensable to others. To achieve the status of "special", the Messiah tries to run faster, jump higher, and advance quicker than others. In response to the Messiahs' devotion to over-achievement, others may call them "superstars", "exceptionally talented", or "achieving well beyond his or her years". If the Messiah does not overachieve, but achieves on an age-appropriate level at pace with natural abilities, he or she often feels like a failure. Messiahs have to be better to feel worthwhile at all.

Elizabeth developed a special program for mentally gifted children in her school and diligently worked to obtain scholarship money for students from low-income and single-parent homes. Messiahs are naturally and unconsciously attracted to other people who share a common childhood pain. Stop for a moment and think back on those people you have helped recently. Do you help everyone that comes into your path? Probably not. You most likely help certain types of people. It is not uncommon for victims of sexual abuse to become therapists who specialize in treating victims of molestations, for children of alcoholic parents to write books on alcoholism, or for children of divorced parents to become attorneys specializing in family law. When caught in the Messiah Trap, you may be driven to help others because you are so woefully neglecting yourself.

A well-balanced individual will be able to comfortably perform in three capacities. There will be a time to lead (superior to subordinate), a time to follow (subordinate to superior), and a time to walk beside someone else (peer to peer). The Messiah is limited in his or her capacity to relate to others. Deep inside, most Messiahs are like a little child who feels powerless to protect him or herself. This frightening feeling is masked by taking on the most powerful role available, that of helper. When we help someone, we are in the superior role while the person receiving our help is in the subordinate role. The helper has more power, more prestige, and is often considered an "expert". The person receiving help, on the other hand, is considered needy and dependent on the helper. While many Messiahs claim to be "serving" others, they are nevertheless playing the most powerful role. Playing the powerful role of helper may not seem too crucial to the Messiah until it is taken away. Then it becomes apparent just how much that power is needed. Think about yourself for a moment. How well do you receive assistance from others? How often do you ask for help? Most Messiahs have great difficulty receiving gifts, letting people throw parties in their honor, or calling a friend when their car breaks down on the highway. Messiahs do not mind giving people rides or dropping off bags of groceries to shut-ins, but will writhe in frustration and even humiliation should they need transportation or need to call a friend to drop by some food when ill.

Many Messiahs may look as if they have peer relationships. Some are quite outgoing and have a wide circle of "friends". But on close inspection, it becomes evident that the Messiah has difficulty in relating on equal footing with these so-called peers. Instead of developing relationships with peers as equals, Messiahs tend to use peers as points of competition, as standards against which to measure a sense of "specialness". It is my observation that Messiahs try to avoid situations wherein they are expected to be one of the group. Messiahs most often avoid peer relationships and social gatherings by giving the great Messiah excuse, "I would really like to come, but I'm just too busy." If unable to avoid the situation, Messiahs may try to move into roles of leadership (disguised as helping): "Sure, I'll come. What can I do to help? Want me to arrange the transportation/bring a video/organize the refreshments/come early and decorate?" Most Messiahs do not relate easily to others as peers and rarely disclose personal, especially problematic, information. As children, Messiahs were unable to acquire the skills necessary for the development of peer relationships, which lay the groundwork for the development of intimate relationships as adults. When robbed of this opportunity, Messiahs inevitably have difficulty in adult intimate relationships. Messiahs pay a high price to be special by ending up being separated from the group and missing out on acquiring fundamental relationship skills.

At a conference, Elizabeth busied herself by browsing at the book tables as the meetings broke for lunch. She hoped no one would notice she was alone, yet she could not bear the idea of joining the special lunch table set aside for newcomers. She slipped out and ate alone at a nearby deli. Messiahs tend to experience

Fig. 14.10 Messiahs often spend hours at work in an attempt to hide their pain.

a deep sense of isolation. While in the presence of other people, the Messiah may feel excruciatingly lonely. This is due, in part, to the fact that the Messiah cannot be a part of the group and feel special at the same time. Many are caught in the Messiah cycle - feelings of worthlessness propel them toward attempting to be special. They try to be special by being different, but being different leaves them feeling isolated and odd. This intensifies their feelings of worthlessness, which once again propels them toward proving their "specialness" - and the cycle continues.

Elizabeth worked every Saturday. People soon stopped calling her for social activities, knowing she would answer, "I've got too much to do." Messiahs do a great deal of pretending - pretending they were not hurt as children and that they do not feel worthless and powerless. This pretense is maintained by doing things other people consider worthwhile and by taking on powerful roles, hoping that no one will find out about the pain inside. Since they are trying to establish a sense of worth through external achievement, the Messiah cannot rest. The Messiah becomes addicted to helping. Successes achieved are not internalized, so they are not trusted. Regardless of the college degrees earned, the professional status attained, and the noble sacrifices made, Messiahs still feel worthless. During periods of inactivity, Messiahs usually experience many uncomfortable feelings such as guilt, depression, and/or anxiety. Messiahs often feel guilty if they are not out helping someone in need or achieving something measurable. Anxiety creeps in with the fear of being seen as selfish or useless. The Messiah may feel depressed but not know why. Waiting is a form of torture for most Messiahs. Restlessness is generated by the inner sense of inferiority that pushes Messiahs into an endless search for activity.

Do you want to know how ensnared you are by the Messiah Trap? Ask yourself these questions: How did you feel the last time someone teased you about taking it easy or loafing around? Did you defend yourself by listing all you had accomplished that day? If you have an evening free, do you feel guilty about spending that time on yourself? Or do you find something to do that is useful to someone else? Do you find it necessary to justify taking a vacation? Or do you never take a vacation because you can never find the time? Since Messiahs have to reach perfection just to feel that they have broken even, Messiahs become quite agitated if accused of "taking it easy" or "loafing around". Messiahs overreact to such terms, because to Messiahs they translate into "worthless" and "unacceptable".

Perfection and Maturity

Perfection is not something that will be attained on this side of Heaven. Yet many ministers caught in the Messiah Trap have perfectionist tendencies. Perfectionists have black-or-white thinking. Everything is broken down into dichotomies ("I am either the hero or the goat!") An absolutistic attitude develops that believes any negative quality is unacceptable. Specific thinking patterns of the perfectionist are as follows:

- **Hurdle Effect:** The tendency is to ALWAYS be looking ahead at the next barrier or hurdle that "must" be crossed.
- **Maximizing and Minimizing:** Every failure is maximized, and every success is minimized. Past goal achievement and compliments are minimized.
- **Negative Attribution:** The tendency to read rejection into the ways others relate to them. They focus on someone's body language or tone of voice as evidence of rejection. This may be the way a perfectionist attributes his or her own negative feelings about self to others.
- **All or Nothing Thinking:** When they look at themselves and others, they only see two possible categories: success or failure, good or bad, smart or stupid, etc.[14]

A perfectionist often sets unrealistic goals. Goals can be set so high that they can never be achieved. For example, "I will never gossip again!" or "I will never miss my quiet time!" Unrealistic goals can alienate others. This happens when they do not live up to the standards of the perfectionist, and the perfectionist gets frustrated with them. Conflict can result. Three favorite phrases of the perfectionist are: "could have", "should have", or "would have". A healthy achiever rates only her performance. The perfectionist rates herself. Loneliness and depression are often the result of a perfectionist's lifestyle. The fear of being rejected and judged leads to despairing isolation.

Striving for excellence must not be taken to the extreme of perfectionism or to the Messiah Trap. Excellence will come from being realistic and knowing who you are in Christ. Become process minded; take joy in the journey, since for Christians it is all a process. Set attainable but challenging goals. Remember that it is fine to do your best, it is all God wants; but always focus your worth on the fact that you are created in God's image.

When maturation takes place, we are better equipped to handle stress and avoid some of the temptations that have been discussed above. There are two major perspectives on maturation. The first is from a psychological point of view. We will then examine maturity from a biblical standpoint. Psychologically, maturity is a realistic view of oneself and others, and it involves an accurate objective evaluation of oneself and others. Often, a realistic view of the self may be obtained by asking oneself several questions such as, "What kind of things can I do best?"; "What are my strengths and weaknesses?" At the same time it is necessary to ask, "Would others agree, and have I had some success in my area of strength?" Often a person finds that he is good at doing things he likes to do, or he can learn to do them more quickly than someone who does not share those interests. The variety of interests an individual has is related to the variety of his abilities. Consequently, in gaining a realistic view of the self, an examination of one's interests may be very helpful in discovering one's abilities and potential. The immature person often makes one of two errors in gaining a realistic view of himself. He assumes he is very capable or talented in one or more areas that he is not. Coupled with this error is the assumption that others have little or no real ability, having achieved their office, job, or position of responsibility by coincidence. This first error is often observed in children and particularly in adolescents who seem convinced that they can do things much better than just about anyone. This is also the error of the "armchair" or "Monday-morning quarterback", who is certain he could have done a much better job than the real player. The second error, which is characteristic of the individual with an immature or unrealistic view of the self, is the reverse of the first. This person says he is untalented and really cannot do anything very well. In fact, he says most anyone can do almost anything better than he can. A person with realistic self-perception knows his strengths and his weaknesses and does not over- or underestimate either. He can also laugh at himself. When a person can perceive his own strengths, abilities, and talents, as well as his lack of ability in certain areas, then he can also perceive the talents of others accurately.

The second aspect or dimension of maturity - accepting oneself and others - is closely related to the first. Acceptance means allowing, believing, or recognizing something as true or real in one's inner experience. It does not imply that whatever needs to be accepted is good, valuable, or right, but only that it really exists. Everyone has a variety of hopes, fears, desires, and aspirations. They are not all good or desirable, but they are all real. Their reality must be accepted if one is to be mature. The reality of these worthwhile desires and fears must be accepted as existing now in order for change or improvement to occur. Suppose a child gets in trouble with the neighbors by walking on their grass and picking their flowers, but his parents say to the neighbors, "He is a good boy and would not do such a thing!" The longer the parents fail to accept the reality of the child's bad behavior (and thus their relationship to it), the more likely is the child to continue the activity and the more the relationship with the neighbors will degenerate. Acceptance means that the self or other selves are approved as persons or personalities apart from however many imperfections exist. The immature individual often confuses some specific habit, attitude, or action with the total person, and he rejects the person rather than accepting the total person as being worthwhile and more important than the undesirable aspect.

The third dimension of maturity is living in the present but having long-range goals. Living in the present means facing and coping with one's present circumstances and situations. This involves dealing with and acknowledging the importance of oneself, job, church, friends, family, etc. All of these situations could be described as "where I am". Each of these situations or circumstances has some positive and negative qualities; that is, it meets some needs but not others. The mature person is aware of these qualities and his needs. He or she is able to see what is good and bad, as well as what can be changed and what cannot in each situation. In each, the mature person has some goals that he or she would like to see accomplished and is aware of the present state of progress toward these goals. The immature person tends to live with the "if only" or the "when" attitude; that is, "if only it were as good as it used to be" or "won't it be grand when". For either case, there is little or no acceptance of the present situation and the person's responsibility in it and for it or for changing it.

The mature person is aware that the present is not all that it could be or all that he would like it to be. Consequently, he develops goals toward which he directs the course of his activity and life. The goals vary as to their clarity, permanence, and desirability. As he moves toward them, the mature person assesses his progress and directs or redirects his effort as needed. He may even change his goals; i.e., he remains master of his goals, and they remain flexible. The immature person tends to be mastered by his goals, becoming rigid and rejecting others or himself for not obtaining or making satisfactory progress toward his goals.

At first, having values may not appear to be a very psychological concept, but most psychologists recognize implicitly, if not explicitly, the existence of values for the mature or healthy person. Values for the psychologist must be self-chosen. They are not values the individual accepts because he is coerced by a society or a religion. Rather they are chosen by the mature person and integrated in the person's self-concept and behavior. They are thus not external but internalized values. The immature person operates without values, e.g. a psychopath or a child or someone with a rigid, threatening set of moral values, such as an obsessive-compulsive individual or a pre-adolescent. The mature person is free of coercion, because his values are self-chosen and he acts accordingly. His values may be that of society or religion, but they have become his own by choice and internalization.

The developing of one's abilities and interests and coping with the problems of living comprise the final characteristic of maturity. This last characteristic focuses on developing one's potentials and skills and then utilizing them to create, make, and do things both from necessity and for fun. Mature people are interested in their job, home, family, community, church, themselves, etc. Of course their degree of interest may vary from area to area, but they have interests. They are not only capable of purposeful, creative action, but they like to do things. They have a high degree of ability to concentrate on the task at hand and also to leave it when necessary. The immature person seems to have more dislikes than likes and has not developed his creative abilities nor the ability or interest to cope with life's daily tasks. Does the person have a task-oriented approach to life or a defensive orientation? The immature person is trying to protect or defend himself from life, the world, others, and himself. The mature person is involved in the tasks of life. He is able to modify his approach and try an alternate approach, and he is also able to accept a substitute goal and make compromises when necessary.

The biblical perspective is seen when man chooses to have a realistic or objective view of himself and others. The basic requirement is to perceive the self, others, and the world from the divine perspective. God views each and every man as fallen and in need of a Savior (Romans 3:23). Once man recognizes his need for a Savior and responds, he becomes a new creature with a new relationship to God, other men, and the world (2 Corinthians 5:17). Another aspect of a realistic biblical view of self and others is the recognition of natural traits and abilities, as well as one's spiritual gifts (Matthew 25:25-26; I Corinthians 12:14-25) and place in the body (I Corinthians 12:14; Ephesians 4:4). A realistic perception of the needs of others, both believers (Galatians 6:2) and unbelievers (Matthew 25:34-40), is the biblical expectation as well as a divine view of the social order (Romans 13:1-3). A second aspect of biblical maturity involves the

Fig. 14.11 Biblical maturity involves accepting oneself and others.

accepting of oneself and others. Perhaps the clearest statement of this principle is given by Jesus: "... Love your neighbor as yourself" (Matthew 22:39 NIV). It is important to note that the love of a neighbor is dependent in quality and amount on the love of self; that is, love of self in the sense of acceptance as described above. Acceptance means allowing the biblical view of sinfulness and our fallen nature to be true or real in my inner experience both before and after I become a Christian. Sinfulness and our fallen nature are not eliminated by being saved. Righteousness always belongs to Christ and is legally attributed to the person by God. It does not become a personal quality so that the person can brag (Philippians 3:9; Ephesians 5:9), either before God or before others.

A second aspect of acceptance of self and others is recognizing that both self and others are more than sinful and fallen. Each person is created in God's image (Genesis 1:27) and is also fallen (Romans 5:12) and is redeemed or in need of redemption. God loves everyone whom He created, which means everyone is worthwhile as a person. Hence everyone should be accepted as a person. Acceptance as a person does not imply approval of all of the person's behavior or motives. The Bible calls the mature believer to a very high level of love for other believers (I John 3:16), to a deep sensitivity to their weakness (Hebrews 12:12), and to the whole body as brothers in Christ (I Corinthians 12:25-26).

The biblical words *agapeo, philo,* and *koinonia* call for a greater depth of warmth and mature relationship than most psychologists emphasize. Living in the present with long-term goals is basic in the Scriptures. Now is the day of salvation, for both the believer and the unbeliever. Salvation has an eternally present aspect. While the Bible describes the future life with God, there is a very heavy emphasis on present actions and attitudes. The believer is to manifest the fruit of the Spirit in his life. Christ makes an observable difference in the believer's ongoing action. It is the carnal or immature who does not show a currently observable change. The words "abide" and "grow up in Christ" are repeatedly used to emphasize the current ongoing focus of the Christian. The Christian life is also described as a race with a prize (Philippians 3:14). In verse 10 Paul says, "That I may know Him, and the power of His resurrection, and the fellowship of His sufferings, being made conformable unto his death" (Philippians 3:10 KJV). This last verb is a present participle and is the strongest possible way of stressing ongoing action - the focus is on the present. Paul continues by saying that he knows that he is not yet perfect (mature) but that: "I press toward the goal for the prize of the upward call of God in Christ Jesus" (Philippians 3:14 NKJV). Thus the model of the Christian has a present focus with long-range future goals.

Having values that are self-chosen can be seen as Joshua is in the process of conquering and possessing the land in his appeal to the Israelites, "... choose today whom you will serve ..." (Joshua 24:15 NLT). Values are a "package plan" because they involve an integrated set of motives and actions, not just something one says he thinks is right. The value-packages are clearly indicated in the descriptions of the works of the flesh and the works of the Spirit. In Philippians 3 Paul describes a complete values reorganization in which a total set of values and accompanying actions are reinterpreted and reversed. This value reassessment is an ongoing process that merges with the realistic evaluation of the self and the focus on the present, but it is pulled forward and clarified by the long-range goal of the "high calling of God". It is the commitment of the self to a set of values that reorganizes the person and gives him an identity. For the Christian this is union with Christ, which is so characteristically described by Paul with the phrase "in Christ".

The development and use of one's talents and gifts (Ephesians 4:7) is a necessary part of Christian maturity, since they are given to the church for the work of the ministry (Ephesians 4:12). Timothy is encouraged to rekindle the gift of God within him (2 Timothy 1:6). The encouragement of growth toward Christian maturity seems to be the purpose of the gifts and the goal of the ministry (Ephesians 4:15-16). Interest in everyday living involves working to support oneself (2 Thessalonians 3:10) as well as one's family (I Timothy 5:8). Interest in the daily tasks is not to be neglected or done grudgingly (Ephesians 6:6; Colossians 3:22). The developing of one's abilities, talents, and gifts begins to merge with Christian values and a biblically appropriate perception of oneself and others. This merger produces congruence in the mature Christian of all that he says and does (James 2:26; I John 3:18). Perhaps this is best illustrated in the epistle of I John, where the apostle describes three criteria of mature Christian faith: believing the truth (Jesus is the Christ), loving the brotherhood, and practicing righteousness. These criteria tend to focus on three different aspects of the human person. Believing the truth has a strong cognitive component, while practicing righteousness has a strong behavioral focus and loving the brothers involves the emotional-motivational aspects. The mature Christian's behavior, beliefs, and emotions are thus organized in a consistent, congruent, and unified pattern. He is interested in his daily life because this is where God has placed him (Philippians 4:11; Hebrews 13:5; I Corinthians 7:21), and he acts as unto the Lord (Ephesians 6:8). Every task or sphere of activities is infused with spiritual meaning and interest. He recognizes that every good thing in life is from God (James 1:17), and that there is much that is worthy of his attention and enjoyment in this life (Philippians 4:8). The mature believer is aware that the mandate to subdue the earth (Genesis 1:28) has never been revoked. The immature Christian is torn by conflict, because he is pulled in two directions (James 1:8; 4:8) and because he is unclear about his identity. That is, he has not reckoned himself dead to sin and alive to God (Romans 6:11). He has not embraced his identity as a new man or self but rather tries to operate as the old man, which he is not.

Maturation will also cause the chaplain to examine his motivations for caregiving. There are some unhealthy motivations for ministry. The need for relationships can be motivation for some. Our motivation should be the care of others, not companionship for ourselves. An authoritarian caregiver likes to be in control, to correct others, to give advice (even if not requested), and to play the role of problem solver. Some dependent people may want this, but eventually most people resist the controller-type caregivers because they do not really help. Additionally, we need to instruct others to become dependent on Christ, not on the chaplain. The need to rescue can be in place for some community ministers. The rescuer often has a sincere desire to help, but this helper takes responsibility away from the person by showing an attitude that conveys a lack of confidence in the individual. This will be frustrating for all involved in the end. Other caregivers have a need for information. When a caregiver is curious, he sometimes forgets the person in crisis, pushes for extra information, and is often unable to keep confidences. Finally, some community ministers seek out this type of position because of their own need for personal healing. Most of us carry hidden needs and insecurities that could interfere with people-helping. Caregiving sessions are less helpful when the caregiver has a need to manipulate, atone for guilt, please some authority figure, express hostility, resolve sexual conflicts, or prove that he is intellectually capable, spiritually mature, and psychologically stable.

The stress that can come from being a caregiver in the community can be lessened through having healthy relationships, especially with your children and spouse. Emotional health is impossible to

Fig. 14.12 Healthy family relationships can lessen stress.

get and maintain apart from deep, rich relationships with others. Yet I am aware how difficult it can be to begin to trust anyone with the delicate pieces of our emotional life. Many of us have learned that it is much safer and easier to keep our emotions to ourselves. Yet God created us with the wonderful capacity to know another in a deep fashion. Genesis 2:18 reveals to us man's relational capacity. "The LORD God said, 'It is not good for the man to be alone. I will make a helper suitable for him'" (Genesis 2:18 NIV). Man was designed for intimacy with God and others. The centrality of relationships to the child of God is reinforced when Jesus affirms a lawyer who said the law could be summed up in loving God and your neighbor. Jesus continues this thinking when He says, "A new commandment I give to you, that you love one another; as I have loved you, that you also love one another. By this all will know that you are My disciples, if you have love for one another" (John 13:34-35 NKJV). The Apostle Paul says this about relationships in his letter to the Galatians, "For all the law is fulfilled in one word, even in this: You shall love your neighbor as yourself" (Galatians 5:14 NKJV). At the center of the heart of God is relationship. Relationship is intended to be a vital part of our emotional health.

Relational Development

I want you to get an idea of where you are in your relationship development. Emotional growth most readily occurs in the soil of rich relationships. To make this easier to grasp, I have used each letter of the word "close" to describe the necessary characteristics of intimate relationships.

C- Communication: Growing relationships are characterized by a lot of sharing of ideas, dreams, hopes, etc. If you were to listen in on their dialogue, you would get the sense that talking for them is easy and natural. You may get the impression that they have known each other for a long time. The shared unity between them makes talking and sharing normal. It may be helpful to review some communication barriers.

L- Let down the walls: My assumption is that most of us have learned that it is not always safe out there in the relational jungle we call life. We have developed ways to protect ourselves from the hurts that others may launch at us. Often I have felt like one of King Arthur's knights covered from head to toe with thick armor plating. I had the belief that if I wore enough protection that I would never be hurt or disappointed again. Not so! You will need to take some of that armor off to build the types of relationships that produce emotional health. We relate best to others when they know who we really are and vice-versa. I am not suggesting that you remove all your armor at once, but you can remove one piece at a time as the relationship develops. You will find our Heavenly Father more than adequate to protect you. He is better than any armor that you will ever wear.

O- On purpose: Relationships that produce emotional health must be built intentionally. They will not happen on their own. You will have to be proactive rather than reactive or passive. What if you find that you have no relationships that are mature enough to encourage emotional health? The first thing you can do is tell God you want a mature relationship and will look to Him to provide it. This is a proactive and intentional step toward health. Another thing you can do is go to people where they are. It is hard to develop depth relationships if you are not around people. Make yourself available to God and others, and see what happens.

S- **Self-disclosure:** I know of no better way to develop a relationship to a soul-mate level than by the use of self-disclosure. It will take time to get comfortable and secure enough to open up in a way that allows the person to see who you really are. There is no need to get in a big hurry. Allow God to work at His pace. When the time comes to share a deep piece of your life, it will still take a little courage. Go ahead, for this is the path to maturity. I remember being a bit anxious and fearful the first few times I shared my heart with another. I was just hoping that they would accept it and not think badly of me. The more I practiced, the easier it became. The more my relationship with Christ grew, the safer it was to let others see the real me. I believe the reason for this was an assurance of His acceptance, no matter how my friend reacted to my self-disclosure. For many of us, this will be a big step.

E- **Expect challenges:** Anytime you begin to follow God in building a close relationship, you can expect to face problems. It seems to be the nature of relationships. You need only thumb through the pages of the Bible to see just how difficult relation ships can be. You are in good company! You are on a most wonderful adventure as you grow with others in Christ. Nothing this fulfilling would ever be accomplished without some trials and disappointments. Persevere, my brothers and sisters! Our Savior has run the race before us, so we need not be dismayed. Endure in your pursuit of "soul-mate" intimacy, and I promise you will not be disappointed.

Relationship development enables us to have a ready resource in times of trouble. The road to emotional health will have many barriers for us. Often we will need help along the way; we will need someone to "burden-bear" for us (Galatians 6:2). The picture painted in this verse is of one who is overburdened with life's problems and is unable to free himself alone. He must have someone to assist him, or he may never get free. That is when God uses the soul-mate. There is nowhere that this is more needed than in our emotional lives. Oh, what a blessing it is to have someone walk along with us as we travel the path of the Kingdom of God! Take a few minutes and assess how you are doing with relationships. Use the acronym CLOSE to do this. What steps do you need to take this week to begin growing in this area of soul-mate development? Share your plans with someone.

Driven to Success

How driven are you to success? There is a difference between possessing a solid work ethic and being driven only by success, seeing people only as pawns that can help in the accomplishment of a task. Can driven people be spotted? Yes, of course. There are many symptoms that suggest a person is driven. A driven person is most often gratified only by accomplishment. Somewhere in the process of maturation, this person discovers that the only way he can feel good about himself and his world is to accumulate accomplishments. This discovery may be the result of formative influences at an early age. As a child, affirmation and approval may have been received from a parent or influential mentor only when something had been finished. The only way he could find love and acceptance was through accomplishment. A person begins to reason that if one accomplishment resulted in good feelings and the praise of others, then several more accomplishments may bring an abundance of good feelings and affirmations. The driven person begins to look for ways to accumulate more and more achievements. He will soon be found doing two or three things at one time, because that brings even more of this strange sort of pleasure. He becomes the sort of person who is always reading books and attending seminars that promise to help him to use what time he has even more effectively. Why? He does this so that he can produce more accomplishments, which in turn will provide greater gratification. He sees life only in terms of results. As such, he has little appreciation for the process leading toward results.

A driven person is preoccupied with the symbols of accomplishment. He will be aware of the symbols of status: titles, office size and location, positions on organizational charts, and special privileges. There is a concern for one's own notoriety when in a state of drivenness. Who, the driven person wonders, knows about what I am doing? How can I be better connected with the "greats" of my world? A driven person is usually caught in the uncontrolled pursuit of expansion. Driven people like to be part of something that is getting bigger and more successful. They are usually on the move, seeking the biggest and the best opportunities. They rarely have any time to appreciate the achievements to date. The nineteenth century English preacher Charles Spurgeon once said:

Success exposes a man to the pressures of people and thus tempts him to hold on to his gains by means of fleshly methods and practices, and to let himself be ruled wholly by the dictatorial demands of incessant expansion. Success can, and will, go to my head unless I remember that it is God who accomplishes the work, that He can continue to do so without my help, and that He will be able to make it with other means whenever He wants to cut me out.[15]

You can see it in the context of spiritual activity, for there is such a thing as a spiritually driven person who is never satisfied with who he is or what he accomplishes in religious work. This means that his attitude toward those around him is much the same. He is rarely pleased with the progress of his peers or subordinates. He lives in a constant state of uneasiness and restlessness, looking for more efficient methods, greater results, and deeper spiritual experiences. There is usually no sign that he will ever be satisfied with himself or anyone else.

Driven people tend to have a limited regard for integrity. They can become so preoccupied with success and achievement that they have little time to stop and ask if their inner person is keeping pace with the outer process. People like this often become progressively deceitful; and they not only deceive others, they deceive themselves. In the attempt to push ahead relentlessly, they lie to themselves about motives. Values and morals are compromised. Shortcuts to success become a way of life. Because the goal is so important, they drift into ethical shabbiness. Driven people become frighteningly pragmatic.

Driven people often possess limited or undeveloped people skills. They are not noted for getting along well with others. They were not born without the capacity to get along with others, but projects are more important to them than people. Because their eyes are upon goals and objectives, they rarely take note of the people about them, unless they can be used for the fulfillment of one of the goals. If others are not found to be useful, then they may be seen as obstacles or competitors when it comes to getting something done. There is a "trail of bodies" in the wake of the driven person. Where once others praised him for his seemingly great leadership, soon a steady increase in frustration and hostility appears as they see that the driven person cares very little about the health and growth of human beings. Colleagues and subordinates in the orbit of the driven person slowly drop away, one after another, exhausted, exploited, and disillusioned. Of this person we are most likely to find ourselves saying, "He is miserable to work with, but he certainly gets things done." He gets things done, but he may destroy people in the process. In almost every great organization, religious and secular, people of this sort can be found in key positions. Even though they carry with them the seeds of relational disaster, they often are indispensable to the action.

Driven people tend to be highly competitive. They see each effort as a win-or-lose game. The driven person feels he must win, and must look good before others. Winning provides the evidence the driven person desperately needs that he is right, valuable, and important. He is likely to see others as competitors or as enemies who must be beaten - perhaps even humiliated - in the process.

A driven person often possesses a volcanic force of anger, which can erupt any time he senses opposition or disloyalty. This anger can be triggered when people disagree, offer an alternative solution to a problem, or even hint at just a bit of criticism. The anger can take the form of verbal brutality, such as profanity or humiliating insults. The anger can express itself in vindictive acts such as firing people, slandering them before peers, or simply denying them things they have come to expect, such as affection, money, or even companionship. Many good people who surround the driven person are more than willing to take the impact of such anger, although it desperately hurts them. They reason that the boss or the leader is getting things done, that he is being blessed by God, or that no one can argue with success. Sometimes the anger and its cruel effects are accepted simply because no one has either the courage or the ability to stand up to the driven person.

Driven people are usually abnormally busy. They are usually too busy for the pursuit of ordinary relationships in marriage, family, or friendship, or even to carry on a relationship with themselves - not to speak of one with God. Because driven people rarely think they have accomplished enough, they seize every available minute to attend more meetings, to study more material, and to initiate more projects. They operate on the precept that a reputation for busyness is a sign of success and personal importance. They attempt to impress people with the fullness of their schedule. They may even express a high level of self-pity, bemoaning the "trap" of responsibility they claim to be in, wishing aloud that there was some possible release from it all. However, just try to suggest a way out! The truth is that the very worst thing that could happen to them would be if someone provided them with a way out. They really would not know what to do with themselves if there were suddenly less to do. Busyness for the driven person becomes a habit, a way of life and thought. They find it enjoyable to complain and gather pity, and they would probably not want it any other way. If you try to explain that to a driven person, you will probably make him angry.

Fig. 14.13 You can't go Mach II speed in a camel body.

I am convinced that the busyness of American life itself is detrimental to emotional health. I have heard it said this way, "You can't go Mach II speed in a camel body." The statement humorously points out how our bodies are incapable of handling such a high velocity pace of life. Like the body, this type of intense lifestyle hits our emotions hard as well. Too much, too fast results in what I call emotional meltdown. The meltdown can manifest itself in emotional numbness or over-sensitivity. Either way the person has exhausted their emotional reserves. The person must replenish and fill up!

In Luke 10 we have a wonderful story about one person who had an emotional meltdown and another person who knew how to replenish her emotional tank. Look with me at verse 38. Jesus goes to the home of Lazarus, Martha, and Mary for a visit. This seems to be a place he would frequent to get away from the press of the crowds. They were good friends. Verse 38 says Martha welcomed him into her house. She had a good relationship with Him. As a matter of fact John 11:5 says Jesus loved Martha and her sister (Mary) and Lazarus. They were really close! You will soon see that being close to Jesus does not make a person immune to emotional meltdowns. In verse 40 we are given a close-up view of Martha. The Bible gives us a clear example of someone who gets so stressed-out that she crashes her emotions. The following are some of the characteristics of people who have emptied their emotional tank.

They are distracted with too much activity. The word "distracted" could mean "running in circles." She is so busy and frantic that she is literally disoriented. This hits too close to home for me. I have been a Martha all my life - always doing something. When I was at the peak of the busyness, it felt just like "running in circles." I was an ardent follower of hyperactive Martha. Look at the verse again, and see what it is that she is distracted by: serving Jesus! Her problem had to do with the way she was going about her relationship to Christ. Serving Christ will never substitute for intimacy with Christ. As a matter of fact, intimacy with Christ will produce service in the form of an easy yoke and a light burden (see Matthew 11:28-30). Religious activity is wrong when it prevents you from being with Jesus.

They fuss at Jesus. Martha goes right up to Jesus and gives Him a piece of her mind. She tells Him that He must not "care" about her. Intimacy with God allows us to be honest with our Savior. Emotional meltdowns nearly always distort your view of God. Here she sees Jesus as non-compassionate, maybe insensitive. When your emotions are fried, your thoughts and perceptions of reality are easily skewed. I believe that is what we see happening with Martha. If you were to look at I Peter 5:7, you would see these words, "... casting all your care upon Him, for He cares for you ..." (NKJV). Martha's frantic pace resulted in a sense of being uncared for by Christ. Christ is never uncaring. The problem is that our busyness disconnects us from a sense of His care.

Fig. 14.14 Sometimes we, like Martha, find ourselves having tunnel vision

They feel alone and deserted. As the emotional meltdown progresses, the person begins to feel alone. Martha complains that she is doing all the work, while her sister Mary is not helping. I noticed this same characteristic in myself during the old days of "frenzied activity". I would be sweating up a storm over a task and get the sense that I was the only one in the whole world that was doing anything. Often, I would get a little miffed about it. I would say under my breath, "Why am I the only one working?" in a self-righteous way. Like Martha, I had tunnel vision. I could only see what I was doing.

They can be demanding. The last sentence uttered by Martha to Jesus is this, "Therefore, tell her (Mary) to help me." When a person is feeling this way, his or her goal is to get others to speed up rather than for him or her to slow down. The assumption is that busyness and fast-paced living are the correct way to live, so everyone else should fall in line. You will see Martha ordering or placing guilt on others in an attempt to get them to speed up or pitch in. What really needs to happen is for the Marthas to slow their pace. Jesus responds to this one that He loves in verses 41-42. He says "Martha, Martha." It would sound something like this today, "My dear Martha." He is not upset at her, but he does know that she needs help with this hectic lifestyle she has adopted. He tells her several things that I think are helpful.

Too many things should never crowd out the "Main Thing". He tells Martha that the many things that are pulling at her are not as important as the one thing her sister Mary is doing (sitting at His feet and listening to His words). I do not believe Jesus is against activity or balanced-busyness. Right before this passage, He told the story of the Good Samaritan who was very active. I think he is saying to her that *being* with Him comes before *serving* Him. Being with Him empowers one for service. How easy it is to get busyness ahead of being with Christ.

You have a choice about how you run your life. Jesus tells her that Mary has chosen the best part. The word "chosen" indicates that if a choice was made, then one can reverse the choice. Martha is encouraged to make a choice about how to spend her time. Jesus wants her to choose the part that will not be taken away from her - intimacy with Him rather than religious activity.

Sit at the Feet of Jesus

The most drastic change I have ever made in my life was the decision to slow down. A part of doing life differently was making stillness and solitude with Christ central. Like Martha, I was a "doer", and a pretty good one if I do say so myself. Yet it got me in trouble in the long haul. So I began to try to be still and sit at Jesus' feet. At first I could only tolerate short periods of time before I would have to go "do" something. Gradually I was able to extend those periods of time. Believe it or not, now I long to be with Him. I hunger for His presence. It is like I am not the same person that I used to be. I do not want to make it sound easy, because it is not. Each day the fast-paced culture I live in presses in on me to hurry, hurry, hurry. Yet I have a choice to make. Will I enter the rat race or choose a road less traveled? For me, I want the path that leads to rich intimacy with our Heavenly Father and our big Savior, Jesus. Part of that path is allowing time for my relationship to Him and His relationship to me. Consider then what ways you are like Martha or like Mary. What would have to happen for you to be more intentional about "sitting at Jesus' feet and hearing His words"?

One practical way to "sit at the feet of Jesus" is journaling. Before we jump into the topic of journaling, let me first introduce you to the practices of solitude and stillness. Journaling is a way to practice these two. These practices are unfamiliar to many in evangelical circles today. At different points in the history of the church, they were highly prized and practiced. I understand why they are such oddities today. Who has time for them when all we know is "Go, Go!" and "Do, Do!"? When I speak of solitude and stillness, I get the incredulous look from most folks like I was from some other world, an extraterrestrial. The whole idea is foreign and unattractive. Whoever would believe that doing what looks like nothing would produce something? Besides, is that not just an excuse to be lazy? Boy, that lazy word is a powerful one for me. I can be thrown into all types of frenzied activities if someone suggests that I am the least bit lazy. To me the word is like "the scarlet letter". It is an anathema.

Despite all that, solitude and stillness are two ways we can sit at Jesus' feet and hear His words. Some practice of these two is crucial to growing up into full maturity in faith. Much has been written about them that is very comprehensive, so I just want to whet your appetite for time with the Master.

Dallas Willard has this to say about solitude. It is:

...purposefully abstaining from interactions with other humans, denying ourselves companionship and all that comes from our conscious interactions with others. It is choosing to be alone and to dwell on our experience of isolation from other humans. Nothing but solitude can allow the development of a freedom from the in-grained behaviors that hinder our integration into God's order. The normal course of day-to-day human interactions locks us into patterns of feeling, thought, and action that are geared to a world against God. In solitude we find the psychic distance, the perspective from which we can see, in light of eternity, the created things that trap, worry, and oppress us...We can only survive solitude if we cling to Christ there. And yet what we find of Him in that solitude enables us to return to society as free persons...In stark aloneness it is possible. . . to know that Jehovah indeed is God (Psalm 46:10).[16]

Henri Nouwen has this to say in his various works on taking time to retreat:

Solitude is the furnace of transformation. Without solitude we remain victims of our society and continue to be entangled in the illusions of the false self. Solitude is the place of great struggle and the great encounter—the struggle against the compulsions of the false self, and the encounter with the loving God who offers himself as the substance of the new self. It is the place of conversion, the place where the old self dies and the new self is born, the place where the emergence of the new man and the new woman occurs. In solitude I get rid of the scaffolding: no friends to talk with, no telephone calls to make, no meetings to attend, no music to entertain, no books to distract, just me—naked, vulnerable, weak, sinful, deprived, broken—nothing. It is nothingness that I have to face in my solitude, a nothingness so dreadful that everything in me wants to run to my friends, my work, and my distractions so that I can forget my nothingness and make myself believe that I am worth something. The confrontation with our own frightening nothingness forces us to surrender ourselves totally and unconditionally to the Lord Jesus Christ.[17]

Such powerful words about the importance of solitude and stillness are intended to convince today's Christians that these practices are an essential to life. The place I would like you to begin your journey in these two disciplines is with journaling. I have journaled for over 20 years. I believe it has made a tremendous difference both in my relationship with Christ and in my emotional health. Let me give you several benefits of journaling that I have found.

1. Writing out my prayers has helped me slow down. I frequently found myself praying and my mind racing or wandering. Writing allowed my mind to quiet its pace. I stayed on track much more easily. This was extremely helpful when I was anxious or tense. At those times the writing was soothing and calming.

2. The journal has provided a powerful tool for me to "cry out" to God; for me to say, "I can't!" and to admit my "desperation." It is healing and cleansing.

3. It makes me accountable to my commitment to sitting at Jesus' feet and listening to His words. All I need to do is look at the last dated page to see how long it has been since I last met with the Master.

4. It provides me with a detailed look at my spiritual journey. I can look back through

it and get a sense of who I am and where I have been. I can see patterns of sin and self-protectiveness more clearly. It allows me to see victories and progress, which is very helpful when you are trying to grow spiritually and emotionally.

5. It gives me a way to get help from others. I can let my wife or a good friend read sections of the journal to see if they can help me in my growth. It is important that you have a deep relationship with the person before you attempt this because of the personal nature of the journal's contents.

Now I would like to offer you some guidelines for effective use of a journal. First, I want to remind you that there is no power in the journaling itself. Writing on a tablet or on notebook paper is not a magic formula. It is simply a way to be with Christ, to sit at His feet. LeAnne Payne says journaling "is a way of keeping track of what we say to God and what we hear Him say".[18]

Second, there is not a right way to journal, so feel free to do what is most helpful for you. At times I write out prayers, and at other times I record the events of the day. Try it out until you find what works best for you. It is perfectly fine to experiment. I try to let my pen record my heart as it flows out to the Father.

Third, you can record insight you have from reading the Bible or other helpful resources. I suggest that you ingest a large, steady dose of Bible reading. The Bible is God's life manual for us. Putting His word in us is essential for emotional healing and growth.

Fourth, you can record what God tells you in the journal. This might be a specific verse or passage from the Bible, as was mentioned earlier. But it could also be the "still small voice of God". I believe God's still small voice most often comes to us in the form of thoughts and perceptions. The journal is a place to record these thoughts. We can ask God to teach us to know His voice. In John 10 Jesus says He is the good Shepherd and we are the sheep. Verse 4 says that the sheep "know His (the Shepherd's) voice". That is what we need God to teach us. One safeguard is that as we learn to know His voice, we also know that it will never violate the written word of God. This protects us from listening to the wrong source. Also, I ask those that I know intimately to offer feedback about what I think God is saying to me or what it is He is leading me to do. Use all you can to confirm His voice, because there are so many other voices out there (Satan, myself, the world, etc.).

And lastly, you can keep a clear, long-term record of your emotional growth. I suggest that you record on a daily basis the main emotions you encounter. Ask yourself these questions: When did it occur? What events of the day may have led to the emotion? Who was I with when I had the feeling? Have I had these feelings before? What happened after I had the feeling? What occurred that caused the emotion to subside? Here is an example of journaling about emotions.

Not sure where the anxiety came from but it knocked me flat. It is like the emotional wind was knocked out of me. I don't remember having any sense that it was coming. All I remember was being in the car by myself. When I got out of the car and went in the supermarket I was flooded with anxiety. What a freaky experience! While in the store all I could think was, 'I have got to get out of here, NOW!' And so that is what I did. I went back out to my car. The minute I was in the car the anxiety let up. It is so strange. I have never had an experience like this. Wait! I have been feeling a bit edgy the last week as if I could lose my emotional balance. I just blew it off at the time. Also I remember a time when I was a kid that I was left alone in a store and just freaked-out. Not sure if there is any tie between the two or not. Lord, I don't know what is going on inside of me but I know You do. Thank You for being with me no matter what I am feeling. Open my eyes to understand all this in Your time and way. Let me draw strength from Your presence. May I feel Your embrace. I turn these feelings over to You.

We have spoken a great deal about stress reduction through support systems and connection with the Savior. Remember that not all stress is bad. We all have different levels of stress that we need in order to operate at our optimum level. When you are in that "zone", you will feel alert, confident, and able to perform the job. You will be able to think and respond quickly and effectively. You are involved in the task at hand and carry it out in an energetic manner. When a situation is stressful, beyond the optimal stress level, some actions can be taken to reduce the stress. First, do something to change the situation when possible. Prompt, effective action is a great stress reducer. Consider the meaning of the situation and examine your assumptions about it. Is it really worth getting upset about? Accept what cannot be changed. All of our lives are influenced by events that are outside of our control. Relax. Removing yourself from the stressful situation may be an effective way to handle the stress; take a vacation. Avoid undue stress caused by procrastination. Create a peaceful environment to spend time alone with God. Never forsake your quiet time with the Creator. Practice living in the present, learning to enjoy each moment of life. Strive to see and appreciate the beauty and meaning in each situation. Build a support system. Nurture the relationships you value by being accepting of others and giving service where you can. For optimal health and spiritual growth, we need each other. As iron sharpens iron, we are to help each other be the person God created us to be. There are times that it will be beneficial to call a friend in the ministry to share our stresses and burdens. Additionally, there are times that the use of a professional caregiver is essential. I happen to work for a corporate chaplaincy agency that provides a corporate chaplain for the corporate chaplain staff. This is because even the caregiver needs a caregiver at times. The need for such help does not mean you are weak, crazy, or sick. It only means you are HUMAN!

There are numerous types of counselors available. Often taking the initiative to seek appropriate help is the first courageous step required for you to pursue a more satisfying, meaningful, and productive life. While you cannot remove all of the sources of stress in your life, you should be able to get rid of some. Turn off the radio and stop the noise. Clear up the clutter in your life by giving excess to others or throwing things out. And give up those stressful tasks that you volunteered for when you had extra time. Name five stresses that you could eliminate from your life. Then do something about them. An hour spent removing these causes of stress can give you a thousand less stressful hours in the future. If someone in your mission field irritates you, do not over-react. A quiet conversation with that person is less stressful than quitting your job, as well as being scripturally sound. If someone backs into your car, getting it fixed is less stressful than getting into a fight. When you react to stress with drastic measures, your reaction may often cause you more stress than the original problem. How many times have you voluntarily put yourself into situations that you knew for sure would upset you? Avoid unnecessary stress, such as long lines in supermarkets, busy traffic, and parties with people you do not like. It is time to recognize that most of these situations can be avoided by planning ahead (for example, shopping during off hours) and by learning how to say no to things you really do not want to do. If the cause of your stress seems too big to tackle, break it up into manageable parts. If your home is desperately run down, you might fix it up one room at a time. If you are far behind on your bills, you might talk to your creditors about a long-term payment plan. Use the same approach with things that make you tense. Break up your big stress-producing problems into smaller parts that produce less tension and are easier to manage. Wishing things were different will not make them different and will not make you any more comfortable about the way things are. When nothing can alter an unpleasant or stressful situation, you will find there is a certain peace in acceptance. Think about the stressful situations in your life that you know you cannot change. Only you can decide whether you will accept each situation as it is, recognizing that your refusal to accept these unchangeable situations means that you will continue to suffer from them. Setting effective goals can also help to reduce stress. Goals that are specific, establish a definite date to accomplish the goal, and create a plan to achieve the task will alleviate pressure in the mission field. Goals lead naturally into the need for time management. Without it, goals are often unmet. Use the following guide when prioritizing.

"A" - this is a high priority.
"B" - this is a medium priority.
"C" - this is a low priority.

Prioritize your goals. Then make a list, prioritizing the activities that will allow you to reach your goals. As you complete an item, mark it off your list. Any "A's" left on today's list at the end of the day are placed at the top of tomorrow's list. Delegate all items on the list that can be done by someone else. Always start with "A's," even if "C's" are easier. Procrastination promotes anxiety and makes tasks look bigger than they are. If you have an overwhelming "A" in your life, poke a small hole in it every chance you get. Eventually the "A" will become more manageable, and you can concentrate on it and be finished with it.

Because stress and the related burnout is prevalent in the ministry, there are some actions that you should take as a community chaplain to prolong your life as an effective representative of Christ in the community. As has been stated several times in this text, SPEND TIME WITH GOD. Your relationship with Him is primary. You cannot give away what you do not have. How can a chaplain represent Christ when he does not know Him deeply? Next, relate to others in a positive, soothing way. Enjoy some quiet, noncompetitive activities with your family. Share intellectual, emotional, spiritual, and recreational pursuits with friends and neighbors. Build a network of people on whom you can rely if troubled or in times of crisis. Schedule some time each day for meditation on Scripture and contemplation. Contrary to popular opinion, these two are NOT the same. Meditation is a technique of clearing the mind of all but that on which you are concentrating, in our case God's Word. To do this, get in a comfortable position and consciously relax your muscles. Beginning with your feet, work up to your neck and face, and do not forget to include your hands and arms. Once relaxation has been obtained, think of a "word" that brings a feeling of peace and comfort. You might think of the word "relax" or "peace" or "love". You might want a visual word like "water", "sunrise", or "rest". Next, spend some time reflecting on a passage of Scripture. Doing this twice a day, for 10 or 15 minutes at a time, will re-energize the body and the mind.

Contemplation, on the other hand, is to consider things intently. Use this time to consider future plans, problems that need attention, and to look for solutions and resolutions. Be a good steward of your physical body by learning to eat, sleep, and exercise properly. Eat at least one hot meal each day, and do not skip breakfast, even if you must keep it simple. For optimal functioning, you need three meals a day. Do not get caught up in fad diets. When you eat, plan meals that use all basic food groups. Limit the intake of drinks, foods, and drugs that have caffeine in them: coffee, tea, cola drinks, chocolate, and some headache and cold medicines. Sleep at least 6-8 hours each night. Have one day a week that you can wake up naturally. Exercise regularly. This can be a 20 minute walk, an aerobics program, swimming, biking, or anything else that fits into your schedule. Exercise to the point of perspiration at least twice a week - 3 or 4 times a week is preferred. Recognize that you cannot do everything, all of the time. Be realistic about time commitments; allow enough time for what must be done. Do one thing at a time. Cooperate instead of competing. Delegate. If you cannot do it, ask someone else. Reward yourself every week for just being the person that God created you to be. This can be accomplished by spending time enjoying a leisure activity that develops a non-work related part of you.

In conclusion, availability can mean many things to the chaplain. First, it conveys the idea of being available to God in answering affirmatively to the calling that He placed on you to work in the mission field of the society called America. You must also remember that God is making Himself available to you; without Him this ministry cannot take place. Additionally, availability has the connotation of being available to the people in your mission field. Understanding how to be available to those in your community is a must for success. Building relationships with intentionality is crucial to availability. Finally, realize that availability can be defined as being available for yourself; taking care of yourself so that stress can be reduced and burnout can be avoided.

Stories From the Field: #12
"You Never Know Where It Will Happen"*

You just never know when the opportunity may present itself to see a person come to know Jesus Christ as their personal Savior. A commonly used phrase among chaplains is, "There is always someone waiting to see the chaplain." When my wife and I participated in the 2005 Corporate Chaplains of America Marriage Retreat Cruise, little did we know that somewhere in the Caribbean Sea someone would be waiting to see the chaplain. Allow me to explain.

Each night on the cruise ship my wife and I would meet in the formal dining room, where we were greeted by a group of waiters that would take our orders for the evening meal. From the very beginning I noticed that one young lady from Trinidad named Nicole was always attending our table. On one particular night my wife and I asked Nicole if she was anxious to get back home to her family. Nicole shared with us that she missed her family, especially her son and grandmother. I asked if she had any brothers or sisters, and she told me that she had a brother living in New York.

After our food was served, I began to ask Nicole some questions about what it was like living and working on a cruise ship. She said, "I guess it's a lot of fun, but I cannot wait to see my family again." I then asked her what her brother did in New York. She replied, "He is a minister, a Seventh Day Adventist preacher." I asked her if she came from a religious family. She replied, "Yes, my grandmother constantly tells me that I should do all these things, you know, such as don't go here and don't go there and that I should go to church." Looking very frustrated, Nicole said, "I cannot go to church like my brother does each week, because I am living and working on a cruise ship!"

I then began to probe a little deeper. I asked Nicole if she believed in God. She said, "I don't know if I really believe in God or not. My roommate says that there is no God, and that what you see is all there is to life. When you die you are just dead. Perhaps my roommate is right. I do not worry about these matters. It would be too hard for me to be religious like my grandmother and brother. I don't worry about it."

I agreed with her that these are deep matters to think about. I then asked her,

"What if your roommate is wrong about her views of God and the hereafter? Are you aware that in Hebrews 9:27 the Bible tells us that we are appointed to die, and after death face judgment?' And are you aware that in Romans 14:10-12 the Bible says that one day every one of us will have to give an account of our lives before God?"

At this point my wife and I noticed a tear in her eye. I then shared with Nicole that her brother and I had much in common. By that I meant that I too believed in God and that I too was a minister. I then asked her if my wife and I could share something very important for her to think about in regards to religion. I could sense the curiosity in her expression. I told Nicole not to worry about trying please God by what she wears or how she looks or if she could attend church every week. And do not worry about becoming a Seventh Day Adventist, a Catholic, a Baptist, or for that matter any other name that she associates with being a religious person. These are matters to deal with at a later time. I said, "Nicole, the most important matter you need to be concerned about today is your relationship with God."

My wife and I told Nicole that we do not want her to confuse what is often called Christianity and religion with the most important decision she will make in her life. I challenged her with one question: "Are you convinced that God does not exist?" With tears in her eyes, Nicole said, "No." My wife and I then began to explain to her what Jesus meant when He claimed to be the Way, the Truth, and the Life in John 14:6. The door was now open for us to fully share the gospel with Nicole.

After explaining the life-changing good news of Jesus Christ and the importance of following the teachings of Christ that are taught in the Bible, I asked her if she would like to become a follower of Jesus Christ. With tears in Nicole's eyes, my wife and I held her hand and we led Nicole in the sinner's prayer. I asked Nicole if she knew of any other Christians on the ship. She nodded yes. I encouraged her to seek out those other Christians. But above all else, I encouraged her to begin reading the Bible.

The next day we were able to provide Nicole with a Bible and a gospel tract that explained what she had just experienced. I wrote the date of her spiritual birthday on the first page of her Bible. She cried and we rejoiced, as we could see her doubts replaced with faith in Jesus Christ. And the small still voice of the Holy Spirit reminded me to "... Always be prepared to give an answer to everyone who asks you to give the reason for the hope that you have ..." (1 Peter 3:15 NIV).

– Submitted by Gary W.
Indianapolis, IN

*Individuals in this story have granted permission for its use.

Stories From the Field: #13
"Available to All"*

One of the areas that I have found to be most pleasurable to serve as a community chaplain is in a prison work release program. For some, their crimes are significantly behind them. Many others, however, have been recently paroled or are still on probation. Many are currently going through detoxification for drugs and alcohol, struggling to stay clean and sober—and keep their job—in order to prevent a return trip to prison. Many of these ex-convicts have known no other life.

These individuals are often crude, the language is frequently vulgar, and the personalities can be inflammatory. However, not only is this field white for harvest, these fellow humans are so very appreciative of the care they receive from their community chaplain. Many of these people have never had another person love them unconditionally or serve them with no agenda. Many have never come to know the love of Jesus Christ. In my six months' of service, four of these parolees have accepted Christ as their Savior; and there are many more who are considering making that decision.

You see, relationships here are not easily established and held. Trust is earned. Neither do all these relationships have happily ever after endings. Many must be shepherded from square one, knowing practically nothing about what pleases God. It is an environment where even those accepting Christ or professing Christianity stumble and fall, sometimes over and over. It takes great patience. Yet I would have it no other way. If I choose not to show these people, created and loved by God, just as I am, the love of Jesus Christ...who will?

– Submitted By Greg B.
Phoenix, AZ

*Individuals in this story have granted permission for its use.

Questions

Reflect on the Stories From the Field found in this chapter and answer the following questions:

1. How would you handle the situation that was described?
2. What information found in the story is confidential?
3. What information found in the story can be shared with others? With whom may this information be shared? Under what circumstances may this information be shared?
4. How does the information found in this chapter pertain to the story?

End Notes

1. Ted Goodman, ed., *The Forbes Book of Business Quotations: 14,173 Thoughts on the Business of Life* (New York: Black Dog & Leventhal, 1997), 701

2. David A. Seamands, *Healing Grace: Finding Freedom From The Performance Trap* (Indianapolis, IN: Light and Life Communications, 2003), 38.

3. Quoted in sermon by Frank Cox at North Metro First Baptist Church on 4 December 2004. Dr. Frank Cox is the Pastor of North Metro First Baptist Church, located at 1026 Old Peachtree Road, Lawrenceville, GA 30043. Also, see Richard Madsen, et al., eds., *Habits of the Heart: Individualism and Commitment in American Life* (Berkeley, CA: University of California Press, 1985).

4. Ibid.

5. Ibid.

6. Ibid.

7. See American Red Cross <http://www.redcross.org> Press Release # 010770314151700 (Accessed January 2005).

8. W. E. Vine, "Compassion," in *Expository Dictionary of New Testament Words*, vol. 1 (London: Oliphants, 1940), 218.

9. See *Webster's Encyclopedic Unabridged Dictionary of the English Language*, s.v. "compassion," (New York: Gramercy, 1994).

10. Robert K. Greenleaf, *Servant Leadership: A Journey into the Nature of Legitimate Power and Greatness* (New York: Paulist, 1977), 13-14.

11. Southern Baptist Convention-North American Mission Board, *Involving Baptists in Disaster Relief* (Alpharetta, GA: NAMB, n.d.), 29.

12. Corporate Chaplains of America Quarterly Training Meeting, Paul Carlisle presentation in March 2004.

13. See Carmen R. Berry, *When Helping You Is Hurting Me: Escaping the Messiah Trap* (San Francisco, CA: Harper & Row, 1988).

14. Seamands, *Healing Grace*, 38.

15. Cited by H. Gerald Colbert, "Church Planter Network Resource," <http://www.church plantingvillage.net/atf/cf/%7B087EF6B4-D6E5-4BBF-BED1-7983D360F394%7D/18% 20Paper--Developing%20Your%20Ministry%20Roles.pdf.> (Accessed 15 November 2005), 23.

16. See Dallas Willard, *The Spirit of the Disciplines: Understanding How God Changes Lives* (San Francisco, CA: Harper & Row, 1988), 156-92.

17. Henri J. M. Nouwen, *The Way of the Heart: Desert Spirituality and Contemporary Ministry* (New York: HarperCollins, 1981), 25-26.

18. For LeAnne Payne's thoughts on praying journaling, see Part 1, "Keeping a Listening Prayer

Journal" on *Listening Prayer: Learning to Hear God's Voice and Keep a Prayer Journal* (Grand Rapids, MI: Baker, 1994), 19-120.

Unit Four

Caring in Crisis

Unit 4 concludes with pragmatic principles for equipping the community chaplain to help in the many times of crisis encountered by those in their care.

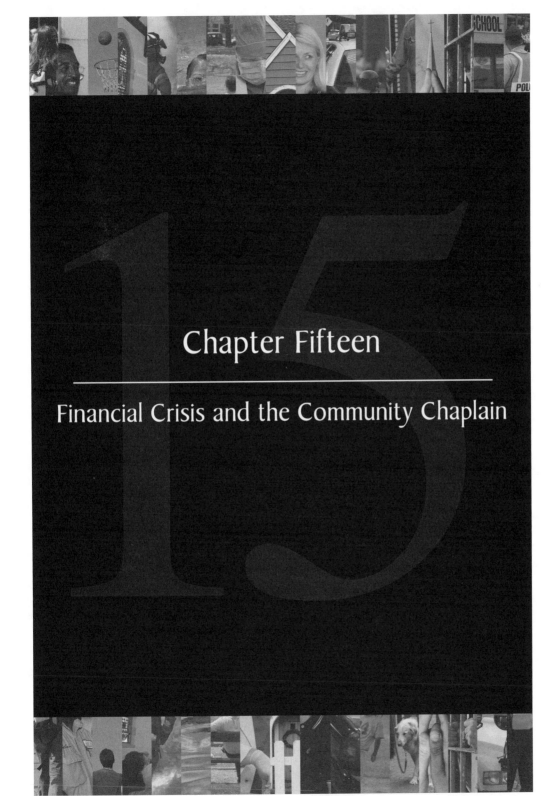

Chapter Fifteen

Financial Crisis and the Community Chaplain

CHAPTER FIFTEEN

Financial Crisis and the Community Chaplain

————————————— Objectives —————————————

During the course of this chapter, we will perform the following tasks::

- Discover the purpose of money

- Explore Scriptural thoughts on money

- List reasons why indebtedness occurs

- Describe the process for setting financial goals

- List methods to manage cash flow to achieve financial goals

- Describe the process for saving for future needs

A ny time the topic turns to finances, most Americans develop a small pit in their stomachs. Why is this so? Most of us, 89% according to most recent studies done by the federal government, owe more than we own. Mismanagement and overspending will be the most common issues that will face the community chaplain in his mission field. We will address many issues regarding finances in this chapter. Before getting into the finances of the families to which we will minister, let us discuss the community chaplain.

In a classic bestselling book, *Rich Christians in an Age of Hunger*, Ronald Sider examines how Christians that have been blessed with financial advantage should leverage those assets to benefit the poor.[1] It is important to address two vital areas regarding finances and the community chaplain. First, as discussed in other chapters, the chaplain should be an example of stewardship and Christ-likeness when it comes to their personal finances. This means that the community chaplain should be a living example of all of the financial principles that will be discussed later in this chapter.

Additionally, the chaplain will need to formulate a balance of grace and accountability when it comes to the finances of others. If he is not careful, a chaplain can place his own personal finances in jeopardy by helping others in a financial crisis. Deciding on a policy before getting into a tempting situation is a good practice. Below you will see a sample policy on giving and/or loaning money to individuals. Simply put, when people ask the chaplain for a loan or a gift, you may reply that the ministry policy prohibits loaning money. When a person has a legitimate need for money, such as a medical emergency or a major car repair, and does not have adequate savings, suggest the individual to go to his employer and discuss the problem with the owner or Human Resources to examine different options that may be available. If you should decide to loan money to an individual, never count on the funds being repaid. Other options include suggesting the company set up an emergency fund that can be available to the employees, based on need and the presence of funds to cover the need. Other agencies, such as United Way or the Consumer Credit Counseling Service, are also good resources for those in financial need.

If the company does want to establish an emergency fund, guidelines that may be helpful can include the purpose of the fund, who qualifies to access the fund, how to apply for assistance, and how the decisions are made. The purpose may include a description, stating that the fund is designed to help all associates who find themselves in a financial crisis situation, explaining that the fund exists to provide a means of support for those who experience a crisis of a medical or catastrophic nature that causes extreme financial difficulty and prevents the associate from functioning in a productive manner. Examples include the inability to afford funeral expenses, travel to the bedside of a terminally ill immediate family member, medical expenses not covered by insurance, health and safety issues outside of the associate's control, assistance to military families, etc. Immediate family of the associate includes the spouse, children, siblings, parents, and other dependents. Individual situations can then be reviewed by a Grants Committee to ensure that the best solution for the associate is identified. Have the person describe the nature of the emergency situation, along with copies of any documentation that may be needed.

Churches, perhaps the one that you attend, often have benevolence funds that are established for the purpose of helping those in need. Some of the same guidelines that have been described above are applicable to church groups as well.

It is always good to explore all options with someone in a financial crisis. Do they have another avenue for assistance, such as a family member or friend, credit cards to use until funds can be obtained, a savings account, 401(k) or other resources that can be liquidated? If the answer is no, then bringing the request to the Grants Commit-tee would be a viable alternative. Often, having information about why and how the expense occurred can assist in making a decision. This can also be helpful in getting the funds to the appropriate party, i.e. paying the rent directly to the landlord instead of giving the funds to the person in need.

Once an individual has gone through proper channels to meet an urgent need,

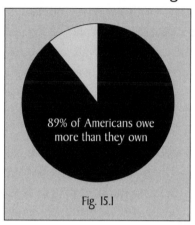

89% of Americans owe more than they own

Fig. 15.1

he will want to sit down with the chaplain and fig-ure out a way to get out of debt. Again, 89% of Americans spend 125% of their total income. That means that not only are they spending all that they are making, they are borrowing another 25% in any given year. The real question when it comes to fi-nances is, "What is my goal?" Therefore, the issue that brings them to the chaplain is financial, but it really has roots that are much deeper and should lead to a spiritual conversation. See other chapters for information on transitioning to spiritual talk.

Being an Example

The first step in being an effective chaplain is to be a good example. This means that reducing and eliminating your own personal debt is the first step. The average American household has $30,000 in debt, excluding their home. This translates into as much as $1000.00 per month in debt reduction and interest payments.[2] Debt is not a tool, it is a method that banks use to become wealthy. Scripture is clear about God's feeling on debt: "The rich rules over the poor, And the borrower becomes the lender's slave" (Proverbs 22:7 NASB). "It was for freedom that Christ set us free; therefore keep standing firm and do not be subject again to a yoke of slavery" (Galatians 5:1 NASB).

When sitting down with an associate or family to determine how to assist with finances, the first thing to do is to determine where the person is currently. This helps them understand that they are worth more than just what a balance sheet might say and to learn how much is enough. Additionally, focus the individual on the purpose of money. It is simply a vehicle to accomplish the goals of the person or family. Once the goals have been outlined, a budget is a tool to help the money facilitate success.

What should this conversation look like? As you sit down with the person, realize that the prospect of developing and adhering to a financial strategy can be overwhelming. However, it does not have to be so complicated. Consider the following three steps:

- Measure your current financial status.
- Identify your financial objectives.
- Identify the steps to get you there.

Measuring your current financial status can be accomplished by preparing a personal balance sheet. An example of a balance sheet will be found later in the chapter. Identifying your financial objectives is simple. Most people indicate that retirement security, funding children's education, increasing current income, reducing taxes and passing accumulated wealth to their families at death are their primary financial objectives. Quantifying what it will take to reach those objectives can be more complex. Here are some points to include in your financial strategy.

Sensible spending: Understand how you spend your money. Prepare a household spending worksheet. It will enable you to prioritize your spending and identify areas with saving potential. Be sure to include on your spending log things like how much was spent, where it was spent, whom you were with when spending, how you were feeling when spending, etc. The goal is to look for trends in spending patterns.

Prudent borrowing: Borrowing can enable you to obtain things that are otherwise beyond your current reach, but borrowing costs money. Loans for things that provide lasting and ongoing value (such as an education, a home, or an auto) are smarter than borrowing for short-term gratification (extravagant vacations or expensive jewelry). Prudent borrowing also includes making sure the rates and terms of your loans are as attractive as you can get. Before borrowing (whether it is a credit card, auto loan, mortgage or other loan), make sure you understand all the terms. The interest rate, length of loan, and method of calculating interest should be clearly understood.

Consistent saving: Utilizing a payroll deduction or another automatic savings program is usually more successful than trying to save on a less regular basis. Automatic saving plans result in consistent deposits and are available in a number of forms. Select one that fits your budget and meets your long-term needs.

Wise investing: Investments come with risks and, hopefully, higher returns to compensate for those risks. Understanding the risks of loss, price fluctuation, and inflation are necessary when creating a sound investment strategy. Diversification, asset allocation (such as dividing funds into stock), bond and cash investments, and investment costs should all be considered as part of a wise investment strategy.

Adequate protection: Periodically, you should review all your insurance coverage. This includes homeowners/renters, health, disability, auto, and any umbrella policies you may have. For peace of mind, make sure you have the right combination of coverage and deductibles. If you use insurance primarily for "catastrophic" coverage, remember that higher deductibles usually translate into lower premiums. For life insurance, evaluate how much you really need. If your family would need significant funds to replace your income, a larger policy may make sense. If you are single, perhaps a smaller policy (and smaller premiums) will be sufficient. Also, compare the benefits and costs of term and whole life policies. For younger, healthy individuals without a need for permanent protection, a term policy may be a better choice.

Use a qualified advisor, if you need one: In areas where you need or want help, find the right advisor. It may be an investment professional, insurance agent, financial planner, credit counselor, or trusted family friend that can provide guidance. Make sure they are qualified and that you can comfortably work with them. Do your homework. The more knowledgeable you are, the better you will be able to evaluate recommendations. Remember, your decisions will affect you and your family for a long time.

A Sample Budget Worksheet

Dave Ramsey, a financial advisor with a call-in radio show, suggests the following budget worksheet.

MONTHLY CASH-FLOW PLAN

Budgeted Item	Sub-total	Total	Actually Spent	% Of Take Home Pay
Charitable Gifts		_____	_____	_____
Saving				
Emergency Fund	_____		_____	
Retirement Fund	_____		_____	
College Fund	_____	_____	_____	_____
Housing				
First Mortgage	_____		_____	
Second Mortgage	_____		_____	
Real-Estate Taxes	_____		_____	
Homeowners Ins.	_____		_____	
Repairs or Mn. Fee	_____		_____	
Replace Furniture	_____		_____	
Other _____	_____	_____	_____	_____
Utilities				
Electricity	_____		_____	
Water	_____		_____	
Gas	_____		_____	
Phone	_____		_____	
Trash	_____		_____	
Cable	_____	_____	_____	_____
Food				
Grocery	_____		_____	
Restaurants	_____	_____	_____	_____

Budgeted Item	Sub-total	Total	Actually Spent	% Of Take Home Pay
Transportation				
Car Payment	_____		_____	
Car Payment	_____		_____	
Gas and Oil	_____		_____	
Repairs and Tires	_____		_____	
Car Insurance	_____		_____	
License and Taxes	_____		_____	
Car Replacement	_____	_____	_____	_____
Clothing				
Children	_____		_____	
Adults	_____		_____	
Cleaning/Laun.	_____	_____	_____	_____
Medical/Health				
Disability Ins.	_____		_____	
Health Insurance	_____		_____	
Doctor Bills	_____		_____	
Dentist	_____		_____	
Optometrist	_____		_____	
Drugs	_____	_____	_____	_____
Personal				
Life Insurance	_____		_____	
Child Care	_____		_____	
Baby Sitter	_____		_____	
Toiletries	_____		_____	
Hair Care	_____		_____	
Education/Adult	_____		_____	
School Tuition	_____		_____	

Budgeted Item	Sub-total	Total	Actually Spent	% Of Take Home Pay
School Supplies	_____		_____	
Child Support	_____		_____	
Alimony	_____		_____	
Subscriptions	_____		_____	
Organization Dues	_____		_____	
Gifts (incl. Chr.)	_____		_____	
Miscellaneous	_____		_____	
BLOW $$	_____	_____	_____	_____

Recreation

Entertainment	_____		_____	
Vacation	_____	_____	_____	_____

Debts (Hopefully 0)

Visa 1	_____		_____	
Visa 2	_____		_____	
Mastercard 1	_____		_____	
Mastercard 2	_____		_____	
American Express	_____		_____	
Discover Card	_____		_____	
Gas Card 1	_____		_____	
Gas Card 2	_____		_____	
Dept. Store Card 1	_____		_____	
Dept. Store Card 2	_____		_____	
Finance Co. 1	_____		_____	
Finance Co. 2	_____		_____	
Credit Line	_____		_____	
Student Loan 1	_____		_____	
Student Loan 2	_____		_____	
Other _____	_____		_____	

Budgeted Item	Sub-total	Total	Actually Spent	% Of Take Home Pay
Other _____	_____		_____	
Other _____	_____		_____	
Other _____	_____		_____	
Other _____	_____	_____	_____	_____
Grand Total		_____	_____	
Total Household Income		_____		
		Zero		

RECOMMENDED PERCENTAGES

Item	Actual %	Recommended %
Charitable Gifts	_____	10-15%
Saving	_____	5-10%
Housing	_____	25-35%
Utilities	_____	5-10%
Food	_____	5-15%
Transportation	_____	10-15%
Clothing	_____	2-7%
Medical/Health	_____	5-10%
Personal	_____	5-10%
Recreational	_____	5-10%
Debts	_____	5-10%

The Total Money Makeover - Dave Ramsey[3]

Basic Financial Principles

Since most of us, including community chaplains, do not have an adequate grasp of finances for households, a basic primer will be needed at this point. Taking care of your long-term financial affairs can be one of the easiest things to put off. It often seems that dealing with daily finances and the other things of everyday life take precedence over the need to create a workable financial plan. Here are some ideas that will help you come up with a plan that will cover the basics and put you on the road to a secure financial future.

Develop a financial reserve: Being prepared (with 3 to 6 months' living expenses) can help relieve some of the financial anxiety we often feel. Consider an automatic savings plan with some amount being deposited into a savings account from each paycheck. The fund will grow and you may end up not even missing what is saved each month.

Get rid of high interest rate credit card debt: Interest rates on some credit cards are high. If you are carrying over balances and paying interest, cut down on your card use, pay more than the required monthly minimum and eliminate this expense. Also, you may want to consider a different credit card that has a lower rate.

Develop a household budget: This is often one of the most dreaded parts to being financially responsible. To make the process less dreaded, call it a "household spending analysis". Determining how you spend your money will probably lead to identifying how to reduce some expenses. You may want to use some common financial management software (Quicken or Microsoft Money) to help. These relatively inexpensive programs will also help organize your finances and may save you time.

Save for retirement: Your financial lifestyle during retirement is largely dependent on the financial decisions you make before retiring. Social Security and the traditional company defined benefit plans are becoming less important. The responsibility is shifting to the individual. Start with your employer's retirement plan. Many plans, especially 401(k) plans, make it easy to save, offer investment flexibility, and enable you to reduce your taxes. Many plans also have provisions for the employer to make contributions on your behalf. Review your plan details, contribute as much as you can, and at least contribute enough to get the full employer "match". If you have taken full advantage of company sponsored plans and can still afford it, consider contributions to an IRA or Roth IRA. The tax deferred compounding aspects of these plans enable your funds to grow faster.

Fig. 15.2 Pay careful attention to taxes.

Be sensitive to taxes: No one likes to pay more income taxes than absolutely necessary. Be aware of the opportunity of deducting certain items like mortgage interest, state and local taxes, charitable contributions, and certain medical expenses. Also, consider the preferential tax treatment from capital gains on your investments.

Have a sensible investment strategy: Start with an asset allocation goal that divides your investments into equity, fixed income, and cash investment categories. Your initial asset allocation should be based on your time horizon (age) and how you feel about taking risks. The younger you are, and the more comfortable you feel with risk, allocating a larger portion of your funds to equities may help you earn the higher returns of stocks that have historically been available. However, remember that all investments involve risk and that past performance is no guarantee of future results.

Be adequately protected: Insurance provides protection against the unknown. Make sure your possessions, life, and health are adequately insured. Examine the level of deductibles and the coverage amounts to get the protection you need at the lowest cost.

Take care of estate planning: Having a well thought-out will can ensure that your assets are distributed as you desire upon your death and can help reduce any estate taxes that may be due. However, estate planning is more than reducing taxes. Your estate plan should include documents that designate someone to make financial decisions if you are incapable of making them (durable power of attorney for finances) and that designate someone to make medical decisions if you are incapacitated (durable power of attorney for health care).

Finally, organize your records: Having a system for handling monthly expenses can reduce the stress and time needed to handle your everyday finances. Using a system to keep track of investment and tax records will make every tax season less "taxing". Keep other important information organized. Having to hunt for the name of your insurance agent, an account number, a frequent flyer number, or any other bit of information can be a waste of time.

Eliminating Debt

There are many debt helps available for people. Be sure that you are completely comfortable with whom you recommend to others. For instance, typing the keywords "Debt Negotiators" into a search engine produced over 35,000 web sites. However, beware of companies that promise to cut your bills in half by negotiating lower payoff amounts from creditors. Sign on with a debt negotiator or debt-settlement company, and your credit rating and your wallet could take some serious hits. If high fees and trashed credit are not bad enough, you may also owe taxes on any debt that gets wiped away. It is easy to wind up in worse financial shape than when you started. Paul Richard, Executive Director of the Institute of Consumer Financial Education in San Diego, indicates:

> Be very, very careful. Because there can be substantially more harm than good. It's the fees, the possible liability to the IRS after you get this negotiated and they're not doing anything for you that you can't do yourself. These slick debt negotiators, they smooth talk people around all these issues. They're really taking advantage of people.[4]

Most individuals have debt of one kind or another. It may be a home mortgage, a credit card, a student loan, an auto loan, or some other form of loan. Using debt as part of an overall financial strategy can be a good thing. Debt becomes a bad thing when you have too much of it, have the wrong kinds, or when its presence causes undue anxiety or bad behavior. Here are some ideas to help you make sure you are controlling your debt and not the other way around.

Set priorities for using debt: Borrow money for things that provide long-term and lasting value. Borrowing for college costs may be considered good. Charging another extravagant vacation on your credit card is probably not a good use of debt.

Use the best type of borrowing: Whether it is choosing a credit card or a home mortgage, be sure the terms match up with your goals and how you manage your finances. If you pay every credit card bill in full and do not incur any finance charges, it may be OK to have a card that has a high interest rate (you avoid it with timely payments) but offers rewards for use (like miles or money back) or has no annual fee. On the other hand, if you carry over balances and pay finance charges, the interest rate you pay becomes more important. If you are considering a mortgage, the type you choose (fixed or adjustable) will affect the interest rate. Choose one that matches your behavior. If you plan to sell your house soon, you may want an Adjustable Rate Mortgage (ARM) with a lower interest rate. If you plan to stay in the home or cannot afford any increase in payments if interest rates rise, consider a long-term fixed rate mortgage.

Eliminate high cost borrowing: If your existing debt has a high interest rate, get rid of that form of debt. Determine if you can convert it to another type of debt with a lower rate. If you are paying interest on your credit card balances, find a card that offers a lower rate; but watch out for "teaser" rates. If you have equity in your home, you may be able to use a home equity loan to consolidate all your debts at a lower rate.

Pay down your debt: This can be a difficult step for many. Incurring interest charges you cannot afford or you do not want is not a good use of your money. Find ways to pay down what you owe. Pay more than the minimum due on credit cards. Do not buy that piece of clothing you do not need or take a fancy trip when a visit with family would be just as enjoyable. Ultimately, paying down debt takes discipline and sacrifice.

What if you cannot pay your bills? This is when you should get help. First, stop incurring more debt. Quit using or destroy your credit cards. Then, work with your creditors. You may be able to work out a payment schedule. Explain your situation and that you want to pay what you owe. They may be able to help. If not, at least you have tried. One caveat: be sure to stop using the credit cards, but do not close the accounts. When an account is closed with a balance owed, the interest rate can increase dramatically.

Do not bounce checks: In some states, it is a worse offense to write a bad check than it is not to pay your debt. In addition, you may be charged for the bad check. It looks very bad to a creditor if your check bounces.

Getting professional help: There are several organizations available that help individuals when all else fails. The Consumer Credit Counseling Service is one of those agencies. They can help you create a plan to work your way out of debt. Look in your phone book for a local office. Their service is free and has helped thousands. Be very wary of organizations that offer to fix your credit rating or want you to pay them a fee to get you out of debt easily. If their "pitch" sounds too good to be true, it probably is.

Check Your Credit Report: Maintaining a solid credit history is an important part of managing your finances. A good credit record can make future borrowing easier and help you qualify for lower rates. Three large credit reporting companies compile credit reports on millions of individuals and make those reports available to businesses. Making sure the information in those reports is correct is important. You can request copies of your credit report, sometimes at no cost, by contacting these companies.

> Experian - 888/397-3742
> Equifax - 800/997-2493
> TransUnion - 800/888-4213

You may also try websites that offer free credit reports, such as freecreditreport.com. Do not be surprised if the reports are somewhat different. Each company gets information from many sources. If you find the information in your file is inaccurate or unfair, you can take steps to correct it or at least get your side of the story attached to your file. If a creditor has made an inaccurate complaint, you can write to the creditor and insist the record be corrected. You should also write to the credit bureau and request their records be corrected. To review the credit record of a business, contact Dun &

Bradstreet at 800-234-3867. There is a charge, but the information is useful. You can also order from their web site. Having an inaccurate credit report can cause problems at the worst possible times. Review your credit report annually and make sure it is accurate. A solid credit record and an accurate credit report are valuable assets.

Once you have made sure that nothing is incorrect on the credit report, begin to eliminate debt in the following ways:

- Stop using credit cards and payment plan systems. You cannot get out of a hole by digging at the bottom. On average, you will pay for an item 3 times when you place it on a credit card.
- Establish a budget. Spend every dollar on paper before payday.
- Agree to work together to be debt free. Mark 3:25 states, "If a house is divided against itself, that house cannot stand" (NIV).
- Use cash for everything. When you spend cash, you feel the loss. Use an envelope system. It worked for your grandparents.
- Reshape your thinking. Eliminate denial along with your debt. The fact is that most people stay in jobs they hate because they cannot afford to leave. People yearn to become healthy, wealthy, and wise with no effort and risk, but it will never happen. Why do you suppose lotteries collect millions and millions of dollars? "Debt is not the problem; it is the symptom of overspending and undersaving."
- Walk before you run. Save some money quickly, about $1000.00. You can go any where if you go one step at a time. You need an emergency fund that will prevent you from using a credit card to bail you out. An emergency fund can turn a crisis into an inconvenience.
- Use the power of focus. When you try to do everything at once, progress can be very slow. When you put 3% in your 401(k), $50 extra on the house payment, and $5 extra on the credit card, you dilute your efforts. Because you attack several areas at once, you do not *finish* anything you start for a long time. That makes you feel that you are not accomplishing anything, which is very dangerous.
- Use the debt snowball. Your income is the biggest debt eliminating tool that you have. You must regain control of your income. List the balances of your debt from smallest owed to largest owed. Put all available money each month on the smallest balance while paying the minimums on the rest. When that balance is paid, focus that payment, and the minimum you have been paying, on the next smallest card,

Smallest to largest

330

and so on until all have been paid off.

- Giving is the biggest reward in being financially responsible. Many Christians have a dark secret; they do not tithe, because if they did, they could not pay their monthly debts. This is called disobedience. Even secular financial planners Suze Orman and Clark Howard recommend giving, no matter how much debt is present, because of the feeling of optimism that is gained.[5]

Using Debt Wisely

There are times when it makes sense to go into debt. Owning a home would be out of reach for many without having access to a mortgage. The sensible use of debt should be part of a sound financial strategy. Debt can enable us to enjoy things that otherwise are beyond our current reach. We have already seen that borrowing can also have its ugly side. Too much, too expensive, or the wrong kinds of debt can make life miserable. Borrowing costs money. That is not necessarily bad. It just means that when you pay it back, you have to pay more than you borrowed. The components of a good debt strategy are quite simple:

- Carefully choose when to borrow and for what to borrow.
- Find the best interest rate and terms, based on your needs and wants.
- Live up to your repayment responsibilities.
- Periodically review your debt. Refinancing your mortgage or auto loan may save you money.

A good credit record does more than just make future credit approval easier to get. Most lenders use your credit record to determine credit limits and what rates to charge. A good credit record can save you money. Maintaining a good credit report can be attained by never borrowing money that you cannot repay or borrowing for a luxury item if you cannot afford the necessities, prioritizing your borrowing, and reserving some borrowing capacity for emergencies. Take action immediately if your borrowing is getting out of control. If credit cards are the problem, stop using them or even cut them up. Contact lenders to develop a workable repayment plan. A qualified credit counselor can help.

Comparing credit cards can be confusing. You have to consider interest rates, fees,

Fig. 15.3 Compare interest rates, fees, and benefits when choosing a credit card.

and associated benefits. The right card for you should reflect how you use it. If you pay the full balance monthly, the interest rate is of little concern. Focus on any annual fee and benefits such as airline miles. If you carry over balances, the interest rate should be a top concern. The "right mortgage" for you should balance interest rate, length, and down payment requirements that fit your situation. Adjustable rate mortgages usually have lower rates, but your payments may rise. Long-term mortgages usually lock at a higher rate. If you expect to stay in one location only a few years, an adjustable rate mortgage may be best. If an increase in monthly payments would be too painful, look at a fixed rate mortgage or an adjustable one with rate adjustment limits.

Being conservative in your use of borrowing can help you take control of your financial future. Borrowing for the right reasons and living up to your repayment responsibilities can make borrowing a useful financial tool.

A "first" credit card can be exciting, tempting, and intimidating. If you are getting your first credit card (or your child is getting his/her first card), here are some ideas to keep in mind. A credit card is serious business. The issuing company is lending you money, and you have responsibilities. One card is probably enough. Avoid the temptation to overspend by only having one card. Keep the credit limit low. Depending on how you are going to use it, $500 or $1000 is high enough for most first-time credit card users. Pay off the entire balance each month. Make the payments on time. This helps build a good record and avoids late payment charges. Use the card for emergencies. Start off slowly with this new convenience. Keep using cash and checks for most purchases, especially until you get comfortable with the card. Never let others use your card. You are responsible for all charges on your card. Do not let others borrow it or give out the number. Keep track of your use of the card, and compare your records to what shows up on the monthly statement. Keep the card active. Even if you are only using the card for emergencies, use it for small purchases every three or four months just to keep it active. Then be sure to pay off the balance before any interest is due. Avoid using the card for cash advances. The interest rate charged for advances is usually high, and interest is charged immediately. Create a spending and budget plan. Do not let your credit card payments exceed 20% of your monthly income.

If having a credit card turns out to be a problem, get rid of it or stop using it for a while. The credit card companies make money by charging interest on long-term balances. Often the rates they charge are relatively high. Choose a card that fits how you are going to use it. Probably for a first time user, find a card that has low (or no) annual fees and low interest rates. If you are not going to use it much, the benefits (airline miles or gifts) will not compensate for the fees usually found with these types of cards. Having a good credit record is important. Those with good records usually find that getting credit is easier, and they often qualify for lower rates on their borrowing. Investigate the details of the card thoroughly. Be sure to understand all the fees and how interest charges are calculated.

Finances For A Lifetime

Having an overall, sound financial strategy requires that you recognize that your finances are in a constant state of change. Not only do financial markets fluctuate, but also your financial needs change over time. Fortunately, it is easier to predict the changes in your financial life stages than it is to predict the direction of the financial markets. According to Ron Blue of Crown Financial, most individuals pass through three primary financial life stages as they age.[6] Income levels, spending patterns, family situations, and areas of financial concern, while not exactly predictable, tend to follow a pattern.

During stage one, young adults face the task of learning how to manage spending and saving within the constraint of their income level. Life events such as entering the work force, marriage, and the birth of children occur. The financial decisions that accompany these events include purchasing a car and a home and developing financial habits. Developing sound financial habits is critical. Learn how you are spending your money to identify ways to save. Prepare a household budget. Use a wise borrowing strategy. Borrow for things that provide long-term value. Control the use of credit cards. Establish a saving pattern. Consider an automatic savings program so that some amount is deposited into a savings account each paycheck. Set some savings goals.

Whether it is accumulating a down payment for a home, paying for a car, or saving for a vacation, connecting a tangible goal with your saving can provide the motivation and discipline you need to save. Make sure you have adequate insurance. Take advantage of employee benefit plans at work.

In the second stage of your financial life, the prime earning years, your income is rising as well as expenses. Nicer homes, nicer cars, and children can easily consume your increasing income. This is also the time when the financial decisions you make will have the greatest impact on the financial lifestyle you will enjoy during retirement. By now you should have developed some savings and the expertise to make sound choices. Start early to save for children's college expenses. Consider using custodial accounts, Section 529 Plans, or Coverdale Education IRAs to get additional tax advantages with the college funds. Take full advantage of employer offered retirement plans. If you have a 401(k) plan available, contribute as much as you can, and at least enough to get the full employer matching contribution. Invest wisely. Consider an asset allocation strategy that matches your time horizon and risk tolerance. Do not ignore the potential long-term returns of equities, but do your homework or rely on a qualified advisor. Be sure your insurance protection has kept pace with your needs. Having adequate life insurance to protect your family, in case of your untimely death, is critical. Prepare an estate plan to minimize taxes and to ensure that your custodial, financial, and medical wishes are carried out.

These years can, and should be, some of the most enjoyable and fulfilling times of your life. Usually, this time in life includes major promotions at work, retirement, grandchildren, and possibly, the death of a spouse. Greater tax sensitivity, preservation of assets, and estate planning become important financial aspects. If children and grandchildren are part of your life, having the financial ability to help them can be rewarding. A successful career, the freedom to live the retirement lifestyle of choice, and a sense of satisfaction with what you have accomplished can make your "golden" years truly enjoyable. However, there are still financial issues that should be addressed. Be sure your medical insurance is adequate. The costs of medical care continue to rise, and the average life span is increasing. Medicare, Medicaid, and private health insurance will all be important. Be sure your estate plan is up to date. Changes in your financial situation, moving to a different state, and changes in your family should all be triggers for reviewing your estate plan with a qualified estate planning attorney. Continue to manage your investments carefully. If you are using an advisor or stockbroker, be sure to fully understand their recommendations before accepting them. Finally, enjoy retirement and the rewards of sound financial decisions made earlier in life.

There are some life events that have financial implications on our homes. Preparing for these universal events can eliminate some of the stress that can be present. Buying a first home or a new home can be one of the largest financial transactions of your life. Investigating the mortgage options before you start looking at homes can help you focus on a home you can afford and help keep you focused on the home selection and purchase negotiation parts of the process. You may want to talk to a lender to get some form of pre-qualification, or at least learn what the current rates are and how much your monthly payment would be for different size mortgages.

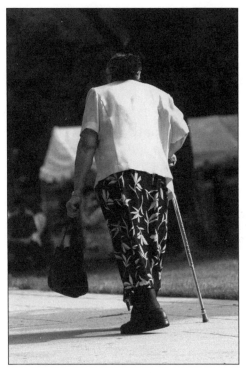

Fig. 15.4 Financial issues must be addressed during the "golden" years as well.

Home equity loans have become a major source of funds used when making improvements to homes. Home equity loans can be ideal funding sources for this use. The application process is usually easy and inexpensive, with funds available when needed. This avoids paying interest on funds you do not need. Home equity loans usually have attractive interest rates, and the interest is tax-deductible. If you are considering a major home improvement, you may want to investigate this source of funds.

Once housing has been addressed, funding for the education of children can be a relatively expensive task. Annual college costs at a private, out of state institution can be more than $30,000 per year. Even state sponsored schools can cost at least half of that amount. Paying those college bills can be tough if you do not start saving early. Make time your ally by establishing a regular savings program and taking advantage of some of the new tax-advantaged programs like Education IRAs and Section 529 Plans.

After a career, venturing into retirement brings many changes. Along with Social

Security benefits, your existing assets must pay for a major portion of your living expenses. Your living expenses will probably fall somewhat, perhaps by 20% to 30%. You will probably want to modify your investment strategies to be more conservative. While you are young and still accumulating assets, it can be easier to absorb a fall in the value of your portfolio because you have time to recoup your losses. During retirement, a significant fall in your portfolio can be troubling. You may want to consider a more conservative asset allocation with more of your funds in cash and shorter-term fixed income investments.

Finally, changing jobs is something that most American employees will face over a lifetime of working. This can have serious financial implications, and it is seldom easy to change employers. New responsibilities, new co-workers, and a new environment can be stressful. In addition, you will probably get a distribution from your old employer's retirement plan. Once you get that distribution, you have important decisions to make. You must move the funds into another qualified plan or IRA within 60 days to avoid paying taxes on the distribution. You must also make investment decisions. Retirement plan distributions are often the largest single sum an individual ever has to invest at one time. Sometimes, a new employer's plan can accept transfers as well. If changing jobs is in your near-term future, investigate your options early and make the transition less stressful.

As you can see, there are few life situations that do not have financial ripples. However, most community chaplains will be assisting individuals and families as they deal with debt elimination. While these discussions about finances can be difficult, there is always the opportunity to transition the conversation to spiritual matters. This is the goal of all interaction within your mission field.

Stories From the Field: #14

"In God We Trust, All Others Pay Cash"*

Jessica, who had been a stay-at-home mom with a four year old son, ventured back out into the workforce. Late one Wednesday evening, I received a desperate page. Jessica and her husband Mark had gotten into a shouting match about an eighteen year old girl who had been temporarily staying in their home, and she was embarrassed, angry, and hurt. Not knowing what to do, she remembered her chaplain and gave me a call.

Jessica shared that her marriage had been in trouble for years, and that they had terrible money problems because of her mismanagement. Finally, the lies, the unfaithful-

ness, the jealousy, Mark's perfectionism, and her low self-esteem pushed her over the edge; she lost it. After encouraging her for several minutes, with her permission, I began to share Christ with Jessica and explain the need for her to have a personal relationship with Him. At that point I was not sure whether the marriage could be saved, but Jessica needed the Lord, and that became my top priority.

We prayed, and Jessica accepted Christ. I shared four things with her that would help her grow in her relationship with the Lord: read the Bible, pray, worship (go to a Bible-believing church), and witness (share her faith with someone). Believing that she needed to tell someone as quickly as possible that she had become a Christian, I asked her who she knew that would be very excited that she had accepted Christ as her Savior. She decided to tell her mother-in-law, who had witnessed Jessica's and Mark's earlier explosion of anger and hostility.

*Jessica went home, and things were very cold and difficult that evening. However, as the week continued, she and Mark talked. She started reading **The Praying Wife**, and he laid down his hunting magazine and picked up the companion book entitled **The Praying Husband**. That Saturday, Jessica witnessed to one of her friends, who then went to church on Sunday and gave her heart to Christ. Jessica and Mark continue to work on their marriage and their relationship with God. I am not sure what would have happened if Jessica did not make the call to her chaplain.*

– Submitted By: Gaylon B.
Birmingham, AL

*Individuals in this story have granted permission for its use.

Questions

Reflect on the Stories From the Field found in this chapter and answer the following questions:

1. How would you handle the situation that was described?
2. What information found in the story is confidential?
3. What information found in the story can be shared with others? With whom may this information be shared? Under what circumstances may this information be shared?
4. How does the information found in this chapter pertain to the story?

End Notes

1. See Ronald J. Sider, *Rich Christians in an Age of Hunger: Moving from Affluence to Generosity* (Nashville, TN: Word, 1997).

2. Mike Wolff, Presenter. Corporate Chaplains of America Quarterly Training Meeting (November 2004).

3. Dave Ramsey, "Monthly Cash Flow Plan," <http://www.daveramsey.com/media/pdf/fpu_monthly_cash_flow_plan_forms.pdf> (Accessed December 2004).

4. Cited by Lucy Lazarony, "How Debt Negotiators Can Crush Your Credit," <http://www.bankrate.com/brm/news/debt/debtguide2004/consolidatehl.asp> (Accessed 22 November 2005).

5. See Suze Orman, *The Road to Wealth: A Comprehensive Guide to Your Money* (New York: Riverhead, 2001) and Clark Howard, *Get Clark Smart* (New York: Hyperion, 2002).

6. Ron Blue, *Master Your Money* (Atlanta, GA: Walk Through The Bible Ministries, 1990), 51.

Chapter Sixteen

Relationships in Crisis
and the Community Chaplain

CHAPTER SIXTEEN

Relationships in Crisis and the Community Chaplain

During the course of this chapter, we will perform the following tasks:

- Discover the relationship for which all of us are searching

- Discuss the items that are sometimes substituted for the real solution to relationship issues

- Explore the methods for relationship caregiving

- Apply the concepts of healthy relationships to the marriage of the community chaplain

R elationships - we are created by God to have relationships. There are so many dating services and other methods of establishing relationships that we need no other proof of the in-born need for connection. In numerous studies, science tells us that infants can die when love and affection are withheld from them, even when they are nourished and basic physical needs are met. When these primary bonds with husband, wife, brother, sister, parent, or friend are functioning properly, they are truly some of the best sources of life support that can be found. When these relationships start to disintegrate, we can begin to feel like our world is falling apart.

We will spend a great deal of time learning about relationships and how to care for those who are in a relationship crisis. You have probably heard the expression that "life is like a three legged stool". Basically, for life to be in balance much like this three-legged stool, all aspects of life must be in balance. One leg of life is the physical. The other two legs are the emotional/intellectual aspects of a person and the spiritual side of their being. Nothing happens in a vacuum. When someone has a physical concern such as a major surgical procedure, it can impact the spiritual life and certainly the emotional aspects of a person as well.

We are created in God's image, and therefore we are designed to have relationships. We are intended to be dependent on God. However, because we live in a fallen world, other things are substituted for the One to Whom we should be addicted. The use of and dependence on drugs and alcohol can throw a relationship into crisis quickly. When someone is dependent on substances, it is a poor substitute for a relationship with Christ. As we begin discussing this topic, it is important to share an understanding of the terms that we will use frequently in this text. The word "design" brings to mind the words "plan", "drawings", and "model". These plans or models may be set aside for certain intent or use. The word "dependent" takes on a meaning in which someone or something relies on another person or thing for help or support.

Designed to be Dependent

Before attempting to direct someone to a state of spiritual wellness and freedom from the bondage of addiction, into a correct relationship with Christ, it is also important to know something about yourself and those for whom you will be caring. We need to come to the realization that man was designed to be dependent. God did not make (design) man to be a substance abuser, nor did He design man to be an addict. God was pleased with His design; "God saw all that He had made, and it was very good ..." (Genesis 1:31).[1] God designed man to look to Him for his needs and provisions. He also designed man with the ability to make decisions. Man made a decision in the Garden of Eden to disobey God (The Designer), and things have not been the same since.

Let us look at the reason for the creation of man. In Genesis 1:27, we learn that man was created in the image of God. This means that mankind was "designed" in the likeness of God. This likeness of God, for which man was designed, was to reflect the image of God, including His wisdom, love, holiness, intellect, emotions, and the ability to make decisions. God designed man with the plan to have dominion over the "... fish of the sea, and over the fowl of the air, and over the cattle, and over all the earth ..." (Genesis 1:26 KJV).

Man had everything in the Garden of Eden. He communed with God daily, and all his needs were satisfied. Mankind was complete and whole, with nothing wanting. However, something changed when Satan deceived Eve, and Adam chose to disobey the command that God gave him. Sin entered in the world, and man lost the moral likeness of God but retained the natural likeness of God. Man continued to have the ability to make decisions, but he lost the holiness of God. Man also broke the intimate fellowship he had with God (Genesis 3:8). This is the relationship for which we are all searching. We often replace it with many things: drugs, promiscuity, a spouse, financial security, etc. Man was no longer complete, because he had lost something great. Man began his quest for that "feeling of completion" and is still searching today. Man realizes that there are unfulfilled relationships, fear and discouragement, loss of hope, pain, and many other unpleasant emotions that would be best avoided. With many efforts to change his life on his own, the design (man) still is in need of help and support for completion.

This leads to the second word, defined earlier, and this is *dependent*. Mankind is dependent on his Maker (God who designed us), and the only way we will be complete is through seeking our Designer, our Heavenly Father, to restore us back to our original design. This sounds simple and easy. However, if it is so easy, why is dependency such an inappropriate state of being?

Addiction

When asked about his or her life achievement or goals, no one will say, "I'm happy to be an addict, and this has been my greatest achievement in life." Nor will they say, "I want to be controlled by a chemical substance and lose my self respect, be despised by those who love me, and be labeled a failure because of a series of losses in my life." What causes a person to get to a point of dependency? Later we will examine what the experts have to say about addiction.

Addiction is no respecter of persons. Anyone, regardless of age, sex, race, culture, social status, religion, or economical status can succumb to addiction. There are people suffering in the bondage of addiction throughout the world. The length of time may vary before the state of dependency is established. Some people seem to

Fig. 16.1 Addiction can effect anyone.

become dependent at the first use, and others take years to form a dependency. However, the fact remains that one who is dependent on a chemical substance, a destructive behavior, or a relationship, has tried to control something or someone in their lives by the use of the substance or engaging in the behavior. Let us look at Proverbs 23:29-35:

> [29] *Who has woe? Who has sorrow? Who has strife? Who has complaints? Who has needless bruises? Who has bloodshot eyes?* [30] *Those who linger over wine, who go to sample bowls of mixed wine.* [31] *Do not gaze at wine when it is red, when it sparkles in the cup, when it goes down smoothly!* [32] *In the end it bites like a snake and poisons like a viper.* [33] *Your eyes will see strange sights and your mind imagine confusing things.* [34] *You will be like one sleeping on the high seas, lying on top of the rigging.* [35] *'They hit me,' you will say, 'but I'm not hurt! They beat me, but I do not feel it! When will I wake up so I can find another drink?'*

The author makes several queries, none of which are unusual. Who does not have problems, experience sadness, or have losses? Who has not had problems in relations that end in arguments? Who does not have complaints or always seem to be running their mouth about something? If we stop with the first four questions, most if not all of mankind would be able to answer with an affirmative, "I have." For some people the next two questions, "Who has needless bruises?" or "Who has bloodshot eyes?" may seem strange or out of sequence. However, for others these are normal questions, and the response may be an affirmative, "I have."

These persons are characterized as "those who linger over wine". This means that they continued to stay and were reluctant to leave the wine. In verse 31, the person was described as gazing or staring at the wine (those with addiction). These persons have tunnel vision. They are preoccupied with the addiction and are unaware of their surroundings. The addictions seem to have had some alluring qualities in the beginning (it sparkles - it goes down smoothly). Verse 32 states that the end is not like the beginning, because it is described as a "snake" that turns and bites the user, leaving him with its deadly, destructive poison. Many addicts recall their beginning use or behavior as pleasurable, but the end is destructive. Verse 33 reminds the reader that people with addictions are under its influence to the point it affects their view of life. With a distorted view, they are unable to see the truth. Their minds are drugged or behavior-affected, and they are unable to think clearly or make appropriate and rational decisions. They are out of touch with the reality of life.

Think of someone whom you have been around who has an addiction problem. Have you tried to talk with them and share the truth? You may recall receiving some resistance, and you wonder in your mind why the communication did not seem effective. It is obvious that they have rejected what you said, which was the truth. However, to admit the truth may cause them pain that they want to avoid. They see or cope with their situation in a way that helps them temporarily avoid pain. The author of Proverbs describes their lives as unstable in the 34th verse. He uses the illustration of a sailor who falls into the sea and drowns. Even the problems that affect their lives and are felt like a blow ("hit") are denied: "They hit me...but I am not hurt." The addict will often say, "I don't have a problem," yet the signs are all around. However, this does not get the attention of the addict. Instead, the problem increases - "They beat me...but I don't feel it." This is not only an increased level of denial of the addiction but a denial of the effects of the addiction. The ultimate denial is to deny any problems at all and to continue with the addiction. "When I wake up...I will find another drink." Unfortunate things happen in all of our lives. Everyone has experienced disappointments and painful situations. However, to try to solve these problems on our own is worthless. We must depend on the One Who designed us to depend on Him, and that is our Heavenly Father.

As mentioned earlier, there are some people that God has gifted with a great deal of knowledge on why people choose an addiction over God and a relationship with Him. An expert can be defined as "having much special knowledge and experiences" or "being very skillful". There are millions of books written on addictions. They focus on what's, why's, causes, and cures for addiction. Sometimes these are labeled as information from the experts. Billons of dollars are spent in researching, studying, and treating addictions. No one is certain of the causes of addiction. However, I would like to spend some time sharing some information on the biological, psychological, sociological, and of course the spiritual aspects of what the experts reveal about addiction.

The physical dependency of a drug usually occurs after continuous use. The body becomes accustomed to having the chemical, or it tries to function with the chemical. If the chemical is removed after the body has become accustomed to it, the body will react. The effects that the drug has on the body depend on the type of drug present in the body. However, most physical dependencies for drugs have one common effect and that is how it affects the brain. In this section concerning what experts have to say about addiction, I will often refer to the term "drug". This will also include alcohol and nicotine. These terms will relate to any chemical which is pleasure producing and can activate the chemical pathways of the brain. When these pathways are activated, feelings of pleasure and euphoria are produced. The definitions of addiction vary depending on the criteria used. For some experts the focus of addiction has to do with the level of tolerance that has developed in the addict. Other studies focus on the severity of withdrawal that occurs, how difficult it is for the addict to let go of the substance, and the likelihood of a relapse occurring.[2]

There are many drugs and behaviors on which one can become dependent. The experts' opinions differ as much as the substances and behaviors. In this section, the primary focus will be on chemical substances including alcohol, cocaine, heroin, marijuana, nicotine, and caffeine. Each of these drugs will be discussed as to the effect it has on the brain, the tolerance, withdrawal, and other factors used to classify them as addictive.

Alcohol Dependence

It is impossible to pinpoint what causes addiction to alcohol or how the alcoholism develops. The opinions are as varied as the types of alcohol sold on the market. The primary focus on alcohol is how it affects areas of the body. Alcohol acts as a depressant on the central nervous system of the brain. The effects of alcohol on the brain can "result in confusion, disorganized thinking, as well as disruption of adequate motor control".[3] Most studies agree that alcohol dependency is a progressive disease that causes a person to lose control over usage. Other studies focus on genetic factors that could determine a person's likelihood of becoming an alcoholic. Children of alcoholics are four times more likely to become alcoholics than children of non-alcoholics.[4] There is also the factor of gender and how absorption and metabolism varies. "Men metabolize alcohol

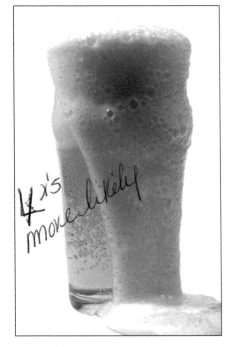

Fig. 16.2 It is impossible to pinpoint what causes addiction to alcohol.

347

quicker than women (this leading to faster intoxication in women)." Alcohol addiction (alcoholism) is defined as a disease. The reason for this is that the disease progresses slowly. If not treated, it gets worse. It spirals and affects other areas of the body. Continual use, regardless of the pattern of drinking, can result in an increased tolerance that will cause the drinker to become dependent. The body adapts to having a certain level of alcohol in the blood stream. As each level is obtained, a greater amount is needed for the body to function. When the body does not have the level of alcohol that it is accustomed to having, it will react. This is called withdrawal. Withdrawal is the body's way of rebelling over the change that is occurring. The best way to remember signs of withdrawal is to know what effects the drug has on the body (brain). Withdrawal symptoms are the opposite. As noted earlier, alcohol works on the central nervous system by producing a depressive affect, which has an impact on the outlook of the user. Without alcohol the opposite occurs, causing signs of irritability and aggressiveness.

Cocaine Dependence

An examination of cocaine will reveal that it is one of the most well-known and talked about of the illicit drugs. "Crack" is a street name for cocaine that has been processed using cocaine and ammonia or baking soda. The term "crack" comes from the sound it makes when the substance is heated. In caring for people addicted to cocaine/crack, you may notice a special way that the person may speak of the drug. Most cocaine/crack addicts will make statements such as, "It makes me perform better. I'm more alert. It gives me a positive sense of confidence." Just as cocaine/crack can cause a rush of excitement and "increase the mental capabilities", the adverse effect is a state or feeling of depression. Because the depression is so intense, the cocaine/crack addict will use again to avoid depressed feelings. The physical effects of cocaine/crack are known to affect the brain, central nervous system, and the respiratory system. "Cocaine's exact action on the brain and central nervous system is not yet understood. Cocaine apparently blocks the nervous system's use of the chemical messengers in the brain: norepinephrine, serotonin, and dopamine. The redirected dopamine apparently causes cocaine's powerful euphoria."[5]

When there is a decrease in dopamine due to excessive use of cocaine, depression will occur. Use of cocaine has also been reported to cause seizures and convulsions. For the cocaine/crack addict who smokes and inhales, there is a problem with the respiratory system. The use of cocaine has caused deterioration of the system. Many people begin experimenting with crack/cocaine as a "recreational drug". This is not considered a recreational drug for those who treat the addict because of the danger of sudden death. "There are several types of cocaine-induced deaths. One is respiratory failure when the brain ceases to control the vital functions of the nervous system. Another type is irregular heartbeats leading to heart attacks. In rare cases, cocaine users die of cerebral hemorrhages." Tolerance for the drug is easily developed; because as the effects of the drug wear off, the depression is so great that the need to use becomes repetitive. Cocaine has been reported as not having as severe withdrawal symptoms as other drugs. This is one of the arguments that many addicts will voice to try to convince themselves and others that cocaine/crack is not addictive. Most users will experience withdrawal symptoms of "depression, irritability, nausea, insomnia, agitation, restlessness, loss of appetite, and incoherence lasting up to five days after they stop using the drug".

Heroin Dependence

The next drug I would like to discuss is heroin. To explain the effects of heroin and its addiction, we must understand how it is obtained. Opium is a natural substance taken from the seedpod of an Asian poppy called opium. There are also synthetic forms of opiates. These drugs are made from the opium. These are commonly called painkillers. You may be familiar with some of these and may have taken some as prescribed by your physician. Two of these drugs are codeine and morphine. Morphine was a drug that doctors made from opium, but they also found that it was very addictive. Heroin was used to replace the addictive problem of morphine. Now, it is considered a more potent painkiller than morphine. There is a common saying among heroin addicts, and that is "live today, for there may not be a tomorrow". Death may occur among heroin addicts, because it slows the heart rate and the breathing of the users. Other studies reveal that heroin "takes over every cell of the body. It makes the teeth rot; bones break easily; vision is damaged (pupils are dilated and become sensitive to light). Heroin addicts are likely to commit crimes for drug money and death from overdose is always near."[6]

Marijuana Dependence

Marijuana is a common name for a plant called "cannabis sativa". Unlike drugs such as alcohol and cocaine, marijuana is not a single drug. "Over 400 known chemicals are in marijuana; its composition is so complex researchers have yet to create an adequate working model of it."[7] Marijuana has been called the "gateway drug" for many years, because research has shown that most people who start smoking marijuana early will progress to other drugs. There are several ways that marijuana affects the body, especially fatty organs, the brain, and reproductive organs. Marijuana is fat-soluble. Therefore, it remains in the body longer than water-soluble drugs such as alcohol. Because it stays in the body longer, one of its chemicals known as tetrahydrocannabinol (THC) can do harm to certain vital organs.

Marijuana smoking causes changes in the brain's chemistry. It inhibits the chemical that transfers information from one nerve cell to another. This accounts for the most noticeable effect of marijuana intoxication. Virtually all of the many studies on marijuana use conclude that it interferes with intellectual performance and impairs thinking, reading comprehension, verbal, and arithmetic problem solving.[8]

Marijuana has been described as more damaging to the lungs than cigarettes, because it has over fifty percent more cancer causing drugs. In males:

...evidence also shows that long-term marijuana use may lead to a decrease in the tissue mass of the testes. This results in interference with testosterone and sperm production. Males who frequently use marijuana have two problems with their sperm. One is low sperm count. The other is a high proportion of sperm with abnormal appearance and reduced movement, both usually associated with low fertility and abnormal embryos.[9]

Marijuana also affects females by causing abnormal menstrual cycles. Because females are born with a fixed number of eggs, there is a possibility that THC can damage the eggs. Like other drugs, excessive use of marijuana can lead to tolerance. This means that more marijuana is needed to produce a desired effect. There is a lot of controversy as to whether there are physical withdrawals or psychological dependency. "Some evidence shows that frequent high doses of marijuana can lead to mild physical dependence. Physical withdrawal (intense disturbances when drug use is stopped) has not been observed among marijuana users. However, some marijuana users do experience withdrawal symptoms, which include restlessness, irritability, mild agitation, decreased appetite, insomnia, sleep disturbances, nausea, and occasional vomiting and diarrhea. This withdrawal, though, is not experienced by all heavy users who quit."[10] Regardless of the vast differences in opinions and studies concerning marijuana, there are some remaining facts: marijuana is a drug, it is a complex drug compared to others, and, as with all other drugs, its use can lead to problems.

Nicotine Dependence

Before we discuss the effects of nicotine on the body, please note that this is a drug that is often overlooked. Let us identify what makes up nicotine. Nicotine is "a poisonous, oily liquid taken from tobacco leaves and used for killing insects."[11] Nicotine can be obtained from cigarettes, cigars, pipe smoking, chewing tobacco, and snuff. There are various reasons why people engage in smoking and chewing tobacco products. One reason is that it has become a socially acceptable drug (like alcohol). They may have seen parents, role models, or friends engage in the activity. Tobacco does not cost as much as some drugs and is easily accessible. Denial is strong among nicotine addicts. Most users will deny addiction and /or harm to their bodies. They usually make excuses for their "need" to use.

Smoking can produce another poison called tar. The nicotine and tar can cause many problems to the body. "Even in tiny doses, nicotine is bad news. It is addicting and harmful. It makes your nerves shaky and unsteady. It speeds up the heartbeat. It raises the blood pressure."[12] Nicotine and tar can produce cancer, emphysema, and heart disease. "Specks of these tars stick to the inside of the lungs."[13] The tar blocks the sacs of the lungs, which will affect the functioning of the lungs. Over a period of time these diseases can develop. Like all other drugs, the more one engages in the use of nicotine, the greater the chance of becoming addicted. The tolerance to this drug is easily developed, because the high (stimuli) is quick and does not last long. This causes the users to crave for another fix. If you will think of places where smoking is prohibited and areas where smoking is designated, you will see the nicotine addicts rush for the opportunity to smoke once they are given a break. This addiction is difficult to quit. Most smokers or chewers attempt several times before they succeed; but remind them that nothing is impossible.

Caffeine Dependence

The last drug to address in this section is caffeine. Many people do not like to classify caffeine as a drug. One of the reasons is because caffeine is found in foods and drinks that are considered harmless. Those foods and drinks are chocolate (candies, etc.), soda products, coffee, tea, and pep pills (no-doze). Caffeine is a stimulus. It stimulates the central nervous system. This buzz lasts for a moment, and the need to use again occurs. Caffeine affects the body in ways that many would overlook or, due to their denial, will give excuses of why the symptoms may be the result of other things. "Caffeine can do a lot of damage. It can cause headaches, diarrhea, irregular heartbeats, and ringing in the ears. Caffeine can make it hard to get to sleep (insomnia)."[14] "Withdrawal of caffeine can cause depression, crankiness, and being short tempered."[15] Like nicotine, caffeine is an acceptable, inexpensive drug used and abused in society.

Criteria of Addiction

Most studies focus on five factors to determine criteria of addiction. These factors are: tolerance, withdrawal, dependency, reinforcement, and intoxication. Dr. Henningfield of the National Institute on Drug Abuse and Dr. Neal Benowitz of the University of California used these five factors to explain the potential for addiction:

■ **Withdrawal:** Presence and severity of characteristic withdrawal system.

■ **Reinforcement:** A measure of the substance's ability, in human and animal tests, to get users to take it again and again and in preference to other substances.

■ **Tolerance:** How much of the substance is needed to satisfy increasing craving for it and the level of stable need that is eventually reached.

■ **Dependence:** How difficult it is for the user to quit, the relapse rate, the percentage of people who eventually became dependent, the rating users give their own needs for the substance, and the degree to which the substance will be used in the face of evidence that it causes harm.

■ **Intoxication:** Though not usually counted as a measure of addiction in itself, the level of intoxication is associated with addiction and increases the personal and social damage a substance may do.[16]

Henningfield used the following substances: alcohol, nicotine, heroin, cocaine, marijuana, and caffeine (see Fig. 16.3). Benowitz also studied the same substances and used the same ratings (see Fig. 16.4).

Fig. 16.3 HENNINGFIELD RATINGS

Substance	Withdrawal	Reinforcement	Tolerance	Dependency	Intoxication
Nicotine	3	4	2	1	5
Heroin	2	2	1	2	2
Cocaine	4	1	4	3	3
Alcohol	1	3	3	4	1
Caffeine	5	6	5	5	6
Marijuana	6	5	6	6	4

Fig. 16.4 BENZOWITZ'S RATINGS[17]

Substance	Withdrawal	Reinforcement	Tolerance	Dependency	Intoxication
Nicotine	3	4	4	1	6
Heroin	2	2	2	2	2
Cocaine	3	1	1	3	3
Alcohol	1	3	4	4	1
Caffeine	4	5	3	5	5
Marijuana	5	6	5	6	4

Based on these ratings, alcohol was the drug that had the most withdrawal symptoms and intoxication. The drug with the least withdrawal symptoms was marijuana. Nicotine was the most serious for dependency, and marijuana was the least serious for dependency. Cocaine was the drug that was the most serious for reinforcement, but the two ratings differed as to the least serious drug. There is one thing that is certain, and that is the fact that drugs do have effects on the body. If a drug can produce artificial pleasures, it can also produce dependency.

There are various signs that addiction is present. The signs and symptoms may have been present for quite some time. However, there are often a series of events or behaviors that take place before the addict or the significant others in their lives begin to recognize that the addict's life is out of control.

Signs of Addiction

Although there is much attention placed on addictions and the many types of addiction, there are still misconceptions of what the signs of addiction really are. I would like to share with you some typical signs observed in more than ten years of workplace ministry to those who are addicted.

- **Loss of control** is the most obvious. The loss may occur in many ways. The addict's ability to control how much and how often he/she engages in the behavior is unpredictable and will vary.

- **An increase** in the amount used, or the behavior in which he/she is engaged. There is the need to increase the amount of alcohol/drugs used or increase the activity as in the case of sexual addiction in order to achieve the desired effect. This is often referred to as "chasing a high" or "seeking" the original feelings.

- **Preoccupation of use.** The addict begins to engage in thoughts of use and plans activities to use. An example may be making sure alcohol is purchased before the cut off time for sales or choosing friends who have this common interest. It may even include making sure that there is money to support the addiction. Addicts tend to spend a great deal of time in preparation, using, and the after effect.

- **Attempts are made to stop using or to control the use.** An example of an attempt to control the use may include making promises to a significant other that they will stop using. The alcoholic may change from drinking liquor to beer or non-alcoholic beer, which still contains a percentage of alcohol.

- **Continuation of use** despite negative consequences. The person has a condition of insanity. It causes him to continue the same behavior and expect different results. Although the addict has experienced negative consequences, each time he uses he hopes to avoid negative results, only to receive them again.

- **Reverse tolerance** is when the normal amount used to get a desired "high" is achieved by using a lesser amount. The alcoholic may have been able to drink 24 beers before becoming intoxicated and now drinks only 3 beers to be intoxicated. This is a result of his body not filtering the impurities as rapidly as it could in the earlier stages of the disease.

- **Withdrawal.** The addict has a physiological dependency. The body and mind will experience signs of discomfort when the body or mind is not being fed with the chemical substance, or the mind is not getting the usual stimuli.

- **Medicate** with the substance. Because of the unwanted withdrawal symptoms, there is a need to continue the cycle by further use or increase of the behavior.

Now that we have talked about the symptoms of addiction, we need to advance to the areas of the effects of addiction. What are some things that occur as the result of one being addicted to a chemical substance or behavior? When an individual is under the control of another person, place, or thing, they can no longer manage areas of their lives.

- Members of the addict's family are often the ones who experience the dreadful effects of addiction. Respect is lacking due to the irresponsible behavior of the addict. **Example:** An alcoholic father/husband is out drinking all night, but he promised to take his son to a basketball game. The alcohol is not what caused the child not to trust his father, but the effects of his drinking and the behavior associated with it has affected this relationship.

- The social interaction. The addict may isolate him/herself from others, especially if they feel that others will condemn their behavior. For some addicts there is an inner magnet that tends to draw them to other users, and they are comfortable only in the presence of those who use. The addict may also lose a very important relationship because of the addiction.

- The moral conduct of the addict is affected. **Example:** A married mother who is addicted to crack may wake up next to a man she does not know. Under the influence of an all-nighter, she may discover that she not only had sexual intercourse with this man but possibly with some other men. Her moral standards may have been affected due to her unmanageable behavior while using the drug.

- Finances are affected because there is a great need to support the addiction. Other areas in the finances that are affected may include a loss of employment due to low job performance, being passed over for a promotion because of excessive absenteeism from work, late paid or unpaid bills, or the addict spending money unnecessarily on the purchase of what I call "guilt gifts". These are items or trips that the addict will purchase for their family or significant other to attempt to control or manipulate them from confronting the inappropriate or destructive behavior (Proverbs 23:21).

- Physical problems are often one of the effects that are easily ignored, because the addict attempts to relate physical problems with other things. **Examples:** Someone who snorts cocaine has excessive nosebleeds but attributes the nosebleeds to sinus problems. An alcoholic will attempt to pass off "hangover symptoms" for cold or flu symptoms.

As you care for the addict, it is important to observe signs and effects of addiction. Do not hesitate to ask questions that will cause the addict to think about what is occurring in his/her life. Remember, addiction affects all areas of the addict's life. It affects the body, mind, and spirit. I would like to bring to your attention how Isaiah compared the behavior of Ephraim to that of drunkards when he was trying to get the people to see the destructiveness of their lives. Isaiah 28:7-8 gives a clear view of someone whose walk is unstable. The rulers were befuddled (confused or stupid) with wine, and it affected their vision and their judgment (ability to make decisions). The tables were covered with filth and vomit. No matter how you look at addiction, it is not a pretty sight to see.

Denial is the refusal to admit what is right. The addict has been through years of convincing himself that he can handle his drinking, using, or pleasure seeking behavior. He isolates himself from those who might confront him with his behavior, or he surrounds himself with others who engage in the same behavior. This allows him to see himself as normal. The addict also uses other tools to protect himself from the truth.

There are three clever tools that the addict often uses to avoid the truth, and they are to **justify**, **rationalize**, and **minimize** the behavior. The addict must find a way or reason to ***justify*** the continued use or engagement of the undesired behavior. The alcoholic may be heard making statements such as, "There's nothing illegal about drinking alcohol." The crack addict may say, "I was feeling down and depressed, and using always makes me feel better." The prescription addict will say, "I'm just taking the medicine that my doctor gave me." The sex addict may say, "There's nothing wrong with looking at pornographic pictures; I'm not hurting anyone." The **rationalizing** statements of the addict consist of reasons or explanations for drinking, using, or engaging in inappropriate behavior. The alcoholic may be heard to say, "I was just drinking with my friends so they wouldn't feel uncomfortable." The cocaine addict will say, "I just use for recreational purposes." The prescription addict states, "I have to take this for my pain; it is unbearable." The sex addict's comment may be, "I started looking at pornographic pictures when I was six years old, when I found them in my father's garage. Therefore, I have been looking at these pictures since then." The **minimizing** comments of the addict are used to make the use or behavior unimportant. An example of minimizing comments for the alcoholic might be, "I only drink on weekends, not during the week while I work." The crack addict may say, "I will only spend $50.00 of my money. If any more is spent, someone else buys it, not me." The prescription addict will say, "It's not like I'm doing those street drugs." The sex addict will say, "I don't go around raping people."

I am sharing these examples with you because in your caregiving, you might be confronted with these comments. What they are really saying is, "I don't want to talk about the truth. I don't want to acknowledge the truth."

Distortion is the clever way that the addict manages to twist and shape a lie into something that looks like the truth. The addict embraces the ability to twist the truth as a survival tool. The reason this is a survival tool is that the addict has to be able to feel good about himself in what he is doing. They believe that telling part of the truth is still telling the truth, and the part that is not truth is just added for special effects. They consider it a skill to be able to distort the truth. Proverbs 12:13 states: "An evil man is trapped by his sinful talk, but a righteous man escapes trouble." The addict is trapped in his lies. He often forgets the lies he has told to try to conceal his addiction. I

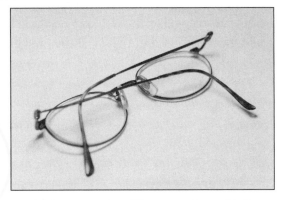

Fig. 16.5 Sometimes the addict gets so trapped in lies that he fails to recognize the truth.

heard a story once that a man called in to work with the excuse that he had a tooth pulled; but during the course of time, the man had sixty-two teeth pulled!

The addict becomes so skilled in a behavior that they fail to recognize the truth or see what is real. I am reminded of an old story shared among those who are caring for addicts who have difficulty recognizing the truth. The story goes like this. Leaving a bar one day, a man encountered two nuns. As the man walked, the sidewalk got narrower as the nuns got nearer. He stood still, and the nuns passed on each side of the man. Because the man was accustomed to seeing double, he stopped, looked back, and said, "How did she do that?"

Escapism may occur as a behavior or statement used by the addict to avoid the truth. When confronted, addicts may agree with statements just to get the one who is confronting them about their behavior to leave them alone. Addicts often use other behaviors to avoid the truth. Often the addict will mask these feelings, fears, or concerns. The addict may not show depressed feelings, because they mask them by telling jokes, especially when they are using. Another type of escapism is to defocus. The addict will try to talk about anything but his problems of addiction or things that are affected by his addiction. The addict will try to talk about family members, the injustice of the system, and even current events in the news. This is intended to get the focus off of him.

The addict may appear to be naïve and say things such as, "I didn't know that," with the goal being to avoid accepting responsibility. It is important to deal with the fear of being out of control, the fear of failure, or whatever the problem may be. However, the most urgent need is to stop the using or the behavior, so that the addict will be able to recognize that he/she needs help. Some addicts will even say that God made them addicts, and that is all they will ever be. Let us look at Romans 1:21-32:

> [21] For although they knew God, they neither glorified him as God nor gave thanks to him, but their thinking became futile and their foolish hearts were darkened. [22] Although they claimed to be wise, they became fools [23] and exchanged the glory of the immortal God for images made to look like mortal man and birds and animals and reptiles. [24] Therefore God gave them over in the sinful desires of their hearts to sexual impurity for the degrading of their bodies with one another. [25] They exchanged the truth of God for a lie, and worshipped and served created things rather than the Creator-who is forever praised. Amen. [26] Because of this, God gave them over to shameful

> *lusts. Even their women exchanged natural relations for unnatural ones.* [27] *In the same way the men also abandoned natural relations with women and were inflamed with lust for one another. Men committed indecent acts with other men, and received in themselves the due penalty for their perversion.* [28] *Furthermore, since they did not think it worthwhile to retain the knowledge of God, he gave them over to a depraved mind, to do what ought not to be done.* [29] *They have become filled with every kind of wickedness, evil, greed, and depravity. They are full of envy, murder, strife, deceit, and malice. They are gossips,* [30] *slanderers, God-haters, insolent, arrogant, and boastful; they invent ways of doing evil; they disobey their parents;* [31] *they are sense-less, faithless, heartless, ruthless.* [32] *Although they know God's righteous decree that those who do such things deserve death, they not only continue to do these very things but also approve of those who practice them.*

The Apostle Paul was inspired to confront the people of Rome (and it applies to us today) about their sinful behavior and choices. Paul stated that man knew the truth; they knew God, but they chose not to glorify him and give him thanks. Man chose to make up in their own minds what they should or should not do. He said their foolish hearts were darkened. Anytime we try to solve our own problems without seeking the guidance of the Lord, we are treading in dangerous water. The people claimed to be wise but were very foolish. I often hear this confirmed when caring for addicts. Most of them will say, "I was hurting and depressed, but I thought I knew how to handle my problems by escaping into drugs, alcohol, sex, etc." Anyone who is thinking sober will tell you that trying to escape a problem is no way to deal with it. Paul continued to say that man exchanged the glory of the Everlasting Immortal God for that which is mortal (limited).

How often in life do we hear of people settling for less? What happens next? God allows them to recognize their powerlessness and unmanageability. He allows them to engage in their selfish sinful beliefs that are contrary to God's standard of truth. "They exchanged the truth of God for a lie." When man chose to be in bondage to darkness (sin), he could not see his way out but continued to stumble around in the darkness. This describes the life of an addict. Addicts think they know what is best; they experience short (temporary) pleasure instead of seeking lasting freedom. They continue making inappropriate decisions, and their lives continue in a downward spiral of one destructive behavior after another. Verse 28 in the NIV states "Furthermore, since they did not think it worthwhile to retain the knowledge of God, he gave them over to a depraved mind and to do what ought not to be done."

Those who have acknowledged reaching a "bottom" will say, "I never thought I could reach so low as to do..." whatever they considered as the worst thing they could have done. Before the addict reaches this state of acknowledging his powerlessness and unmanageability of life, you will encounter great resistance. The reason is that, of all the people to be convinced of the lie, the addict must first believe it himself. The actor must convince his audience in order for them to believe and become a part of the play. As caregivers in the community, it is important to hear what the addict is saying and listen for what they are not saying. Between the struggles of the two lies is the truth that needs liberating.

Relationship Skills

Because relationships are so important and since ultimately we are to introduce associates to the one relationship for which they are looking - a relationship with Jesus Christ - these skills must be developed within the community chaplain.

These skills can be broken down into major categories.[18] The first of these skill sets can be referred to as accepting and attending skills. The purpose of these skills is to alleviate the individual's sense of vulnerability and inadequacy about his inability to solve his own problems, to ease his fears of being judged, and to reassure him that he will not be thought of as sick, dumb, bad, or crazy because of the nature of his problems. These skills will demonstrate that the chaplain is warm, caring, alert, attentive, interested, open, accepting, and non-judgmental. Posture has been discussed in other chapters, but not related to a caregiving session. Open posture is an important skill. This skill should be practiced as erect, not slouching, stiff, or rigid, and leaning towards the speaker while listening to his story. The limbs should be open, conveying an appearance of acceptance to the individual. Open gestures, such as making a basket with your fingers interlaced in a palm up position, carries the message of support. Other skills, such as appropriate eye contact, should be used during a caregiving session, especially when the issue concerns relationships. As the caregiver, you are modeling good relationships and interaction with the associates. Eye contact, when used appropriately, sends the message that you are interested in what the speaker is saying. Look into the eyes of the person speaking, but do not stare. Look away or look down when he is sharing something that could be crucial for connecting with him.

As we seek to make the individual feel accepted, listening is important. A skill called verbal following will help you accomplish this goal. Follow as he tells his story. Let him lead the way. Do not lead, and do not change the subject. Think of this portion of your relationship with the person as him leading you through the rooms of a building, making sure only to enter the rooms when he opens the door. Verbalize as appropriate, to let the associate know that you are following the story. Ask questions or make statements that relate only to what he has already told you. As the story unfolds, the chaplain is often tempted to interrupt to gain more information about a particular subject area. Simply make a note of it, and ask the question later. Practice the lost art of silence. Talk by the chaplain sometimes distracts the speaker and serves the purpose of easing the chaplain's own anxiety. Silence communicates to the person speaking that the chaplain is listening and waiting patiently for him. It further states that what the individual has to say is important. Match the affective expressions of the person for whom you are caring to have appropriate congruency. It helps him feel accepted when the chaplain's affect and flow of speech are congruent with his own. If the individual is speaking slowly and softly and the chaplain responds with loud and rapid words, he may feel that the chaplain does not care or understand.

When preparing for acceptance of someone, especially in a caregiving scenario, the setting can be crucial. The setting should be free from disturbance. This will help to ensure privacy and comfort. Pay attention to all of the senses when ridding the environment from distractions. Seating should be comfortable and in an area that is out of heavy traffic flow. Confidentiality, as mentioned in other chapters, will also go a long way in helping someone feel accepted. There is a great degree of ease that comes from knowing that the chaplain will not share anything, other than the ex-

Fig. 16.6 In a caregiving session, setting is very important.

pressed intent to harm themselves or someone else or disclosure of child abuse, with anyone without the permission of the individual.

In addition to the acceptance emphasis that was just discussed, exploring and encouraging are crucial for success in dealing with relationship issues. Exploring skills are used to give the person in need the latitude necessary for telling his story. These skills will also help him focus on meaningful information and encourage deep self-exploration. One method that aids in the exploration process is the open-ended question. Open questions begin with "what" or "how". Any question that begins with "who", "when", or "where" is closed. Any question that begins with a verb is closed: is, are, do, did, etc. Although "why" questions seem to be open, they frequently elicit a closed response. They should be avoided. Instead, use "How come?" or "What is the reason?" Some examples of open-ended questions include the following:

- How did that affect you?
- What did you do when you felt angry?
- How do you feel about not being invited?
- What was the reason you didn't want to join him?

In addition to the open-ended question, open statements are important in directing the exploration of the individual. The open statement tells the person what you want him to explore. It is a directive rather than a question, and it is more potent than the open question. Control your tone of voice so the open statement does not come across as an authoritarian command. Open statements begin as follows:

- Tell me....
- Give me an example
- Explain
- Elaborate
- Expand
- Explore

If the open statement is introduced with "could you", "would you", or "can you", the potency of the statement is decreased. The permission of the individual is not needed to make an open statement. The following are some examples of open statements:

- Tell me more about the situation with your in-laws.
- Explain how you felt when she clammed up.
- Elaborate on your goal of a happy marriage.
- Give me an example of how she puts you down.
- Expand on that part of the argument.
- Explore how you responded to that.

Communicate Values

Once the chaplain has put the person at ease enough to begin sharing, cues that communicate value in what he is saying become more important. Some of these skills are verbal and others are non-verbal in nature. Body language expresses acceptance and encourages exploration. The chaplain should utilize body language to communicate non-verbally by nodding his head up and down and moving his hand, open with the palm up, toward the person with whom he is speaking. Minimal verbal encouraging can take place when the chaplain uses as few words as possible to encourage the individual to keep talking. "Yes", "I see", "Uh huh", "Go on", "And then?", "How?", etc. While using this skill, make eye contact and include a non-verbal encouraging skill.

There are times that verbal communication becomes more important to facilitate the exploration of the individual. Highlighting is a technique that involves taking a key word or words that he has just spoken and repeating it back to the caregivee with a rising inflection so that it sounds like a question.

Key words to highlight include strong feelings, such as "mad", "terrified", or "trapped". Extremes and exaggerations, such as "always", "never", and "constantly" should be brought to light. "Heavy", "game", and "good" are all examples of vague words and expressions that need clarification. High-energy action words such as "running", "screaming", and "fighting" all deserve some exploration through highlighting as well. When the highlighting skill is used properly, the person with whom the chaplain needs to connect will find it very difficult to avoid responding. Below is an example of highlighting:

Individual in need: "The only thing I could do was run away!"
Chaplain: "Run away?" or "Only thing?"

Individual in need: "I was defeated by that dumb machine!"
Chaplain: "Defeated?

Clarification

When the environment has been arranged for acceptance and the chaplain has taken steps that allow the person to open up and share the details of a situation, clarification will need to take place. Some of this can be handled through exploration, as we have seen above. However, further clarification skills will need to be added to the toolkit of the effective chaplain. Some of the tools that will facilitate effective clarification include reflecting skills.

Reflecting Skills

There are three types of reflecting that the community chaplain can use with those in his mission field. Reflecting feelings, reflecting cognitions, and reflecting actions are all ways that clarification can take place. The purpose of reflecting skills is to provide a feedback loop that helps the individual to hear his non-verbalized story - the covert messages beneath the story. In so doing, he will achieve increased awareness by sorting the thoughts, feelings, and behaviors that are not in his awareness. This will also assist him in personalizing the story. Further, reflecting will help the person take responsibility for his thoughts, feelings, and behavior. Reflecting can also serve to communicate that the individual is a person who thinks, feels, and acts in interaction with others and his environment, demonstrating that the chaplain is interested in all aspects of the individual as a person; that no part of him is unimportant. When the community chaplain begins the reflecting skill, he should remember a few guidelines. First, he should think in terms of holding a mirror for the person in need to look into. All reflections should be direct statements, not questions. Use voice, posture, and gestures that are congruent with what is being reflected. The individual will let you know if you are accurate or not. You accomplish almost all of your purposes, even when you are not accurate. Do not be thrown off balance when the cargivee indicates the reflection is not accurate. Simply require the person to make it accurate; give responsibility to him for the refined sorting-out. The individual will often stop talking after a reflection. Do not think that you have done something wrong. Let him have a few seconds to internalize your reflection, then use a minimal verbal encourager or an exploring skill to move on.

Reflecting feelings is the next stage of using reflection skills to enhance the communication level in the relationship between the chaplain and those in his care, and in turn in their respective personal relationships. When reflecting feelings, there are some things to consider. Listen to the story itself. What would be a typical feeling for a person like this in the situation being described? Examine the body posture of the people involved. Below are some sample messages that are being conveyed:

- Slumped = relaxed, sad
- Leaning away = withdrawn, fearful
- Leaning toward = interested, aggressive, angry, excited
- Erect = alert, rigid
- Limbs crossed = defensive, vulnerable
- Head tilted = suspicious, skeptical, judgmental

Take care to watch for certain actions and movements:
- Smiling = amused, nervous
- Head shaking side/side = disagreement, disapproval, awe
- Sighing = relieved, depressed, pressured, bored
- Head shaking up/down = understanding, approval, agreement
- Foot tapping = impatient, trapped, angry, frustrated
- Pointing = righteous, superior, angry, judgmental, aggressive

Fig. 16.7 Pay attention to actions and movements.

Watch the eyes of the person speaking:
- No eye contact = withdrawn, shame, dishonesty, guilt, sad, disinterested, distrustful, intimidated
- Eye contact = trust, open, interested, confident, secure
- Tears = sad, scared, happy

- Shifting = guilty, vulnerable, alert, scared
- Looking up = hopeful, stumped, impatient, rebellious
- Raised brows = skeptical, shocked, interested
- Furrowed brows = displeased, pensive, angry

Tone and patterns of speech also convey information:

- Slow and quiet = peaceful, sad, uncertain, secretive, suspicious
- Fast and loud = excited, angry, confident, fearful, out of control
- The individual's metaphor often provides a picture of his feelings. For example, a person who says, "It was like getting run over by a truck" might be feeling "crushed."

Once you have taken special care to pay attention to all of the signals through outside observation, reflecting feelings can take place through some of the phrases that are found below. Use one of these statements:

- "You feel ...."
- "You're feeling...."
- "You felt...."

Reasons:

- Personalizing it with the word "You" helps the individual take ownership of his feelings.
- Using the word "feel" indicates that he is a feeling person, that it is okay to talk about feelings, and that feelings are valid experiences.
- Some want to say, "You are" instead of "You feel", but that makes the reflection sound judgmental.

When reflecting feeling, make it sound like a statement, not a question. If it sounds like a question, it will be experienced as a question (not a reflection); and the person may intellectualize an answer. Remember, if you are not accurate, he will usually let you know. Keep it simple. If you use too many words, the individual will be in the left brain mode and will not be able to experience the feeling. Instead, he will respond by intellectualizing about the feeling. A feeling is usually one word, or a hyphenated word (e.g., "You feel rejected" or "You feel pushed-out"). If the word following "feel" is "like" or "that," you are describing a thought or a behavior. For example, "You feel like running," means "You are thinking of running." Someone who is thinking of running might feel tired or exhilarated or scared or angry - all different emotions associated with the thought or behavior of running. Do not try to practice this skill by asking the individual about feelings. If you do, he will be talking about feelings. It will then be very difficult for you to be able to practice the skill of "reflecting feelings", because this skill involves giving the person feedback about what is not being said directly. It is important for chaplains to be developing and improving their vocabularies of feeling words. Most feelings can be categorized in a few classes:

MAD = angry, cheated, bitter, jealous, _____, _____,
SAD = hurt, depressed, guilty, troubled, _____, _____,
GLAD = happy, joyful, tickled, delighted, _____, _____,
SCARED = anxious, nervous, fearful, tense, _____, _____,
PEACE = serene, content, calm, relieved, _____, _____, _____,
MISC. = tempted, sympathetic, greedy, proud, humble, _____, _____,

In addition to reflecting feelings, thoughts and behaviors can be reflected to those in the mission field. The word "you" should be used when reflecting in this manner. Use the word "you" and the word "think" or a synonym in this manner:

- "You think that you will never have enough money."
- "You assumed that she wanted it right away."
- "You believe that you cannot be forgiven."
- "You're wondering if that would get his attention."

Personalizing it with the word "You" helps the individual take ownership of the thought and to realize that he controls his thoughts. Using the word "You" indicates that he is a thinking person, that it is okay to talk about thoughts, and that his thoughts are important. Make it sound like a statement, not a question. Do not use the word "feel" when talking about thoughts. When the chaplain uses the word "feel" one time to relate to emotions and the next time uses it to relate to cognitions, the person may get confused and the sorting out process may be impeded. For example, "You feel like something bad is going to happen" would be more accurate as a reflection of feeling ("You feel scared") or a reflection of thought ("You think that something bad is going to happen").

In addition to reflecting feelings, thoughts can be effective for caring for those in the community. By reflecting thoughts, we help people become aware of their cognitive processes and the influence of these thoughts on their emotions, behavior, body, and spirit. The chaplain needs to be able to discern the individual's more immediate thought processes (e.g., "I might fail"), as well as the more pervasive and continuous attitudes and belief systems that govern the caregivee's life in general (e.g., "I am a failure"). Sometimes peoples' feelings are more readily apparent than their thoughts. When that is the case, first discern the feeling; and then ask yourself, "What would a person have to think in order to feel like this person feels?" Sometimes the story itself is most revealing. Ask yourself, "What would be a typical thought for a person like this in the situation being described?" Sometimes the individual expresses conclusions, opinions, or judgments. Ask yourself what assumption might have led to the statement, and express the assumption as a reflection of thought. We often do things that are not in our conscious awareness (e.g., smiling, foot tapping, holding the throat, winking, etc.). The chaplain needs to assume that these kinds of actions are meaningful - our bodies do not simply do their own thing totally unrelated to whatever else is going on. The actions are either related to what the person is saying, or they are related to what is happening between the chaplain and the individual in his mission field. Bringing him into conscious awareness helps the person to further sort out the story. The reflection of behaviors points out significant things the individual is doing as he tells his story.

Fig. 16.8 Mirror the counselee's behavior along with your verbal description.

Focus on posture, actions, limbs, hands, eyes, and speech. Use "you" as the subject of the verb (e.g., "You are tapping your foot", not "Your foot is tapping"). Physically mirror the behavior observed along with your verbal description. It is sometimes effective to just mirror the behavior without a verbal description. It is frequently more helpful when the reflected behavior is connected to his story (e.g., "You got a tear in your eye when you mentioned your first born child"). If this skill is used too frequently, the person may become so self-conscious that he puts his effort into controlling the reflected behavior instead of sorting out his story. Use it sparingly!

Paraphrasing

Another skill for the community chaplain to place in his tool belt that is effective for relationship caregiving is that of paraphrasing. Paraphrasing works to provide a feedback loop that helps the speaker hear his story and to help him achieve self-awareness by clarifying the content of what he has been sharing. In addition, this will help the individual sort out his story, all the while demonstrating that the chaplain is hearing the story accurately. When paraphrasing, simply restate what the individual has said, using your own words while keeping the meaning of the speaker. The paraphrase should be more concise and clear, and therefore more meaningful. The focus is on the content of the story - the up-front, overt material shared by the person, not the covert feelings or thoughts about the material. While the reflecting skills focus on what he has not said, the paraphrase feeds back what has been said. Effective paraphrasing will sift out the part that does not contribute to understanding and feed back what is left. In general, keep it short! Deliver the paraphrase as a statement, not a question. Use voice, posture, and gestures that are congruent with the material being paraphrased. Remember that it is okay to be wrong or inaccurate with your paraphrase, because even a wrong one will help the individual to sort out the story if you give responsibility for correcting it to him. A common example of paraphrasing may include the following:

Person in need: "My dad worked all the time. When he was home, all he did was watch TV and drink beer. My mom spent all her time taking care of the little ones."
Chaplain (paraphrasing): "Your parents weren't there for you."
Person in need: "Right! When I had problems as a teenager, I didn't get any help at home. If it wasn't for my coach, I don't know how I would have made it. He was more than a coach to me."
Chaplain: "He was like a dad." *Person in need:* "Exactly!"

Paraphrasing can be followed up with summarizing. This skill is used to help the person sort out the story by organizing information. This is accomplished by identifying the main points in the story, serving as a memory aid for the individual and the chaplain, and helping the chaplain remember important topics that need further exploration. Think of the summarizing process in the format of an outline. As information is received, decide where it fits into the outline:

> I. FIRST MAIN POINT
> 2. SECOND MAIN POINT
>   A. First sub-point under 2.
>   B. Second sub-point under 2.
>   i. First sub-point under B.
>   ii. Second sub-point under B.

Example:

Discourse: "When I was growing up, my family was not very close. Mom was gone two or three nights a week doing things for the church. If she wasn't taking classes, she was teaching them. It seemed like she was always involved in something more important than us. Dad wasn't any better. He worked seven days a week. He said he had to in order to pay the bills. When they were home at the same time, they were constantly fighting about something - money, the house, us kids. When they weren't fighting, they would yell at us kids about making messes or not doing well enough in school. School was really hard for me."

- Childhood
- Family not close
- Parents gone
- Mom - church
- Dad - work
- Parents fighting

Chaplain (Summarizing): "Your childhood was difficult because your family wasn't close and school was hard."

Individual in need: "Right."

Chaplain (Realizing that the heading "family" only has sub-headings relating to the parents and that information is lacking about the kids in the family, the chaplain decides to seek more information using an Exploring Skill.): You said your family wasn't close, and you described how your mom and dad were distant. Tell me about any distance of the kids, and then we'll talk about how school was hard for you."

In order to be able to summarize, the chaplain needs to be able to remember lists of things. The mental outline is helpful, but it is useful to develop additional techniques for remembering. Another technique is to repeat the words in your mind while counting on your fingers, thus anchoring the words with numbers and something physical. Remembering this information takes practice. If we practice our memory systems in social conversations outside of caregiving, while listening to the radio, or watching TV or movies, we will be able to do it better during caregiving. Summarize at the following times:

- When it is necessary to help remember.
- When a topic seems to be completed (the caregivee stops, or introduces a new topic).
- To start a session.
- To close a session.

Frequent summarizing improves cognitive processes, so ask the person to summarize once in a while (particularly at the start or close of a session). Invite him to validate the summary by asking what else should be included. The summarizing skill should sound like a statement, not a question; and the tone of voice needs to be congruent with the material. Below are some examples of summarizing:

Chaplain: "Today, you shared about the hassles you're having with your mother, your wife, and your supervisor. What other relationships are hassles to you?" (Summarizing Skill followed by an Open Question)

Chaplain: "So the decision about school requires a consideration of the money involved, having to give up a job you enjoy, and uprooting your family. What else is involved?" (Summarizing Skill followed by an Open Question)

Recapturing and Sentence Completion

Recapturing and Sentence Completion are two skills that should be in the arsenal of the effective community minister. Recapturing is a skill that shifts the focus of the individual's story to a topic that was mentioned previously in order to explore that topic in greater detail. This skill is really a procedure that combines two other skills:

summarizing or paraphrasing and exploring through an open-ended question or open statement. Use this skill when the person has fully explored the current topic and is ready to move on or when further exploration of the new topic is necessary to facilitate exploration of the current topic. An example of recapturing is found below:

Chaplain: "Previously you gave two other considerations about this new job: the challenge and the location. Let us explore the challenge."

Chaplain: "In our last session, you indicated that you had a rough childhood. What was rough about it?"

With Sentence Completion, the chaplain starts a sentence and invites the person to finish it. It is used to encourage deeper exploration. Sometimes, it is helpful to ask him to complete the sentence several different ways. This helps the individual overcome defenses against exploring deeply. Examples of Sentence Completion:

Chaplain: "Finish this sentence in as many ways as you can, 'One thing that could keep me from doing this is _____'." (Chaplain looks the person in the eye and moves hand toward him with palm up. After he completes the sentence, the chaplain repeats the sentence to be completed and keeps doing it until the individual cannot come up with any new answers.)

Cargivee: "They don't show me any respect!"

Chaplain: "You want them to show respect by _____ (moves hand toward individual with palm up)."

Symbolizing

Symbolizing is another skill that should be present in the arsenal of the community chaplain, in order to aid in clarifying the problem at hand so that the hurting person can see the need for Christ. Symbolizing is the skill of creating and communicating word pictures that are representations of the caregivee's situation. The picture helps the individual to clarify and understand his story. In a sense, all words are symbols for the real thing. For example, the word "arm" is not an arm; rather it symbolizes an arm. When we hear the word "arm", we do not picture in our minds the three letters that make up the word "arm". We picture an upper limb. Similarly, the use of a word, phrase, or story becomes a symbol when it helps the chaplain to picture what the speaker has been describing. The symbol is not the thing itself, but it helps us to picture the thing.

The old adage that a picture is worth a thousand words is just as true if the picture is painted with spoken or written words instead of oil on a canvas. Symbolizing causes one to create a mental picture, and the mental picture may include far more detail than words would allow. Another benefit of symbols is that words are quickly forgotten, but pictures are long remembered. Anyone who has watched a satellite launch on television probably easily recalls the sight of the ignition and lift off but cannot remember the words of the commentator describing it. The same is true with a picture that we create in our own mind as the result of a verbal trigger. The caregivee will remember the symbol longer than a literal description of the same thing by the chaplain.

Symbols, if accepted, are immediately personalized to each recipient's frame of reference. For example, when I say, "John has a wall around him," people realize that I am not talking about a literal wall. I am instead describing someone whose behavior seems to keep people at a distance; people have difficulty getting close to him. Everyone will have his own picture of the wall. Some will picture it as a complete wall that lets nothing in; but some will see it as applying only to emotions, ideas, or physical touch. Some will see the wall as impenetrable, while others will see openings in it. Some will see it as made of brick, others as straw, and even others as anything in between. Some will see it reaching to the sky, and others as low enough to step over. Some will see it as very long and difficult to get around, while others will picture it as short and easily bypassed. The point is that the recipient of the symbol paints his own picture. Therefore, it is relevant to his experience.

Since the individual will complete the picture in his own unique way, it is important for the chaplain to explore the details of the picture verbally, never assuming that he has produced a picture identical to the speaker's. Sometimes the symbol is so familiar that the person does not even form a mental picture. In this case, the chaplain may have to encourage him to actually picture the symbol in his mind. Also, the individual will frequently draw an incomplete picture; and by exploring it, the chaplain can encourage him to fill in the missing details. If the symbol accurately represents his situation, it provides a format for filling in the missing pieces of the situation.

Any figure of speech is a symbol. We do not need to distinguish between the various types of figures of speech (metaphor, simile, parable, fable, allegory), like we would if we were studying language. We are studying caregiving; and for our purposes, we will call them all symbols. A good symbol can become helpful to the caregivee in several ways:

- Providing an easily remembered paraphrase.
- Helping to provide a more complete description.
- Enabling an understanding of spatial relationships.
- Exposing cause and effect relationships.
- Carrying within it the seeds of change.

There are many examples of symbolizing in the Bible. Here are just a few:

- Matthew 5:3: "Blessed are the poor in spirit..." The word used for "poor" has an economic meaning, but here it is used symbolically to describe a spiritual situation. We could expand on this symbol by calling it spiritual bankruptcy if we thought the spiritual poverty was the result of the person's own mismanagement.

- Matthew 5:6: "Blessed are those who hunger and thirst for righteousness, for they will be filled."

- Matthew 5:13: "You are the salt of the earth. But if salt loses its saltiness, how can it be made salty again? It is no longer made good for anything, except to be thrown out and trampled by men." A simple metaphor, "You are salt," would not work. This one required some additional explanation.

- 2 Timothy 2:3-6: Paul symbolizes with "soldier", "athlete", and "farmer". In v.7 he says, "Reflect on what I am saying," with those symbols, "for the Lord will give you insight into all this." Paul gives the symbols, and the Lord gives the insight.

As you read the Bible, notice the symbolizing. God models the use of symbols as an important aid to understanding. Below are some examples of symbolizing that the community chaplain may encounter in day to day ministry situations:

- One person talked about being an automatic teller machine for his kids. They were making withdrawals but no deposits. In discussing this, he concluded that if he quit spitting out the money, the kids would stop coming to the machine. He did not want that. His choices were to accept it or to continue feeling sorry for himself. Upon accepting it, he began to see that the kids were making some valuable deposits in his life. The machine had not been giving away money; it had been making advances on future deposits. The individual then gained peace about it.

■ One person said he felt like he was in a jail cell. Instead of saying, "You brought it on yourself," (which is what I was thinking) I said, "Who has the key to the door?" He gave a long pause, then got wide eyed, smiled, and said almost in a whisper, "I have the key." That situation changed.

Other symbols used in caregiving:
■ The addiction train ride
■ The intimacy tight rope
■ The heart flasher (pouring out your heart to everyone; people react to a flasher by getting scared and running away)

When using symbols in a caregiving session, there are some important principles to keep in mind. Present the symbol as a direct statement, not as a question. The symbol must be in the individual's frame of reference. As is the case when the chaplain uses other clarifying skills, the person will invariably acknowledge the symbol as accurate or not. If he says it is not accurate, work together to make it accurate. If it cannot be made accurate quickly, or if he does not understand the symbol, drop it. It is probably not in his frame

Fig. 16.9 The intimacy tightrope is one symbol used in caregiving.

of reference, and it therefore will not work. Do not try to force it. Let it go, and look for a different symbol. Be careful about how far to go with a successful symbol. It is possible to overwork it. Every symbol, no matter how good, eventually loses its referential effectiveness. Do not give up if you have difficulty with this. With practice, anyone can improve his skill with this technique. Many caregivees will initiate their own symbols. Unless yours is clearly better, use the one that is developed by the person in need.

Confrontation

The effective community chaplain will also be aware that there comes a point in the caregiving process where a confrontation will take place. In his discussion of nouthetic confrontation, Jay Adams says, "The idea of something wrong, some sin, some obstruction, some problem, some difficulty, some need that has to be acknowledged and dealt with, is central. In short, nouthetic confrontation arises out of a condition in the person that God wants changed. The fundamental purpose of nouthetic confrontation, then, is to effect personality and behavioral change." [19] The Greek word in the New Testament, which is closest to our understanding of the meaning of "confront", is *noutheteo*. It is translated as "warn", "admonish", or "instruct" in the eight verses in which it appears. This word *noutheteo* is from two root words, one of which means "to put" or "lay in" and the other means "mind" or "understanding". Therefore, a confrontation involves putting something into someone's mind or adding to his or her understanding. The way in which it is used implies that the result is some kind of change. When we talk about insight, we mean an understanding in someone's mind concerning the nature of a problem. Our process model of caregiving emphasizes that insight leads to change. The purpose of confrontation, then, is to point out to the person in need of change that something is wrong. It provides insight concerning cause and effect. It identifies what has to be changed. The object of the confrontation, then, relates to an attitude or behavior on the part of the person which is self-defeating or dysfunctional in some way.

Self-defeat involves many things. The basic self-defeat is to be out of God's will, but this is often difficult for the individual to comprehend or accept. Although it is the underlying component, putting too much emphasis on this often results in increased resistance. This resistance is manifested somewhere on a continuum between hostile rejection and intellectual argument over the interpretation of God's will. The result is that the focus is directed away from specifying the attitudes and behaviors that are causing problems and need to be changed. Most ineffective confrontation is of the judgmental, parenting, or preaching variety. The chaplain tells the person what is wrong with him and either implies or states that he had better change. The individual hears that he is sick, dumb, bad, or crazy and may feel guilty, depressed, anxious, or angry, all of which can inhibit communication and increase his resistance. The aggressive person will get angry and walk out; the assertive individual will intellectualize why the chaplain's statements do not fit him; the passive-aggressive caregivee will sabotage the process; and the compliant person will agree with everything the chaplain says but revert to previous attitudes and behaviors when the caregiving is finished. For these reasons, confrontation needs to be accomplished in a non-judgmental, non-accusing manner.

Confrontation is most effective when the individual confronts himself or when the chaplain enlists his active participation in the confrontation. This helps the person to acknowledge the validity of the confrontation and to take ownership of the situation. Without this acceptance of the truth and ownership of the problem, he will not take responsibility for changing. We have to earn the right to confront. This is done by respecting the one in need of change enough to proceed at his pace and to hear his story accurately, without judgment. All the previous skills covered in this training provide the essential foundations for confrontation.

> *23 Don't have anything to do with foolish and stupid arguments, because you know they produce quarrels. 24 And the Lord's servant must not quarrel; instead, he must be kind to everyone, able to teach, not resentful. 25 Those who oppose him he must gently instruct, in the hope that God will grant them repentance leading them to a knowledge of the truth, 26 and that they will come to their senses and escape from the trap of the devil, who has taken them captive to do his will. (2 Timothy 2:23-26)*

Confronting, as a skill and method of caregiving, hopes to accomplish certain goals. Confrontation should seek to help the person take responsibility for the problems in his life, to help him discover insights about the causes of problems in his life, and to help him see that some change will be necessary on his part. When using confrontation during a caregiving session, some general guidelines should be remembered. Ask yourself, what is causing this to be a problem and why is it not solved? When you have an answer, use one of the confrontation skills to communicate it to the individual. Use a calm but direct and matter-of-fact approach. Do not get angry or judgmental. Do not point, glare, or smile. Maintain eye contact. Do not make excuses for the confrontation. If you find yourself doing any of the above "do nots", then recognize that you are either too personally involved or you do not have the necessary foundation for the confrontation. At that point, back up in the process (i.e., develop more rapport, get more of the story out, or increase the person's self-awareness). Make the confrontation internal to them, not external between the two of you. Frame the confrontation in such a way that the individual has to argue with himself, not with you. Always ask for a response.

There are times that the person will reject the confrontation. If he responds with "I don't know" to any invitation to explain, respond with "What's your guess?" If he needs assurance, you may want to say, "That's okay, you don't have to know, just make a guess." If the caregivee denies the confrontation, ask him to explain what he sees as the cause. If he responds with his own interpretation, explore it fully until he sees his folly or until he convinces you that he is right. Do this in a non-defensive manner. Do not try to force your interpretation down his throat. If he does not offer an interpretation of his own, he either does not have enough self-awareness, he has not gotten enough of the story out, or you do not have enough rapport. Decide which it is, and go back to the skills in that stage of the process.

There are eleven types of confrontation skills of which you should be aware. They include:

- **Interpreting**: telling the person what you believe to be the cause
- **Linking**: feeding back two apparently unrelated things: actions, feelings, thoughts, situations, and asking the individual to describe what links them together
- **Describing incongruency**: feeding back two things about the person that are not congruent and asking him to explain
- **Identifying consequences**: telling the person what could happen
- **Confronting with the Bible**: exposing him to what the Bible says
- **Inviting self-confrontation**: asking the caregivee to confront himself
- **Reframing**: causing him to see something differently by describing it in a new frame of reference
- **Using paradox**: prescribing more of the same
- **Identifying distortion**: pointing out the distorted thinking
- **Self-disclosure**: sharing an insight from the chaplain's personal life that relates to the person's situation
- **Contrasting question**

Let us begin with interpreting. Interpreting is telling the individual your interpretation of the reason for the problem. Example: "You don't like working for a woman, because you expect her to treat you the same way your mother treated you." Of all the confrontation skills, interpreting runs the greatest risk of being rejected by the person in crisis, because you are giving him your interpretation of the reason for the problem. It is easy for the person to conclude that it is just your interpretation (and he is right) and decide to minimize its importance or reject it completely. Therefore, use this skill sparingly. You may soften the interpretation with an introductory statement, such as "It seems as if you're doing this because . . ." This would reduce the probability of rejection by the individual.

Linking is a skill in which you hypothesize a link between two situations, and it is your purpose to get the caregivee

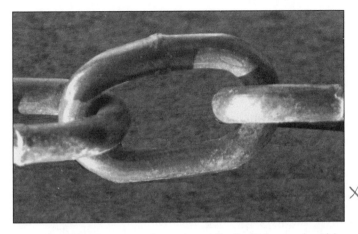

Fig. 16.10 Linking is one confrontation skill of which you should be aware.

to also see how they may be connected. Example: "Previously you said that you couldn't work for a woman, and now you're describing how degraded you felt when your mother was displeased with you. How do you think these are related?" In the above example, if you explain how you think those two situations are related, it becomes an interpretation. Instead, by requiring the person to make the interpretation, you increase the likelihood that he will accept it and act on it. State clearly both situations that you want linked, and then ask him to explain the connection. It helps to gesture with one hand to emphasize one situation and the other hand to emphasize the other situation.

Describing incongruency is a skill that is used to give the individual feedback that you assess to be incongruent or inconsistent. Simply repeat the inconsistency and ask him to explain it. Do not make any value judgments about the disparity. Encourage the person to make the judgment by saying, "What do you think of that?" "How does that strike you?" "Explain that for me," or some other similar phrase. An example of this skill may look like this: "You said that you want to qualify for a job at a higher skill level, and now you say that you don't want any more schooling. Explain that for me." There are differing types of incongruency.

- **Content v. content:** What the person says is not consistent with what he said previously. Example: "When we began our session, you said you wanted to stop using drugs. Now you're saying that it's okay to smoke a couple of joints on weekends. How does this make sense to you?"
- **Content v. affect:** The individual's demonstrated emotions are not congruent with

what is being talked about. Example: "You're telling me that your wife found out about your affair, and you look like you're feeling calm. Explain that for me."

- **Intention v. behavior:** What the caregivee does is not consistent with what he says he intends to do. Example: "You said that you were going to verbally affirm your husband every day, and you've only done it once in the last week. What does that mean to you?"

- **Affect v. behavior:** What the person feels is not congruent with what he does. Example: "You're feeling sad, but you're frequently telling jokes. What's going on with you?"

When challenging those in your mission field to change, there is a process to use for this type of confrontation. When a person gains insight into the nature or cause of a problem, the chaplain challenges him to change. It is a confrontation. The individual gets the message that it is no longer acceptable to explain or complain; he now has to take some action. He has to change. As he experiences this, it can be very upsetting; but it motivates him to change. This skill challenges him to begin to move into the integrated state. It challenges the person to explore new attitudes or new behaviors that would implement a newly gained insight. First, repeat the insight, and then ask him how he intends to use it. "Now that you see that you can't control your drinking once you start, what are you going to do about it?" "Now that you understand that your marriage is threatened by your need to control your wife, what will you do differently?" "Now that you realize that your kids need firm limits, what changes will you make?" Be certain that you have the caregivee's attention before you state the challenge. State his name, pause, fix eye contact, touch an arm or shoulder, and then say it. You may have to say, "John, look at me," in order to get his attention. Avoid a condemning or accusing tone of voice. Instead, use a gentle, encouraging, and serious tone.

Beyond identifying incongruencies, we can work to help the individual identify consequences of choices that are made. The use of this skill helps him understand that there are consequences for what he thinks, feels, and does, and that he can influence the consequences that he experiences by controlling what he thinks, feels, or does. Some common examples include:

- Thought: "That kind of thinking could make you depressed."
- Feeling: "If you allow that anxiety to continue, you could get an ulcer."
- Behavior: "If you get another DUI, you could go to the penitentiary."

When confronting with the Bible, be sure to gain permission first. Biblical confrontation involves exposing people to the Bible so that the Word of God can confront them. 2 Timothy 3:16 states, "All Scripture is God-breathed and is useful for teaching, rebuking, correcting and training in righteousness." This skill may be used when someone is contemplating or already engaging in activity that is prohibited or discouraged by the Bible. It may also be used when the Bible prescribes something that would be helpful to the person for dealing with a specific problem, and he is not doing it. First, ask him if he wants to know what the Bible says about the subject. Some phrases to gain this permission may be, "Would you like to hear what the Bible says about forgiveness?" or "Would you like to hear what the Bible says about what you are planning to do?" If he says "yes", you have some choices about how to respond. You may read the passage or have the individual read it out loud (but do not assume that he can find the passage). You may recite it from memory or paraphrase it. Whichever you do, ask for a response from the caregivee, like "How does that apply to you?" "What do you think that means?" or "What is that saying to you?" If he says he does not want to know what the Bible says, do not tell him. "Do not rebuke a mocker or he will hate you . . ." (Proverbs 9:8). Rather, explore in depth his reasons for not wanting to know. Have him identify the advantages and disadvantages of not knowing what the Bible says about the particular subject being discussed. You may then have the opportunity to use one of the other confrontation skills to deal with this issue of not wanting to know what the Bible says. Some examples:

- **Interpretation:** "I suspect that the reason you don't want to hear it is that you don't think you're going to like what it says."
- **Linking:** "You grew up in a very condemning church, and now you don't want to know what the Bible says about your situation. How are those connected?"
- **Describing Incongruency:** "You said last time that you want to know God's will for your life, and now you're saying you don't want to hear what the Bible says about what you're planning to do. Please explain that for me."

Many people resist hearing confrontations, even when they are done gently, respectfully, and with subtlety, as described herein. This is when the skill of self-confrontation can be very useful. If we can find a way to get someone to confront himself, and as a result he accepts the insight, it will be well worth the effort. But he has to be capable of insight, and many are not unless they have help. Simply ask the individual,

"What do you think is the reason that you don't change?" or "What would it take for you to change this?" If he does not know, you may ask once or twice again with different words; but do not push too hard. He may not be ready, in which case it would be helpful to revert to more use of the skills which aid rapport: exploration and clarification.

Confronting with Change

We know that changing the frame of a picture can completely alter the impact of the picture. In chaplaincy, we can help people see things from a new perspective by altering the frame of reference. This frequently frees him to try a new approach. Example: The individual is an alcoholic who refrained from drinking for three months and then got drunk again. He is focusing on the incident as proof of failure and is feeling discouraged, depressed, and defeated. He is talking about giving up and saying, "What's the use?" The chaplain is concerned that the addict will convince himself to go back to drinking. The chaplain reframes the interaction by saying "Congratulations! You succeeded in stopping the binge after only two days. This was a serious test of your commitment to sobriety, and you passed the test! Aren't you glad that Christ has defeated Satan's attempt to separate you from sobriety?" This is a double reframing. First, the chaplain reframed the drinking episode from a failure to maintain abstinence to a success at stopping the binge, thereby encouraging him to continue abstaining. Second, the chaplain reframed it from a physical battle he has to fight on his own to a spiritual battle in which he can rest in the victory Christ already won over Satan.

Paradox is another method that can be effective in confronting an individual with change. Using paradox is very similar to what lay people call "reverse psychology". It involves making statements with the expectation that the person will do the opposite. The use of this skill can be very risky and should only be done by, or under the supervision of, someone experienced in its use. Obviously, if we tell people to do something with the expectation that they will do the opposite, they may do exactly what they are told. This can be very distressing to the chaplain; dealing with it requires experience and special training. Using paradox is frequently referred to as "prescribing more of the same". In other words, using paradox involves telling the person to do what he is already doing. Let us look at some examples:

The caregivee complained of wanting to sleep all the time and not having the energy to do the housework. The chaplain told him that his body was trying to tell him that he needed more rest. Therefore he should sleep at least 12 to 16 hours per day, whether he thinks he needs it or not; and he should quit worrying himself about the housework. The next week, the individual sheepishly reported that he could not spend all that time in bed, he was not tired anymore anyway, and he was doing some of the housework and beginning to get out of the house again.

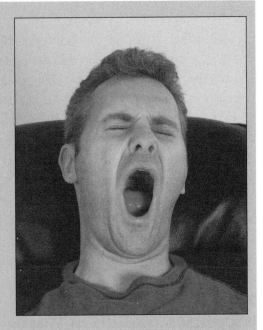

The director of a nearby Christian camp brought an out of town teenage boy to the chaplain, because he was very withdrawn and would not participate in any of the camp activities. In getting the story out, it was determined that the boy was doing the same thing at home; and that he seemed to be moving toward extreme paranoia. Knowing that he probably would have only this one session with the boy, the chaplain used a paradox. He told the boy that his problem was that he was not doing a good job of protecting himself at home. When he gets home from camp, he should systematically improve his security by withdrawing completely behind a barricade. He should board up the windows and door to his room and require his parents to place his meals outside the door. Then after ensuring they are gone, he should disassemble the boarded up door, get his meal, and board up the door again. This discussion was carried on with extensive elaboration and great seriousness. The chaplain even feigned taking offense whenever the boy questioned the sincerity of his suggestion. The boy returned to camp. A few weeks later the camp director said, 'I don't know what you did with that boy, but he was completely different after seeing you.'

Distortion

Identifying distortion can be a valuable tool for the community chaplain. This skill involves pointing out the distorted thinking process of the person in crisis. This skill is very effective for dealing with emotional problems. It is an application of the Cognitive Therapy approach, which says that emotions are the result of thoughts. With the application of this skill, people improve their emotional health by improving their thought processes. In his book *Feeling Good*, David Burns lists the following ten "cognitive distortions".[20] A cognitive distortion is an illogical way of thinking which results in inappropriate emotions. Chronic distorted thinking results in chronically unhealthy emotions. Even if medication alleviates the emotional distress, it is important to change thinking patterns in order to alter emotions in the long term. In order to use this skill, it is important that both the chaplain and the individual read the book. Below is a checklist of cognitive distortions:

- **All-or-nothing thinking:** You look at things in absolute, black-and-white categories.
- **Overgeneralization:** You view a negative event as a never-ending pattern of defeat.
- **Mental filter:** You dwell on the negatives and ignore the positives.
- **Discounting the positives:** You insist that your accomplishments or positive qualities "don't count".
- **Jumping to conclusions:** (A) Mind reading - you assume that people are reacting negatively to you when there is no definite evidence for this;
  (B) Fortune-telling - you arbitrarily predict that things will turn out badly.
- **Magnification or minimization:** You blow things way out of proportion or you shrink their importance inappropriately.
- **Emotional reasoning:** You reason from how you feel: "I *feel* like an idiot, so I really must be one." Or, "I don't *feel* like doing this, so I'll put it off."
- **"Should" Statements:** You criticize yourself or other people with "shoulds" or "shouldn't". "Musts", "oughts", and "have to's" are similar offenders.
- **Labeling:** You identify with your shortcomings. Instead of saying, "I made a mistake," you tell yourself, "I'm a jerk," or "a fool", or "a loser".
- **Personalization and blame:** You blame yourself for something you were not entirely responsible for, or you blame other people and overlook ways that your own attitudes and behavior might contribute to a problem.

Once you are both familiar with the ten cognitive distortions, the chaplain can confront the individual when he uses the distortions. The Identifying Distortion skill is the way the chaplain needs to challenge the person to correct the distorted statement and to help him if necessary. Follow the skill in practice below:

Person in need: "I didn't get hired. Employers don't want people like me."
Chaplain: "That was overgeneralization. Restate it without a cognitive distortion."
Person in need: "I didn't get hired. That employer chose someone else."
Chaplain: "That's better. What are you going to do?"
Person in need: "I just know I'm going to blow that interview. My degree won't matter to them. I shouldn't have applied."
Chaplain: "You just used three cognitive distortions. What were they?"
Person in need: "Fortune telling, discounting the positive, and 'should' statements."
Chaplain: "Good job! Now, correct the distortions."

Self-Disclosure

On occasion, it is important that confrontation take place through self-disclosure. The skill of self-disclosure can be used as a confrontation by implying or directly stating a contrast between the chaplain's personal experience and the individual's. One of the risks of chaplain self-disclosure is that the caregivee may shift his focus from his own story to the chaplain's; it can become a way for the person to avoid uncomfortable issues. To deter this, the chaplain refers back to the other's story immediately after the self-disclosure. An example of this skill may resemble this:

> The person in crisis is sharing her resentment and bitterness toward her husband and insists that he doesn't deserve forgiveness. The chaplain says, 'When I was in a similar situation, I was so full of resentment and bitterness that I was unable to sleep, I couldn't eat, I was crabby with the kids and the people at work, and my spouse and I couldn't communicate without fighting. How is your resentment and bitterness affecting you?' In this case, the chaplain first attempts to establish an identity with the individual. After she identifies with the chaplain's story, the chaplain says, 'When I was able to forgive, all of that changed. I was able to sleep and eat, and I got along with everybody much better.' The person hears this and identifies again, thinking, 'Maybe things will get better for me if I forgive like the chaplain did.' The chaplain then says, 'What would keep you from forgiving like I did?'

Contrasting Question

Sometimes asking a contrasting question can be an effective method for confronting the problem in the life of an individual. A contrasting question is a rhetorical question - a question asked merely for effect with no answer expected. It is a substitute for a statement. It has more impact than a statement, because the person is thinking the obvious answer and is compelled to make the statement himself. Since he makes the statement himself, he is more likely to accept the statement and ultimately to act on it. To be effective, the answer to the question needs to be obvious. Phrase the question by contrasting reality with the caregivee's mistaken concept of reality. The Apostle Paul has some outstanding examples. In Galatians 3:2 he states, "I would like to learn just one thing from you: Did you receive the Spirit by observing the law, or by believing what you heard?" Galatians 3:5 states, "Does God give his Spirit and work miracles among you because you observe the law, or because you believe what you heard?"

Implementing Change

The goal of all of these methods of accepting, exploring, clarification, and confrontation is to seek out change. Scripture is clear that change must take place when old life is replaced with the new. For this reason, it is crucial that we, as caregivers in the community, possess skills for change implementation. These skills should help those in the mission field explore alternative solutions, identify possible consequences of alternatives, and clarify values that are influenced by the basic problem, the alternatives, and the consequences. The skills should also help the person to prioritize values, challenge him to decide what changes to make, teach the individual an effective decision making process, help him experiment with and practice new behaviors, and encourage him to implement new behaviors outside the caregiving session. The exploration of alternatives flows naturally from the confrontation skill, challenging them to change. Use the exploring and encouraging skills, but focus on alternatives. Here are some examples:

- "How could you fix that?"
- "What ideas do you have?"
- "What other options are available?"

People will frequently want to explore only one alternative, thereby reducing the decision making process to a "yes" or "no". Keep them at this task until they have at least three alternatives. If he cannot think of any alternatives, prime the pump by giving him one or two of your ideas and then say, "What ideas do you have?" or "What can you add?" Before giving him your alternatives, ask him if he would like you to do so. It is helpful to write the alternatives on a marker board or piece of paper as they are mentioned. If you do not have a way to do this, frequent summarizing will be necessary. The purpose is to develop a list of values that need to be considered in contemplating change. For the most part, you will have to initiate this; but encourage the caregivee to participate freely. Ask him, "What other values do you think are involved in this decision?" Write down the values as they are identified, then explore them so that you both understand what they mean. Do not judge the values, just list them. For example, if he highly values his material possessions, money, or physical comfort, do not try to convince him he should change. Problems with values will emerge more clearly when exploring consequences and prioritizing (the next two skills). Use confrontation skills at that time. Most pertinent values will have emerged prior to now. They may have been verbalized, or you may have interpreted them. You may have to speculate and ask for verification. Ask the person which of the listed values is most important to him and assign that value a weight of "ten". Then ask him to assign weights to the remaining values in relation to the "ten". Some values may have identical weights. There may even be more than one "ten". Be alert to his incongruities and biblical inconsistencies. Use the confrontation skills where appropriate.

Exploring consequences of the choices made, based on the values explored, can then be accomplished. Identify the possible consequences for each alternative by asking, "What will probably happen if you do this?" or "What are the possible consequences of that option?" After exploring the general consequences, get specific by exploring the impact of the alternatives on each identified value. Examples:

- "How will this affect your family?"
- "How will this affect your job?"
- "How will this affect your health?"
- "How will this affect you spiritually?"

Add any consequence that is overlooked. Write these with the list of alternatives.

After a list of alternatives has been determined, challenge the individual to decide. Display all of the above information on a matrix as follows:

Fig. 16.11 DECISION MAKING

Values	Weight	Alternatives			
A.					
B.					
C.					
D.					
Totals					

Ask the person how each alternative affects value A. Does it have a positive effect, a negative effect, or no effect? For each alternative that has a positive effect on value A, enter the weight of value A as a plus factor in the appropriate column on line A. For each alternative that has a negative effect on value A, enter the weight of value A as a minus factor in the appropriate column on line A. For each alternative that has no effect on value A, enter a zero in the appropriate column on line A. Then follow the same procedure for value B, C, etc. Add the numbers in each column and enter the totals. This will enable you to eliminate undesirable alternatives, but do not simply pick the alternative with the highest score. Ask the individual how he feels about the alternative with the highest score. If he is pleased, that alternative is selected. If he or you are not pleased, explore the following:

- Perhaps an important value was not included.
- Perhaps the weighing does not accurately reflect the person's priorities.
- Perhaps alternatives can be improved by combining the best parts of two or more or by eliminating negative aspects.

Keep reworking the values, weights, and alternatives until a decision is made that is acceptable to both of you. Sometimes the process goes very rapidly and is not done as formally as described here.

Often change has to be implemented in steps rather than all at once. Also, many times a step will not by itself produce the desired end result, but it will contribute to it in consort with other steps. An example would be a person whose goal is to overcome depression. Steps in that direction might include abstinence from mood altering chemicals and foods, regular exercise, daily goals, daily Scripture reading, meditation and prayer, attendance at a support group, confession of specific sins, and forgiveness of specific acts of significant people. Any one of these probably would not accomplish the goal of overcoming depression, but the combination of all steps probably would. If the sequence of steps is important, it needs to be specified. For example, drug detoxification would be accomplished before relational caregiving. Use the exploring and encouraging skills to help the individual come up with at least some of the steps. This helps him to take ownership of them and will increase the likelihood of following through. When dealing with resistant or manipulative people, it is especially important that the steps be measurable. Specify who is to take the step, what the step is in behavioral terms, when it is to be taken, how often, and how long. Do not expect the person to be able to do this without your prodding and priming.

The probability of successful implementation of change is increased by anticipating possible obstacles to completion of the steps and developing a strategy for what to do if the obstacles arise. It takes away excuses for failure ahead of time. Ask "how" and "what" questions directly. Here are some examples:

- "What could happen that would keep you from doing this exercise three times this week?"
- "How could you sabotage this plan?"
- "What might somebody do that you might allow to discourage you from completing this step?"

Develop strategies for overcoming the obstacles. Again, use "how" and "what" questions. Here are some examples:

- "How could you protect yourself from that happening?"
- "What would help you to get in three practices this week, even if that obstacle arises?"
- "How could you overcome that obstacle?"

If the change is something that involves the caregivee's thought processes, have him write the new thoughts. This is called rehearsing. It is a sort of script that reinforces the decision that has been made in the caregiving session. Keep rewriting them until they are clear. Have him read them repeatedly outside of caregiving sessions. If the change is something that the individual does alone, have him imagine doing it successfully. If the change is something that the person will do in interaction with another person, have him role-play the new behavior. You play the role of the other person.

Assign practice for the caregivee. Explore with him how he can practice the change outside of the caregiving session. Identify and clarify the specifics (who, what, when, where, why, and how). Set a goal that is possible, challenging, and measurable, and ask him to repeat it and commit to it. Explore with the individual what might keep him from accomplishing the goal and how to overcome it.

Healing and Prayer

There are times that healing will take place. God is, after all, the Divine Physician. As a society, we understand pretty well and are very sensitive to and supportive of the healing process for physical injuries. However, we act as if emotional injuries are not really serious. We expect people to take time off to get over the flu or a broken leg, but we are reluctant to see them take time off for depression or a broken relationship. In the old days we admired the football player who shot Novocain into his broken ankle and continued the game. While we look down on such practices today, we often admire the person who gets Valium from the doctor and continues the game of life in the midst of a broken heart. Emotional injuries need healing at least as much as physical injuries do. In fact, it seems as if the process for both is the same. God provides the healing for both, and we are responsible for taking certain steps to allow the healing. If we do not do our part, the healing will be inhibited. Our part is first aid, treatment, and rehabilitation, and God provides the healing. He also helps us with our part.

God can heal us in an instant, but his normal method is to use a process of healing. The process takes time and effort on our part. Considerable study and prayer must go into understanding the healing process and how to facilitate it. Help individuals to heal by encouraging and monitoring activities associated with first aid, treatment, and rehabilitation and by leading them in prayer during the process. A critical step in healing emotions involves expressing them and reconciling the past. In discussing the process of becoming mature, Paul says, ". . . [13]Forgetting what is behind and straining toward what is ahead, [14]I press on toward the goal ..." (Philippians 3:13-14). We cannot run a good race toward maturity if we repeatedly look behind. Healing the past frees us to grow. After talking about the past and expressing our feelings about it, forgiveness is a key element of forgetting the past. We need to help others forgive those who have hurt them, and we need to help them repent of their own sins and receive forgiveness. Many people reach an impasse with these issues. Some can agree intellectually that it is necessary but balk at actually doing it. Some

Fig. 16.12 We cannot run a good race toward maturity if we repeatedly look behind.

say the words but do not experience relief because they did not really mean it. Many people cannot get through this impasse without God's direct help. Prayer is the best way to get that help, but many need help with praying. In these cases, it is important for the chaplain to lead by telling them what to say. Those in need of healing also need to be encouraged to participate in support groups where they can be honest and real with other Christians. Galatians 6:1 tells us that confessing sins and praying for each other allows healing and restoration to take place.

Some people are handicapped by their view of themselves and situations. They would respond differently if they believed they could. Simply telling them that it is all in their head does not work. However, using imagination to reprogram their mind can work. When they can imagine themselves doing something different, they can be freed of their own mental block that has been preventing them from doing it. Prayer can also be used to gain that freedom. The use of prayer and imagination together allows us to communicate with God in pictures as well as words. In most cases, the chaplain has to imagine it first and then guide the individual's use of his imagination. An example of this skill may resemble the following: A woman had been severely victimized as a child. She said she felt like an injured bird that people kick around. She said she wanted to fly. The chaplain asked her to imagine that she is that injured bird. She then imagined Jesus being there and healing the bird and the bird flying.

Reinforcement

Once the decision is made to change, reinforcement of that decision should be put in place. The groups of skills that we will discuss at this point are designed to reinforce changes in order to encourage repetition and continuation. Psychologists discovered God's method of influencing behavior - reward and punishment. Rewards increase the probability of an action; punishment decreases the probability of an action. A reward can be the addition of something pleasant or the subtraction of something noxious, whereas punishment can be the addition of something noxious or the subtraction of something pleasant. We typically think of rewards and punishments as consequences, because they follow the action being rewarded or punished.

Consequences can be experienced physically, verbally, cognitively, emotionally, or spiritually. A physical consequence is experienced through one of the senses (e.g., touch, smell, sight) and is of itself either pleasant or noxious. A verbal consequence is experienced through thought processes that can be intentionally pleasant (happy, excited, peaceful) or unpleasant (mad, scared, sad). Spiritual consequences are experienced as pleasant (God's presence, forgiveness, peace, joy) or unpleasant (isolation from God, oppression, shame, fear).

The four ways that consequences occur are intentional, natural, vicarious, and imagined. Consequences are intentional when they occur in response to a predetermined decision. Someone decides to reward a particular action and then provides the reward when the action occurs. The decision can be made and executed by the person who receives the reward, by someone else, or by both in consort. With humans, the effect of the consequence deteriorates when the person who intends to provide the consequence does not appear to be observing or capable of following through. Consequences are natural when they occur as a natural result of the behavior. The action has a high probability of resulting in the consequence without outside interference. Another way of saying it is that the consequence can normally be expected to follow the action. For example, touching a hot stove produces pain and eating chocolate produces a pleasant taste. Consequences are vicarious when they are observed happening to someone else. For example, we may wince when we see someone receive a grave injury, and we may smile when we see others laughing even if we do not know what they are laughing about. We associate someone else's consequence with his or her action, and the vicarious experience serves as a consequence for our doing the same thing. Vicarious consequences are frequently the motivator behind imitating a model. Consequences are imagined when they are created in the imagination. Through the imagination, the person experiences the consequence as if it actually happened. It is as if the body does not tell the difference between an actual event and an imagined one.

Fig. 16.13 What is rewarding to one person may be punishing to another.

Reward and punishment are subjective experiences and are therefore highly personal in their differentiation. One person's junk is another person's treasure. What is rewarding to one person may be punishing to another, even with consequences that are experienced physically. For example, a sauce made of fermented fish entrails is highly valued by Vietnamese people but considered repugnant by most Americans. It is therefore important to determine the response of the individual when devising rewards and punishments. It has been found that the frequency of reinforcement is also important. Providing rewards 100% of the time (i.e., every time the desired behavior occurs) results in very rapid acquisition of the behavior, but it also results in very rapid extinction in the behavior when reinforcement is ceased. On the other hand, providing rewards intermittently on an unpredictable schedule results in slow acquisition of the desired behavior, but it also results in persistent retention of the behavior after reinforcement is ceased. A practical application of these research results would be to provide 100% reinforcement when a person is first learning the behavior, and then switch to an unpredictable intermittent schedule of rewards for the behavior. This would result in rapid learning followed by persistent retention.

2 Peter 1:5-7 talks about developing faith, goodness, and other qualities of the spirit-controlled person. It then says in v. 8, "For if you possess these qualities in increasing measure, they will keep you from being ineffective and unproductive in your knowledge of our Lord Jesus Christ." This indicates that most qualities are not possessed once and for all, but in increasing measure. The principle of successive approximations emphasizes the importance of rewarding movement toward growth, not just the final attainment of it.

Five reinforcing skills can be developed to facilitate success for the people in your care. The skill of invoking reinforcement involves laying the reinforcement on the individual. It can be simply a verbal compliment or word of encouragement or it can be a gift or privilege. Example: "You're looking so much better. There's a sparkle in your eye and a spring in your step." The skill commonly referred to as evoking reinforcement involves drawing the reinforcement out of the caregivee. This is very effective because it teaches him to reinforce himself and provides the wherewithal to continue outside the caregiving session. Example: "Tell me how good you feel walking in the house sober every night." Contracting rewards involves developing a contract with the individual, which identifies rewards for specific achievements. He makes the contract with himself, but you hold him accountable by asking about it next time. Example: Someone says, "When I have maintained my weight at 125 pounds for six weeks, I can spend two hundred dollars on new clothes." Keeping a record of changes provides reinforcement each time the caregivee makes an entry. A 3X5 card is a handy record because it can be carried in a pocket or purse. Example: An individual has set a goal of demonstrating love to his wife. He has decided that he will take the following actions to demonstrate love:

- Compliment her twice a day.
- Do one of her chores three times in the next week.
- Go for a walk with her three times in the next week.
- Give her a love note once in the week.
- Pray with her five times in the next week.
- He has to initiate these. If she initiates any, they do not count.

Always ask to see the record and discuss it with him while invoking and evoking additional reinforcement. For example, some follow-up statements for the above card would be: "I see that you met your goal for compliments on four of the days and even exceeded the goal on Friday. That's great!" (invoking reinforcement). "I bet you were pleased with yourself on those days. Tell me how good it felt" (evoking reinforcement). Since he was successful that last four days in a row, I would not ask about the two days that he did not accomplish his goal. Instead, I might say, "It looks like you really have that down pat now that you did it four days in a row" (invoking reinforcement). "Tell me how good you feel about that" (evoking reinforcement). "You did really well with the chores" (invoking reinforcement). "How good did you feel when you experienced her response?" (evoking reinforcement). "Wow! You even got in two of the three walks" (invoking reinforcement). "What was it like when you did it?" (exploring and evoking reinforcement). "What happened that you weren't able to get the third walk?" (exploring). "What can you do to prevent that interference this coming week?" (challenging to change and exploring alternatives).

When the change seems to be apparent, terminating the caregiving relationship will be necessary. This does not mean that the relationship between chaplain and caregivee is ending, but simply the caregiving for this particular issue. Terminating the caregiving relationship may be viewed by the caregivee as punishment if you do not handle it properly. It is desirable to make the termination of caregiving rewarding to the caregivee and the chaplain. Begin by having the individual summarize what he was like when he started, the key insights that were discovered, and changes in behavior and attitude that were accomplished. Encourage him to use "I" statements. Ask the person to critique the sessions. What was the most helpful, and what was most harmful? Provide lots of reinforcement throughout the termination. Evoke reinforcement by asking him how he expects the rest of his life to be different as a result of the changes he has made. Be sure to attribute the changes to the work of the individual and the work of the Lord. Many people slip back after caregiving is completed. They need to be encouraged to continue working on growth without the chaplain. In the termination session, the chaplain needs to explore growth possibilities and seek a commitment by the caregivee. Simply ask, "What will you do to continue the growth process you have begun in our meetings?" Then help him to explore opportunities for service in the church and the community, for fellowship in the church, and for expanding knowledge of God.

The Most Common Entrance into a Relationship

While we have discussed some important skills that are needed for building relationships with people, caring for them when they have relationship issues, and introducing them to the greatest relationship that they can ever have, we have not examined when you are most likely to step into relationships with them. You, as a community chaplain, will most likely come into the relationship of an individual and his significant other on two occasions: to perform a wedding ceremony or to help with a problem in the marriage. If you happen to be an ordained minister, the chaplain is qualified to perform marriages; and it is quite likely that an individual will make that request. It is best to have a policy on officiating wedding ceremonies before you are asked to do so. Scripturally, you should not unequally yoke. We understand that to mean that we will not marry a believer to an unbeliever. Obviously our goal will be to evangelize the couple to bring both to a saving knowledge of Jesus Christ. Please pay particular attention to these criteria. Additionally, it is recommended that the couple must submit to premarital counseling consisting of a minimum of six 50-minute sessions. The decision to perform marriage ceremonies is up to each chaplain, but the above criteria should be met. So what is your reaction when someone asks if you do weddings? Is it any of the following?

Fig. 16.14 What is your reaction when someone asks if you do weddings?

- Oh no, another stinking wedding!
- Oh boy, 6 weeks of premarital.
- Oh boy, $150!
- I hope the wedding is in Vegas.

The chaplain has a great opportunity for evangelism when he performs a wedding ceremony. In fact, there are four chances for this to take place. Sharing the life-changing Good News of Jesus Christ can take place during the premarital counseling, the rehearsal and the rehearsal dinner, on the wedding day, and during the reception.

Let us first take a look at the pre-marital counseling sessions. Follow the recommended schedule for meeting. If you see any reluctance to put the time in for the counseling, maybe you should not be performing this wedding.

Week #1: Will they be equally yoked?

Are they born again (witnessing opportunity)?

Remind them about your confidentiality agreement.

Give overview of next five sessions.

Discuss your fees and their agreement to attend these meetings.

Week #2: Skeletons in the closet

Get them to open up about anything that might be a deal buster later on in the marriage. These are things that the other party does not know about (ex-spouses, abortions, children by previous marriages, health issues [VD etc.], credit problems, addictions, former drug use, alcohol abuse, arrest and convictions, and so on.

Week #3: All about finances and budgeting

Will they have joint or separate accounts?

Who will pay the bills?

Is one a spender and the other a saver?

Have they made a simple household budget?

What about the debts they are bringing into the marriage?

Week #4: All about children

Have they discussed the issue?

How many will they have and when?

What if God has other ideas, and they cannot conceive?

What about discipline?

Week #5: Family matters

How will they deal with the pressures of family?

What about Thanksgiving, Christmas, and Mother's Day?

Will either of them run home to mom and dad when conflict arises?

What about sibling matters that might impact this marriage?

Discuss the biblical concept of leaving and cleaving.

Week #6: Recap previous weeks/prepare to tell their story

Go over the plans for the actual event.

Find out how they want you to dress for the wedding.

Nail down all the dates.

Get phone numbers for relatives and friends that are involved.

Clarify your responsibilities and what you plan to do.

Make sure they know how, where, and when to get their license.

The very best gift you can give the couple is a framed copy of the marriage license. Simply pick up an inexpensive frame and put everything together after the wedding and give it to them at the reception.

The next opportunity you will have to share the gospel will be at the rehearsal of the wedding ceremony and the dinner that usually follows. Be sure to ask permission of the couple to share about the important role that God will play in their marriage. Conduct two wedding walkthroughs, using the second walkthrough to share the Good News. Say something like, "Tomorrow will be a large crowd, but tonight we're part of an intimate gathering," to break the ice. Remind others that are attending the rehearsal that God wants to be involved in their marriages as well. Many people that are there may be in a church building for the first time in their lives. Remember this crucial point.

After the rehearsal comes the wedding day. This is yet another wonderful opportunity to share with those attending the wedding. Make the day special by telling their story. Include vows that have spiritual meanings and teach about marriage. Minister to those whose marriages are suffering, and share the Gospel. A good lead-in to the Gospel may go something like this: "Having earlier asked John and Sue for permission to do so, let me pause for just a moment to speak some words of encouragement to those joining this couple in this special event. John and Sue walked in here this afternoon with a desire for one another, a desire to honor God, and a desire to speak words of commitment to one another. Some of you walked in here this afternoon hurting. Some are here this afternoon and you're saying, 'That sounds so idealistic' - and that may be true, but here's the word I want to speak to you - it's God's ideal! Remember to keep Christ at the center of your own marriage. Some of you are here, and weddings make you feel guilty because you have had a marriage fail and maybe you need to hear God say I forgive you. Others are here who need that most important relationship. Romans 5:8 states, 'But God showed his great love for us by sending Christ to die for us while we were still sinners' (NLT). Perhaps today is the first time in a long while you've given any thought to God. It would be a tremendous blessing for John and Sue if the day they began their marriage relationship were the day you began your relationship with God."

The reception is one more chance that is given to the officiating minister to have an eternal impact on the lives of the wedding attendees. Be alert to opportunities for ministry and evangelism when people comment on certain aspects of the wedding ceremony.

The other opportunity presented to the chaplain to be in relationships that are important to the others who are in the mission field is when the relationship is in peril. They have tried many other things, all to no avail. This is when the relationship that you have with your spouse can really reflect the relationship between Christ and His Church to those in need.

Have a Model Marriage

Our own marriage can be used as an evangelism tool if we demonstrate knowledge of God and the marital relationship.[21] We need to communicate knowledge of God's vision for marriage. It is a God-created institution and not to be taken lightly. It is a covenant made with your spouse and with God. Additionally, God created roles for both husband and wife, unifying them with a permanent bond that is dissolved by death. We need to demonstrate in practice what a Godly marriage is like. Having a marriage that reflects Christ and His Church is accomplished by having Jesus Christ as a priority in your marriage. Make sure that every decision made honors Him. Praising your spouse in front of others and making your spouse's needs superior to your own are also important. Praying together daily for each other, in troubled times, about mission field issues, salvations, surgeries, care sessions, and the like is crucial. Remember that you are partners in ministry. The gifts that our spouses possess can help us witness in the community around us. Your spouse can help by being a prayer warrior and attending funerals, weddings, and hospital visits whenever possible. Sharing effective ways to have a fulfilling marriage is useful, but be sure to use care to avoid revealing too much of your own marriage, spouse, and self. Participate in church weekly as a couple, seeking to protect your spouse from the flaming missiles of the enemy, taking care to avoid the dragons of doubt, depression, and destruction that are assaulting you both.

There are often relationship issues that stem from spiritual roots. One of the most common spiritual problems in a marriage is that the "Spiritual Head of the House" is spiritually weak. This is especially important for the minister to notice as he tends to his own family, his first ministry. Notice that Adam failed in Scripture. He changed the message that God had given to him. In Genesis 2:15-17 God told Eve not to eat from the tree of the knowledge of good and evil. In Genesis 3:1-3 Eve stated that God told them not to eat *or touch*. Adam stood by and watched his wife make a bad decision. Genesis 3:6 says that Adam was "with her". He hid from God. He cried "victim". The consequences were severe. They included the fall of man and the fall of the family. The first step in leading your family toward Christ is to prepare yourself. Adam walked with God in the garden during the cool of the evening, and it was not enough for him to resist temptation when it was offered to him. We should follow Christ's example set forth in Ephesians chapter five, by keeping ourselves pure for God and for our spouse.

Infidelity and Intimacy

Another issue that the community chaplain will face in his mission field is the infidelity in a marital relationship.[22] It is amazing that people will put everything at risk for a brief encounter. A working knowledge of the affair and how to prevent one is crucial for vital relationship care in the workplace. As Willard Harley, Jr. writes in his book *His Needs, Her Needs*, intimacy is important in a marriage relationship. He states that there are five needs that are specific to men and women:

It is important to her:	It is important to him:
Affection	Sexual Fulfillment
Conversation	Recreational Companion
Honesty	Attractive Spouse
Financial Support	Domestic Support
Family Commitment	Admiration

Scripture has much to say about the physical aspects of a marriage. Sex was created by God and is good. God gave us instructions for physical relationships in His Word; sex is for propagation and for pleasure. God creates a partner for us to experience such intimacy. Sex is created for the husband/wife relationship (see Genesis 1:27-31, Song of Solomon 6:3, I Corinthians 7:3-5). There is intimate communication in Scripture:

> *I liken you, my darling, to a mare harnessed to one of the*
> *chariots of Pharaoh.* (Song of Solomon 1:9)

This means: Your very presence creates intense excitement in me (a young mare next to a stallion would create intense desire).
This does not mean: You know, for a woman, you are as strong as a horse.

> *Your cheeks are beautiful with earrings, your neck*
> *with strings of jewels.* (Song of Solomon 1:10)

This means: Your jewelry only enhances your beauty.
This does not mean: Without jewelry, your face is plain.

Biblical intimacy can be defined as a dynamic collection of intimate thoughts, passionate emotions, spicy words, and committed actions exchanged with reckless abandon between husband and wife, thus producing a joy-filled life-long relationship to the glory of God. But we have placed barriers in our intimate lives that derail this important aspect of marriage. Gentlemen should guard where their eyes wander, while ladies should be careful to avoid sharing intimate details with others. There are also lies that are told in marriage. The liar is commonly referred to as the protective liar, the stay out of trouble liar, or the born liar.

So how can we pursue the passion God intended for our marriages? Look at the following points found in Scripture:

- **Be Attractive:** Song of Solomon 7:6 states that we should be captivated each by the other's appearance. I Peter 3:3-5 warns against neglecting the internal beauty for a short term external result.
- **Be Available:** Song of Solomon 6:3 gives freedom to enjoy the physical relationship only within the marriage relationship. I Corinthians 7:3-5 provides guidelines for periods of abstinence.
- **Be Anticipatory:** Proverbs 5:19 describes what can happen when you anticipate an encounter with your spouse.

Seek to ignite passion and intimacy through writing. Letters are the history books of your love, the echoes of your story, and the memorials of your marriage. Love letters are not simply pages of ooey-gooey sweet talk. They contain information, thoughts, emotions, passion, encouragement, and gratitude. If you are having trouble coming up with love letter starters, reflect on these:

- "Do you remember the time we..."
- "I love you more today than yesterday because..."
- "The best part of my day is when I see you for the first time. You..."
- "Today I prayed for you about..."
- "You are my best friend. Thank you for the times you..."
- "You are the world's greatest _____ because..."
- "Our relationship is like a candy store..."
- "I daydreamed about you today..."

Always keep the relationship fresh by making dating an adventure. Here are some ideas to pass along to the people in your mission field. Be sure to try them before you recommend them to others:

- **Queen for a day:** Gift wrap a toy tiara and give it to her at night before going to bed. Let her know that tomorrow you will be her royal subject, and she will be the Queen. Treat her like royalty for the entire day.
- **Tell her about her value:** Go to a toy store and purchase some toy jewelry or some costume jewelry at a department store. Take her out to dinner and while you are waiting for the meal to arrive, give her the jewelry and explain that she is worth far more than jewels. Fill in the following passage from Proverbs 31 with how you feel about her:

> I have found an _____ wife! You are worth more than _____
> ___, more than the jewels on the earth.
> I trust you because _____.
> When you _____, you really make our house feel like a home.
> You are very generous. When you _____, it makes me glad that I am your husband.
> You impress me when you _____. Many women do noble things, but you surpass them all.
> When you _____, you inspire me to greater devotion. I pray that God will give you the desires of your heart.

- **Bookworm date:** Go to the library and look through old newspapers for significant dates in your relationship. Search for each of your birthdays, your wedding day, the birth of a child, etc.
- **You're simply the best:** Spend some time during your date praising your spouse.
- **Best seat in the house:** Find a place to view a great sunset. Pack a picnic basket and watch God's brushstrokes paint the canvas of His creation.
- **Take a stroll down memory lane:** Recreate your first date, the first time you said, "I love you", or when you asked her to marry you. Go to the same place, if possible, and talk about how you were feeling about each other during these significant milestones in your life.

Most importantly, be intentional; look for what communicates love to the other. Learn what the other loves, and make sacrifices to bless and romance each other. Dates, phone calls, e-mails, love letters, gifts, getaways, and other surprises should be used in various ways to spark emotion and encourage communication. Become a student of your spouse. Men, look at your wife. She wants to be complex. Do not try to "solve" her

Fig. 16.15 Make dating an adventure!

formula. It is not MUSIC + CANDLES = INTIMACY. Sacrifice your own goals (sexual fulfillment) to understand her. Commitment means that there are no threats, loopholes, or escape hatches. Relationship does not mean simply doing things together, it means experiencing them as a conduit for intimacy. Time means that you place each other in high priority. Ladies, look at your husband. He wants your respect, in words and actions. He needs to feel sexually needed. He wants to be affirmed through the sexual relationship with his wife. He wants to know how to please you; for this part of your relationship to be satisfying, you must risk being open and vulnerable with each other. He needs your adventurous companionship. Spend time together in memory-making activities designed for just the two of you. He wants sexual satisfaction. The male sex drive, designed by God, is not something shameful. The wife has the power to affirm or to wound her husband by her response to this part of marriage. Spend the extra time and effort that is required to make your master bedroom a master retreat. This may include soft lighting, pleasing aromas, music, poetry, and a spirit of adventure. However, it definitely includes a door that locks, if there are children in the home!

Touch should work to establish a good emotional climate of warmth, love, and affection.

Hold Hands	Temple Rubbing	High Five	Play With Hair
Foot Massage	Kissing	Snuggling	Footsie
Sit In Lap	Spooning	Palm Pressure	Nose Rub

The characteristics of passionate touch can be found in the simple acrostic TOUCH:

T- **Tender:** the weight of your touch

O- **Often:** the frequency of your touch

U- **United:** the reciprocal nature of touch

C- **Considerate:** the thoughtfulness behind your touch

H- **Head To Toe:** the destination of your touch

Unhealthy Boundaries

The final major issue that the chaplain may come into contact with in the community is the subject of abuse in the home or domestic violence. A successful relationship is composed of two individuals each with a clearly defined sense of his or her own identity. Without our own understanding of self, of whom we are and what makes us unique, it is difficult to engage in the process of an ongoing relationship in a way that is functional and, though not always smooth, is a safe environment that generally enhances each of the partners. We need a clear sense of self in order to clearly and unambiguously communicate our needs and desires to our partner. When we have a strong conception of our own identity, we do not feel threatened by the intimacy of the relationship and can appreciate and love those qualities in our partner that make him or her a unique person. When two people come together, each with a clear definition of his or her own individuality, the potential for intimacy and commitment can be astounding. The similarities between two people may bring them together. However, in an ideal partnership, sometimes called interdependent, their differences are respected and contribute to the growth of their relationship, which aids in the growth of the individuals in that relationship.

One feature of a healthy sense of self is the way we understand and work with our emotional boundaries. Personal boundaries are the limits we set in relationships that allow us to protect ourselves from being manipulated by or enmeshed with emotionally needy others. Such boundaries come from having a good sense of our own self-worth. They make it possible for us to separate our own thoughts and feelings from those of others and to take responsibility for what we think, feel, and do. Boundaries are part of the biological imperative of maturation as we individuate and become adult people in our own right. We are all of us unique, and boundaries allow us to rejoice in our own uniqueness. Healthy intact boundaries are flexible. They allow us to get close to others when it is appropriate and to maintain our distance when we might be harmed by getting too close. Good boundaries protect us from becoming engulfed in abusive relationships and pave the way to achieving true intimacy (the flipside of independence) as we grow to interdependence (the relationship of two mature individuals). They help us take care of ourselves; and if we can receive it, to respect the selves of others.

Unhealthy boundaries are generally a result of being raised in dysfunctional families where maturation and the individuation process was not properly understood, nor was the child respected as an individual. In these types of families, the unmet needs of parents or other adults are sometimes so overwhelming that the task of raising children is demoted to a secondary role, and dysfunction is the likely result. Consider the role of the father or mother who screams at his/her children or becomes physically, verbally, or emotionally abusive with them as a self-centered way of dealing with his/her own stored up anger/grief from their own traumatic childhood. The emotional fallout of these unmet developmental needs, depending on the severity of the original pain, is often close to the surface and can be triggered by totally unrelated present circumstances. The pain of their own childhood experiences repressed for so long is felt again, insisting that these experiences be dealt with, relegating the present needs of the children for safety, security, respect, and comfort to second place at best. Because of what they represent and the negative self worth of the parent, the child can sometimes be perceived as the "enemy"; and so dysfunction is passed on from one generation to the next. This is not to say that the childhood experiences of the parent were necessarily horribly abusive; it is just that what may have been acceptable parenting practices in their family of origin for generations were abusive. More often than not these practices and their underlying attitudes were based on false or abusive religio-cultural premises. What the children are likely to learn in this situation is that boundaries do not matter and that they as individual human beings do not matter, except where they are useful for the emotional needs of others. As they grow up in their families of origin, they lack the support they need from parents or caregivers to form a healthy sense of their own identities. In fact, they may learn that to get their needs met, they must get their way with others. To do this they need to intrude on the emotional boundaries of other people, just as their father or mother may have done. They would in all likelihood grow up with fluid boundaries that cause them to swing between feelings of engulfment on the one hand and abandonment on the other, inevitably leading to dysfunctional relationships later on in life. They would have at best a hazy sense of their own personal boundaries, not able to properly define where they end and the other begins. Conversely, they may learn that rigid and inflexible boundaries might be the way to handle their relationships with other people. They wall themselves off in their relationships as a way of protecting their emotional selves and as a consequence will, in all likelihood, find it difficult to form lasting close interpersonal bonds with others in adulthood, as they are still trying to individuate from their parents. The exception in this is relationships predicated on the same rigid rule-based structure as their family of origin, where nothing came into the family or out from it; but in this case the bond is likely to be enmeshment.

When we lack a sense of our own identity and the boundaries of the self that protect and define us as individuals, we tend to draw our identities and our sense of self-worth from our partner or significant other. This is what we did in the earliest stage of our biological growth in our family of origin, drawing our sense of worth from their perceptions of us. The structure of the relationship in this case is not that of equals in a partnership, but that of parent and child. This leads in some cases to that most unequal of relationships, master and slave. It is quite possible that children developing in a family where the important relationship of the parents is an unequal one will be forced to take on roles as either surrogate spouse and/or adopt roles with the hope that they will restore dignity to the family and balance to the system. If we cannot imagine who we would be without our relationship, chances are we come from a dysfunctional family of origin and have learned co-dependent behavior patterns. Unable to find fulfillment within ourselves or a relationship with God, we look for such fulfillment in others and are willing to do anything it takes to make the relationship work, just as we may have done in our enmeshed family of origin. We do this even if it means giving up our emotional security, friends, integrity, sense of self-respect or worth, independence, or employment. We may even endure objectification (an attitude in which we are no longer perceived as a feeling human being, but just an object, a part of the family system) in the form of physical, emotional, or sexual abuse just to save the relationship.

The more rational alternative is to find out whom we are and what makes us unique, and we will rejoice in the freedom of this discovery. We will come to realize that our value and worth as a person is not necessarily dependent on having a significant other in our life, and that we can function well as an independent person in our own right. When we move into accepting ourselves for who we really are, warts and all, we will be able to accept others for who they are. Our relationships and our selves will actually have a chance to grow into an emotionally mature state, able to give freely out of choice and flourish in the newfound freedom. This journey of self-discovery can be challenging and painful, but highly rewarding. Working with a trained therapist, as part of a support group, or a combination of both can provide the structure and support we need to take on this task. Whatever way we may choose, the first step is to acknowledge to ourselves, God, and possibly another person that our lives have become unmanageable in their current state. The second is to give ourselves over to the cleansing and renewal processes.

When boundaries are unhealthy and we are not in line with what God's Word clearly teaches about relationships, we may cling to the irrational belief that things are good enough the way they are. We tend to feel a measure of security in the relationship, that change is a difficult and fearful prospect, that we do not deserve any better, our life has always been a sacrifice of the self, and that this is as good as it is likely to get. However, in the process we give up the chance to be the person we were meant to be and to explore our sense of personal fulfillment in life. We give up not only our own life dreams, but also our sense of worth in order to maintain the security of a relationship. A healthy relationship is one in which boundaries are not only strong, but flexible enough to allow us to flourish with our own uniqueness; but we are also known and respected by each other. There is a sense of respect on the part of both partners that allows each to live as full a life as possible and to explore their own personal potential in Christ. We do not have to give up ourselves for a relationship but can become interdependent. Healthy boundaries allow trust and security to develop in a relationship, because they offer an honest and reliable framework by which we can know each other. If we do not know where our self ends and the other begins, it is impossible.

One characteristic of growing up in a dysfunctional household is that we may learn to feel guilty if we fail to ensure the success and happiness of other members of the household. We may feel responsible, or be made to feel responsible, for the failure or unhappiness of others. Thus in adulthood we may come to feel, or be made to feel, responsible for our partner's failures. The guilt we feel when our partner fails may drive us to keep tearing down our personal boundaries so that we are always available to the other person. When we feel the pain, the guilt, and the anger of being overly responsible for another person's behavior or life experiences, we may seek to alleviate this feeling by rescuing them from the consequences of their behavior, as we learned in our family of origin. We thereby deprive them of one of the most important features of an independent, healthy, and mature life: the ability to make their own life choices and accepting the responsibility for and the consequences of their decisions. Alternatively, we may bear the burden of their unacceptable behavior for many years.

A healthier response is to show our partners respect by allowing them to succeed or fail on their own terms. You, of course, may choose to support your partner's fulfillment of life goals, but it is unhealthy to rescue them from all of life's consequences. When you do agree to help, ask yourself two questions: Is it something they can do for themselves? Do I resent the giving of my own resources (self, time, money, etc.)? This may be a difficult choice if we have confused love with rescue. You can be there to comfort or encourage your partner when times become difficult, and you can rejoice with them when success is the outcome. When boundaries are healthy, you are able to say, "I trust and respect you to make your own life choices. As my equal partner, I will not try to control you by taking away your choices in life."

People who grow up in a dysfunctional family may fail to learn the difference between love and sympathy. Children growing up in these conditions may learn to have sympathy for the emotional crippling in their parents' lives and feel that the only time they get attention is when they show compassion for the parent. They feel that when they forgive, they are showing love. Actually, they are rescuing the parent and enabling abusive behavior to continue. They learn to give up their own protective boundaries in order to take care of the dysfunctional parent, becoming a surrogate co-dependent spouse. In adulthood, they carry these learned behaviors into their own relationships. If they can rescue their partner from the consequences of their behavior, they feel that they are showing love. They get a warm, caring, sharing feeling from helping their partner, a feeling they call love. But this may actually encourage their partner to become needy and helpless, enabling the negative behavior to continue. An imbalance can then occur in the relationship in which one partner becomes the rescuer or enabler and the other plays the role of the helpless victim. In this case healthy boundaries, which allow both partners to live complete lives, are absent. Mature love requires the presence of healthy, flexible boundaries. Sympathy and compassion are worthy qualities, but they can be confused with love, especially when boundaries have become distorted or are virtually non-existent. Healthy boundaries lead to respect for the other and equality in a relationship, an appreciation for the aliveness and strength of the other person, and a mutual flow of feelings between the two partners, all features of mature love. When one partner is in control and the other is needy and helpless, there is no room for the give-and-take of a healthy relationship.

Children from highly dysfunctional households often feel that things will get better someday, that a "normal" life may lie in the future. Indeed, some days things are fairly "normal", but then the bad times return again. It is the normal days that encourage the fantasy that all problems in the family might someday be solved. This is a common cycle in highly dysfunctional families. When they grow up, these adults carry the same types of fantasy into their relationships. They may portray to others the myth that they have the perfect relationship, and they may believe, to themselves, that someday all of their relationship problems will

Fig. 16.16 Children from dysfunctional households hold on to the fantasy that they will one day have a "normal" life and all family problems will be solved.

somehow be solved. They ignore the abuse, manipulation, imbalance, and control in the relationship. By ignoring the problems, they are unable to confront them; and the fantasy of a happier future never comes to pass. Unhealthy boundaries, where we collude with our partner in believing the myth that everything is fine, make it difficult to come to terms with the troubles of the relationship. Healthy boundaries allow us to test reality rather than rely on fantasy. When problems are present, good boundaries allow us to define the problems and to communicate with our partner in finding solutions. They encourage a healthy self-image, trust, consistency, stability, and productive communication.

In conclusion, the following are some common areas that associates find as pitfalls and a brief action statement for the course of correction:

- **People sometimes fall in love with someone's potential.** They may choose a mate or choose to stay in a relationship with the hope that the other person will change. They should be encouraged to explore the possibility of loving that person exactly as he/she is now with no expectation of change.

- **Individuals will at times confuse lust for love.** In a rush to feel close, people will have sexual relationships with someone, creating a false intimacy, which leads to disappointment. Direct them to take the time to create a genuine emotional connection that will facilitate true intimacy in God's timing.

- **Someone may overlook red flags out of desperation to have a relationship.** Examine statements that reflect that the person is emotionally and situationally not available.

- **People will assume that their partner knows what they want or need.** Facilitate the person taking responsibility for expressing his feelings and needs to the other. This will preempt conflict and deepen the emotional connection between them.

- **Individuals will take their partner for granted.** When couples get past the honey moon stage, they often become complacent with one another. Institute date nights and other strategies to continue romancing each other throughout the relationship, not just in the beginning stages.

- **People are not always empathetic with their spouse.** They need to put aside the need to be right and put themselves in the shoes of the other person. Being understanding and validating the feelings of another person does not mean that you will always agree with them. Often feeling understood will advance the relationship.

- **Someone may focus on what their partner has done wrong.** Encourage them to focus on what has been done right. Be specific, give examples.

- **Individuals enter into serial dysfunctional relationships without understanding or taking action to correct the problems.** In a healthy relationship your love is re turned, no one has to withhold true feelings for fear of lack of approval, and worth and value is increased.

To be in an intimate relationship, couples need to expose their authentic selves. That entails being able to be vulnerable and show some emotional courage. People are often afraid of revealing who they really are for fear that they will not be accepted.

A healthy relationship, hopefully one modeled by the community chaplain, will occur when people feel safe revealing their true selves to each other and eventually to God.

Stories From the Field: #15
"Getting Even With One Another"*

In December I began working closely with a neighbor who had committed adultery about a year earlier. He felt so guilty that he finally told his wife. She got "revenge" by doing the same, only she continued for a few months. I prayed for them daily and encouraged him as much as possible. He grew up in the church and went to a Christian school, but he did not embrace Christianity. One night, about ten or twelve weeks ago, he called me and told me that his wife wanted to get saved. I went to their apartment and presented the plan of salvation, and they both accepted Christ. He broke down as he prayed. They began going to the church he grew up in, were baptized, and are raising their children in the faith. The first time I spoke to Lee he was really skeptical about church; now they go two to three times a week! The first time I did rounds in my apartment complex after leading him to Christ, I had four or five unsaved guys come up to me and say that they had heard what I had done for Lee. (Of course, I gave God the credit.) He has been telling people unashamedly what Christ has done for him, and God has worked on the language problem, too!

– Submitted By: Troy T.
Pittsburgh, PA

*Individuals in this story have granted permission for its use.

Stories From the Field: #16
"A Girl In Every Port"*

One day I was doing rounds in a white-collar environment, when one of my associates, Steve, said he wanted to talk to me. After finding out what times were good for him to meet with me, we scheduled a lunch appointment in one of the conference rooms in his building. As I listened to what was bothering him, he talked about how he knew he had a problem with stringing women along. He had about ten girlfriends. In talking, he mentioned that he liked some things about each, but he was really using them to fill different emotional needs. As I listened to the pattern that consistently developed for his reason for dating each woman, I discerned that he was not saved. I asked him if anyone had ever mentioned to him how we each have a God-sized shape in our heart, which feels like an empty void in our life until it is filled. With his permission, I explained that God created us to have a relationship with Him and how He wanted to fill that void in our lives. I then shared the gospel with him, and he eagerly prayed with me to accept Jesus into his life as his Lord and Savior. Now God is helping to transform him as he renews his mind through reading Bible verses related to the issues in his life in the Bible that I gave him. He is being discipled and is growing. It is exciting and refreshing to see how God is changing his life. As a result, he is less depressed and more focused at work.

– Submitted By: Sherry K.
Charlotte, NC

*Individuals in this story have granted permission for its use.

Questions

Reflect on the Stories From the Field found in this chapter and answer the following questions:

1. How would you handle the situation that was described?
2. What information found in the story is confidential?
3. What information found in the story can be shared with others? With whom may this information be shared? Under what circumstances may this information be shared?
4. How does the information found in this chapter pertain to the story?

End Notes

1. All Scripture quotations are from The New International Version (NIV), unless otherwise specified.

2. Piedmont Associated Industries Rapid Eye Movement Training Seminar, Attended March 2003

3. Ibid.

4. Ibid.

5. Ibid.

6. Ibid.

7. Ibid.

8. Ibid.

9. Ibid.

10. Ibid.

11. Ibid.

12. Ibid.

13. Ibid.

14. Ibid.

15. Ibid.

16. Ibid.

17. Ibid.

18. Corporate Chaplains of America Training Manual

19. Adams, Jay, *Competent to Counsel* (Grand Rapids, MI: Baker, 1972), 45.

20. See David D. Burns, *Feeling Good: The New Mood Therapy* (New York: New American Library, 1980).

21. Corporate Chaplains of America Quarterly Training Meeting, Brian Ayers, Presenter (November 2004).

22. Corporate Chaplains of America Quarterly Training Meeting, Chris Hobgood, Presenter (November 2004).

Chapter Seventeen

Legal Issues and the Community Chaplain

CHAPTER SEVENTEEN

Legal Issues and the Community Chaplain

———————————————— Objectives ————————————————

During the course of this chapter, we will perform the following tasks:

■ Discover the legal boundaries of community ministry

■ Explore relevant laws for the community chaplain

■ List legal terms with which the effective chaplain should be familiar

■ Describe the process of the legal system and court proceedings

■ Apply Scripture to the legal functions of chaplaincy

■ Describe methods for effective ministry during legal crises

---

A s you, the community chaplain, take your first step onto the property of a neighborhood, a school, a sports field, a hospital, or a jail, all of which are a mission field, there is often a pit in your stomach. Those in the mission field and the community chaplain may both hold major concerns: How far can the chaplain go? How can I avoid a lawsuit in a litigious society? How can I be effective without infringing on the legally protected rights of others? While obtaining permission is addressed in another chapter, we will focus a large bright light on the legal parameters in which a community chaplain must operate. We will then look at some of the legal issues that face individuals in the society at large.

Overcoming the fear can be accomplished by educating yourself about the obstacles that can be in place for the effective chaplain. The first step is to relax. Remember, you are called by God, the Creator and Sustainer of the world. He is in control of all of the situations that will be encountered in the business world, the community clubhouse, a hospital room, or in the dugout. Secondly, realize that there is a trend that exists in many American communities. That trend is the acceptance of faith in places that it had not previously been accepted. Take a look at the following quote, and there are many more like it:

The marketplace, a synthesis of business, education, and government, is to a metropolis what the heart is to a human body. Yet millions of men and women who have been called to ministry in the marketplace feel like second-class citizens when compared to those who serve in a church or missionary context, and they often fail to rise to their God-appointed position. It is time to give marketplace people their rightful validation as full-fledged ministers; because the last revival, the one prophesied by Joel and quoted by Peter in Acts 2:17-21, will take place all over the city and not just inside the church building. Traditionally, we picture Jesus more as a monk than as a manager. However, He was a businessman much longer than He was a preacher. He was also born in the marketplace, in a stable at an inn, and later identified with the marketplace, when He became a carpenter. His teachings dealt extensively with the marketplace. A closer look at His life can help validate the role of marketplace Christians.[1]

There is openness to faith in America. In most of this country, it is illegal to leave a child or an animal in a car unattended, especially on a hot day. Each summer, since I live in a warm climate, there is a story about a person who left a child or a pet in the car; and the effects of that decision were tragic. And yet, so many Christians in America would prefer to lock their Lord and Savior into the car as they walk into work Monday

Fig. 17.1 The results are just as tragic when Christians lock their Lord and Savior into the car as they go to work.

through Friday. This compartmentalization of our faith leaves us operating in the flesh all during the workweek, some of the times that we need Christ the most. People often speak of having made peace *with* God. By this, they mean to say that they know that upon death, they will be present with their heavenly Father. They are Christians. However, after almost eleven years as a minister, first on a church staff and later as a corporate chaplain, my experience lends credibility to the belief that many Christians may have made their peace *with* God, but few are demonstrating and living out the peace *of* God. Therefore, there is the demand for access to spiritual guidance in your sphere of influence.

According to northernway.org, a recent *Business Week* article states that a spiritual revival is sweeping across corporate America.[2] Our goal, again, is to be available for those in need through relationships that develop to the point of sharing the gospel, all without offending. However, how can this vision be accomplished? How far can we go as ministers in the community? What are the legal parameters in which we must operate? First, we need to study the boundaries. Remember, free exercise of religion is the first and most fundamental right of Americans protected in the Bill of Rights. It is the most basic and inalienable of all human rights.

For more than 50 years the American Civil Liberties Union, or ACLU, along with other groups, has attempted to eliminate the public expression of our nation's faith and heritage. This has been accomplished through fear, intimidation, disinformation, and the filing of lawsuits. This last tactic seems to be most effective. These lawsuits would seek to eliminate Christian and historic faith symbols from government buildings, documents, and monuments, in addition to banning public prayer in schools and at school functions. Denying Christians the right to use public facilities that are open to other groups and the prevention of Christians from expressing their faith in the workplace are other objectives of some groups. These attacks have sought to limit the spread and influence of the gospel. Many court cases have been won by Christians, setting precedents for stopping discrimination of Christian employees, enabling Christian groups to use the public facilities on the same terms as other organizations, and preserving historic and Christian acknowledgement in public places.

Many public places are open to Bible studies and other religious activities. John Ashcroft, for example, has been known to hold prayer meetings in the White House. Read the following summation of a story from the May 14, 2001 edition of *The Washington Post*:[3]

The Bible study begins each day at 8 a.m. sharp, with Attorney General John D. Ashcroft presiding, *The Washington Post* reported.

According to the *Post*, a group of employees gathers at the Main Justice building in Washington, either in his personal office or a conference room, to study Scripture and join Ashcroft in prayer.

Ashcroft held similar meetings each morning as a United States senator from Missouri and sees the devotionals as a personal matter that has no bearing on his job as attorney general, according to aides.

Spokeswoman Mindy Tucker said Ashcroft wants to 'continue to exercise his constitutional right to express his religious faith'.

Any employee is welcome, but not required, to attend, his aides said.

But within the massive Justice Department, with about 135,000 employees worldwide, some who do not share Ashcroft's Pentecostal Christian beliefs are discomfited by the daily prayer sessions -- particularly because they are conducted by the nation's chief law enforcement officer, entrusted with enforcing a Constitution that calls for the separation of church and state.

'The purpose of the Department of Justice is to do the business of the government, not to establish a religion,' said a Justice attorney, who like other critics was unwilling to be identified by name. 'It strikes me and a lot of others as offensive, disrespectful, and unconstitutional . . .. It at least blurs the line, and it probably crosses it.'

Several aides said many of Ashcroft's top staffers -- including the chief of staff, the deputy chief of staff, and the communications director -- have never attended the devotional meetings, nor have they been pressured to do so.

They say that the sessions are open to all Justice employees, Christians or otherwise, and that one of the regular participants is an Orthodox Jew.

The federal government's 'Guidelines on Religious Exercise and Religious Expression in the Federal Workplace', issued in 1997 after bipartisan negotiations, say supervisors and department heads must be especially careful with religious activities or statements.

Ashcroft, who is the son and grandson of Assemblies of God ministers, considered a run for the presidency with support from leading Christian conservatives and has regularly cited God and Scripture in speeches and policy statements. In

1998, Ashcroft said at a Christian Coalition event that 'a robed elite have taken the wall of separation designed to protect the church and they have made it a wall of religious oppression'.

The next year, he told Bob Jones University graduates that America was founded on religious principles, and 'we have no king but Jesus'. That statement became the subject of some controversy at his confirmation hearings.

Under Ashcroft, the Justice Department issued new style guidelines for correspondence carrying Ashcroft's signature. They forbid, among other things, the use of 'pride', which the Bible calls a sin, and the phrase 'no higher calling than public service'.

'He's running the department like a church, complete with rituals and forbidden words,' said Barry W. Lynn, executive director of Americans United for Separation of Church and State. 'That is deeply troubling.'

Ashcroft refers to his daily devotionals as RAMP meetings -- Read, Argue, Memorize and Pray.

Ashcroft hands each participant a devotional book from a stack he has used for years, Tucker said. The book highlights a Bible verse or passage for each date of the year, and the group spends the first minutes discussing its meaning, according to a participant.

The group then moves on to a memorization, with the goal of committing to memory a psalm or Bible story through repeated readings.

The session ends with a prayer, often including a reference to a relative or acquaintance who is ill or in need.

Many members of Congress and their employees participate in Bible studies, prayer meetings, and other religious gatherings. A Christian magazine, *Charisma*, recently estimated that about 30 Bible study and prayer groups regularly meet on Capitol Hill.

Laura W. Murphy, director of the American Civil Liberties Union's Washington office, said Ashcroft is at least violating the spirit of the federal rules on workplace prayer.

'Ashcroft has a right to pray in office, but he does not have a right to implicitly or explicitly force others into praying with him,' she said.

'Ashcroft is the chief defender of the nation's civil liberties. He can't pretend to be just another citizen leading prayers,' she added.

A career Justice lawyer agrees, calling the devotionals 'totally outrageous'.

'It feels extremely exclusive, that if you don't participate in that kind of religion, that your career could be affected by it,' the attorney said. 'If I had some political aspirations and wanted to work for the front office and didn't have the same religious feelings as he does, my non-participation could adversely affect me.'

Harassment Law

Because many of the environments in which the community chaplain will operate are private property, where certain speech laws are not applicable, we will focus on laws pertinent to businesses and government buildings. Other examples, originally published in the *UCLA Law Review, Freedom of Speech and Workplace Harassment* written by Professor Eugene Volockh, will be cited in this portion; they will be excerpted, but with substantial modifications. Through harassment law, the government is x suppressing speech that it believes is harmful and offensive. This speech is not limited to threats or insults, but includes political statements, religious proselytizing, art, and humor, material that is at the core of the First Amendment's protections.[4]

This can demonstrate that harassment law is presumptively unconstitutional. Is there, however, some existing exception to First Amendment protection that justifies such a broad speech restriction? Even if there is not, should courts create a new exception? For matters of religion in the workplace and other public places, laws regarding free speech and harassment are considered to be relevant.

Below, it is seen that an argument can be made that the answer to both questions is "no":

- Harassment law is state action -- a restriction imposed by the government, acting as sovereign.
- There is no "workplace or community speech" exception to the First Amendment.
- Harassment law is not a valid time, place, or manner of restriction on speech.

- Harassment law is not justified by *R.A.V. v. City of St. Paul*, a recent Supreme Court case that mentions harassment law in passing.
- Harassment law is not justified by the "captive audience" doctrine.
- Harassment law cannot be supported in other ways; for instance using the fighting words exception, the government as employer doctrine, the speech-as-evidence principle, or other arguments.
- Creating a new exception would be tremendously dangerous for free speech, both in the workplace and out of it.

Speech Restrictions in the Workplace

As applied to one-to-many speeches, harassment law is an unconstitutional restriction on free speech.

According to UCLA Law Review, 1791, harassment law is a government-imposed speech restriction on people's speech: The government is enjoining certain kinds of speech, or awarding substantial compensatory and punitive damages based on speech. This is most obvious when harassment law punishes an employer's own speech or when a court enjoins employees themselves from speaking. When the government is imposing liability on a private employer because of the speech of its employees -- thus giving the employer an incentive to restrict its employees' speech -- the situation is a little less familiar. Nonetheless, state action is clearly present there, too.

The best way of seeing this is through a simple hypothetical. Say Congress commanded, "Any employer that tolerates criticism of American soldiers shall be liable to any coworkers who are offended by such criticism, for instance those whose relatives were injured or killed in action" (this is actually not that far-fetched a hypothetical; such speech might well qualify as something akin to "veteran status harassment", a recognized claim under existing law).

For state action purposes, this law is identical to harassment law. Instead of the government restricting people's speech directly, the government is pressuring private employers -- through the threat of liability -- into restricting the speech. But surely this cannot be constitutional. Private employers, of course, may restrict employees' speech with no First Amendment difficulties, just as private householders and private publishers may restrict speech on their property. However, when the government pressures private employers into restricting speech, the First Amendment steps in.

The Court has recognized this distinction between what a private employer can do to the employee and what the government can force the employer to do. For instance, in *Truax v. Raich* a state law required that at least 80% of each employer's employees be citizens. Raich, a non-citizen who was discharged because of this law, sued, alleging that the law was a denial of equal protection, and the Court agreed. Though Raich's employer could have fired Raich at any time, the Court said, the state's attempt to force the employer to fire him was unconstitutional; the state, by imposing the 80% requirement on the employer, was acting directly upon the employee.

Similarly, in *Peterson v. City of Greenville*, a Greenville city ordinance required restaurants to be segregated, and plaintiffs were arrested for trespass when they ignored a lunch counter manager's demand that they leave. Though the Court agreed that the manager could have kept his lunch counter segregated, it held that

Fig. 17.2 The Equal Protection Clause prevents forced discrimination. The First Amendment prevents private parties being forced to restrict speech.

the city could not have required the manager to do this. Imposing the requirement that the manager eject blacks was tantamount to the city's ejecting them directly.

Just as the government cannot avoid Equal Protection Clause scrutiny by forcing private parties to discriminate, so it cannot avoid First Amendment scrutiny by drafting private parties to implement speech restrictions. This includes religious speech.

What about free speech and the workplace? The First Amendment protects workplace speech from government abridgement, so long as the communications "do not contain a 'threat of reprisal or force or promise of benefit '".[5] "An employer's free speech right to communicate his views to his employees is firmly established and cannot be infringed;" and likewise, courts of appeals have held, for

423

employees' free speech rights.

The Court has been more willing to find a threat or a promise in an ambiguous statement made by an employer or a union than in other situations. Workplace communications by the employer must be viewed in light of "the economic dependence of the employees on their employers, and the necessary tendency of the former . . . to pick up intended implications of the latter that might be more readily dismissed by a more disinterested ear." Additionally "[the] threat of retaliation based on misrepresentation and coercion [is] without the protection of the First Amendment."

However, where no promise or threat is present, workplace speech both by employers and employees is fully protected. Federal appeals courts have regularly upheld free speech rights in cases in which no threat or promise could be implied, such as where a manager told his subordinates that they lost benefits by voting for a union; where a union put out leaflets to plant employees revealing, contrary to an administrative judge's protective order, what happened at an administrative hearing; where an employer asserted that unionization, by increasing costs, might lead to the plant's closing in the future; where an employer encouraged injured workers to go through a company's claims representative instead of going to court; and so on.

Harassment law cannot fit within the threat-or-promise exception. Except for actual threats and possibly certain kinds of sexual propositions made by a supervisor to a subordinate, no other forms of harassing speech could be viewed as threats or promises of benefit. The cases make clear that there has to be some fairly tangible evidence of threat. Abstract assertions that certain kinds of speech might be potentially menacing are inadequate, just like abstract claims that all employer speech on labor issues is necessarily threatening are inadequate.

As offensive as bigotry or pornography may be, courts thus cannot view it as inherently threatening, at least until some evidence is shown in the particular case that the employee was actually threatened (rather than just offended) by it. Similarly, harassment that is largely the work of a single coworker who has little power over the victim should rarely be threatening, though it could easily be very offensive. It may be true that some of the targets of bigoted speech might perceive such speech as inherently threatening, but one can also say that some employees might perceive any antiunion commentary by an employer as threatening. *Gissel's* "threat" exception does not reach far enough to cover either situation.

Gissel makes perfect First Amendment sense. Speech in the workplace has no less value than the same speech outside the workplace. It might be that, as a statistical matter, "for the most part workplace speech will not [help form public opinion]," but neither will most speech in some homes, magazines, or television shows. Surely this does not mean that the government can freely limit speech in those places. Jokes, posters, and political discussion are just as valuable in the workplace as elsewhere and should be just as protected.

Of course, employee speech can always be restricted by private employers, who are not bound by the First Amendment. This cannot, however, authorize greater restrictions *by the government*. A householder is entitled to kick out dinner guests who say certain things. A commercial landlord can refuse to rent to tenants who put up certain posters. A newspaper publisher can refuse to publish articles with which he disagrees. A private university may restrict what its faculty members say in class or even what its students say on campus. Speech on private property can generally be controlled by the private property owner. However, this in no way increases the power of the government to restrict speech in private homes, private shopping centers, private newspapers, private universities, or private workplaces.

Harassment law cannot be justified as a "time, place, or manner" regulation. Time, place, and manner regulations are permissible only if they are content-neutral; harassment law is content-based, suppressing some kinds of speech (say, bigoted, religious, or political statements) and not others.

Nor can harassment law be seen as focusing on the "secondary effects" of speech, and thus being "justified without reference to the content of the regulated speech." The Court has many times held that the "direct impact that speech has on its listeners or the emotive impact of speech on its audience is not a `secondary effect.' " Thus, in *Boos v. Barry*, where the government tried to "protect the dignity of foreign diplomatic personnel" by restricting demonstrations hostile to foreign governments, the Court held:

Listeners' reactions to speech are not the type of 'secondary effects' we referred to in [*City of Renton v. Playtime Theatres*, the case that pioneered secondary effects analysis]. To take an example factually close to *Renton*, if the ordinance there was justified by the city's desire to prevent the psychological damage it felt was associated with viewing adult movies, then analysis of the measure as a content-based statute would have been appropriate. Harassment law is precisely the sort of thing that the *Boos* language describes -- a law justified by the desire to prevent psychological damage to the targets of the harassment -- and is therefore content-based.

Viewpoint of Speech

Furthermore, time, place, or manner restrictions must in any event be viewpoint-neutral. The *Renton* Court explicitly justified its upholding of a speech restriction by saying that the ordinance does not contravene the fundamental principle that underlies our concern about "content-based" speech regulations: that "government may not grant the use of a forum to people whose views it finds acceptable, but deny use to those wishing to express less favored or more controversial views."

However, much of the speech that harassment law suppresses is suppressed precisely because of its point of view; saying that women make bad policemen can give rise to liability, but saying that men and women should be treated equally cannot. Such a viewpoint-based law cannot be justified as a mere "time, place, or manner restriction" -- as even the two most prominent defenders of the constitutionality of workplace harassment law, Suzanne Sangree and Deborah Epstein, agree.

R.A.V. v. City of St. Paul, which held that the government cannot impose viewpoint-based restrictions even on bigoted fighting words, especially distinguished (in dictum) workplace harassment law: "Even the prohibition against content discrimination that we assert the First Amendment requires is not absolute. It applies differently in the context of proscribable speech than in the area of fully protected speech."

Since words can, in some circumstances, violate laws directed not against speech but against conduct (a law against treason, for example, is violated by telling the enemy the nation's defense secrets), a particular content-based subcategory of a proscribable class of speech can be swept up incidentally within the reach of a statute directed at conduct rather than speech [citing *Barnes v. Glen Theatre, Inc., FTC v. Superior Court Trial Lawyers Ass'n*, and *United States v. O'Brien*]. Thus, for example, sexually derogatory "fighting words", among other words, may produce a violation of Title VII's general prohibition against sexual discrimination in employment practices. Where the government does not target conduct on the basis of its expressive content, acts are not shielded from regulation merely because they express a discriminatory idea or philosophy.

This dictum makes clear that harassment law can constitutionally restrict sexually derogatory fighting words; and it suggests the same about an unspecified set of "other words", which seems to be referring to other *proscribable* words -- for instance, threats, obscenity, slander, and the like. This does not by any means dispose of harassment claims based on nonproscribable speech, such as art, jokes, political statement, or religious proselytizing.

In fact, it is clear that the First Amendment generally prohibits speech from being punished based on its *communicative impact*, even when that impact places the speech "within the reach of a statute directed at conduct". For instance, the government may ban conduct that interferes with the war effort, but it may not constitutionally apply the ban to antiwar publications whose communicative impact interferes with the war effort. Likewise, many kinds of conduct may lead to liability under the torts of intentional infliction of emotional distress and intentional inference with economic advantage -- but when the liability is triggered by the communicative impact of speech, as in *Hustler v. Falwell* and *NAACP v. Claiborne Hardware*, such a tort judgment must face First Amendment scrutiny.

When speech violates a general law because of its *non-communicative* qualities, it may indeed be more readily punished. Thus, the government may generally apply a ban on interference with the draft to people who are demonstrating in a way that blockades a draft office, because the speech implicates the law because of its non-communicative qualities -- because the speakers are blocking the door. This is even more clearly so when expressive conduct violates a general law because of its non-communicative qualities: As *R.A.V.* says, "Nonverbal expressive activity can be banned because of the action it entails, but not because of the ideas it expresses." The three cases that the *R.A.V.* dictum cited -- *Barnes, Superior Court Trial Lawyers Ass'n,* and *O'Brien* -- all involved laws that were violated by the non-communicative aspects of the challengers' conduct (public nudity, economic boycott, and destruction of a draft card).

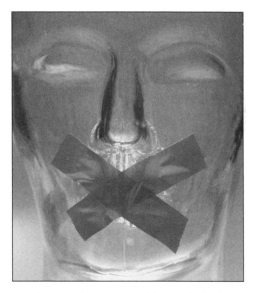

Fig. 17.3 Speech is more readily punished when it violates a general law because of non-communicative qualities.

R.A.V. held that proscribable categories, such as fighting words, would to a large extent be treated as conduct rather than speech: "The exclusion of 'fighting words' [and other proscribable categories] from the scope of the First Amendment simply means that, for purposes of that

Amendment, the unprotected features of the words are, despite their verbal character, essentially a `non-speech element of the communication." The government may punish fighting words because of their tendency to cause a fight, though not because of the "hostility -- or favoritism -- towards the underlying message expressed".

The *R.A.V.* dictum thus reaffirms a basic principle: When a law is violated by the non-expressive impact of speech, or by the proscribable impact of proscribable speech, then applying it to the speech will not require the strictest First Amendment scrutiny. But as *Hustler v. Falwell, NAACP v. Claiborne Hardware*, and the anti-draft speech example show, protected speech may not be punished *because of its communicative impact*, even if the punishment is accomplished through a general law.

Harassing speech in the workplace, even when seen as a violation of the general ban on creation of work environments hostile to particular groups, violates this ban precisely because of its communicative impact. Just as it was the communicative impact of the offensive parody in *Hustler* that inflicted emotional distress on Jerry Falwell and the communicative impact of the boycott advocacy that hurt Claiborne Hardware's business, so it is the communicative impact of verbal workplace harassment that creates a hostile work environment for its victims. The fact that Title VII does not specifically mention speech cannot immunize it from First Amendment scrutiny when it operates to restrict speech because of the offensive or disfavored message the speech conveys.

Edith Jones of the Fifth Circuit, writing (also in dictum) in *DeAngelis v. El Paso Mun. Police Officers' Association*, had it right:

> The Supreme Court's offhand pronouncements [about harassment law] are unilluminating. . . . The Court's pronouncement in *R.A.V.*, that 'sexually derogatory `fighting words,' among other words, may produce a violation of Title VII's general prohibition against sexual discrimination in employment practices' does not mean that Title VII trumps First Amendment speech rights. Rather, as the next sentence in *R.A.V.* explains, conduct not targeted on the basis of its expressive content may be regulated. Citing *R.A.V.*, the Court in *Wisconsin v. Mitchell*, 113 S. Ct. 2194, 2200 (1993), reiterated that conduct not targeted on the basis of its expressive content may be regulated by Title VII. However, application of Title VII to the 'conduct' in the case sub judice [which involved sexist newsletter articles] would do precisely that -- regulate speech on the basis of its expressive content.
>
> *R.A.V.* suggests that the Supreme Court is sympathetic to the aims of harassment

law. Quite likely it would be willing to stretch First Amendment doctrine to allow regulation of some harassing workplace speech, which is what I to some extent propose. But this sympathy for harassment law does not mean that the Court would uphold all of harassment law's speech restrictions under all circumstances, especially those that are far from the 'fighting words' context in which the *R.A.V.* dicta arose.

Captive Audience

Employees in the workplace are often said to be a "captive audience", and in a sense they are: Their jobs require that they remain in a particular place. But what does this mean for others' rights to speak?

When we say that people are "captive" to posted matter -- for instance, flyers on people's cubicles or bulletin boards -- we generally do not mean that they are compelled to stare at it for hours. Rather, we mean that they have to pass by it every so often and risk seeing it out of the corner of an eye. Even if they studiously try to avoid looking at it, the very act of averting their eyes might only serve to remind them of the offensive message.

Of course this sort of "captivity" is extremely common and is no justification for a speech restriction. Employees who have to cross a picket line may see, twice a day, picket signs that call them "scabs", or even hear similar statements made by the picketers. If they have to run errands or if their workstations face the street, they may see the picket line even more often. But this does not allow the government to ban offensive picketing.

Likewise, people whose work takes them out into the street -- traffic police, pushcart vendors, workers who have to come and go from nearby buildings -- are "captive" to street demonstrations; and yet this does not cancel the demonstrators' right to speak or even to speak offensively. Gardeners in UCLA's Sculpture Garden or students or staff walking by on their way from parking to class cannot avoid seeing the sculptures of nudes that stand there. Drivers who must keep their eyes on the road may be "captive" to billboards that are unavoidably visible from their only route to work or school. Nonetheless, the government cannot ban offensive sculptures or billboards.

Being "captive" to occasional oral remarks (or occasional e-mail) also does not mean literally being forced to listen to an extended harangue. The speech is thus pretty much over -- or is fairly easily avoidable, for instance by deleting the e-mail or by walking away from the speaker -- shortly after one realizes it is offensive. The captivity, though, comes from the fact that you may at any time be surprised by offensive speech: Every week or month or however often it happens, you will unavoidably find yourself hearing things that you did not want to hear.

Of course this is also true outside the workplace. We may at any time run into someone on the street wearing a shirt that says something offensive. We may at any time overhear someone using profanity or even hear someone using it directly at us. We may at any time run into someone making an offensive political statement, whether it be burning a flag, criticizing a religion, or wearing a swastika. Averting our eyes will not erase the offensiveness of the speech or prevent us being offended in the future. Employees or not, we are all equally "captive" to occasional offensive remarks whenever we are surrounded by people whose behavior we cannot control. Again, though, this cannot justify restrictions on such speech.

The court system has acknowledged that "we are often 'captives' outside the sanctuary of the home and subject to objectionable speech" and concluded that despite this, such speech cannot be restricted. This was first made clear in *Cohen v. California*, where the government sought to bar public profanity. Even though constitutionally protecting such profanity made us all captive to it -- wherever we go on the street, we might run into profane or otherwise offensive speech -- the Court held that banning such profanity, even in the presence of a "captive audience", is unconstitutional.

Likewise, people who must cross a picket line, whether they are employees or patrons of important services, are captive to the picketers. For instance, as the Court seemed to acknowledge in *Madsen v. Women's Health Center*, abortion patients are "held 'captive' [to antiabortion picketing] by medical circumstance". Despite this, the Court refused to uphold even content-neutral restrictions on displaying images observable by the incoming and outgoing patients and on approaching patients within 300 feet of the clinic. The Court did uphold *content-neutral* restrictions on picketing within 36 feet of the clinic door and on loud noises audible from inside the clinic, but both of these were justified by concerns other than the patients' "captivity". Abortion clinic patients may be captive to antiabortion picketing, but the Court has not seen this as reason enough to suppress it.

The one case most often cited for the proposition that captive audiences can be protected through content-based restrictions, *Lehman v. City of Shaker Heights*, actually holds no such thing. *Lehman* upheld the policy of a city government, acting as proprietor, allowing only nonpolitical ads on government-run municipal buses. The four-Justice plurality argued that the advertising space on the buses was not a public forum; and therefore, the city policy needed to meet only a deferential reasonableness test. The four-Justice dissent argued that the advertising space was a public forum, and that the content-based restriction violated the First Amendment.

The one opinion that stressed the bus passengers' captivity was Justice Douglas's concurrence (the plurality considered captivity only as one factor in deciding that the advertising space was not a public forum). However, even Justice Douglas believed that captive audience considerations would only justify content-neutral restrictions. In his view, "The content of the message [was not] relevant either to petitioner's right to express it or to the commuters' right to be free from it. Commercial advertisements may be as offensive and intrusive to captive audiences as any political message." Justice Douglas agreed a year later in *Erznoznik v. City of Jacksonville* that a ban on drive-ins showing movies containing nudity was unconstitutional:

> ...the interests of captive audiences [citing *Lehman*] .... cannot ... justify attempts to discriminate among movies on the basis of their content -- a 'pure' movie is apt . . . to be just as intrusive [as an 'impure' movie] upon the privacy of an unwilling but captive audience. Any ordinance which regulates movies on the basis of content . . . impermissibly intrudes upon the free speech rights guaranteed by the First and Fourteenth Amendments.

Justice Douglas voted to allow the ban on political ads, not because he thought the city could constitutionally discriminate among ads, but because he thought the city was constitutionally forbidden from putting *any* ads on its buses: The "captivity" of the bus passengers "preclude[d] the city from transforming its vehicles of public transportation into forums for the dissemination of ideas upon this captive audience." This view (first articulated by Douglas in his dissent in *Public Utilities Commission v. Pollak*, which his *Lehman* concurrence frequently cited) prevented Justice Douglas from agreeing with the *Lehman* dissent and forcing the city to take political ads, because such a course would have only been a violation of the passenger's right to be free from government-imposed propaganda (political or commercial). The correct remedy, to Justice Douglas, would have been to bar commercial as well as political ads;

but it was a remedy that he was procedurally unable to grant, since no challenge to the commercial ads was before the Court.

Thus, five of the *Lehman* Justices -- the four dissenters and Douglas -- did not agree that content-based restrictions may be justified by the presence of a captive audience, even on government property. As importantly, *none* of the Justices suggested that the government may impose such content-based restrictions on private property. (The four-member plurality upheld the city policy because the advertising space was a nonpublic forum; content-based restrictions are generally allowed in nonpublic forums.) The Court has twice specifically held that *Lehman* can only apply to government property, and surely this must be right -- surely, for instance, *Lehman* does not allow the government to ban political ads on *private* buses.

The only other serious mention of captive audiences outside the home is a dictum in *Erznoznik v. City of Jacksonville*, where the Court said that certain content-based restrictions may be permissible if "the degree of captivity makes it impractical for the unwilling viewer or auditor to avoid exposure" and when at the same time "substantial privacy interests are being invaded in an essentially intolerable manner". But as the examples mentioned above suggest, this must be a narrow exception indeed. Even where it is in fact impractical for people to avoid exposure to picketing, demonstrations, and the like, the government may not restrict them. And in fact, the Court has never acted on this dictum.

The rare cases in which the Court has upheld content-based restrictions aimed at shielding captive audiences have specifically relied on the audience being in the home, though even there the Court has been hesitant. *Rowan v. United States Post Office Department* upheld a Federal statute allowing a householder who has received sexually-oriented ads to demand that the Postmaster General order the sender to refrain from further mailings to that householder. An advertiser argued that this statute violated its First Amendment rights, but the Court disagreed, "The right of every person `to be let alone' must be placed in the scales with the right of others to communicate."

Most people categorically reject the argument that a vendor has a right under the Constitution or otherwise to send unwanted material into the home of another. If this prohibition operates to impede the flow of even valid ideas, the answer is that no one has a right to press even "good" ideas on an unwilling recipient. That we are often 'captives' outside the sanctuary of the home and subject to objectionable speech and other sound does not mean we must be captives everywhere.

Clearly the rule would be entirely different outside the home. The viewers in *Co-*

hen v. California, for instance, were actually more captive than the householder in *Rowan*. The householder could have easily thrown out the mailer, but the viewers would have had to either leave Cohen's presence or consciously keep their eyes averted from his jacket, which would likely only remind them of the jacket's offensive message. Despite the viewers' greater captivity, the *Cohen* Court refused to shield them, precisely because "we are often 'captives' outside the sanctuary of the home and subject to objectionable speech."

Similarly, in *FCC v. Pacifica Foundation*, the Court upheld an FCC regulation which banned the use of certain vulgarisms in radio broadcasts, in part because radio broadcasts "confront the citizen, not only in public, but also in the privacy of the home, where the individual's right to be

Fig. 17.4 "The right of every person 'to be let alone' must be placed in the scales with the right of others to communicate."

left alone plainly outweighs the First Amendment rights of an intruder [citing *Rowan*]." Though the listener could hardly be considered to be "captive" to a broadcast that he could easily turn off, Justice Stevens concluded that "to say that one may avoid further offense by turning off the radio when he hears indecent language is like saying that the remedy for an assault is to run away after the first blow."

Finally, even in the home, the Court is quite properly skeptical about content-based speech restrictions. Thus, though content-neutral bans on residential picketing are allowed, the Court has (in *Carey v. Brown*) struck down content-based bans precisely because of their content discrimination. Similarly, though the law upheld in *Rowan* referred only to householders demanding an end to "arousing or sexually provocative" mailings, the Court stressed that, "In operative effect the power of the householder under the statute is unlimited; he may prohibit the mailing of a dry goods catalog because he objects to the contents . . . . Congress provided this sweeping power not only to protect privacy but to avoid possible constitutional questions that might arise from vesting the power to make any discretionary evaluation of the material in a government official."

Even *Pacifica*, which upheld a content-based ban (albeit one that touched only speech that the plurality saw as "low-value"), emphasized that:

> ...the fact that society may find speech offensive is not a sufficient reason for suppressing it . . . For it is a central tenet of the First Amendment that the government must remain neutral in the marketplace of ideas. If there were any reason to believe that the Commission's characterization of the Carlin monologue as offensive could be traced to its political content . . . First Amendment protection might be required.

Bigoted speech, of course, is offensive precisely because of its political content and the message of inferiority that it sends. Even bigoted epithets are barred by harassment law not because they are epithets (and thus ugly because of their form and not merely their content), but because they express bigoted views. An analogy would be an FCC regulation that banned only the words "fascist", "imperialist", or "capitalist pig". Even if these words were viewed as "low-value" enough that they could be banned as part of a general ban on epithets on the radio, a selective ban on pejorative words used to describe supporters of the government would clearly be based on the words' political content.

Thus, the best restatement of current captive audience doctrine is this: The government has some power to restrict offensive speech that reaches into the home, though even there the restriction cannot be justified by the offensiveness of its ideas as opposed to its form (see *Carey, Rowan,* and *Pacifica*). Outside the home, the government acting as sovereign cannot shield people from offensive speech even if the speech is genuinely hard to avoid.

Cohen and *Madsen* hold this as a matter of doctrine, but the examples with which I began show this as a matter of basic First Amendment logic. We are as captive to offensive picketing, offensive demonstrations, and offensive jackets worn in public and the like as we are to most offensive workplace speech. So long as these kinds of speech are constitutionally protected despite our captivity, workplace speech must be protected as well.

Exceptions to Speech Restriction

There are some exceptions to speech that are protected by the First Amendment. This exception, called "fighting words". applies only to face-to-face insults that are likely to arouse an immediate violent response. Very little workplace harassment fits this mold.

The rules pertaining to government employee speech -- which is protected only if it addresses issues of public concern -- are completely inapplicable to private workplaces. The government employee speech doctrine is based on the theory that, "The State has interests as an employer in regulating the speech of its employees that differ significantly from those it possesses in connection with regulation of the speech of the citizenry in general." Harassment law is imposed by the government acting as sovereign, not by the government acting as employer; the rules for the two contexts are radically different.

The government acting as proprietor may regulate speech on certain publicly-owned property that is not a public forum. Again, though, the doctrine is completely inapplicable to the government acting as sovereign to restrict speech in privately owned places.

Some commentators have argued that harassment law is justified by "congressional power under the Commerce Clause to impose content based speech restrictions in the workplace to effectuate values embodied in the greater constitution", or even by Congressional power under the Thirteenth Amendment. This argument, however, is entirely unsound.

Of course Congress has Commerce Clause powers and Thirteenth Amendment Enforcement Clause powers -- powers which extend far beyond the workplace. However, the Bill of Rights is meant precisely to constrain Congress, even when it is acting within its enumerated powers. The positive grants of power to Congress in no way diminish the restraints imposed by the Bill of Rights.

The First Amendment does not prohibit the government from using speech *as evidence* of another element of the offense -- for instance, as evidence of the speaker's conduct, intent, or motive. Thus, for instance, during World War II, a person's pro-Nazi statements could be used as evidence that his conduct was intended to help the Nazis and was therefore treasonous. The law punished the treason, not the speech, even though the speech was evidence of treason. Similarly, a manager's racist statements might be used as evidence that his firing of a subordinate was racially motivated.

However, as the Court has explicitly held, this doctrine does *not* allow the speech to be made part of the offense itself. Harassment law does not use the speech as evidence of some other action or intention; under harassment law, the speech itself is an element of the claim.

One-to-One Speech

A new trend in free speech law, the regulation of unwanted "one-to-one" speech -- speech between two people that could be potentially overheard by another and produce offense or printed materials that communicate to many employees in general is gaining strength of protection under the Constitution. Suppressing such speech would improperly prevent the speaker from getting his message out even to potentially willing listeners.

Workplace speech is a critical part of our national public discourse. People spend more of their waking hours at work than anywhere else except (possibly) their homes. Much of most Americans' political speech happens in the workplace. The average American does not go to public demonstrations, burn flags outside the Republican Party convention, write books, or go to political discussion groups. However, the average American does talk about current affairs with his coworkers. This is especially true of any issues that have to do with the workplace, that is, affirmative action hiring, the rights of women, union politics, the impact of faith on life, and the like.

The opportunity to speak outside work is thus a poor and constitutionally inadequate substitute for speech in the workplace. The Court has consistently rejected this argument when content-based distinctions were involved; and it is particularly untenable in this case, where the opportunities for an employee to communicate to his coworkers outside the workplace are theoretical at best. Telling an employee that he cannot talk politics, religion, or values to his coworkers at the office generally means that he cannot talk about these subjects at all.

Harassment law is also a viewpoint-based restriction, the sort of restriction the Court has most strongly condemned. One person in the lunch room may speak eloquently and loudly about how women are equal to men, and harassment law will not stop him. However, when another tries to respond that women belong in the home, harassment law steps in. It seems to be both extremely dangerous in this case, and an exceptionally perilous precedent for the future, to let the government control the parameters of public debate in this way.

Moreover, every place is someone's workplace. The classroom is a teacher's workplace; a university professor who dislikes art that is posted in a classroom may claim that it constitutes harassment. Lots of people work in public buildings, parks, and other public spaces -- to "protect" them, harassment law may restrict speech there, too.

Restaurants are full of employees who might complain about offensive jokes that they overheard patrons make; under harassment law, the employer would be obligated to suppress the speech of those patrons. In every library, there are employees who might be offended by sexually suggestive material that they see patrons display on the library's computers. The Loudoun County Public Library has in fact used this as the main justification for using shielding software that blocks access to sexually explicit material, including "soft core pornography."

Even private homes are often workplaces for housekeepers and other workers, who might complain about offensive art on the walls or offensive conversations by the residents or guests. Muzzling speech "only in the workplace" means muzzling it in very many places indeed.

An even more serious problem arises if the speech that creates the hostile work environment is an inherent part of the employer's business. A store's decision to stock (or specialize in) racist, sexist, or religiously offensive literature could easily create a hostile work environment for many employees.

Fig. 17.5 Harassment law may restrict speech to "protect" employees.

Thus, one employee filed a sexual harassment suit against her employer, a convenience store company, for stocking pornographic magazines in the store which she managed; the suit is now pending. Several employees of Stroh's Brewery have recently sued their employer for workplace sexual harassment that was allegedly caused by the employer's ads, which feature women in bikinis. Part of the remedy that the employees seek is the discontinuation of the ads.

In a slightly different context, New York's highest court came within one vote of holding that it was illegal for a gift shop to display items bearing Polack jokes, because they sent a message to Polish customers that they are not welcome in the shop. The case was brought under public accommodations statutes, but it could equally well have been brought by an offended employee. Additionally, there is nothing in harassment law that would keep it from being applied in such cases; if offensive materials on a coworker's office door can create a hostile work environment, then so can the same material offered for sale in a bookstore or copied for a customer by a print shop.

Of course, speech in the workplace is already restricted: Clearly, an employer may prohibit offensive speech in the workplace, either to minimize tension between employees because he thinks that bigoted speech is wrong, or for any other reason. The First and Fourteenth Amendments simply do not bind private actors. It can be seen that there is a vast difference between allowing an employer to restrict workplace speech and allowing the government to do so.

The line between one-to-one and one-to-many speech is not without its difficulties. What if two employees intentionally go to a coworker's work area to carry on an offensive conversation, hoping that the coworker will overhear? What if someone puts up a derogatory cartoon on his office door, knowing that *all* the other employees in the department belong to the group that the cartoon would offend? Is the speech one-to-one or one-to-many?

These are hard questions, questions of the sort that arise whenever a line needs to be drawn. It is probably best to describe both of these hypotheticals as involving one-to-one speech, in keeping with the policy behind the one-to-one/one-to-many distinction. In both of the above examples, the harassers are clearly trying to offend unwilling listeners, without any real desire to communicate to willing ones. On the other hand, one may reasonably argue that the speech is nonetheless one-to-many, because of the difficulties involved in determining the speaker's intent.

But despite these difficulties, the one-to-one/one-to-many standard avoids greater difficulties. First, there are large core areas of speech on both sides that are clearly either one-to-one or one-to-many. Under this standard, an employee will generally be able to speak his mind to willing listeners or to post written material without fear of discipline and without arousing in his employer a fear of liability. Similarly, an employee will know that when he speaks directly to another employee, he should be careful not to make statements that he knows are unwelcome.

Second, a rule that would look to the content of one-to-many speech -- such as whether the speech is political, bigoted, vulgar, degrading, or pornographic -- would create even more dangerous uncertainties. As discussed above, one-to-many speech, even in the workplace, is a valuable part of public discourse. Allowing liability for one-to-many speech and letting the liability turn on whether a joke is political or not, whether a discussion about racial issues is bigoted, whether a borderline epithet is vulgar, or whether a picture is "pornography" or "art", would have an unacceptable chilling effect. Unless one is willing to suppress any workplace speech that may create a hostile work environment or to condemn harassment law as entirely unconstitutional when applied to speech, the one-to-one / one-to-many line may be the best line to draw.

Free speech, religious or otherwise, often exacts a high price. It has forced us to tolerate speech that urges revolution, that undermines the nation's war effort, or that advocates what some see as immoral and dangerous personal behavior. Much of this speech, like much bigoted speech in the workplace, is material that many think valueless and that many wish did not exist. Still, even such speech must be protected because the price the alternative exacts -- the power of the government to impose an orthodoxy of speech and thought or to cleanse public discourse of ideas it finds dangerous and threatening -- is even higher.

So, for a good summation of all of the laws that govern the workplace and faith, it is important for the community chaplain to be aware of the following:[6]

- Title VII of the Civil Rights Act of 1964 prohibits religious discrimination.
- Title VII applies to all employers with 15 or more employees.
- Religious institutions are exempt from Title VII.
- Title VII allows that religion may be a bona fide occupational qualification where the employer can show it is a business necessity.
- The United States Supreme Court has defined religious belief as "a given belief that is sincere and meaningful and occupies a place of in the life of its professor parallel to that filled by the orthodox belief in God of one who clearly qualifies for the exemption".
- Religion must address fundamental and ultimate questions having to do with deep and imponderable matters, comprehensive in nature, a belief system as opposed to an isolated teaching, and recognized by the presence of certain formal and

external signs.

■ An employer has a duty to accommodate religious practices and beliefs, if it does not cause undue hardship for the employer.

Legal Issues Associates Face

We will now shift the topic from a framework of the legalities of religion in the workplace to legal issues that associates in the mission field may encounter. Because the chaplain will walk through these matters with an employee, to support and offer encouragement, a working knowledge of the legal system is crucial. Most likely, the community chaplain will interact with the legal system for cases like divorce, child custody matters, financial and bankruptcy issues, and criminal activity. Criminal activity can cover a diverse group of issues including, but not limited to, driving under the influence of drugs or alcohol, theft, domestic violence, and driving offenses.

Criminal Activity

Most often, the chaplain will receive notification that an individual has been arrested and/or charged with a crime, such as domestic violence. This is not an immediate urgency; remember the incarcerated will not be going anywhere. The process to get someone out of jail is slow. Jails are difficult places with which to work. Because he has already registered with the facility, the community chaplain can immediately identify himself as a chaplain on file at that jail. It is then recommended to ask the jailer what the charges are for that individual. It may be the case that the charge is not what was communicated to the chaplain by the incarcerated. It is important then to find out the bail amount. This will help when attempting to facilitate bail. If it is an individual with whom you are trying to build a relationship that is in jail, a visit every other day is recommended, unless they are in for a long term.

Find out if the incarcerated person has simple toiletry items. Frequently they do not, and the jail does not supply them. Some facilities will allow you to bring these items to the individual, but more often the incarcerated will be required to purchase these items through the jail store. Money can be placed in the account of the person for these needs. Inquire about access to Scripture. If there is no access to a Bible, find out if the inmate would like one. Follow the procedures put in place by the jail to get the Bible to the person who is incarcerated. Often, the chaplain will not be allowed to give a Bible directly to a jailed person. The Bible may need to be mailed from a book store or other recognized publisher/provider of books. Always respect the set procedures for that jail. Ministry to the individual is crucial, but do not neglect the family members and others that may be involved with the case. Remember that this too is a ministry opportunity.

The greatest skill for the community chaplain is listening. Expect the individual to tell you that they are innocent. That is not really an issue for you. Your issue is ministry.[7] Find out when they are going to have a bond hearing. Plan to attend the bond hearing. This hearing is to determine if the associate will be allowed to post bail to get out of jail until the hearing to determine guilt or innocence. If this hearing, also called a first hearing in some areas, is held in the jailhouse courtroom, no outsiders including the chaplain will be allowed in. If you are allowed to be present, when the person's name is called at the bond hearing, you will stand. At that time the judge will ask why you are standing, and you will inform the judge that the individual is part of the community where you are a chaplain. Introduce yourself by name. As much as possible, vouch for the person and inform the judge that you see the person periodically in your duties as a community chaplain.

Your attendance may or may not sway the judge in setting the bail amount. It will never hurt. You can ask the judge to consider a pretrial release. If you wish to get directly involved, get the permission of the associate to speak with their employer or their employer's Human Resources Department and let them know what is going on because their job may be in jeopardy. Because of matters of confidentiality, you must have the person's permission before informing his company. The hope is that the incarcerated can be placed on "short term leave of absence". This will frequently allow their medical insurance to stay in force, and it will keep the company from firing them. Additionally, the company may be willing to count any available vacation or sick leave time toward the absence.

Finally, if the individual must

Fig. 17.6 Plan to attend the bond hearing.

remain in jail, take steps to help maintain other important concerns of life. Payment of bills, getting an impounded vehicle released to avoid additional charges, etc. can be on the mind of the jailed. While it is never recommended for the chaplain to contribute personal funds to cover expenses of anyone, a responsible party should be found to handle these items.

When someone in your mission field has a court appearance that is not a jail offense, such as a divorce, if possible inform the individual that you will meet him at the courthouse. Meet the person, pray with him, and be there for moral support and encouragement. If the courtroom is closed to those other than the litigants, as is sometimes the case, you may then dismiss yourself for other work. This is only if the offense cannot end in incarceration. If the offense may end in incarceration, you should try to make arrangements to stay with the charged person throughout the appearance. If there is a chance that you will get to testify on behalf of the individual, you should be in court. There are few cases where you will be allowed to testify (DUI, Simple Assault, Assault on a Female, and Spousal Abuse). Do not give character references or endorsements on behalf of the person where you do not know it to be true. Be sure to wear professional clothing to these hearings. Regardless of what type of case it may be and no matter how much experience you may have with the legal system, *it is critical that the community chaplain does not give legal advice!*

When it is time to go to court, the following information will put you at ease.

1) Remember, you and the charged should dress like you are going to church. Yes, some will never have been to church. However, I have not been disappointed very often when giving that advice. Look for dress codes in the local rules at the Clerk's office; some are even placed in a conspicuous place right outside the courtroom.

2) Obey any and all posted rules. As with many other things, preventive measures serve to avoid many unpleasant scenes at the courthouse.

3) Know your mission field - ask about proper attire or at least tell them if you are not headed to court with them. Do they have "Sunday clothes"? At minimum, shirt and tie for men/boys and a dress or pantsuit for women/girls is expected. Talk to them about this prior to court. If you have visited this court before, let them know the expectations and posted rules. If they do not have appropriate dress, see what can be done to help them (borrow from a family member).

4) Know the rules yourself - consider visiting the court first and ask questions. Sit in the courtroom and observe, if possible. Remember to be kind when addressing

this issue. Some people really do not have dress clothes. They have work clothes and casual clothes (jogging suits, etc.).

5) Many times people will go to court before or after work depending on the time. If it is a choice between making it to court or going home to change clothes, do not be late. Many judges will understand a working person's need to be dressed for work even if it is not the preferred dress code. HOWEVER, let the judge know this in advance if possible!

6) Young people are scrutinized more than adults. Many judges like to make examples of young people who are improperly dressed. Maybe they feel that with the "right incentives", they might change their ways. Be careful with young people; they seem to be a lightning rod. Never allow them to wear jeans, cut-offs, baggy pants, or T-shirts (especially with rock bands or profane words on them) to court.

7) Gentlemen should take off hats, and ladies should not wear halter tops or shorts. Remember that first impression - you never get a second chance! All eyes will be on you and the person charged with a crime - let everyone know how important and serious you consider the matter. These rules should apply to anyone with the individual, friends, family, etc. The judge or attorney may ask for someone to speak on the defendant's behalf. Remember, they represent this defendant as well. Dress accordingly, even if you are not planning on addressing the court. As a professional, you can direct and influence the court; so take measures to prevent any hostility from the judge.

8) If court begins at 9:00 AM, have the charged be there at 8:30 AM. Much may be accomplished before court, not the least of which may be an opportunity to get to the proper place and find a seat. Sit up front so you may be able to hear well. Many courtrooms are old and have terrible acoustics. Your associiate will want to respond when called upon; otherwise an order for their arrest may be issued for "Failure to Appear".

9) Listen carefully- answer the call of the docket or calendar as instructed. You will always be instructed by the judge or district attorney/solicitor. Nothing gets people in more trouble faster than answering the wrong way after just being instructed in the proper way. You can help a nervous defendant by listening for instructions and reminding him/her to follow them.

10) Do not talk while in the courtroom, unless spoken to by the court, court official, or the client's lawyer. My advice is to avoid all co-defendants in your case.

11) Do not read the newspaper in the courtroom. It is disrespectful and shows that you are more interested in the box scores than your own case, and some judge may just remind you about it when it is your turn to stand before him/her.

12) Do not have or allow any one with you to have a loud outburst in court. Regardless of the outcome, try to remain calm and assure family members that the outbursts will not be tolerated, nor will they change the outcome.[8]

Special caution should be taken when speaking with the judge. Remember to whom you are talking! If asked by the judge to speak in the courtroom, follow these rules:

1) Speak loudly enough to be heard, especially if no microphones are available in the courtroom. Remember, acoustics are often poor, so speak up!

2) Do not repeat things that others have already said. If you have something new to add or a comment on something previously said, please do so; but do not just repeat what everyone else knows.

3) It is good to put your comments in writing when possible, especially in Superior Court. If given notice, this is still the best policy.

4) You will want to confer with the individual's lawyer, if possible, before offering your comments. You may not be given the chance in open court. Therefore, talk with him or her about your knowledge and information concerning the case before court.

5) If you prefer not to talk, let everyone know before the case is in front of the judge.

6) Always introduce yourself, either before court or through your client's attorney and let them know you are there for support of the accused, whether you intend to speak or not.

7) Speak with the person in your mission field beforehand and ask permission to speak.

8) Have your facts straight before you stand up. Know your situation!

9) TELL THE TRUTH! This may sound odd; however, honesty with the court is always the best policy. Most experienced judges know when you are fudging a little. They listen to people exaggerate all the time. Be different - it will be appreciated.

10) Be brief and to the point. Say it and sit down!

11) Ex parte communications with a judge are conversations held outside the court room or sometimes inside the courtroom which exclude other parties to the lawsuit or case. DO NOT DO IT! It looks bad, and even though it may be harmless chit chat, it damages the system of fair play and disclosure. It may be seen as unduly trying to influence the court in an improper way.

12) You may be asked to approach the bench by a judge - do so only at his/her instruction. Others are interested in these conversations, so the attorneys will be asked to approach even when it may not apply to them directly. Be aware of this. This does not mean that you cannot say hello to the judge or other court officials outside the courtroom.

13) Be courteous but mindful of the great care that must go into using the system in a fair and impartial manner. I do not believe you will have problems in this area if you are sensitive to this concern on the part of judges and courtroom officials.

14) You will see lawyers and judges talking in almost any hallway in a courthouse; do not assume they are discussing your case. My experience is that most are fair-minded and go overboard in avoiding even the appearance of impropriety. You should conduct yourself likewise. I cannot stress enough the need to visit the courtroom and the judges and other court officials before your first court appearance with a client. So much can be learned, and you can solve many problems ahead of time. Become known and the familiarity will open many doors for you and enable you to minister more effectively to those in your mission field.

15) Always address the court with "Your Honor". It makes no difference whether the judge is male, female, older, or younger than you. Get used to answering with respect, and advise those with you to do the same. "Yes, sir/ma'am and No, sir/ma'am" are the proper responses and provide a needed framework of civility and respect within which to conduct the court's business.

16) Learn and teach the ability to listen without interrupting. You will not agree with every witness, lawyer, or judge, but allow each to have his/her say uninterrupted by you or the defendant. Judges handle objections by lawyers in the course of every trial or hearing. Remember to allow the judge to rule on an objection before answering a question. Most judges will instruct witnesses about this before it arises, and you may be able to help the client by reminding them of this. Lawyers often do this as part of their preparation of witnesses before trial.

Sentencing is best understood by the sequence in which it occurs in the courtroom process. The general sequence is as follows:

- **Charging phase:** normally occurs outside the courtroom by police officers; in some cases, magistrates or individuals. This produces an arrest warrant.
- **Pre-Trial phase:** this includes any kind of preliminary hearing, bond hearing,

probable cause hearing, or pretrial motions. This prepares the case for hearing either by judge or jury.

■ **Trial:** the fact-finding process where both sides may possibly present evidence and the judge or jury decides guilt or innocence.

■ **Sentencing phase:** this is where the judge applies the necessary and appropriate punishment for the conviction(s) in the trial phase. Remember, if defendant is found NOT GUILTY, we skip this phase!

A sentence given by a judge must follow applicable state or federal law. All states have statutes covering all possible punishments for each crime set out in the statute (we will concentrate on state law here).

Remember that all judgments are done in open court and are directed to the defendant. Many courts will have the defendant stand during the sentencing phase as the judge imposes the sentence on him/her. All judgments are recorded and either hand written or typed on a computer in the courtroom. In Superior Court, the judgment will be recorded by the court reporter for verification later. The judgment will tell the defendant what his/her punishment will be, when that punishment will begin, and if any delay is granted by the court. Judges do have some discretion within the law on most sentencing matters. The trend in most states is to limit sentencing discretion. Judgments are part of the public record in most cases and can be reviewed or retrieved from the clerk's office (exception is juvenile cases). The chaplain will be able to help during this phase by listening to the judgment as it is written or recorded in open court; learning the terms of the judgment and how they affect the individual; being ready for negative reactions from the charged and family/friends; being there to support the person after the judgment if possible; and even when an active sentence is imposed, following up with the incarcerated, if probation or other sentence is imposed. If they are unsure, refer to the judgment or call their lawyer for clarification.

There are certain terms that should be familiar for the community chaplain dealing with legal matters.

■ **Probation:** sentence imposed most often when an active sentence is suspended for some time period. Defendant must follow conditions of probation - generally remain sober, continue or find employment, not violate the law, refrain from associating with certain people and visiting certain areas, remain in school, attend substance abuse classes if required, do community service, meet with probation officer on a regular schedule, pay probation fees and restitution to victim, abide by curfew, undergo a term of house arrest, and submit to random drug tests.

- **Probation Officer:** supervises people while on parole and sets up all requirements of judge's order (judgment), tracks progress or lack thereof, and reports violations to the court. Most often a state employee who works in local area or county.

- **Community Service:** required of some defendants, usually involves work in a government agency, recycling center, animal shelter, private agency, etc. Approved list kept by the court and used on a rotating basis. Hours required differ depending on the crime. There is a set time period, sometimes by statute, for the client to complete the hours. Representatives from community service regularly appear in court and meet with defendants.

- **Restitution:** money required to be paid to victims. Stated time period for repayment schedule set by probation officer.

- **Curfew:** Defendant must be in his/her home during certain hours of day or night. Subject to checks by probation officer; violations may activate sentence.

- **House arrest:** Defendant required to wear electronic device that is phone activated (must be digital dial phone), normally a leg bracelet. Amount of time required set out in judgment.

- **Random drug screens:** usually administered by probation officer. Used in cases besides drug convictions.

- **Suspended Sentence:** this means the active part of the sentence is "suspended" for some time period (usually set by statute). If the defendant completes probation successfully, the active term is not imposed. Later violations can sometimes invoke the suspended sentence.

Fig. 17.7 Be prepared for the possibility that they may face jail time.

Become familiar with each one of the professionals the court refers to in sentencing: Drug Counselors, Probation Officers, Community Service Counselors, Domestic Violence Counselors, Victims Assistance Counselors, or any others. You may be able to help in the tracking of the defendant, providing workplace assistance, and other areas. Expect that some of these people will be wary of your offer of help. If you provide helpful information when asked, you will help the defendant as well. Be there if you are needed and follow up on all commitments made. Many of these professionals see people fail on probation all the time. The alternative in most cases is an active jail sentence for the friend from your mission field; remind him of this. Each person must take responsibility for his actions. This is the biggest factor in successfully completing probation.

An active sentence generally means the individual will either spend time in the county/city jail or, if the crime is very serious, state or federal prison. Be prepared for this and try to help him and his family deal with this possibility. You may be able to arrange visits and provide directions to employers and family and friends.

Active sentences may also require a period of probation before or after the active sentence is served. Most individuals will know the sentencing possibilities after discussions with their lawyers or negotiations with the state. With sentencing statutes in many states the ultimate result (amount of time) is not a surprise.

Sometimes an active sentence will be delayed for some reason by the court, usually in lower or district courts. Reasons range from weekend jail for Driving While Impaired convictions, job responsibilities, or sickness of the defendant or family member. Delays are hard to deal with because they offer the possibility that the defendant will not show up when required. Therefore, their use in regular sentencing is limited. However, it can and does happen.

Separation and Divorce

Cases involving separation and divorce will constitute a large part of your ministry in the community. In a time when even Christian marriages fail at the rate of one in every two, you will encounter these problems with those in your sphere of influence on a regular ongoing basis. Why? People not only have legal problems, but also personal and emotional problems. However, I believe the problem is much deeper. I believe it comes from a lack of knowledge, understanding, and belief in God's Word. While this text covers the "legal aspects of separation and divorce", I do not believe it can be understood without looking at what God's Word has to say about the subject.

Selected Scripture readings:

Genesis 2:24
Deuteronomy 24:1
Malachi 2:16
Matthew 5:31-32
Matthew 19:3-9
Mark 10:1-12, 19
1 Corinthians 7:1-16
Ephesians 5:22-33
1 Peter 3:1-7

I suggest that you read these Scriptures and pray over their meaning and application in your ministry in this area.

Divorce actions in most states generally refer to one of the following:

- A "no fault" divorce based on one year's separation - sometimes referred to as an absolute divorce.
- Divorce based on some fault of either party: adultery, natural impotency, pregnancy at the time of marriage not known or caused by the husband, or imprisonment for a stated period (usually one year or more).

Gather as much information as possible. This is one type of court action where a thorough knowledge of those involved will help. Why? There is a possibility of "forgotten details" that may harm his/her case. You can help by asking very general questions that provide you with information necessary to properly minister to this individual and possibly other family members. Always remember, in cases of divorce and separation you may need to deal with whole families, not just individuals. So ask questions.

- **Full names:** client, spouse, girlfriend, boyfriend, children - his, mine, ours (see the problem!).
- **Ages of everyone including children:** some will not have a clue, even married couples - a great place to start your ministry. Divorce affects children; do not forget them.

- **Addresses of everyone.**
- **Places of employment:** you may already know one or both.
- **About the marriage:** date and place of marriage, date they separated, previous marriages or relationships (live-in or otherwise).
- **Present status:** still married, separated, or divorced.
- **What happened?** Be careful here; you are asking for a flood of information, and it may come with a flood of tears. You may also get only a trickle of information. As tough as it may be, keep being persistent until the flood comes - you will need all of this information to minister properly to these persons. Be prepared to spend the time necessary to get the information.
- **Personal visit:** this is a great time to establish your willingness to help, so offer to visit with the individual somewhere besides the place that you normally see him or her. You want plenty of time and a comfortable atmosphere to seek answers to your questions.

Much of the information lawyers will seek from the same client will also include financial information. I would stay away from this type of questioning and leave the property questions to the individual's lawyer. You are likely to be asked or questioned by the person about his/her property and what to do about it. Resist the temptation to advise or even comment on these matters, as property matters are covered by state laws in most cases. Title and property interests differ in community property states. Do not advise people about their property rights in a divorce case. Be aware that many times marital property is fought over for years and represents a method of claiming some sort of victory in a situation where there are truly no winners. Do not be influenced by the power struggle over property.

Almost every state allows the parties to sign agreements resolving many issues involved in separation and divorce, if they can agree! Separation agreements may be incorporated into divorce judgments and thereby become orders of the court. They are important documents and, like the marriage to which they refer, should not be entered into lightly. You are likely to see and be asked to read a Separation Agreement. Do so only in the rare case that information you need may be included within. Do not offer opinions as to whether or not they got a "good deal"! Basic separation agreements cover some but not all of the following topics:

- **Division of property:** personal, real estate, and hopefully all marital property -

450

property owned, purchased, or used during the marriage.

- **Child custody:** who has custody of the minor child/children and visitation by the non-custodial parent.
- **Child support:** who pays and how much is paid.
- **Alimony:** in cases involving fault, grounds usually alleged in the break up of the marriage.
- **Insurance and other special matters:** who keeps the health insurance, the children's medical needs and educational needs - special schooling, etc.

Reality: you may have to provide it. Many people in these circumstances do not know or cannot fathom the reality of what has or is about to happen to them and their family. They are hurt, confused, and angry, which also means they are in desperate need of God's Word and your ministry to them through the Holy Spirit. Embrace them and this opportunity. As I have stated before, be prepared with God's Word and be bold. People in the midst of these problems need your guidance and love. Be prepared to give both.

Reconciliation: this may be possible; however, is it reality? Work towards reconciliation, but understand that in their minds it may be over. Counsel from God's Word, and do not shy away from the effort it will take from both sides to restore the marriage. You will find that sometimes people simply quit trying. Remind them of this. Do not be discouraged if reconciliation does not occur. You have not failed!

Caregiving: be constant in prayer and available in body and spirit. Nothing else will help these persons more. You will be an anchor for many and a life preserver for others. Be mindful of both roles. Adapt your ministry to the individual as much as possible. Having discussed with you the intimate and often painful details of a separation or divorce, you are now a trusted friend. Do not abuse this trust.

Chaplain Representation

Often, especially if an individual cannot afford an attorney, he will ask the community chaplain to represent him in court. NEVER represent anyone in court. Instruct the person that there are public defenders who will work pro bono, or for free, and there are some things that he can do to represent himself, if he so chooses. The best way for a non-lawyer to survive the courtroom is to avoid it altogether by settling their dispute or arranging to have it diverted to mediation, where:

- things are done in plain English,
- procedural rules are kept to a minimum, and
- no decision is made unless you agree.

Failing this, the person will either need to hire a lawyer or learn how to navigate a formal court proceeding, which may be his only realistic approach if his dispute is not for enough money to justify paying a lawyer. As with learning any other bureaucratic process, learning to represent oneself will take some effort, but it is not impossible.

Fortunately, the basics of how to bring or defend a case are not difficult, although trying to get on top of every nuance of procedure and strategy is. For those who want to represent themselves, there will be a need to learn how to handle routine representation tasks. For example, before they even go to court, they may have to participate in a deposition or ask or answer written questions (interrogatories). Also, when the trial begins, he will obviously need to know where in the courtroom to sit and stand; and more importantly, what to say and how to say it. He will also need to call his own witness or cross examine those of his opponents, which he will have to learn to do efficiently and effectively.

Second, they can hire a lawyer in the limited role of self-help law coach, to provide advice as needed on strategy and tactics. In many situations, hiring a lawyer to coach self-help efforts will cost only about 10% to 20% of what it would cost to hire the lawyer to go to trial for them. The legal coach may simplify the legal research, suggest evidence the client should look for to prove his legal claims, explain rules of evidence, inform him of deadlines, alert him to courtroom procedures peculiar to his local court system, or suggest ways of making his arguments more persuasive.

Even if he decides that he does not have the time or inclination to represent himself and he wants to hire a lawyer to handle his case, there are several ways he can minimize his stress and maximize his chances of success. First, the charged should find a skilled lawyer with whom he can work comfortably at an affordable cost. Next, he should find out what to expect during the course of his lawsuit -- and how he can work with his lawyer to achieve the best possible outcome. He should ask his lawyer to keep him apprised of developments in his case and tell him what role he can play in each stage of the proceedings. To this end, he can consult a self-help resource for detailed information about what goes on in a civil lawsuit. Finally, the individual should work with his lawyer to take advantage of pretrial opportunities to settle his case by approaching settlement talks, mediation, and negotiations with an open mind. Remember, the vast majority of civil lawsuits never go to trial. Even though he has hired a lawyer and entered the litigation arena, he can still leave the legal system quickly behind if he makes good faith efforts to resolve his dispute.

Fig. 17.8 Never place bail for an individual with your own money.

There are times when someone in your mission field will need to be bailed out of jail. You may with permission talk with an employer, family, or friends of the individual to obtain help with the bail. You may go through the bail process with revenue supplied by a family member or friend, but you must never place bail for an individual with your own money. You may simply explain that ministry policy prevents this. Any other individuals involved should also be made aware that you do not provide bail.

In the event you are bailing with revenue supplied by someone else, you should have a bail bond contact in your resource list. Bail is generally 15% of the bail-bond. That is, if bail has been set at $2,000, they can bail (purchase an insurance policy) out of jail for $300. They will not get the $300 back. Whoever bails the individual is responsible for the individual appearing at the scheduled court time. Should the accused not show, the person that provided bail is then responsible for the balance of the bail-bond.

If an out-of-town family member is going to send bail, have the family member send a cashier's or certified check payable to the local court. This check should be sent by FedEx to the business where the individual is employed. They should never send this check to your home or to a ministry office. This check should never be made out to the chaplain. By keeping this transaction at "arm's length", the chaplain will avoid any appearance of impropriety. Notify someone at the business that a FedEx package is coming for you and to please contact you when it arrives. You will then take this check to the magistrate or the jail. Be prepared to spend considerable time. This process may easily take 3 to 5 hours. Make sure that you or someone else is there to meet the individual when he gets out. He probably does not have any transportation and may have other ministry needs as well.

Dealing with legal issues can be stressful for the community chaplain, since this is an area in which most of us have had limited experience and exposure, if that. The unfamiliar can be intimidating; but time and experience, with reliance on the Holy Spirit for guidance, will help to dissuade these fears. Remember, we are commanded in Scripture to visit those in jail, for we may be entertaining angels unaware.

Stories From the Field: #17
"Not Supposed To Be There"*

I wasn't supposed to be there. It was 9:00 p.m. and I was walking up the stairs of my company's loading dock. I had been a chaplain just a few months, and I was still trying to adjust my ministry schedule along with my job with the trucking company's crazy schedule. But I was determined to do it, so I tried various times. This particular day, I was ready to see some of the part-timers that worked on the dock. Knowing that they worked from 6 to around 10 p.m., I decided this was a good time to show up.

Alejandro wasn't supposed to be there. As a pick-up and delivery driver, he usually set out in the morning and would normally be done by 6 or 7 p.m. I had spoken with him a couple of times as I did my rounds in the early morning hours but was not expecting to see him that night. But there he was.

As I approached him, I called him by name and shook his hand. He had been delayed on his route, had just finished clocking out, and was on his way to the car. Even though he knew he could talk to me at any time, not being on the clock helped to ease his mind about stopping and chatting some with the chaplain.

We talked about work, heritage, and family. He expressed feeling empty and being unable to see victory and success, especially in his family life. Even though he was a "good guy", something seemed to be missing. He had attended church as a boy and knew about God and Jesus Christ, but that did not help either. With his permission, we delved into the gospel. As I spoke, you could see him understanding what I was explaining. In a while, Alejandro was praying to receive Christ as his personal Savior and Lord.

In the 3 years that have followed, we have seen God do some great things in his family through prayer and obedience. His walk with Christ has grown over the years. What a blessing he has been in my life!

I wasn't supposed to be there. Alejandro wasn't supposed to be there. But I was there and so was he. God had planned a "divine appointment" and right to the precise minute. It was an appointment where a thirsty soul found the water of life. His thirst was quenched that night on the stairway to a loading dock.

– Submitted By: Albert B.
Miami, FL

*Individuals in this story have granted permission for its use.

Stories From the Field: #18
"A Voice Crying"*

On Saturday, August 9th, I was doing my morning devotion. While praying I heard what sounded like voices crying in my spirit, saying, "Help us, help us!" I said out loud, "Who is crying, Lord?" I opened my Bible and began reading in 1 Samuel 9. Amazingly, when I got to the second part of verse 16, it seemed like it was illuminated: "...for I have looked upon My people, because their cry has come to Me" (NKJV).

I didn't understand, but I felt as though God was trying to impress something on my heart. Later that morning, I decided to take my 12-year-old son down the road to a church to play some basketball. Interestingly, the church was located on a street called **"The Lord's Way"**. *A short time later, the groundskeeper, who was cutting the grass, took a water break and spoke to me. He commented about how it blessed him to see my boy and me spending time together. We exchanged Christian pleasantries, and then he went his way. About 10 minutes later a white car approached with really dark tinted windows. Someone inside motioned my son over to them. Since I was further away and could not see the individuals, I yelled to my son not to approach the vehicle but to direct them to where I was. The car stopped in front of me, and a lady got out of the passenger side. She said, "Do you work here?" "No, I just came over here to play some basketball with my son," I responded. She said, "I was told about this church and that they might be able to help me find a place to stay." I said, "I really don't know anything about this church, but you probably could come back on Monday and speak with someone in the office." Right then I felt the prompting of the Holy Spirit, so I said, "Is there something I can do to help you?" "I really need to talk with a minister," she stated. I said, "I am a minister. Actually, I am a chaplain here on vacation." She said, "Oh, my God!" and immediately* started crying. "What's wrong?" I asked. She said, "I was just gang-raped!" I asked her if she had reported it to the authorities. As it turns out, this woman was 32 years old and was in a drug rehab program. That morning she had relapsed, blacked out, and then was raped on the balcony of her mother's first floor condo.

While her mom sat in the car, I asked this young lady if she had a relationship with Jesus. She said, "I know He is with me." I said, "Have you ever asked Jesus not just to be with you on the outside but to come live with you on the inside?" Her response was, "No." "Would you like to invite Him in so that He can show you what to do and can guide you in everything, **including where to live?**" I asked. She said, "Yes, because I really don't know what to do." I then had her repeat after me and ask Jesus to take up residence in her heart. After we prayed, I gave her one of my cards and suggested that she and her mom drive to the other side of the property to see if they could find the groundskeeper that I had met. They drove on off, and my son and I followed in our vehicle. As only God could arrange, as soon as the ladies drove up, the groundskeeper happened to be walking out. She told him that she had just prayed with the chaplain (and pointed toward me) and accepted the Lord, but she needed a place to stay. The groundskeeper was blown away, not knowing that I was a minister, by how God had placed me there at just the right time. In addition, the house he had just walked out of was a drug and alcohol rehab center of which he was about to graduate! He said, "I cannot promise anything, because I am not the decision maker; but as of Monday I believe we will have two beds available! Could you come back on Monday morning so I can introduce you to the Pastor who oversees the program?" She said she thought so. I then interjected and said, "Why don't you plan to come to church tomorrow since you now have a new relationship with Jesus and so you can fellowship with some other believers?" She agreed that the plan sounded great. The groundskeeper then told her, "If you come to the 11 am service, I will make sure you meet the Pastor and we will make you feel right at home." Before they drove off, I asked the mother if she knew Jesus. She said, "Yes, I am a born again Christian—but now my daughter is too!" I told them it was going to be all right, and then I prayed for them. They pulled off, both crying and giving us the thumbs-up sign. The groundskeeper and I then embraced and praised God for His divine intervention. I may never see her again here on earth, but one thing I know – the angels in heaven are rejoicing! That morning, God heard the cry of one hurting young lady...

– Submitted By: Brian P.
Chicago, IL

*Individuals in this story have granted permission for its use.

Questions

Reflect on the Stories From the Field found in this chapter and answer the following questions:

1. How would you handle the situation that was described?
2. What information found in the story is confidential?
3. What information found in the story can be shared with others? With whom may this information be shared? Under what circumstances may this information be shared?
4. How does the information found in this chapter pertain to the story?

─────── End Notes ───────

1. Ed Silvoso, *Anointed for Business* (Ventura, CA: Regal, 2002), I.
2. Corporate Chaplains of America Internal Training Materials, Rick Butler, Esq. Presenter
3. Ibid.
4. Eugene Volokh, *Freedom of Speech and Workplace Harassment*, 39 UCLA Review 1791 (1992).
5. Unless indicated, the following citations were presented by Rick Butler, Esq. for the Corporate Chaplains of America Internal Training Materials.
6. Dudley Rochelle, Presenter, Ministry In The Workplace Conference, Atlanta, GA (March 2004).
7. Corporate Chaplains of America Training Manual
8. Corporate Chaplains of America Internal Training Materials, Rick Butler, Esq. Presenter

Chapter Eighteen

Health Crisis and the Community Chaplain

CHAPTER EIGHTEEN

Health Crisis and the Community Chaplain

──────────────── Objectives ────────────────

During the course of this chapter, we will perform the following tasks:

- List strategies for caring for those with an unfavorable health diagnosis

- Define methods for accepting the change that comes with a loss of health

- Discuss the intricacies of hospital visitation

- Analyze the loss of independence and the ramifications on living situations

- Examine methods to care for the family of the patient

- Determine strategies for navigating the legal aspects of death

- Explore the process of death and the customs surrounding death of a loved one

A fter the community chaplain has made inroads in establishing relationships with those in his mission field, to build and nurture them, and to gain permission to share with them, a crisis of health may occur. Statistically, each one of us will traverse through some type of stressful event, positive or negative, in any given 12 to 18 month period. This portion of the text will focus on a specific type of crisis and the care that is needed during such a crisis. Health concerns will be the primary area in which we will examine the caregiving methods for this chapter.

This can be a stressful type of care to give. It forces the chaplain to face his own mortality and finiteness. Having spent more than 13 years in the medical industry, and believe me it is an industry, doing a hospital, hospice, or even a funeral visit can still be very uncomfortable for me. As a beginning community chaplain, there will be many "firsts" for you. A support system that is developed specifically for the community caregiver to share some of these anxieties is crucial. We will take an in-depth look at what to expect when someone receives news about his health that is concerning, when someone is hospitalized, the various steps in long term care facilities, and finally, death and the time of grieving.

Those Dreaded Words

Most health crises begin with symptoms that propel an individual to seek medical attention, either through an emergency room in a hospital or a primary care physician. Many times the symptoms are treatable, and there is minor life interruption. However, at other times major life alterations are required to treat an illness. Even more life altering, symptoms can be an indication of a terminal illness. Any time our expectations are not in line with reality, grief takes place. It happens in some small ways in everyday life. Children misbehave and do not live up to a parent's desired expectations, leading to grief. An expected income tax refund is not as large as anticipated or worse yet, becomes a payment to the government for not withholding enough, and there is grief. Grief can best be defined as "a normal response to the loss of any significant person, object, or opportunity".[1]

Within this normal response, then, there is a commonly accepted process that goes something like this:

shock and denial
anger and anxiety
bargaining with God
depression and sadness
acceptance[2]

These stages of grief happen during a period of time that lasts from 6 months to 24 months, depending on the depth of the loss and the individual experiencing the loss. The grieving process does not happen in the same manner for everyone. Some people go through the five stages in sequence, while others may bounce from stage to stage, repeating some of the stages to varying degrees. There is no right or wrong way to experience grief; the goal of the caregiver is to facilitate the process. This means that the community chaplain will assist the grief-stricken to avoid getting stuck in any one of the stages.

Grief comes to people in different ways. What do we do when somebody in the family gets sick? If the illness is minor, the sick person takes it easy for a few days, family members adjust to the temporary change in schedule, and soon everything is back to normal. For an estimated 14% of the population, however, activities are limited permanently by chronic medical conditions. This is a serious illness that takes over the person's life and consumes the energy and resources of the whole family. Examples of this are cancer, AIDS, aging, and finally death. The neighborhoods in which we live, the opportunities available to us, the people we know, the political and economic status of the times, and countries in which we live all can have an impact on how our families cope. As culture changes or disintegrates, often families change and sometimes fall apart as well. Financial loss can have a tremendous impact on families and their communities. Infertility can be a major point of grief for some families. They have to face the fact that they will never be a biological parent. Often they turn to adoption. This too is most challenging. As it can be seen, grief comes to us through several vehicles. One interesting aspect to note about grief is that the more the person likes to have control over a situation, the more profound the grief experience will be. Loss breaks a person's illusion of control. While every person grieves in a unique way, the loss of a loved one requires about two years re-stabilizing. After a significant loss, grief comes from realizing that life has changed forever. The cause of loss is different for each person. One significant loss triggers a multitude of smaller losses. When someone in the mission field of the community chaplain experiences a loss, leading to inevitable grief, the following suggested strategies will help facilitate the grieving process:

- Provide a non-anxious presence.
- Being "with" them is your main objective.
- Use words that help them and avoid words that protect you, the caregiver.
- Experience their pain.
- Learn to release your pain to Jesus and help them to do the same.
- Express your care in a way that makes sense to the griever:
  Cards
  Words
  Appropriate touch
- Stay connected to the person or connect the person to support persons.[3]

Change: Our Best Friend

Regardless of the source of the grief, it is tied to a change that is not desired, is unknown, and is often avoided. But Quotes like: "Change is good", "The only thing constant is change", and "You have to change with the times", are just a few of the common phrases we have heard regarding change. Change, and the grief that comes with it, are too large to summarize in a single statement. Mark Cress, Founder and President of Corporate Chaplains of America, often says that change is our best friend. I have often replied that flexibility is the cousin of change, so they come in a package plan. Unfortunately, many, if not most of us, do not handle change well. There are changes that we dream about, plan for, and then through much effort, seek to bring to pass. These changes can be taking on the challenge of ministering to those in your sphere of influence, rearing a child through the changes of maturity, or fighting for those who do not have a voice like the unborn. Though the desired outcome is not guaranteed, we can seek to create change through our individual and collective efforts. Some changes we anticipate with joy, while others sneak up on us, such as our children growing up, a face with wrinkles, and retirement. But there is another kind of change that happens in life, the kind that we do not see coming that can turn our lives upside down in an instant. These changes, like a sudden death through a car accident, the doctor diagnosing cancer, or discovering drugs in the pocket of your teen's clothing, present the biggest challenges to us. Change that is sudden can shake the foundation of our lives and remind us that we do not have as much control as we think we do. Our willingness to embrace change has an impact on how we process change and our outlook on the future.

Once we move past the illusion that we have control over life and the circumstances that we encounter, we can begin to address the fear that is associated with change. Remember, grief is the result of re-

Fig. 18.1 Sudden change can remind us that we do not have as much control as we think we do.

alizing that there can be a disparity between expectations and the realities of life. That gap between expectation and reality is the unknown. Human beings, regardless of status and experiences, universally fear the unknown. Some people may be innate risk takers who welcome change as eagerly as rock climbers thrive on working without ropes and safety equipment. They like the thrill of the unexpected. It makes them feel alive. However, for those of us who like things to be predictable, who like the security of routine, change can be scary.

We do not want to see our kids grow up or dear friends move away. We do not want to see our hometowns burgeon with new growth. We do not like all the traffic or seeing the old buildings torn down to make room for the new. We do not want to see our friends (or ourselves) get old. Even when our circumstances are miserable, we may choose the familiar misery over the frightening unknown. I have seen battered women stay with their abuser because of the fear of the changes necessary to live in a safe place. "Leave it like it is," we insist. "I do not want to make new friends. I do not want to learn new things or have to change my habits or attitudes. I have formed my opinions; do not complicate my life with new information!" You may be able to pre-serve the status quo for a little while with such an attitude, but the price is high: You stubbornly cling to habits, events, and people you have outgrown. It gets harder and harder to make things "stay the same". While others move on, you grow more isolated and out of touch. Eventually, you find yourself the lone inhabitant of your cocoon, where nostalgia and fantasy are all that remain to keep you company and feed your imagination. In effect, you have stopped living.

As Roberta Rand of Focus on the Family states:

> It is true, change forces us to come out of our comfort zones, stretching us in ways that might hurt for a while. But the rewards can be astounding. In releasing the stale familiar, we clear the way for new experiences that can feed our thirsty souls and re-animate our lifeless dreams. Purged of the fears that held us back, we emerge as better people, more free and certainly more interesting.[4]

One of the trendier phrases to come down the pike in the last decade is, "He/She's in denial." Unfortunately, the sentiment has become trivialized through overuse; now we hear it uttered most often as a punch line. But clichés tend to become clichés because they are true. Many of us *would* rather deny what we do not care to accept.

Think about Job in the Old Testament; a comfortable man whose life was the epitome of worldly success. He had wealth, position, friends, and a great family. Then the bottom dropped out. God took it all away to prove to Satan that Job's faith was solid — not just the product of a charmed life. At his lowest point, having been stripped of family, home, health, status, and his good name, Job cried out, "[15] Terrors are turned upon me; They pursue my honor as the wind, and my prosperity has passed like a cloud [16] ...The days of affliction take hold of me. [19] He has cast me into the mire, and I have become like dust and ashes." (Job 30:15-16, 19 NKJV). Talk about cataclysmic change! Job's big question to God at that point was (to paraphrase), "What did I do to deserve this?" He then vents his frustration: "[35] Oh, that I had one to hear me!... *That* my Prosecutor had written a book! [36] Surely I would carry it on my shoulder, *and* bind it on me *like* a crown; [37] I would declare to Him the number of my steps; like a prince I would approach Him" (Job 31:35-37 NKJV).

What started out as a wager between God and Satan evolved into something else altogether for Job — mainly, a lesson in humility. God responded to Job's cheeky complaints with a withering "Who-do-you-think-you-are-to-question-me?" reproof that left Job shaken and chastened. His final reply to God was brief and abashed, "... I have uttered what I did not understand, things too wonderful for me, which I did not know" (Job 42:3 NKJV). Job, who thought he had all the answers, left his encounter with God with a much clearer understanding of the word "omnipotence". Though his was an extremely painful experience, he grew spiritually as a result. He was *changed* — and for the better.

What an exercise in futility to try and second-guess God's methods! When it comes to change, we are limited in our ability to see how hard-to-fathom, uncomfortable changes play into God's Big Picture. As we are reminded in I Corinthians 13:12, "For now we see in a mirror, dimly, but then face to face. Now I know in part, but then I shall know just as I am known" (NKJV). How God gets us to the point of blessing is His business. He owes us no explanations. To paraphrase Job, His ways are "too *wonderful* for us to understand" — the operative word being "wonderful". Whether we label changes as "good" or "bad", "happy" or "sad" is irrelevant. It is simply one of the media God uses to shake us out of our complacency and ruts.

We all seem to come equipped with a nostalgia gene: something in us that thinks the past is preferable to this present moment, something that yearns for the warm, soft-edged memories of times gone by. That same gene airbrushes out all the bad parts of the less-than-perfect past and convinces us that the present moment is defective, not a place in which we want to linger. What a waste! All it really takes is a drive past the home you lived in as a child. Remember it? It was large, nice, and beautiful. Drive to it as an adult, and you may think that it is now small; the lawn is not nearly as big and fun as you remember. We have romanticized the past. We certainly do not want to forget what we have learned from the past. In our old age, when our bodies can no longer do what we command them to do, memories can be a special comfort. For those of us whose minds and bodies are still vibrant, we must remember that the present is a gift to experience in its fullness right NOW — not to just look back on in nostalgia and regret. It is time to embrace change.

Change is a river, and in its deliberate journey, eternal journey, it carries away our most bitter tears just as surely as it folds into itself the moments we had hoped would last forever. If we allow ourselves to trust God, He will help us not only cope with change but also learn to celebrate its wonders and possibilities. Change will happen, whether you choose to go with the current or cling desperately to the crumbling riverbank. Only when you learn to surrender control of your circumstances and release yourself to God's direction and care will you begin to experience the fullness of a life entrusted to Jesus Christ and the miracles He has waiting for you. In the meantime, take these words as God's promise in the midst of change: "'Though the mountains be shaken and the hills be removed, yet my unfailing love for you will not be shaken nor my covenant of peace be removed,' says the Lord..." (Isaiah 54:10 NIV).

Remember, as Mark Cress says, change is our best friend. My caveat to that is: flexibility is the cousin to change and must be applied in all situations. Now, as Jesus says, get out there and change the world!

Health Issues and Local Hospitals

Once the reality of change is addressed, looking at the practical aspects of ministering to those navigating change through a loss of health can be examined. We will begin our journey with hospital visits. You may have experience as a church leader performing hospital visits. The hospital visit of a community chaplain is typically a little different than that of a church pastor. We are usually going in to see a co-worker, neighbor, public servant, etc. or one of their family members. Where do you draw the line? For immediate family members, it is best that the community chaplain visit as soon as possible. As the distance of the relationship increases, for examples uncles or aunts, the visit may take place at a more convenient time, still conveying importance of the relationship to the person in your mission field. A hospital visit for a distantly related family member can be delayed until later in the day. Remember that there is a ministry opportunity with every hospital visit.

When a call is received, first qualify where the call came from. Verify that you have the correct information by repeating it back to the caller. The effective community chaplain will gain permission to inform the patient who told you that he was in the hospital. Remember that all health information is confidential and can not be shared without the permission of the patient. More about permission is covered in another chapter. Let us take the example of an individual having a surgical procedure. There are two times of which you need to be aware: the time that they have to arrive for the pre-op appointment and the time of the surgical procedure. In standard hospitalization, your first order of business is to be there at least one hour before the surgery. Hospitals are currently requiring patients to arrive approximately two hours prior to surgery. You will allow the patient some time to get settled and then arrive one hour prior to surgery. This will also allow you to meet family members that you have not met before. Take the initiative and introduce yourself to family members. The person having the surgical procedure may not be comfortable introducing you.

Early in the visit, ask permission to read some Scripture. A preferred passage is Romans 8:18, Psalm 91, or Psalm 121. We might advise that you use some literary license, and do not read "You shall tread upon the lion and the cobra..." (Psalm 91:13 NKJV), etc. It is recommended that you have a Bible specifically for hospital use.

Please pray with the patient as early as you can. It is suggested that you pray for the family, the patient, the doctors, and the nurses. The nurses will often hear you praying for them, and this may open valuable lines of communication for you and the family. The patient will eventually be taken to surgery. Ask permission to wait with the family. At that point, before the patient is taken, explain that you would like to stay with the family until the doctor comes out. If you have received permission to do so, you can then state, "After the doctor comes out and we hear how (the patient) is doing, I will be leaving and I will let all concerned parties know how the surgery went." You have then received permission to leave without the family feeling as though they have been abruptly abandoned.

Know that there will be some very long surgeries. Take advantage of that time to minister to the entire family. The family will have many questions about their loved one. It is permissible to act as an advocate for the family to obtain answers to questions they may have, but keep in mind that newly adopted HIPAA laws prevent doctors and nurses from sharing some information with you. Be respectful of these laws; and understand that once the medical professionals know who you are, they may share the information with you regardless of regulations.

Another reason for staying until the doctor comes to meet with the family is that family members are very stressed by the circumstances of the surgery. It is not unusual for the family to get the doctor's report confused. The chaplain should listen carefully to the doctor's report and make sure the family completely understands the report. Feel free to ask the doctor any questions where you feel clarification is needed.

Do not offend, but do not be intimidated by the doctor. You and the family only get one chance here; take advantage of it.

It is best that the community chaplain not visit a patient of the opposite gender in the hospital alone. Take your spouse, a friend, or another chaplain. Do not make age determinations here. Where this comes into play most often is when women have a baby. Contact the hospital and see if the husband is with her. If the husband is present, inform them that you are coming right over and would like to see both of them. This can be a wonderful time to strengthen the relationship with both the patient and his or her spouse.

Fig. 18.2 The chaplain should stay and listen to the doctor's report and make sure that the family understands the report.

How often do you visit the hospital? A good rule of thumb is to take into consideration the importance of the relationship to the individual in your mission field. Generally, the closer the relationship, the more troubled a person will be over a health crisis, providing more opportunities for ministry and evangelism. Then, use your discretion after the initial visit and come by as needed, depending on the medical situation and spiritual condition of all involved. Obviously, if you are at the hospital visiting someone else, take that opportunity to visit others you know who may be in the hospital. Visit as often as practical. Be attentive to the prompting of the Holy Spirit. Give great attention to just how important it is to visit the sick. Christ refers to it in the Scriptures.

Health Issues and Out Of Town Hospitals

If a person is hospitalized out of town, you should still immediately visit, if feasible. Often, the community chaplain's church may offer to assist with these additional expenses. It is important to realize that you may visit, but it is not necessary for you to visit every day when the hospital is out of town. It is not necessary to visit relatives out of town. Building a network of resources in different cities becomes especially important for this circumstance. Special attention should be given to children of those with whom the chaplain is trying to build a relationship regardless of where they are hospitalized. Building a network of ministry friends across the country can be beneficial, because then a local pastor may be contacted for a hospital visitation out of your local area.

Always, always be in dress code that would identify you as the community chaplain when visiting the hospital. Your local hospital will come to recognize the logo and will be a great asset to your ministry.

If you get a call when someone has been taken to the hospital for some type of medical emergency, find out everything that the contact person knows, such as which hospital, why, has the family been contacted, and who knows about it. Call the hospital and find out if the person is there. Have all hospital telephone numbers in your PIM (Personal Information Manager). Always identify yourself as a chaplain when you call the hospital. This will help to open doors of communication with hospital personnel; remember HIPAA laws.

Always leave a business card and a tract at visitation. When doing follow-up visitation with the relative of an individual in your mission field, telephone the person upon leaving and let them know that you have just visited. Permission, a subject covered thoroughly in another section of this text, must be sought when considering hospital and other health related information. The goal is to be a friend to whoever needs it during the hospital visitation. With permission, pray for the family and the ill person. Be sure to maintain contact with the spouse of the ill person to gain information. Disseminate information to others only with the permission of the patient. Integrate your spouse into this part of your ministry. During hospital visits your spouse can help you to see more of the family members that are in the waiting area in a shorter amount of time and to avoid any potential issues with visiting anyone of the opposite gender.

Hospital visits should be done as soon as possible, when possible. They should most assuredly be performed as soon as is practical on non-critical issues. These types of visits may take place in the hospital room itself, the emergency room, the lobby or waiting area of the hospital, or even the cafeteria or designated smoking area of the hospital. Flexibility and understanding are important. These visits should be done graciously, lovingly, sensitively, and consistently. With permission, share Scripture that is relevant, like Psalm 91, Romans 8, etc. Be sure to defer to the family pastor, if he is involved. We do not want to intrude on anyone's territory. Be sure to call and verify by phone that the person is in the hospital and will not be discharged before you get there. Also, stop by the nurses' desk to see if they will give you any information on the status of the patient. In this manner, you will know what you are facing in terms of ministry. When dealing with nurses and other hospital staff, it is best to refer to yourself as "a family minister" or as a "community chaplain" to gain more information. Finally, the Clergy identification badge offered by many hospitals will often allow unencumbered visitation throughout restricted areas. This badge can be obtained through the office of the hospital chaplain. It is best always to introduce yourself to the hospital staff chaplain as a professional courtesy and to add one more asset in your ever increasing arsenal of resources.

Health Issues and Independence

There are times that an illness causes a loss of independence. Those in your mission field will be looking to the community chaplain for help. This means that as our population ages, an increasing number of adult children will be helping parents search for a solution to living as independently as possible while having needed services available. For many people, this solution is an assisted living facility. For an adult child, it is a decision that contains many questions and often guilt. Knowing the facts about assisted living care can ease the decision making process. The first step in choosing an assisted living facility is to take a candid examination of the aging person's physical, financial, and lifestyle needs. If an elderly parent or someone who needs around the clock care seems like a candidate for assisted living, the next step is to shop around for a facility that has a well trained, reliable staff offering quality care. The hospital discharge planner, physician, social services case manager, a financial planner, and friends who have moved to a facility are all good resources to recommend viable options.

It is then time to visit as many of the available facilities as possible to get a sense of the kind of options that are available. Notice how you are greeted as you come into the facility. Do the administrator and other staff members call the residents by name as you tour the facility? How much training does the staff receive? What is the average turnover rate? How will the facility meet the specific needs of the loved one in question? What type of medical attention will your loved one receive in the facility? Is there a doctor in the facility? If so, how often is the doctor there? Developing a list of questions before investigating the facilities will make the decision making process easier. It is important to consider how close the facility is to the home of the closest relatives. Residents who have frequent visitors tend to receive the best care, so proximity is a plus. As you inspect the physical surroundings, take care to notice things like the presence of handrails, easy reach cupboard space, accessibility to the dining room, and color coded hallways. A new trend is to incorporate skylights into the facility design of common areas such as dining rooms and corridors; this brings in more natural light and creates a friendlier, less "institutional" environment. Ask about special amenities. For example, some assisted living facilities have beauty salons with shampoo bowls that elevate several inches to accommodate people in wheelchairs.

When you have narrowed your selection to the top three, return to the facilities with your elder for a more in-depth look. Visit at different times of the day and on a weekend to observe the routines and activities. Make surprise visits to the places you are seriously considering, and arrange for an overnight stay before making a final decision. Eat in the dining room. Speak to several of the residents and ask them questions like these found below:

- Do you have a choice of main courses at meals? Do you help decide the menu?
- How long do you have to wait for service?
- What happens if you have a problem?
- Does the staff smile and respond to you as an individual?
- Is there an active resident council?
- Are pets allowed?
- Can grandchildren of the residents spend the night?
- What kinds of things do you do in a typical day?
- Are you glad to be living here?
- What happens if someone dies?

- What observances are performed here (both secular and Christian)?[5]

Ask the administrator for a copy of the rules and the contract, and read them carefully at home. Then ask a lawyer (preferably one who specializes in elder law) to review the contract for you. If you do not know an elder-law attorney, search for "elder law" on the Internet. You will find dozens of sites, including some that have searchable databases of attorneys in your area. Ask to see the facility's licensing inspection report. Your local long-term-care ombudsman can advise you and provide you with a recent listing of complaints.

Additionally, the Consumer Consortium on Assisted Living (CCAL) has developed a lengthy questionnaire you can take with you when you meet with the director of the assisted-living facility. Here are some questions excerpted from the questionnaire:

- What services are provided in the fee?
- What happens if funds run out? Is there any type of financial assistance?
- Does the contract clearly describe a refund policy, in the case of transfers, discharges, changes in ownership, or closing?
- If a resident displays a difficult behavior, what steps will the facility take?
- Is there special training for staff about dementia and Alzheimer's disease?
- Is there a separate area specifically for people with dementia, and if so, how do the services differ from services in the rest of the facility?
- What kind of emergencies are staff expected to handle and how are they trained for them?
- To what extent will the facility monitor the patient's health?
- What safeguards are in place to see that your loved one receives his medications on schedule?
- Is transportation to health appointments available? Is it wheelchair accessible and what are the fees?
- How are religious/spiritual needs met? Is there transportation to church? Are there arrangements and room for worship programs in the facility?
- If your elder does not like a meal, what alternatives are there?
- Are background checks made on all staff?[6]

Assisted-living residents or their families generally pay the cost of care out of their own funds. Medicare does not pay for assisted-living services. Medicare pays the bills only for a limited number of days when a more intensive form of care, called skilled nursing care, is needed and provided in certified facilities. Some facilities offer subsidies and financial aid on a limited basis, although a waiting list typically exists. A growing number of private insurance companies are beginning to offer assisted-living coverage as part of their insurance package. However, services covered under these policies vary widely, and many elderly people do not have long-term health care insurance. Most facilities accept only private pay, although some states offer limited assistance through Medicaid or Supplemental Security Income. Thirty-seven states reimburse or plan to reimburse for assisted-living services as a Medicaid service. Check with your state Medicaid office for more information. The Assisted Living Federation of America website will also provide some much needed information before beginning the search. View the website at www.alfa.org for more resources.

Health Issues Requiring Hospice Care

There are some physical issues that go beyond the type of care that can be provided in an assisted living facility, a nursing home, or home health care. Additionally, these health issues are not appropriate to be addressed through a hospital facility. Hospice care is an excellent option for these situations. The goal of hospice is to provide support and care for people in the last phases of an incurable disease so the remaining time on earth can be lived as comfortably as possible. The program is built on the hope and belief that through appropriate care, patients and their families may be able to prepare mentally and spiritually for death.

Fig. 18.3 Hospice can allow terminally ill patients to live in the comfort of their own home.

Hospice programs offer services to terminally ill patients and their family members around the clock in various settings. This care can be in the home of the patient or in a facility. A team of caregivers provides physical, social, emotional, and spiritual care. Families, professionals, and volunteers work together to treat patients in the last stages of illness, attending during the dying process, and helping families during bereavement. Patients must have a terminal diagnosis (life expectancy of less than 6 months) to receive hospice care. If the patient is able-bodied and independent, the hospice will treat the patient in the home with help from the patient's family, if available. If the patient is unable to care for himself, the hospice will arrange for care in a hospice-operated, in-patient facility or work with a nearby nursing home or hospital on a contract basis to care for the patient. Hospices try to provide as close to a home-like setting as possible for the patient.

The primary goal of hospice is to manage or control pain and other symptoms and to alleviate as much fear as possible, commonly found in those dealing with a terminal illness. According to the U.S. National Hospice and Palliative Care Organization, common fears include the fear of pain related to the illness, the fear of becoming a burden to the family, and the fear of financing the cost of the treatment.[7] The hospice team of doctors, nurses, psychologists, spiritual counselors, and volunteers provide such support services as administering medication, lending equipment, shopping, cleaning, and running errands for the patient. Generally, the hospice staff can be reached 24 hours a day and will visit a patient when needed. The staff and volunteers tending to the needs of hospice patients are professionals with a true heart of a servant. When interacting with them, the community chaplain should always express gratitude. Those seeking hospice care for a friend or relative can find a listing in their local telephone directory's yellow pages. However, most people find out about a particular hospice through a friend, neighbor, or family member who has been involved with hospice care. Other ways to obtain information about a hospice program are through friends who have used a facility, social workers, a doctor, and some faith-based referral services. Hospice care not only cares for the individual, but for the family as well. Hospice staff members and volunteers attempt to meet the needs of family and friends by performing some of these functions:

- Assessing the physical needs of the patient, such as a hospital bed, commode chair, or walker.
- Attempting to fulfill the heartfelt needs of the patient, no matter how big or small.

- Serving as go-betweens for the patient and his or her doctor.
- Teaching the family how to administer pain medications.
- Instructing the family on how to make caring for the patient a team effort.
- Encouraging the family to surround themselves with a network of support from friends and church members.
- Challenging family members to reminisce and take time out for lighthearted moments with the patient.
- Urging the family members to express their true feelings about what is happening.
- Preparing the family for when the patient passes away, adjusting expectations, and discussing whom to call first, etc. when the time comes. This training is often a comfort to the family.
- Giving the family breaks and running errands for family or patient.
- Offering companionship to the patient.
- Helping the family plan the funeral (which volunteers and staff members often attend), sending cards and letters, and offering continuing psychological and spiritual counsel to the family for as long as needed.

Hospice care can be a very cost-effective way of caring for a terminally ill person. Hospice care is covered under Medicare, Medicaid (in some states), most private-insurance groups, and HMOs. Families may be asked to meet some uncovered costs. However, hospices rarely, if ever, turn down patients for financial reasons. Public and community support through donations, grants, memorial gifts, and fund-raising events assist to help cover the cost of care.

Health Issues and The Family

When a family member has been diagnosed with a terminal illness and the health crisis begins, relationships can be put to the test. The community chaplain can then be a much needed resource. Emotions run high and fears that have already been discussed can play havoc on those who will be caring for the ill family member. This is not an easy task. There will be decisions to make and duties to divide. You may need to referee disagreements and identify unfair workloads. Outside expertise or caregiving may be needed if discussions are too volatile or the issues regarding the patient are particularly complex. However, the more prepared you are to handle a crisis when it occurs, the more successful you will be in resolving it.

As the aging population grows, the ranks of family caregivers are swelling. Although there is usually one primary caregiver, the context of family (siblings, spouses, children, and extended relatives) provides a built-in network of partners for caregiving. This family network can offer emotional support and a kind of backup system, as well as the security of knowing that if something should happen to the caregiver, the loved one in need of care will not be left alone. Sharing a strong sense of family is a powerful motivator to share the caregiving responsibilities for terminally ill and aging loved ones. It is vital for the effective chaplain to be aware that the stability of the family as a whole is affected by changes or disturbances among its members. In times of crisis, they need all the support they can get. Where do they find support when their aging loved one is incapacitated, and their own siblings or immediate family members are in the vortex of the tempest with them? The time-consuming tasks, tough decisions, and caregiving arrangements for which typical caregivers are responsible can strain and drain the most loving of families, both emotionally and financially. Feelings of guilt, frustration, and resentment are common when the demands of caregiving are prolonged and family members disagree about caregiving decisions. An outside party with a clear perspective can be invaluable. The community chaplain or minister can effectively facilitate the decision making process, being careful to *never* make a decision *for* the family.

Fig. 18.4 Caregivers of dementia patients are likely to feel tired, stressed, and unappreciated.

Those caring for someone with dementia are more likely than other caregivers to have less time for other family members or leisure activities. In many situations, it seems one person does all the work and that person may feel tired, stressed, put-upon, and unappreciated (despite the fact that he or she is more than willing to care for the aging loved one). The other family members that are not serving as primary caregiver may feel left out, ignored, and guilty for not doing more. Some extended members prefer to stay out of the picture entirely, except to hear how their elder is doing. This can cause problems both with the family members and the patient for whom the family is caring. As it can be seen, there are many complex dynamics in health related caregiving. We will also discuss later in this text that the community chaplain can take on a great amount of stress when caring for those with health related crises.

Caregivers who are single or without siblings may encounter less family interference, but they can tend to feel overburdened and intensely lonely in the caregiving role. Caregiving daughters and sons who have no children of their own are sometimes plagued by uncertainty: *When I'm old, who will take care of me?* To protect yourself and your loved ones, it may be helpful to expand your circle of support to include friends, neighbors, clergy, volunteers, and other professionals. Neither you, nor the people to whom you are ministering, should feel guilty because you cannot do everything. Be willing to delegate tasks and to turn to community programs and professional resources for help. Have discussions with the family and other supporters at the start of any acute situation in order to establish roles and responsibilities. Fostering good communication and solidarity will help keep finger pointing to a minimum when it comes time to make life-changing decisions for a loved one.

If the caregiver has a supportive spouse, someone who will listen and sympathize with caregiving stress, this can be a precious resource; even if he or she does not share in the hands-on care. Having a spouse also provides the caregiver with someone who can share in the decision making. However, spouses of caregivers may tire of the lifestyle restrictions: disruptions to vacation and travel plans, constraints on the family budget, increased household chores, and less time spent with each other and the children.

According to eldercare.com, a website providing resources for those caring for elderly loved ones, children in caregiving households are often silent witnesses to changing family dynamics.[8] As children get older, they often become part of a caregiving backup system, both emotionally and practically. They can sense the importance of sacrifices made to care for grandparents or older relatives. They frequently are able to develop a special relationship with the patient, even if the loved one has some form of brain deterioration. When children and adults share a household with an aging loved one, the potential for love increases with each additional family member. However, so does the possibility of interpersonal conflict. Children's social lives might be disrupted and their personal freedom restricted. They might feel uncomfortable bringing friends home. Parents find themselves mediating conflicts between the children and their aging loved one, especially when the elder's health is critical. Caregivers, who are pulled in both directions by the demands of their elder and their children, often feel restless, isolated, and depressed. As a caregiver, the desire to meet everyone's needs and set a good example of elder care for children can contribute to the pressure that is felt. Ultimately, it is the decision of the caregiving family members to decide how much is too much. It is important to take breaks from caring for the loved one to recharge. An adequate support system is crucial. Utilizing the resources that are available through hospice services can be vital to relating to others going through a similar experience.

Minimizing A Health Crisis

While a health related crisis can have an impact on the entire family, with far reaching consequences, some actions can be taken when everyone is healthy that will help to diminish the crisis. This section of the text will assist the chaplain who is seeking to minister to the needs of someone who is at the beginning of a health crisis or to prepare his own family for any potential health issues. No one likes to talk about death and funerals. Why deal with these matters when everyone is healthy? It will help to reduce costs at an expensive time for most people. There is compassion in preparing for the inevitable. Remember, family members will be grieving the loss of a loved one and preparation can help to reduce stress. Property and other assets the family needs to finance final expenses may be in probate for 6 to 18 months without a will. Additionally, costs will be greater if no preparation has been made. Attorney and court fees are usually 8% to 10% of the value of the estate.

Preparations can be made to make the death of a loved one a smoother transition. The first document to consider is the personal will. Basically, it should include some of the following information to be considered valid: an expression of his or her wishes, his or her signature and the date signed, the minimum required number of witnesses and their signatures, and a notarization. Items to address in the will include a designation of a guardian for any children, the selection of an executor, and the distribution of assets. A will that is most helpful will also include information about assets like a home, personal property, stocks, bonds, mutual funds, annuities, CDs, cash, IRAs, profit sharing, 401(k), life insurance, and other insurance policies. Information about liabilities against the estate will also be vital. Liabilities are any debts that are held against the assets. The more specific the will is, the better for the family. Plan for all contingencies. Include explanation of special terms, administration expenses, taxes, powers of administration, children's and incompetency trust provisions, simultaneous death instructions, effects of birth or adopted children, and copies of the last four tax returns for tax history. Place the will in a file that will be easy for loved ones to locate. Give the executor of the will a copy before your death. Do not include your funeral plans with your will, as the will may not be read prior to the funeral services. A trust for the children is usually part of the will. It will help to avoid court control of minor assets, appoint a guardian for the children and establish trustees for the children, and safeguards the inheritance for the children.

Creating other legal documents, like a durable power of attorney, may also be in order. A durable power of attorney will allow others to manage your affairs if you are unable to do so, while avoiding court control of your property. The author will appoint an attorney in fact, a decision maker, and a secondary for contingencies for the primary attorney in fact. This will allow the caregiver to make business decisions that are in your best interest: borrow on your behalf, enter into a contract on your behalf, collect benefits on your behalf, and enjoy usual and customary benefits legally guaranteed to you. A durable power of attorney for health care should also be included. This document would provide for others to make health care decisions on your behalf, including but not limited to personal care, medical treatment, hospitalization, access to medical records, and the withdrawal of care, even though it may lead to death. Finally, a family trust can be written to allow complete privacy through confidentiality. It saves estate taxes, provides for asset management, manages property for incompetent beneficiaries, and avoids ancillary probate, but requires more attorney involvement.

When The Inevitable Occurs

Instruct those to whom you minister that when someone does pass away, first they should call you, the community chaplain for support. Then the death should be reported to other interested parties and to government agencies at 1.800.772.1213.

Fig. 18.5 The chaplain can offer much needed emotional support in a time of grieving.

At that point, one should begin the probate process and obtain several copies of the death certificate. During the probate process, the executor will accomplish certain tasks. He will file an inventory of the deceased's assets with the court, file any income tax and estate tax returns that may be due, make decisions about how to pay any debts, make sure that the assets are dispersed correctly, and follow up with court filings to complete the probate process.

Taxes can be one of the most challenging aspects for the family of the deceased to handle. For this reason, we will spend some time discussing the tax implications, at the time of this wrting, according to the Internal Revenue Service. It is helpful to have at least the last four tax returns to determine any patterns specific to the taxpayer, paying special attention to the gifts given to others in the last years of life. File estate tax returns within nine months of the death if assets exceed 1.5 million or 3.5 million, depending on the year of death. The current tax year's return is still due by April 15th of the year following the death. Income received until the time of death is handled on the personal tax return of the deceased. Income received after the time of death is handled on the estate tax return. Deductions taken must have been utilized in life, with the only exception being medical expenses. Standard deductions and exemptions are not pro-rated, so the entire amount may be used. If there is a refund from the final tax return, it will go to the surviving spouse if it is a joint return, executor, or to a person legally entitled to the refund. Be sure that the deceased's date of death is in the date section of the return. Also, write DECEASED where he would have signed the return. This should also be written across the top of the form. The executor should file IRS form 6905 to discharge personal responsibility for the deceased's financial obligations, along with IRS form 4810 requesting prompt assessment. The IRS can audit this tax return for up to four years. Recipients of the inheritance can be held responsible for any taxes due. Taxes can be reduced through Payable-On-Death accounts, assigning beneficiaries to accounts, Transfer-On-Death Registration of Securities, joint owner-ship, Revocable Living Trusts, and gifts ($11,000 in a calendar year).

Sometimes families willingly turn over all decision making to someone else so they will not have to think about these issues. Under the circumstances, this is certainly understandable. However, except in rare instances, no one can deal with most of these issues but relatives of the deceased. It is important to have a policy that the survivors not make any long-range financial decisions during the first year. Also, under no cir-cumstances should finances be turned over to someone for investment until there has been sufficient time for emotional recovery and clear thinking processes. Whenever a chaplain, survivor of a decedent, or anyone experiencing the grief process feels down or overwhelmed by the decisions you have to make, remember: "A father to the father-less, a defender of widows, is God in his holy dwelling" (Psalm 68:5 NIV). Pray for His guidance, and trust in His love for you during this difficult time of adjustment.

As a chaplain in a community, a school system, a jail, a hospital, or small business, death will be a normal part of your ministry. While this is not something with which we will ever be completely comfortable, experience does bring some familiarity to the process. It is important, as a lay caregiver, to build your own support system and to have a circle of companions that can "bear one another's burdens" that come from ministry. In fact, a recent study confirmed what many of us already knew or suspected: a vibrant spiritual life offers older people mental and emotional health benefits. Ac-cording to Lynn Waalkes:

The study of 28 recently bereaved seniors from various Christian backgrounds found a clear link between spiritual belief and personal well-being. Of the 28 par-ticipants, nine stated they had low or weak spiritual beliefs, 11 indicated moderate levels of belief, and eight had strong beliefs. Researchers interviewed participants on the first anniversary of their spouses' deaths, again six months later, and also after the second anniversary of their loss. Those with strong beliefs indicated they were adjusting well, while those without some foundation of faith showed signs of depression.

Earlier studies have overwhelmingly shown a strong correlation between an ac-tive spiritual life and good physical health. More than 40 studies comprising some 125,000 participants have indicated that those with strong religious beliefs live longer. One six-year study of elderly North Carolina residents, predominantly Protestant, reported that those who prayed or read religious material daily had a much better chance of staying healthy.

Some researchers surmise that prayer and Bible study act as stress relievers, protecting the immune system and offering an emotional cushion in difficult times. The notable exception was people with religious beliefs that put a heavy emphasis on God's judgment over His love and mercy. The research indicated that guilt and fear of eternal punishment may actually damage health and increase stress. For those of us who profess Christ as Lord and Savior, the take-away from these studies is not simply a confirmation of the benefits of our belief in God. As we spend time with friends and family who are undergoing difficult times, we can offer them not only an eternal perspective to help them past temporal troubles, but a reminder that our health and emotional comfort can be found in our loving, heavenly Father.[9]

As a community chaplain, you will be attending many funerals. These funerals will have a different tone and experience based on the culture of the decedent. Because the likelihood is high that the chaplain will be involved in an interfaith or multidenominational service for a funeral, familiarize yourself with some customs of other people groups when there is a death. Take a look at some of the common practices at a funeral service:

Bahai

Bahai followers view life on earth as a preparation for the life in the next world. Embalming is not allowed, and cremation is forbidden. Interment must take place within one hour's drive from the place where death occurs. As there are no clergy in the Bahai movement, the family or other Bahai members conduct the service. It would take place at a Bahai chapel or at the graveside. Women and men are permitted to sit together, and no head covering is required. It is considered appropriate to send flowers or cards. Attendees should dress respectfully according to their culture. Mourners would usually wear dark colors and no makeup.

Buddhist

Buddhism allows that most funerals take place in a funeral home, not a temple. It is appropriate to send flowers. Only one night of viewing the body is held, and this generally takes place the evening before the funeral. Shoes are left on; footwear is removed only in the temples. Inside the funeral home, a table is set up with candles and incense, which burn until the body is moved to the cemetery. The family sits at the front of the room in which the casket is placed. Visitors greet the family, offer their condolences, and then go the casket and bow. They may either stay and sit for a while or leave, according to personal preference. Visitors will often make a financial donation to the family. A monk conducts the funeral service, held the following day. There will be a lot of chanting in which visitors are not expected to participate. Men and women sit together. No headgear is required. While white is the color of grieving, friends often wear black.

Protestant

While there are a multitude of denominations within Protestantism, all revolve around the Christian theme that there is life after death. Funeral services most commonly take place at a funeral home, although some may be held at a church. There are generally visiting hours arranged one day prior to the actual funeral. Funerals usually take place within three days of the death. Sending flowers, cards, and charitable donations in the name of the deceased are appropriate displays of sympathy to the family. Today, it is unusual for people to wear only black or to cover their head. A minister will usually conduct the service, although increasingly there is more participation from family and friends in the actual service. Visitors are not expected to participate, although some services include a time for spontaneous testimonials about the life of the deceased.

Roman Catholic

Roman Catholic cultures have many variations in practice, but there are some constants. One such constant is that the body is usually viewed in a funeral home, and then transported to a church for a funeral mass. At some point during visiting hours in a funeral home, a priest will lead official prayers. Visitors may join in or sit quietly, but it is considered disrespectful to talk or to leave. The prayers usually last about 15 minutes. Catholic adherents bow at the knee when they enter the church, a gesture that a non-believer should not imitate. Only believers should take communion, but everyone should rise and kneel at appropriate times throughout the service. Friends of the family will often send flowers, sympathy cards, and/or give a donation. Catholics may also purchase Mass cards, which would be displayed in the funeral home. Only those closest to the family would go to the cemetery.

Mormon

Mormonism states that funerals held by members of the Church of Jesus Christ of Latter-day Saints (LDS), although solemn and grieving, should also project a spirit of hope based on anticipation of reunion with the deceased after this life. Services are usually held in an LDS chapel or a mortuary under the direction of the local church leaders. Circumstances also may dictate a memorial service or a graveside service only. The service would open and close with sacred music and prayer, sometimes involving congregational singing or a choir, and usually include reminiscences and eulogies as well as talks about Jesus Christ's Atonement and Resurrection, life after death, and related doctrines that comfort and inspire the bereaved. Some families choose to have members or friends of the family talk about the life of the deceased or sing an appropriate hymn. Traditionally, a simple graveside dedication service is held following the funeral service, attended by family and intimate friends. Local law in some countries may dictate cremation rather than burial; but in the absence of such a law, burial is preferred because of its doctrinal symbolism. Often, there will be a reception or luncheon held following the services, where friends may offer condolences to and greet the family. Cards and flowers are considered appropriate.

Hindu

Hinduism attempts to hold a funeral service before the sun goes down on the day of the death. Traditionally, the first-born son conducts this. The service is held at a funeral home. Flowers may be sent, although this is not considered a tradition. Mourners would wear white, and visitors are expected to simply wear subdued colors. At the funeral, the family may lay flowers on the deceased. All Hindus are cremated. A short service takes place at the crematorium. Afterward, the family is expected to enter a period of formal grieving for at least 13 days depending on the caste of the family.

Muslim

Muslims try to bury their deceased as soon as possible, usually within a day of death. The funeral service always takes place in a mosque. Women and men sit separately, and women must wear a veil or scarf and loose clothing. Both sexes sit on the floor, having left their shoes at the door. The service is short and consists of ritual chanting and recitation from the Koran. Before the body is taken to a cemetery for burial, visitors and mourners would file past it to pay their last respects. Those close to the family wear black. Sending flowers and cards is appropriate. After a short ceremony at the burial grounds, visitors return to the mosque for more prayers and the offering of additional consolation to the family. Later, a meal would be eaten at the mosque.

Fig. 18.6 Instead of sending flowers, people honor the deceased through a donation to a charity or cause.

Jewish

Jewish funerals take place as soon after the death as possible, either the same day or the next. People pay their respects in three ways: by attending the funeral service, by attending the burial service at the cemetery, or by supporting the family the week of Shiva (a time when activities are restricted in order to grieve) following the service. While there are three different types of Judaism, Orthodox, Conservative, and Reform, funeral services for each are similar. A head covering is required for both sexes at Orthodox Jewish funerals, for men only at a Conservative, and is optional at a Reform service. Head covering is provided for anyone arriving without it. Until the body is buried, the focus is centered entirely on the deceased person. As a result, it is not appropriate to approach the family until the body is buried. Sending flowers is not part of the Jewish tradition. Instead, people would honor the deceased by making a donation to the family's favorite charity or cause.

Sikh

Sikhism funerals usually take place within 48 hours of the death. They are held at a funeral home, not a gurdwara (temple). While men and women sit separately in a temple, this is not necessarily so at a funeral home. Headgear is required for both sexes. A scarf covering the head is adequate for men and women. At the funeral service, passages from Guru Granth Sahib (the Sikh holy book) are read and prayers are offered. Relatives and close friends are not supposed to cry but recite spiritual hymns. Sending flowers or cards is appropriate.

Why Have A Funeral?

In a society that places less emphasis on traditions and more value on time, many people "opt out" of funerals altogether. Because they view you as an expert on the subject, the chaplain may be asked by grieving family members why they should have a funeral or the purpose of the service. Funerals are an important step in the grieving process, as well as an opportunity to honor a life lived. Additionally, it is a time to offer surviving family members and friends a caring, supportive environment to explore and share their feelings about the death. Funerals will often be the first step in healing the grief associated with the death. "Funerals are for the living, to rejoice in the one who has caused this coming together," according to Maestro Leonard Bernstein.[10]

Decisions must be made. Should we hold a traditional funeral like our parents and grandparents did? Should we go for the whole ritual with the casket open and viewed by mourners? Or is it time to consider a more modern and innovative way to pay our last respects? Or would you prefer a memorial focusing on the achievements and contributions of the deceased? It is actually all the same, according to Fares J. Radel of Radel Funeral Home, who says, "You celebrate a life lived. The difference is a body is not present in a memorial."[11] When a person dies, we acknowledge what is the traditional way in this country to honor and pay last respects to a dear departed. A call is made to a funeral home, which takes care of removing the body, often from a nursing home, hospital, or hospice. The body is prepared or embalmed, dressed, and readied for viewing. For some families, viewing is imperative. Says author Elizabeth Kübler-Ross, "It is important that the family can view the body before the funeral in order to prevent any late denial of death."[12] A brief ceremony is usually held at the funeral home and then continued at the church, with hymns, scripture readings, a short sermon, and sometimes a eulogy. A procession to the cemetery follows (for either ground or above-ground burial in a mausoleum or crypt) and concludes with a brief graveside service. Afterwards it is customary for friends and other mourners to gather at the family home for more expressions of sympathy. For many, having this whole ceremony with viewing is beneficial. "They need to see the body of their loved one, be close to it," says funeral director Fares J. Radel. "It also provides closure and makes them realize that indeed a life has ended."[13] Additionally, that life is celebrated when you hold a funeral. "It's a coming together of families, sort of a reunion to honor the deceased,"[14] offers one Cincinnati, Ohio, funeral director. Funerals in whatever form are beneficial to the survivors, not only as a reminder of their own mortality, but also as a means of helping them accept the loss and move on with life.

Much like a funeral, a memorial service celebrates the life of the deceased. The only difference is that there is no body present. Memorials are often held in a church, a fraternal hall, or other appropriate location and take place a few days or a couple of weeks after the death of a loved one. In recent years, more and more people choose memorials, especially those whose loved ones have been cremated and whose remains have already been disposed. Maybe the ashes are already stored in a columbarium or have been scattered at a place of personal significance. There is no format to the service, but proponents say it is simple yet dignified. There are prayers and music. Sometimes a short sermon or meditation and friends speaking about the deceased and his or her achievements and contributions to society follow. In lieu of a body, photos are displayed showing the high points of the deceased's life.

The definite advantage here is the cost - no embalming, no casket, no grave liner or vault. The organized memorial service movement wants to do away with elaborate funeral rites, advocating "dignity, simplicity, and economy" instead. The feeling is that spirituality is sacrificed with all the materialist trappings associated with funerals. An opponent to memorials, Dr. George E. LaMore, Jr., argues, "There's minimum confrontation with death, minimum ministry and ceremony for the living. . . . A terrible cheapening of both life and death is implied by all this. . . ."[15]

Most will choose to have a funeral service involving a funeral home in some form or fashion. Funeral homes are in business to make money; and therefore charge, sometimes exorbitantly, for their services. The best consumer is an educated one, even when it comes to funerals. Remember that funeral directors are there to help you through a very difficult time in your life. They are listeners and counselors, tribute planners and crisis managers. Through discussions with you, based on information you share about your wishes and details about your loved one, they are able to offer guidance and help you coordinate a very personal tribute that honors the life of your loved one. They can guide you through planning the service, complete necessary paperwork, and coordinate doctors, ministers, florists, newspapers, and other vendors to make your funeral experience as seamless as possible. However, they also listen to your stories about your loved one, answer your questions on grief, link you to support groups, and recommend sources of professional help. By acting as an experienced source for support and guidance, a professional, ethical funeral director can provide you with relief during one of your greatest times of need. It is recommended to, as much as possible, preplan the funeral. Doing so can offer emotional and financial security for both you and your family. By preplanning a funeral you will get the kind of service you want, and your family will be unburdened from making decisions at a stressful time. Preplanning does not necessarily mean prepaying.

Because cremation is on the rise, there are new doors that are opened to different funeral options. From traditional services to contemporary celebrations, cremation often gives a family the flexibility to personalize the services. The cost can be a large concern for many families. As the caregiver, remind them that a funeral can be as extravagant or as simple as desired. Preplanning the funeral can help to control costs. Also, by making decisions ahead of time, the family can avoid making choices at a time when emotions are heightened. It is vital to keep in mind that this is an important time for ministry to take place and that receptivity to the gospel is high.

There are many terms that a community chaplain will hear when funeral arrangements are in process. Below is a list of terms with which to be familiar. These terms are listed as defined by an association of funeral directors and listed on Funeralnet.com.

Arrangement Room: A room in the funeral home used to make the necessary funeral arrangements with the family of the deceased.

Bereaved: The immediate family of the deceased, suffering from grief upon the death of a loved one.

Burial: Placing a dead body in an underground chamber, earth burial interment.

Burial Garments: Wearing apparel made especially for the dead.

Burial Insurance: An insurance policy in which the principal is paid in a funeral service and merchandise instead of cash.

Canopy: A roof like structure projecting from the outside wall over the driveway allowing passengers to board and alight from vehicles without being directly exposed to the elements, sometimes construed as a portable canvas shelter used to cover the grave area during committal service.

Casket: A receptacle of wood, metal, or plastic into which the dead human body is placed for burial; sometimes referred to as "coffin" or "burial case".

Casket Coach, Hearse: A motor coach designed and used for the conveyance of the casketed remains from the place the funeral service is conducted to the cemetery; also known as a Funeral Coach.

Casketing: Placing the body in the casket upon completion of embalming.

Casket Veil: A silk or net transparent covering for the casket for the purpose of keeping flies and other insects from the remains.

Fig. 18.7 The chaplain should familiarize himself with funeral arrangement terms.

Catafalque: A stand upon which the casketed remains rest while instate and during the funeral service.

Cemetery: An area of ground set aside for burial or entombment of the deceased.

Cenotaph: An empty tomb or monument erected in memory of a person buried elsewhere.

Certified Death Certificate: A legalized copy of the original certificate, issued upon request by the local government, for the purpose of substantiating various claims by the family of the deceased such as insurance and other death benefits.

Chapel: A large room of the funeral home in which the farewell service is held.

Coffin: A wedge shaped burial case, usually eight-sided.

Committal Service: The final portion of the funeral service at which time the deceased is interred or entombed.

Coroner: A public official, and in some cases constitutional officer, whose duty it is to investigate the case of death if it appears to be from other than natural causes, or if there was no physician in attendance for a long time prior to death.

Cortege: The funeral procession.

Cremation: Reduction of the body to ashes by fire.

Crematory: A furnace for cremating remains or a building housing such a furnace.

Crypt: A vault or room used for keeping remains.

Cot: The stretcher-like carrier used to remove deceased persons from the place of death to the funeral home.

Death: Cessation of all vital functions without the capability of resuscitation.

Death Certificate: A legal paper signed by the attending physician showing the cause of death and other vital statistical data pertaining to the deceased.

Death Notice: That paragraph in the classified section of a newspaper publicizing the death of a person and giving those details of the funeral service the survivors wish to have published. Most such notices list the names of the relatives of the deceased.

Deceased: (N) one in whom all physical life has ceased; (V) dead.

Disinter: To remove the remains from the burial place; to dig up.

Display Room: That room in the funeral home in which caskets, urns, burial garments, and sometimes vaults are displayed.

Door Badge: A floral spray placed on the door of a residence wherein a death has occurred.

Embalm: The process of preserving a dead body by means of circulating preservative and antiseptic through the veins and arteries.

Embalmer: One who disinfects or preserves dead human bodies by the injection or external application of antiseptics, disinfectants, or preservative fluids; prepares human bodies for transportation which are dead of contagious or infectious diseases; or uses derma surgery or plastic art for restoring mutilated features.

Embalming Fluid: Liquid chemicals used in preserving a dead body.

Embalming Table: An operating table usually constructed of metal with a porcelain surface upon which the remains are placed for embalming.

Ethics: The moral code which guides the members of the profession in proper conduct of their duties and obligations.

Exhume: To dig up the remains; to remove from the place of burial.

Family Car: That limousine in the funeral procession set aside for the use of the immediate family.

Family Room: A specially arranged room in the funeral home which affords the family privacy at the time of the funeral service.

Flower Car: A vehicle used for the transportation of flower pieces from the funeral home to the church and/or cemetery.

Flower Racks/Stands: Wooden or metal stands and racks of varying heights used for banking flowers around the casket.

Final Rites: The funeral service.

First Call: The initial visit of the funeral director to the place of death for the purpose of removing the deceased and to secure certain information for which he has immediate need.

Funeral Coach: See Casket Coach.

Funeral Arrangements: Funeral director's conference with the family for the purpose of completing financial and service details of a funeral.

Funeral Director: A professional who prepares for the burial or other disposition of dead human bodies, supervises such burial or disposition, maintains a funeral establishment for such purposes, and counsels with survivors. Synonym: mortician, undertaker.

Funeral Home: A building used for the purpose of embalming, arranging, and conducting funerals.

Funeral Service: 1) The profession which deals with the handling of dead human bodies; 2) The religious or other rites conducted immediately before final disposition of the dead human body.

Funeral Spray: A collective mass of cut flowers sent to the residence of the deceased or to the funeral home as a floral tribute to the deceased.

Grave: An excavation in the earth for the purpose of burying the deceased.

Grave Liner: A receptacle made of concrete, metal, or wood into which the casket is placed as an extra precaution in protecting the remains from the elements.

Grave/Memorial Marker: A method of identifying the occupant of a particular grave. Permanent grave markers are usually of metal or stone which gives such data as the name of the individual, date and place of birth, date and place of death.

Honorary Pallbearers: Friends or members of a religious, social, or fraternal organization who act as an escort or honor guard for the deceased. Honorary pallbearers do not carry the casket.

Inquest: An official inquiry or examination usually before a jury to determine the case of death.

In State: The custom of availing the deceased for viewing by relatives and friends prior to or after the funeral service.

Instruments: The varied tools required in the embalming operation.

Inter: To bury a dead body in the earth in a grave or tomb.

Inurnment: The placing of the ashes of one cremated in an urn.

Lead Car: The vehicle in which the funeral director and sometimes the clergyman rides. When the procession is formed, the lead car moves to the head of it and leads the procession to the church and/or cemetery.

License: An authorization from the state granting permission to perform duties which, without such permission, would be illegal.

Limousine: An automobile designed to seat five or more persons behind the driver's seat.

Lowering Device: A mechanism used for lowering the casket into the grave. Apparatus is placed over the open grave which has two or more straps which support the casket over the opening. Upon release of the mechanism, the straps unwind from a cylinder and slowly lower the casket into the grave.

Mausoleum: A public or private building especially designed to receive entombments; a permanent above ground resting place for the dead.

Medical Examiner: A government official, usually appointed, who has a thorough medical knowledge and whose function is to perform an autopsy on bodies dead from violence, suicide, crime, etc., and to investigate circumstances of death.

Memorial Service: A religious service conducted in memory of the deceased without the remains being present.

Minister's Room: A room in the funeral home set aside for the minister to prepare for services and meet with family of the deceased in private.

Morgue: A place to where bodies found dead are removed and exposed pending identification by relatives.

Mortician: See Funeral Director.

Mortuary: A synonym for funeral home; a building specifically designed and constructed for caring for the dead.

Mortuary Science: That part of the funeral service profession dealing with the proper preparation of the body for final disposition.

Mourner: One who is present at the funeral out of affection or respect for the deceased.

Niche: A hollowed space in a wall made especially (in this connotation) for placing of urns containing cremated remains.

Obituary: A notice of the death of a person, particularly a newspaper notice, containing a biographical sketch.

Pallbearers: Individuals whose duty is to carry the casket when necessary during funeral service. Pallbearers in some sections of the country are hired and in other sections are close friends and relatives of the deceased.

Plot: A specific area of ground in a cemetery owned by a family or individual. A plot usually contains two or more graves.

Prearranged Funeral: Funeral arrangements completed by an individual prior to his/her death.

Prearranged Funeral Trust: A method by which an individual can prepay their funeral expenses.

Preparation Room: A room in a funeral home designed and equipped for preparing the deceased for final disposition.

Preparation Table: An operating table located in the preparation room upon which the body is placed for embalming and dressing.

Procession: The vehicular movement of the funeral from the place where the funeral service was conducted to the cemetery. May also apply to a church funeral where the mourners follow the casket as it is brought into and taken out of the church.

Purge: A discharge from the deceased through the mouth, nose, and ears of matter from the stomach and intestine caused by improper or ineffectual embalming, due to putrefaction.

Putrefaction: The decomposition of the body upon death which causes discoloration and the formation of a foul smelling product.

Register: A book made available by the funeral director for recording the names of people visiting the funeral home to pay their respects to the deceased. Also has space for entering other data such as name, dates of birth and death of the deceased, name of the officiating clergyman, place of interment, time and date of service, list of floral tributes, etc.

Remains: The deceased.

Reposing Room: A room of the funeral home where a body lies in state from the time it is casketed until the time of the funeral service.

Restorative Art: Derma surgery; the process of restoring mutilated and distorted features by employing wax, creams, plaster, etc.

Rigor Mortis: Rigidity of the muscles which occurs at death.

Service Car: Usually a utility vehicle to which tasteful ornamentation may be added in the form of a metal firm name plate, post lamps, etc. It is utilized to transport chairs, church trucks, flower stands, shipping cases, etc.

Slumber Room: A room equipped with, besides the usual furniture, a bed upon which the deceased is placed prior to casketing on the day of the funeral. The body, appropriately dressed, lies in state on the bed.

Spiritual Banquet: A Roman Catholic practice involving specific prayers, such as Masses and Rosaries, offered by an individual or a group for a definite purpose.

Survivor: The persons outliving the deceased, particularly the immediate family.

Trade Embalmer: A licensed embalmer who is not employed by one specific funeral home but does the embalming for several firms either on a salary or per case basis.

Transit Permit: A legal paper issued by the local government authorizing removal of a body to a cemetery for interment. Some cities also require an additional permit if the deceased is to be cremated.

Urn: A container, into which cremated remains are placed, made of metal, wood, or stone.

Vault: A burial chamber underground or partly so. Also includes in meaning the outside metal or concrete casket container.

Vigil: A Roman Catholic religious service held on the eve of the funeral service.

Visitation: An opportunity for survivors and friends to view the deceased in private, usually in a special room within the funeral home.

Wake: A watch kept over the deceased, sometimes lasting the entire night preceding the funeral.

Stories From the Field: #19
"Pam's And Ted's Excellent Adventure"*

Shortly after I arrived here in Western Pennsylvania, Ted's wife, Pam, developed lung problems. Thanks to Cindie, who is my friend at the company where Ted is employed, I learned that she was in Farrell UPMC Hospital in the intensive care unit. Ted had gone home by the time I was able to get to the hospital that evening, but Pam's sister was there. I introduced myself and explained that I am Ted's chaplain (that's what he calls me). I asked her to ask Pam for permission to come into the room and pray with her. She allowed me to do so, and the three of us joined hands and prayed.

The next day Pam had to be put on life support because the infection was so bad. Ted, his two sons, and five of Pam's relatives were in the waiting room when I arrived. We discussed the pros and cons of having Pam life-flighted to a hospital in Pittsburgh. Their doctor came in and gave his advice. We then prayed together, and Ted decided to send Pam to Pittsburgh.

Over the next two weeks Ted and I traveled to Pittsburgh to be with Pam on three occasions. Ted opened up to me considerably, and our friendship grew. In answer to prayer, the Lord smiled upon Pam and she came home three weeks later. Again she developed similar physical problems, and again was put on life support and taken to Pittsburgh.

This time when she came home, she called me and said that she and Ted had been talking. They wanted God to be involved in their lives. She asked if I would come to their home and explain to them how this was possible.

*In their home a couple evenings later, we discussed this further and I then asked permission to explain how I met Christ. They consented. When I was done, they said they wanted that experience as well. With permission, we sat together on their sofa and went through the **Steps To Peace With God** booklet. Pam and Ted prayed aloud together, confessed their sins, and opened the doors of their hearts and lives to Christ.*

Thankfully, Pam has not had to go back to the hospital, although she continues physical therapy for some different issues. Ted and I continue to meet together at the workplace, as well as offsite. We have meals together as families, and they continue to grow in their faith.

– Submitted By: Jeff S.
Pittsburgh, PA

*Individuals in this story have granted permission for its use.

Stories From the Field: #20

"My First Day As A Chaplain"*

*Monday morning I arrived early to begin my rounds, alone as a new chaplain working with a company that a friend of mine owned. I had been through training and had been introduced to the company I would serve on this day. I was "prayed up", knowing I could **not** do this in my own strength, but that I "**could** do all things through Christ who strengthened me". I asked the Lord to give me His love for these employees – that I would see them the way He sees them. So, I took a deep breath and began. The start of my day was pretty much what I had expected. I spoke to each employee, introducing myself as the new chaplain and giving him or her my business card. There was small chitchat, but basically I just let them know who I was and that I was there to serve them, encouraging them to call me if they ever needed my assistance.*

By lunchtime, I was wrapping up my first set of rounds. Everything had gone well. As I approached my last set of cubicles, however, I realized that something was wrong. The manager of that department told me that one of her employees, Cindy, had suffered a massive heart attack the day before. All of her co-workers were in shock. They told me that Cindy was the picture of health - ate right, exercised five days a week, and was only 45 years old. They all wondered how it could be possible.

After spending some time with them, I left for the hospital. As I drove, I prayed again, not knowing what to expect when I arrived. I asked God to use me and enable me to be the person He needed me to be in this situation. I arrived at the hospital and made my way to the ICU waiting room. I was glad that I had already registered as a chaplain and had my hospital clergy ID badge. As I approached Cindy's family and friends, I introduced myself, asked how they were doing, and was informed of her current condition. She was in a coma with minimal brain activity. From that point on, I was immersed into the life of this family. Though I didn't know Cindy, I got to know the members of her family quickly.

On Tuesday, her teenaged son, Todd, was scheduled to have outpatient surgery at another hospital. I arrived to pray with him, his dad Mike, and grandparents. Other members of the family remained at the hospital where Cindy was in ICU. As we waited for Todd to be called back, I spent time with them, listening and talking, hearing their concern for Cindy. I wasn't sure what to say or do. I was just there. I have heard that called the ministry of presence. Todd's surgery was postponed until later in the afternoon, so I left to go back to the other hospital to visit his mom. Cindy's daughter Ashley, her mother, and her brothers were in the waiting room. They asked me if I'd like to go back and see Cindy. It was hard to see this woman who had gone to church with her family on Sunday, had cooked dinner, and then had laid down with what she thought was indigestion, lying here in this comatose state. Ashley held her mother's hand and talked to her. I asked them if I could pray for Cindy and for them. They said, "Yes." They told me there were people praying all over the country. Todd's surgery went fine, and he was back at the hospital to see his mom the next morning. The days that followed were long and difficult for family and close friends. I spent a lot of time at the hospital. Sometimes I would come in the morning, leave, and return in the afternoon. I tried to make a few rounds, check on the ladies in the department where Cindy worked, and visit relatives of employees at other hospitals. My heart was with the Lewis family. They took me in and often introduced me as not only Cindy's chaplain, but also a friend of the family. I was supposed to be there for them, but I must say that it was an honor to be with this family. Their faith in God, in this most difficult of situations, was humbling. Cindy's husband Mike, in the midst of much pain, was a rock. They prayed, trusted the Lord, and pulled together as a family and community of friends.

The end of Cindy's life here on earth came on Friday afternoon. I was in the room when she took her last breath. I have been around death before, but I was surprised at the bond the Lord had formed between Cindy's family and me in only five days. They said good-bye to their loved one, we prayed, and I walked downstairs with the family. Earlier that day I had called my husband, who is also a chaplain in our community, to assist in caring for some of the many family members at the hospital. Reflecting on the day, I realized that I had stood there in a hospital room with my husband and Cindy's mother while Cindy passed from this life into eternity. What a privilege to be able to care for a family at such a pivotal time.

I notified my business of Cindy's death and talked with management about how to minister to employees on Monday morning. I attended the visitation on Sunday afternoon. I just mingled with the family. I wasn't sure what I could do to be helpful. Then I heard a sister-in-law say how thirsty she was, so I found paper cups and filled them with water and took them to the family, who had been greeting a long line of visitors for over two hours. It was a small thing, but the Lord used it as a practical way to serve this family.

Monday, a week after I had begun, I arrived early at the company to be in the area where Cindy had worked. I wanted to just "be there" if someone was struggling and *needed to talk. The memorial service was later that day. I attended like everyone else. I was able to see the family afterward and hug them good-bye. Many were from out of town, and I may never see them again. Much was said about Cindy's walk with the Lord. Her mother said that they trusted God and His decision.*

*Over the next few days, I would go by to check on the ladies in Cindy's department. Most of them are still in shock as they pass her cubicle and realize she won't be back to work. They are in different stages of grief. One is really struggling with anger at God. I left a copy of **Recovering from The Losses of Life** by H. Norman Wright for them. I have called and checked on Mike, Ashley, and Todd. The kids are back in school.*

I'm not sure what my role will be in ministering to my employees and this family in the days ahead, but I am open to whatever God would have me to do. I am back to making regular rounds and love what God has called me to do as a community chaplain.

– Submitted By: Susan H.
Columbia, SC

*Individuals in this story have granted permission for its use.

Questions

Reflect on the Stories From the Field found in this chapter and answer the following questions:

1. How would you handle the situation that was described?
2. What information found in the story is confidential?
3. What information found in the story can be shared with others? With whom may this information be shared? Under what circumstances may this information be shared?
4. How does the information found in this chapter pertain to the story?

---------------------------------- **End Notes** ----------------------------------

1. Gary R. Collins, Christian Counseling: A Comprehensive Guide (Waco, TX: Word), 345.

2. CCA Training Meeting, Paul Carlisle Presenter (Summer 2004).

3. Ibid.

4. Roberta Rand, *Focus on the Family* (Annual Newsletter 2004).

5. Physicians Resource Council, Complete Guide to Caring for Aging Loved Ones (Wheaton IL: Tyndale, 1998); cited in Focus on the Family's Physicians Resource Council, "Choosing an Assisted Living Facility," <http://www.troubledwith.com/stellent/ groups/public/%5C @fotf_troubledwith/documents/articles/twi_037626.cfm?channel=Relationships&topic= Caring%20for%20Elderly%20Parents&sssct=Life%20Applications> (Accessed 8 December 2005).

6. For more information about this lengthy questionnaire, see Consumer Consortium on Assisted Living (CCAL) <www.ccal.org/bookstore.htm>; cited in Focus on the Family's Physicians Resource Council, "Choosing an Assisted Living Facility," <http://www. troubled with.com/stellent/groups/public/%5C@fotf_troubledwith/documents/articles/twi_ 037626.cfm?channel=Relationships&topic=Caring%20for%20Elderly%20Parents&sssct=Life %20Applications> (Accessed 8 December 2005).

7. See National Hospice and Palliative Care Organization <http://nhpco.org/templates/1/ homepage.cfm> (Accessed 8 Dec 2005).

8. See <www.eldercare.com> (Accessed January 2005).

9. Lynn Waalkes, "A Spiritual RX for Healthy Mind and Body," <http://www.troubledwith.com /stellent/groups/public/%5C@fotf_troubledwith/documents/articles/twi_012753.cfm ?channel=Transitions&topic=Death&sssct=Other%20Things%20to%20Consider> (Accessed 8 December 2005).

10. Cited by Eline Funeral Home <www.elinefuneralhome.com> (Accessed 8 December 2005).

11. "Funeral or Memorial Service—Which One's Right for You?" <www.funeralplan.com/ funeralplan/about/funmem.html> (Accessed 8 December 2005).

12. Ibid.

13. Ibid.

14. Ibid.

15. Ibid.

Also available through Lanphier Press:

The Complete Corporate Chaplain's Handbook

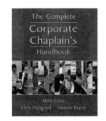

This handbook is the only "how to" guide for the corporate chaplain available today. Written by seasoned corporate chaplains and industry leaders with over twenty years of full time corporate chaplaincy experience, this is a very practical handbook designed to foster genuine caring in the workplace. It is truly a "soup to nuts" approach to the world of corporate chaplaincy. The nation's leading corporate chaplaincy agency uses this book as the primary text in its initial training process for all new chaplains and offers rave reviews for its effectiveness in quickly acclimating new recruits to the field. Leaders across the country in the workplace chaplaincy movement call it a "must have" and an "exceptional resource". (Fourteen chapters, 496 pages soft cover)

The Compass

The Compass, with its ultra-high production value DVD, high impact audio CD, and 48-page booklet, introduces the believer to all aspects of their new walk with the Lord. This innovative kit immerses the user in the five basic fundamentals of a serious Christian walk. Issues such as learning to pray, loving communication with God through meaningful Bible study, finding a great church, saturating their lives with Christian music, and sharing their faith with others are addressed.

C-Change

Print or Audio Book available. Workplace leaders across the country are offering high praise for the caregiving and leadership principles that follow each chapter of this exciting, realistic story of a committed company chaplain who spends his days making a difference in the lives of every employee he encounters. A surprising number of American business leaders have offered reviews stating that this book not only taught them new leadership principles, but it also brought them to tears. (127 pages hard cover)

The Third Awakening

Print or Audio Book available. This is a fast, fun novel of intrigue and romance that shows how the Holy Spirit works in the lives of ordinary people and how through them a third great awakening may occur. Follow the story of how BB, his grandmother, wife, and friends travel to a place they never expected to reach and what happened to their plans. (131 pages hardcover)
Plus: Now available in Spanish

To order more of our products, please visit us at:

www.lanphierpress.com

Index

R

S

T